LORD
OF THE
LOOSE
ENDS

LORD OF THE LOOSE ENDS

LLOYD OGILVIE

WORD PUBLISHING
Dallas · London · Vancouver · Melbourne

Library of Congress Cataloging-in-Publication Data

Ogilvie, Lloyd John.
    Lord of the loose ends: the secret to getting your life
under control / by Lloyd Ogilvie.
        p. cm.
    ISBN 0-8499-0749-7
    1. Christian life—Presbyterian authors.   I. Title.
BV4501.2.O333   1991
248.4—dc20   91-15151
                                                            CIP

Printed in the United States of America

1 2 3 4 9 MV 9 8 7 6 5 4 3 2 1

This book is dedicated
to
Herbert and Lillian Downey
in gratitude for
their love, faithfulness, and encouragement
to my wife, Mary Jane, and me,
and countless others through the years

ACKNOWLEDGMENTS

Deep appreciation is expressed to those who have helped me in the preparation of the manuscript for this book.

I am thankful for discussions with David Moberg, Charles "Kip" Jordon, Joey Paul, and Ernest Owen of Word, Inc., that helped shape the scope and focus of the book.

Cathy Powers, my Manager of Publications, was responsible for typing and editing the manuscript through several revisions. I appreciate her skill and expertise as an editor and her encouragement and enthusiasm for this project.

Once again, it has been a pleasure to work with Pat Wienandt of Word. She did the final editing and preparation of the manuscript for Word, Inc.

Through the years, my friend William McCalmont, our church's librarian, has assisted me in research for preaching and writing.

And special gratitude to my beloved congregation of the First Presbyterian Church of Hollywood for the privilege of extending our ministry together through the printed page.

To all these friends, I express my special debt of gratitude.

CONTENTS

1.

LORD OF THE LOOSE ENDS

LOOSE ENDS. THEY DANGLE AND DISTURB. AGITATE AND alarm. With frustration we say, "I feel at loose ends!"

We desperately try to get caught up. Each morning we resolve to get our act together. "Today's the day!" we say to ourselves in the morning shower. *"Today* I am going to stop procrastinating and finally get up to date." We set an impossible agenda, and at the end of the day, we are more hassled than when we started.

Life in the nineties is accelerated and exasperating. The junk mail piles up and we feel junky about the important letters we failed to answer. The phone rings off the hook. Our list of unreturned calls gets longer. Our schedules get loaded and we feel victimized by the demands, and guilty about the lack of quality time with family, friends, or even a few moments alone to keep our sanity.

Problems mount. We live with the illusion that someday we'll get them all solved. Our goal is to tie up all the loose ends. We can do it, if we only try harder — or so we think. But some loose ends just won't stay tied! And then, of course, as soon as we tie up a problem in a neatly packaged solution, we get hit with other problems.

I think this happens because so many of our problems are caused by people. Talk about loose ends! There's always someone who feels misunderstood, unrecognized, or unappreciated. Relationships take time. When there's just not enough time to deal with everyone's needs in the family, or at work, we get that awful feeling of being pulled in all directions; we can feel our relational loose ends flopping around inside us. Even after we've done our best to stretch our limited reserves to care for everyone on our agenda, a loose end cracks like a whip as we remember someone we've neglected.

Loose ends . . . the unfinished, the unresolved, the unexpected, and, most of all, the unfulfilled. More than things to do or people to see, more than the duties and details of life, the real loose ends are, rather, the total accumulation of what someday we'd like to do or what we'd like to accomplish with our lives.

When we say, "I feel at loose ends," we are really confessing that our lives are out of control. We are like a sailor who has lost his grasp on all his lines and whose sails are flapping in the wind. Even without taking a drink, our lives are "three sheets to the wind." We bob about in the sea of life unable to catch the wind that will get us moving toward our destination.

Nine Desperate Words

The feeling of being at loose ends is expressed in what I hear as the nine most desperate words of the nineties — "I've just got to get control of my life!" I hear this plea of panic wherever I go. Try as we will, we can't seem to get control of circumstances, people, or ourselves. Instead, so many of us feel that pressures, problems, and people are controlling our lives. We aren't getting what we want out of life and don't know what to do about it.

Often, the feeling on the inside of being out of control outwardly produces a very controlling attitude in our relationships and responsibilities. We tighten our grip on life to be sure nothing goes wrong. Naturally, tenseness and anxiety result, and almost everything usually does go wrong.

Each year I do a survey of the concerns of the American people so that what I preach and write can be an up-to-date response to the deepest needs and most urgent questions people are feeling and asking. (I've discovered there's nothing more ineffective than an answer to an unasked question or a response to an unexpressed need.) Listening to people before I speak or write presses my heart next to the pulse beat of their current concerns. Those of you who have read some of my other books know how important this discipline of listening is for me; it makes writing a book like this a personal conversation.

So, last summer, with the results of this yearly national survey packed in a big trunk, I headed off for my study leave. Alone, I read the deep needs of people young and old, rich and poor, successful and struggling. At the end of a full week of sensing the pulse beat of their longings, I realized that those nine words "I've just got to get control of my life!" were expressed with urgency in thousands of different ways.

Listening to this need in other people moved me to remember times when I had felt at loose ends and had sensed an urgent need to try to get control of my own life. (I'll share some personal illustrations of these times as we travel through this book.) With empathy, I began to search for an answer to this perplexing problem.

Weeks were spent in solitary reflection and prayer. Questions kept tumbling around in my mind: "What is the deeper cause of this anxiety in people, this feeling of being at loose ends and out of control?" and "Why do so many Christians express this same frustration?"

I knew that the answer was more than simply the pace and pressure of life today. Every past age has had its own set of complexities. The very difficulties often brought out greater strength and courage. Why, in our time, are Christians feeling like they are losing control?

One night as I lay awake thinking about this dilemma, it hit me. I knew the answer to the weeks of wrestling with the problem! Struggling to get control of our lives is a sure sign that we're already in control and really want more control!

That may seem contradictory—at first. Why would a person who is in control feel out of control? Because a basic, primal problem of life is the fact that in our frantic attempts to stay in control, we desperately grasp for *more* control over ourselves, others, life, relationships, and situations. Mounting pressures and perplexities make us more imperious in our lust for power, and more frustrated when it eludes us.

So the nine desperate words, "I've just got to get control of my life!" are really the nine most dangerous words of our time. You see, God never intended for us to be in control. That assignment was given by the Father to the reigning Christ. He is the Lord of the Loose Ends. And our biggest problem is yielding control of our lives to Him.

Controlling And Out Of Control

A woman who came to see me opened the conversation with this request: "Please, I want you to help *me* get control of *my* life."

"I'm sorry," I replied, "I won't do that."

The woman was shocked. She had expected me to listen to her anxieties and give her some easy steps to feeling more in charge. What she really wanted was *greater* control.

I went on to explain, "There's only one Person who can control your life. His name is Jesus Christ. He alone is adequate for the task. Turning the control of your life over to Him is the only way you will find the security and strength for which you are searching."

15

This woman was a Christian, but a very controlling person. She believed in Christ, but she had never
confronted her need to yield control to Him as Lord of
her life. Some serious failures at running her own life
were giving her the sense of being at loose ends and
out of control. Her addiction to human power and control kept her from experiencing Christ's authentic
power to take charge of her life. It took several long
conversations before the woman was willing to admit
her addiction and turn over to Him her gnawing anxiety
of feeling at loose ends.

Millions of us share her problem. We face the dilemma of feeling out of control while wanting more
control. At the same time, the dangling loose ends of
life intensify a feeling of helplessness. We are brought
to a crisis when external problems remind us of our
inability to be in control; it will either break our control
addiction, or tighten its grip on our lives.

It's amazing how little impact the preaching and
teaching of the Lordship of Christ makes on how we
live our lives. Even though we say we believe in Him
as our Lord, we hang onto our self-destructive control
of people, situations, problems, finances, plans, goals,
as well as our personalities and characters.

How Would You Answer?

Recently I asked a group of Christians three
questions: Have you ever yielded control of your life to
Christ? When did it happen? What difference has it
made? For many, the challenge of actually giving up

16

control of their lives to Christ was not a part of becoming a Christian. Most could not pinpoint a time when they intentionally turned the control over to Him.

In many churches of America, the need for a radical, new beginning is often not clearly taught, or even included, in the process of receiving new members and confirming young people. There is no call to surrender to Christ's character-reorienting, personality-reforming, mind-repatterning Spirit. And there's far too little emphasis on how to live our daily lives under His moment-by-moment management.

The result? The fact that the majority of contemporary Christians remain in control of their lives, merely adding the *conceptual* belief in Christ to their self-determined lifestyles. Sure, we pray in times of trouble, but what we ask for is the Lord's intervention to accomplish our plans. We're still in charge. We remain essentially what Paul called "carnal Christians"—believers who are governed by our own wills instead of the Spirit of Christ.

A Constricted Christ

Could one of the reasons for this be that our experience of Christ is too constricted? J. B. Phillips wrote that "your God is too small." It is my conviction that our comprehension of the power of God available to us through the reigning Christ is too confined. Christ is restricted to our stained glass windows and to His historical ministry as Jesus of Nazareth. We define Him with glib but vague theological phrases.

What we need is a robust Christ—a dynamic Savior and a powerful Lord who can help us know that our lives are in control—His control. He is the only One who can liberate us. He can set us free once and for all from the wretched feeling of being at loose ends.

For me personally, the Christian life was a constant struggle until I had a one-to-one encounter with the preexistent, prevenient, personal, all-powerful Christ. But wait! Before you groan inside thinking I've just pulled together some more fancy theological terms, let me explain.

One Worthy To Take Control

The Christ who is able to control our lives existed in eternity before time and creation. He was co-equal with God the Father. "In the beginning was the Word, and the Word was with God, and the Word was God. He was in the beginning with God" (John 1:1–2). These opening words from the Gospel of John help us catch the magnitude and majesty of the preexistent Christ. As the Word, He was, and is, the generative power of the universe, the One through whom all things were made at the Father's command.

The One we like to think of as Friend, Teacher, our Good Shepherd, is also Christ, the Word, the uncreated creator of universes within universes, who created life on the planet Earth. When the Father said, "Let us make man in our image," the Word created humankind. Life Himself brought life into being. The Father was the instigator, the Son the implementer.

18

And through the ages, the Word was the One through whom God spoke to His people—to the prophets, priests, kings, the mighty men and women of Israel.

If we are to experience true power to control our lives, we must first meet the One who created the process by which we were born! Christ made us. He alone has the authority to take charge of us. Only He can help us function at our full potential under His control.

None other than the preexistent Christ who was *with* the Father (the word "with" in Greek is *pros*, meaning here "face-to-face unity") came to us and dwelt in human flesh—light for our darkness, grace, unqualified love and truth, ultimate reality.

John again helps our minds to soar and think magnificently. "No one has seen God at any time. The only begotten Son, who is in the bosom of the Father, He has declared Him" (John 1:18). Some original Greek manuscripts read *Monogenes Theos*, "only begotten God," not *Monogenes Huios*, "only begotten Son."

Paul also catches the wonder of it all. "He is the image of the invisible God, the firstborn over all creation. For by Him all things were created that are in heaven and that are on earth. . . . All things were created through Him and for Him. And He is before all things, and in Him all things consist. . . . For it pleased the Father that in Him all the fullness should dwell . . . " (Col. 1:15–17, 19).

In our quest to get control of our lives it is so important to reaffirm who Jesus Christ was in the incarnation. Without negating His humanity in the least, we need to behold with awe and wonder the preexistent, divine Son of God, who made us and who came to remake us, who was born among us so we could be reborn.

In His humanity Christ revealed how life was to be lived under divine control. As the Son of God, He called His followers to faithful and obedient discipleship. As Immanuel, God with us, He left no ambiguity about who He was. With authority He said, "Before Abraham was I AM," asserting His preexistent oneness with Yahweh. With equal force He spoke with I-AM, Yahweh power as He declared that He was the Bread of Life, the Light of the World, the way, the truth, and the life.

The Control Factor

Throughout His ministry, Christ exposed the deepest raw nerve in humankind—the control factor. People's lives were out of control because they sought to live under their own control. The cause was sin, separation from God, manifested in the pride of wanting to be in charge of themselves, as well as of others, of life itself, and even of their own destiny. From this basic sin of estrangement from God came all the other sins of rebellion and, finally, the danger of control by Satan.

Control was the issue at the core of Jesus' conflict with the leaders of Israel. When they could not control Him, they put Him to death on the cross. They tried to control the uncontrollable and lost. Death could not defeat Him nor could the grave hold Him. Christ rose victorious over the forces of death and Satan. The triumphant Lord ascended into heaven, was glorified, and was delegated by the Father to reign as Lord.

The preexistent Christ is also our prevenient Lord, always beforehand with us. He chooses us before we choose to be His disciples! He calls us when we are neither worthy nor adequate. He singles us out and engenders in us the gift of faith, so we can receive His amazing love and awesome forgiveness. When we accept Him as our Savior we are given the assurance of eternal life. We are Christians, destined for heaven.

What About Now?

That's fine for openers, but what about living now? The really good news is that Christ is always present and all-powerful. What he did as Jesus of Nazareth He is ready and able to do in our lives today. He offers to fill us with His Spirit, to give us supernatural strength, and to transform our personalities, guiding us each step of the way. All He asks is that we give Him complete control of our lives!

There's the rub! Christ demands unreserved surrender of our wills, and our desire to be in control, to Him. Sounds great . . . or does it?

Imagine! The Christ who existed with the Father before time and creation, the One who created the process by which we were born and now have been reborn—offers us power to live life to the fullest. We are back to where we began when we asked: Why do so few experience this power? Why do so

21

many Christians feel powerless? And why the persistent plea, "I've just got to get control of my life!"?

It bears repeating: we are capable of a drastic duality: we can say that Jesus is Lord while at the same time we crave imperious control over our lives. I certainly know about that from my own experience. I'd been a Christian for eight years when I had to face both my powerlessness and my need for Christ to take control of my life. I've shared aspects of my experience in previous books, but here I want to explain more fully how I really came to know the Lord of the Loose Ends. It happened early in my ministry.

My preaching was biblically sound and Christ-centered, and I taught good, orthodox reformed theology. Yet, I still had a problem: few lives were moved or changed—something was wrong, something was lacking. I had no power for a supernatural ministry; I depended on human energy, talents, and personality. But popularity and outward success did not satisfy a gnawing, inner spiritual hunger—a real need and longing for authentic power. Years of Bible study had hit wide of the mark of the most crucial truth the Word contained. I had a purpose without power. As a result, I became exhausted and frustrated. I was at loose ends.

This led me to take a prolonged, solitary retreat on a lonely beach. I was alone, but not really. Christ was there, and I felt He guided me to spend the time studying John, chapters 14, 15, 16, and Paul's Letter to the Colossians.

Up to this point in my life, I had tried to follow Christ to the best of my ability. As a man "in Christ" I knew I was a recipient of salvation through the gift of His death and resurrection. I knew I was forgiven, that death had no power over me, and that I was alive forever.

But there on that beach, I was stunned intellectually by a truth I had missed; I was stirred spiritually by a power I had not appreciated. Most of all, I was startled by a vision of what a Christian is meant to be—the post-resurrection home of the risen Christ.

Again and again, I stumbled over the Lord's words, "Apart from me, you can do nothing." The words contradicted my aggressive, self-assertive addiction to human power. Repeatedly, I read Christ's promise that He would make His home in me. Though I knew what it meant to abide in Him, I longed to experience His promise to abide in me. Then I read these words in Colossians: "Christ in you, the hope of glory" (Col. 1:27). They sounded like a trumpet blast. "That's it!" I exclaimed.

During those days, the secret of true power became very real to me. The preexistent, reigning, all-powerful Christ is also the indwelling Lord. The glory that was promised was to be a manifestation of Christ in me. He offered me a character transplant that would help me become more like Him in attitude, action, and reaction. A liberating conviction captured my mind: Christianity is not only life as Christ lived it, it is more than my life in Him, it is Christ living in me!

I had read those Scriptures before. How had I missed the experience of these promises? It had taken the crisis of powerlessness to make me ready to receive what had been offered all along.

The Lord wanted a surrender to Him of all that there was of me—mind, soul, will, and body. It happened the last day of my retreat; I was determined not to miss the opportunity to respond.

I can remember it as if it happened yesterday . . .

The tide was out on the seashore, so I took a stick I found nearby and wrote out in the firm sand all of my needs, yearnings, and failures. Then I scratched out a list of the sad results of a powerless life and ministry. After I'd finished, I got on my knees and asked Christ to fill my total life. I prayed, "Lord, I've missed the secret. I've been ministering for You and have not allowed You to work through me. Come live Your life in me. I'm empty, and I need to be filled. Love through me. Care through me. Preach through me. Lead through me. . . . All that I am, or ever hope to be, I yield to You."

Christ's presence flooded my entire being, from the top of my head to the soles of my feet. I felt loved, forgiven, empowered. I don't know how long I was on my knees. It must have been a long time, because when I got up I realized that the tide had come in and had washed away all that I'd written in the sand.

That experience of the indwelling Christ transformed both my personal life and my ministry. I returned home a different person. After being gripped by such a liberating revelation, I was set free from my compulsion to try to earn my status with the Lord. The parched places of my soul were drenched, bringing an end to the drought that had kept my Christian life like a barren desert. The indwelling Christ gave me all that

24

I had previously worked so hard to achieve, all that I had studied to understand and struggled to accomplish. Now I was free to love without restraint. I felt a new boldness, an exuberant joy I couldn't contain.

But don't misread my enthusiasm for what happened so many years ago. That experience has had to be renewed every day and especially in each new challenge or difficulty. I have known my share of suffering and pain, disappointments and problems. And I've been called to attempt some humanly impossible tasks. Looking back, I can't imagine living through it all without the power of the indwelling Christ.

Over the years, His presence has given me incredible resiliency and almost untiring expectancy. I've discovered that guidance is not something I must beg to receive, but something Christ signals within my mind and spirit. Each person I meet or work with gives me a fresh opportunity to let go and allow Christ to speak or love through me. I continually rediscover that my task is only to pray for openness to let Him through, and then to marvel at what He says and does.

Problems and difficulties are really gifts for new levels of depth in experiencing the limitless adequacy of what Christ can do. What a relief it is no longer to feel that I have to find answers and solve problems on my own. He is at work in me. I know that as surely as I feel my heart beat and my lungs breathe.

And I know something else equally important: Christ's indwelling power is for servanthood, not for private, esoteric piety. When Christ takes up residency in us, it follows that He will lead us into situations and to people who need Him most. And the more we serve, the more power He releases.

All my other experiences of growth through the years have been but diminutive repetitions of that ultimate discovery there on the lonely beach where I was not alone. And each one has brought me back to a renewal of the secret of the abundant life I experienced. "And this is the secret: that Christ in your hearts is your only hope of glory" (Col. 1:27, TLB).

So, constantly feeling at loose ends is a sure sign that we think our lives are out of control. Our control. I fervently hope that the chapters to come may help you recognize the loose ends of life for what they are— warning signals. Powerlessness makes us grasp for more power and control, but the ugly reality is that the more we are in control, the more powerless we are and the more we feel at loose ends, unable to cope.

He Is Able

This book is about the Lord of the Loose Ends who is able to help us. Throughout the epistles of the New Testament there are eight "He-is-able" exclamations that show us how Christ helps us overcome the feeling of being at loose ends and how He actually ties down our most distressing loose ends. The Greek word for "able" comes from *dunamis*, "power." To say with Paul, Jude, and the author of Hebrews, "He is able," is like an exuberant shout, "He has all power!" Our confidence is not "I am able," but "He is able!" Christ is able to free us to soar, to open the floodgate of His power for our problems, to help us when we are tempted, to deliver us from frustration, to keep us from stumbling over our previous stumbles, to conquer financial worries, and to give us lasting security.

As we move through this book, we'll be talking about all the loose ends that you and I share and how Christ's power makes us able to live truly powerful lives.

But before we can receive all that Christ "is able" to do for us, we need to take the five steps to experiencing authentic power. They are in the next chapter. Let's take them together with the Lord of the Loose Ends!

2.

THE POWER STRUGGLE

THE BOLD LETTERS ACROSS THE TOP OF A FULL-PAGE advertisement by a famous manufacturer of men's clothing caught my attention. "Get Suited Up With Power!"

The ad pictured an executive decked out in what was called "the power suit," shown in pin stripes, of course. In the corner of his mahogany-paneled office was a full suit of armor. The idea I was supposed to grasp was that both the executive's suit and the suit of armor were to achieve the same purpose—the assertion of authority and power.

On the massive desk of the smoothly groomed executive were the symbols of power—his impressive title, his own FAX machine, a battery of phones, and the memorabilia of his athletic achievements. Junior executives stood at attention with notepads in hand, waiting for orders from the top gun. A secretary, who looked as if she would be more adept at an office cocktail party than at a word processor, sat demurely in front of the desk.

The rhetoric of the ad played on the human quest for power. "Power is everything," the copy read. "You've worked hard to get it. It's been a long way up the ladder of success and power. So why not look the part in the latest power suit? A suit that emphasizes the trim figure you've pumped iron to acquire—that signals the influence you wield."

Then came the hook, the appeal to the universal longing for power. "And even for those of you who are not yet in the positions of power you deserve, look like a warrior in armor who has taken command. So get suited up with power—now!"

Secular clothing manufacturers aren't the only ones who have adopted the word "power" to sell their wares. An article in the Raleigh (North Carolina) *News and Observer* announced the sale of Dunamis Sportswear, a new line of casual clothing for active Christians. Every item is emblazoned with a crest that says "Dunamis" (the Greek word for power, as noted in chapter 1). There are "Prophet Sweats," "Sea of Galilee Sweaters," "Jerusalem Jerseys," and even a "Bible Smuggler's Bag"—all displaying the word "Dunamis."

There was a time when the key word in advertising was "new," and it was said that you could sell anything if you called it new. Now the impact word is "power."

Ours is an age addicted to human power. Read your daily newspaper. Leaf through your weekly news magazines. One word dominates the news: Power. Raw, human power. The pull of power is magnetic; the taste of it is intoxicating. The kind of power I'm talking about is the exercise of our will in manipulative ways to achieve our own goals and to gain and maintain control over people and situations.

We all want power. Those who have some want more. Those who think they have little or no power long to acquire it. And we all play our power games to get what we want.

Perhaps the reason the ad about the "power suit" and the article about Dunamis Sportswear caught my eye was that I'd just been reading about a very different kind of power clothing. It was not in an ad or a newspaper story, but in a promise made by a leader beginning a worldwide movement. At a time when this leader's followers were experiencing both the longing for power and the lack of it, this leader said, "Behold, I send the Promise of My Father upon you; but tarry in the city of Jerusalem until you are endued with power from on high" (Luke 24:49).

A Different Power Suit

The word "endued" means "clothed"; the One who offered this distinctly different power suit was Jesus of Nazareth, the risen Lord. The power He offered was more than human power. He would be the holy haberdasher of divine power, power from on high, God's power, the same power He had displayed in His ministry, the very power that had raised Him from the dead.

Authentic, nonmanipulative, noncoercive, liberating, enabling power to be, to do, to accomplish: to live life as He lived it, and would live it in His followers.

The powerless disciples desperately needed this kind of power. They had seen human power exercised at the crucifixion. In the execution of Jesus, the tributaries of political power flowing from Rome converged with the religious power of the leaders of Israel in a collusive surge of hate. But the disciples had also beheld an awesome release of God's power in raising Jesus from the dead. And now, here was their resurrected Master telling them that they would receive the very same power!

Not many days later, just before His ascension, Christ repeated His Promise of authentic power. "You shall receive power when the Holy Spirit has come upon you; and you shall be witnesses to Me in Jerusalem, and in all Judea and Samaria, and to the end of the earth" (Acts 1:8).

But this power would not be squandered; it would be released for a reason—for a purpose. The power clothing Jesus promised to send would enable his followers to be witnesses.

The word "witness" comes from the Greek word for "martyr," one who lives the truth as he or she has experienced it, regardless of the cost. Jesus offered to clothe His followers with power to love and serve as He had during His ministry.

The actual clothing with power happened at Pentecost. The disciples of Jesus were entrusted with the authentic power of His Spirit and were given the authority to exercise that power as His servants to change the world. The church of true power was born.

But What About Now?

Meanwhile, back to you and me. Back to our marriages, our families, our friendships; back to our jobs, our relationships, and our responsibilities; back to the arenas of our struggle for human power. With the promise of this kind of power given to us, why are we so often caught in the struggle for coercive, human power?

To repeat our question and put it even more directly: Why are so many Christians so powerless—so out of control, at loose ends? What's missing? Our first response is, "Why, of course, impotent Christians lack the indwelling power of the Spirit of Christ."

But let's go deeper. What causes that lack? Does Christ play favorites? Does He give His power to a select few who pray hard enough, study the Bible persistently enough, live piously enough? No. There's more, much more, to living in the consistent flow of superabundant power.

"All right, then," you say, "what must we do to be endued, clothed, with Christ's authentic, abundant power?"

My response is to suggest five crucial steps to power. They may not be what you expect, and certainly they are more challenging than we're accustomed to hearing. Let's think together about power addiction, power purpose, power failure, the power connection, and power flow.

THE FIRST STEP

The first step to receiving authentic power is to admit our addiction to the misuse of human power. I believe the love of power is really the false love of ourselves. We all have some measure of human power, and at times we all use this power to manipulate, coerce, barter, and struggle for dominance. We all want to be the first to answer the question "Who's in charge here?" with "I am, of course—hadn't you noticed?"

There are lots of ways to exercise human power. The shout and the pout are equally effective. Compliments and complaints both express power as well. Intellectual power can be used as manipulatively as sheer physical force. We can rape a person with words as drastically as we can use physical dominance.

Some people are very up front in their quest for power, demanding the rights and recognition of human power. Positions, titles, and authority are the requirements for these power brokers.

Others prefer to work behind the scenes, exercising primary power through secondary pawns, that is, by quietly manipulating the people around them. The important thing is getting what they want when they want it.

Still others barter for power. Their power base is secured by the negotiable commodities of influence, money, sex. Often their modus operandi involves a simple quid pro quo: "If I do this for you, I can assume you will do that for me." We all know how much of life is based on this exchange of power. When people let us down we can't help blurting out an agonizing "After all I've done for him, how could he do this to me?"

Our addiction to power forces us to play power games. "Control" is really the name of these games which are played in the parlor, the bedroom, the boardroom. Lately, it's not uncommon to hear of people breaking off a relationship with someone because the other person has too many "control issues." Power is the issue troubling many marriages in need of genuine affection . . . the problem that festers and erupts between many parents and children . . . the debilitating obsession that causes competition on the job.

Churches are not exempt. Clergy often try to use power to control and are defensive about challenges to their authority. The laity sometimes seek to control clergy with threats, criticism, withdrawal of support, or resistance to leadership.

But one of the saddest, most deprecating misuses of power is the withholding of love, affirmation, and delight from other people. Few things keep people in line with our wishes more than an attitude of reserve or aloofness. It is paradoxical that in the power struggle of relationships, *the one who loves and encourages the least, gains the most power.* This puts people on edge, keeps them guessing, and plays on their need for assurance about their worth.

Why is it so hard to tell people how much we love and appreciate them? Because we've learned early in life that we hold the trump card as long as we withhold ourselves and dangle people over the abyss of uncertainty.

This is a major problem in many marriages. The partner who plays the withholding game soon gains control. And all of us have friends who are stingy affirmers, who keep us struggling to try to win their approval, let alone their accolades. Managers often try to control employees by keeping them insecure about their future employment and advancement. As one boss put it, "If my people knew how much I appreciated them, they would take advantage or get a big head. It wouldn't be long before someone would hire them away." Control!

But by far the most serious result of addiction to human power is how it blocks our ability to receive and communicate the power of God. This, surely, is the reason so many Christians ardently express their lack in experiencing God's power! Even those of us who talk the most about the power of the Spirit find that we woefully lack power in the pressures of life. Why? I'm convinced it's because we are still under our own control, committed to the struggle for human power.

Psalm 8 declares the blessing that often becomes our bane. "When I consider Your heavens, the work of Your fingers, the moon and the stars, which You have ordained, what is man that You are mindful of him, and the son of man that You visit him? For You have made him a little lower than the angels, and You have crowned him with glory and honor. You have made him to have dominion over the works of Your hands" (vv. 3–6).

You see, it's this gift of dominion that gets distorted and makes us lose touch with the Giver. We claim this entrusted dominion to be our own and use it to manipulate life and others. Some even try to manipulate God with good works! We barter our efforts and accomplishments for His approval rather than serving Him because we know we are loved.

The only way out of the power bind is to recognize how powerless we are over our misuse of power. This is absolutely necessary if we are to begin, or grow in, the Christian life.

Now let's consider the power purpose.

THE SECOND STEP

The second step to authentic power is to affirm Christ's purpose for the release of power. This purpose is made awesomely clear in His life, message, and death. If we want authentic power, which is the power of Jesus' Spirit, we must come to grips with what He called us to be: nothing less than the high calling to be a servant.

During His incarnation, Christ took "the form of a servant" (Phil. 2:7). Throughout His ministry, He revealed what we were meant to be as servants. He exemplified an entirely new quality of servanthood. Out of unqualified love, He served with no thought of reward or desire to manipulate. Humbly and unselfishly, He gave Himself away; He cared for the poor, the disadvantaged, the sick, and the brokenhearted. His motive was clear: "For even the Son of Man did not come to be served, but to serve, and to give His life a ransom for many" (Mark 10:45). Christ's purpose was equally clear: "It is enough for a disciple that he be like his teacher, and a servant like his master" (Matt. 10:25a). He called followers who would be a new breed of servants in His style, to whom eventually He could entrust the power of His own Spirit.

The disciples found Jesus' calling to be servants very difficult to accept. They were more concerned about positions of power and recognition. Even on the night before Jesus was crucified, the disciples were embroiled in divisive competition. Luke tells us that "there was also rivalry among them, as to which of them should be considered the greatest" (22:24). This helps us understand what was on the disciples' minds when Christ dramatically focused in with a never-to-be-forgotten example of all that He had taught them about servanthood. It is recorded in John, chapter 13.

When Christ and the disciples arrived at the house where they planned to celebrate the Passover meal, someone was missing. The host who had provided an upper room in his house had not arranged for a servant to meet them at the door to wash their feet. I've often wondered if Jesus had instructed him to forgo this customary act of hospitality in order to see if one of the disciples would rise to the occasion and wash His and the other disciples' feet. None did; each was too occupied with thoughts of human greatness. And so, with dusty feet and competitive hearts, they sat down to the meal.

During the meal, Christ rose and stripped Himself down to a loincloth, the garb of a servant. He took a towel and basin of water and washed the disciples' feet. Their amazement mingled with embarrassment as Christ performed this task. What He said intensified the living parable He had enacted: "Do you know what I have done to you? You call Me Teacher and Lord, and you say well, for so I am. If I then, *your Lord* and Teacher, have washed your feet, you also ought to wash one another's feet. For I have given you an example, that you should do as I have done to you. Most assuredly, I say to you, a servant is not greater than his master, nor is he who is sent greater than he who sent him. If you know these things, happy are you if you do them" (John 13:12b–17).

We are called to be to each other what Christ has been to us. Until we accept our calling to servanthood as the key to experiencing authentic power, we will find the Christian life one of struggle, strain, and stress, and we will be troubled by the lust for power and the lack of it. And worse yet, until we understand the vital link between servanthood and power, we will limp along in our own delusions—our inadequate facsimiles of power.

How May I Serve You?

Recently, I had the privilege of spending an hour with a great thinker and theologian whose benchmark writings I had read and admired for years. After the pleasantry of greetings, this giant of wisdom and knowledge looked at me intently with his warm, brown eyes and said, "Now, how may I serve you?" He had no need to impress or wield the power of his intellect. The purpose of his scholarship and concern for people is simply to serve.

After the visit, I thought a lot about the question "How may I serve you?" That question really is the antidote to false power, competitiveness, and self-centered ambition. It's a question to ask at the beginning of every day and in every relationship and situation—how can we serve?

In marriage, with our friends, on the job, in the community—our purpose is to serve and not expect to be served. Our concern is not what we can get, but what we can give.

What a difference it would make in our marriages if we thought of what we could do to serve our mates rather than keep a scrupulous account of what he or she has done (or not done!) for us lately. This means listening, bearing burdens, doing the practical (and sometimes gloriously impractical) things that communicate we care. Our calling is to initiate affection, simply giving ourselves away unselfishly, and forgiving unconditionally. A tall order? Yes, but there's no true power without it.

Now let's focus on being a servant with our friends. Try this on for size—it takes time and involvement. When we serve our friends, we are given the chance to share our faith, introduce them to Christ, and experience the profound joy of a creatively powerful relationship.

On the job, there are few things more liberating than serving the people for whom we work, who work for us, or who work around us, if we surrender to the Lord our worries about future advancement.

We do not need to jockey for position or use other people as rungs on the ladder to success. When we replace defensiveness about our own power with a commitment to serve, the Lord will make it abundantly clear where He wants us. Then if we are given greater advancement, recognition, or the trappings of success, it will be to serve the Lord with greater opportunities.

There are manifold opportunities to be a servant right where we live. The power of our Servant-Master is released when we serve the poor, the homeless, the sick, the disadvantaged, the hungry. We are all called into ministry. The very word "minister" means servant, as does the word "deacon." Christ, our Eternal Deacon, calls us to serve in His name.

THE THIRD STEP

Now we are ready to consider the reality of power failures. To do this, we need to think about the third step to authentic power: to acknowledge our powerlessness. This difficult step of acknowledging our vulnerability is the exact opposite of defensively manipulating situations and people. Vulnerability is the freedom to confess our weakness and need, and therefore to receive the power the Lord has to give us. Always needing to be strong closes us off from His power. Paul affirmed, "When I am weak, then I am strong." Put another way, when we can acknowledge our need for power from Christ, we are strongest of all. No human being in Christian history was stronger than Paul, and no one confessed his weakness more readily.

The problem with this, however, is that we are so accustomed to maintaining control over others by appearing to be strong, adequate, and sufficient. But the Lord cannot bless with supernatural power those who want to be superstars. No one can present himself as sufficient in himself and at the same time communicate Christ's power!

Yet there's an even deeper issue. Our Lord was willing to become vulnerable. He came and lived among us and experienced our humanity. He suffered our hostility, rejection, and crucifixion. The cross forever stands as the symbol of God's vulnerability. Paul went so far as to call the cross "the foolishness and weakness" of God. *"But we preach Christ crucified, to the Jews a stumbling block and to the Greeks foolishness, but to those who are called, both Jews and Greeks, Christ the power of God and the wisdom of God. Because the foolishness of God is wiser than men, and the weakness of God is stronger than men"* (1 Cor. 1:23–25).

At the cross, our vulnerability and God's vulnerable love meet. He has opened Himself to us; in Christ He suffered for us. This is why we can be vulnerable with Him, confess our weakness, and receive His power.

Now we can understand and respond to Jesus Christ's call for us to take up our cross and follow Him. To do this requires obedience to Him, and gives us the assurance of the forgiveness of our sins, but it also means humbling ourselves to be vulnerable with people. It means being willing to love even if we are rejected. It also means identifying with the weakness of others by sharing how Christ is using our own weaknesses. Power is given to those who are vulnerable!

This brings us to the need to experience the power connection.

44

THE FOURTH STEP

The fourth step is to accept the gift of authentic power. It is a gift to those who admit their addiction to false power, affirm the true purpose of authentic power, and acknowledge their powerlessness.

At last, we are ready to visualize Christ's awesome description of how power is to be given to us. "If anyone thirsts, let him come to me and drink. He who believes in Me, as the Scripture has said, out of his heart will flow rivers of living water" (John 7:37b–38). John gives a helpful commentary to clarify the promise: "This He spoke concerning the Spirit, whom those believing in Him would receive; for the Holy Spirit was not yet given, because Jesus was not yet glorified" (v. 39). Now add to that a couple of lines from Peter's sermon after Pentecost and Christ's promise becomes vividly clear. "This Jesus God was raised up, of which we are all witnesses. Therefore being exalted to the right hand of God, and having received from the Father the promise of the Holy Spirit, He poured out this which you now see and hear" (Acts 2:32–33).

Don't miss the crucial dynamics for receiving power! It is for the powerless who come to Christ confessing their feelings of being at loose ends, and turn over the control of their lives to Him. In an intimate relationship with Him, He gives the gift of the Spirit. The Holy Spirit is authentic power—Christ's indwelling, abiding Spirit.

First, the living water of the Spirit flows to the inner needs we've endured. Like a geyser of grace or a river of new resources, the powerful flow reaches and fills our empty wells of insecurity, fear, and anxiety. All that causes us to feel impotent and at loose ends before the mounting demands of life is inundated with confidence-building courage. These rivers of living water maximize our intellectual abilities, enabling us to think with the mind of Christ. Our turbulent emotions are calmed and then healed; our wills are set free to desire and accept the Lord's guidance; our physical bodies receive new resiliency.

But the artesian flow of the Spirit fills us so we can overflow: we are to be a riverbed, not a reservoir. Jesus promised that *out* of our heart would flow *rivers* of living water—not a drop, a trickle, or even a rivulet, but a mighty, rushing, whitewater river of power!

So often when we think of the rivers of living water, we think only of the satisfaction of our own thirsty hearts. Sometimes we build a dam around us to keep the flow for ourselves. That's another manifestation of control, and it doesn't work! Have you ever smelled a stagnant pond? That is what happens when what flows in doesn't flow out again. There is a wonderful secret of spiritual power: the inflow of the Spirit is perfectly proportioned by outflow.

THE FIFTH STEP

Now, are you ready for the fifth step to experiencing authentic power? Here it is: *attempt something you could not do without the power of the indwelling Spirit of Christ.* When we dare to attempt what we would consider impossible on our own, we receive the flow of Christ's power.

Think again about those dangling, disturbing loose ends we talked about in the first chapter. Focus on the loose ends of the unfinished, the unresolved, and the unfulfilled. Remember how we identified the feeling of being at loose ends as the total accumulation of things that stand between us and what someday we'd like to be or to accomplish with our lives.

What is it for you?

First of all, living under Christ's control gives us the power to spread out before Him all that is unfinished, unresolved, and unfulfilled on our personal agendas. The inflowing rivers of His Spirit soften the tightly knotted bonds of our control, untying them so we can submit our frustrated desires to Him. We have the courage to pray, "Lord, show me what you want me to be and do, give me your strategy for my life, and give me equipoise to do what you want on your timing."

In response, Christ gives us the power to picture our lives under His management. He flashes onto the picture screen of our imagination what He wants us to be in the pressure-producing situations that confront us. There we see ourselves in a new quality of relationship with people in our lives. Most of all, we picture His priorities for us. We receive supernatural power to envision our lives filled with Christ, serene with Christ's peace, and energetic with actions and words of Christ's love.

You may need the power of Christ to express love to someone who is difficult to love; or you may need it to forgive people you think are neither worthy nor deserving of your acceptance. Perhaps it's tackling a big challenge you've avoided because you've been stewing in self-doubt and feelings of inadequacy. It may be changing your priorities, or canceling things Christ never called you to do in the first place! A change in lifestyle may be demanded.

But don't let me sandbag you with ideas of what the impossible dream "ought" to be for you—that's between you and the Lord. Ask Him what life under His control can be for you. If you ask Him to show you how to live without the misery and frustration of constantly being at loose ends, be sure of this: He will answer. And after a prolonged time of intimate listening, write out the results of His guidance. A good way is to finish this sentence: If I had an unlimited supply of Christ's power, I'd attempt . . . .

And honestly, it may all seem so impossible! *How can I do it? It's beyond me. Too much to ask.* "That's exactly how I hoped you'd feel," says Christ. "If you could do it on your own, you wouldn't need my power. But since you've admitted it's impossible, I'm ready to do it through you."

Living out the five steps to authentic power requires a constant inventory.

• Am I still addicted to fake, human power?

• Am I dependent on playing power games to get and keep control?

• Do I use manipulation rather than love to motivate others?

• Have I accepted Christ's purpose for power, and am I living as a servant?

• Has my lack of power driven me to Christ to receive the living water of His Spirit?

Power To You!

The other day, I had a frustrating lunch with a man who persistently avoided being honest and open about his needs. At the end of our visit, I shook the man's hand and said something I often say as a parting shot along with good-by: "Power to you!" I said.

Amazingly, these words broke through the man's shell. "That's exactly what I need," the man said intently. "Power seems to be what I lack. I hear a lot about the power of the Spirit of Christ, but I just don't have it. What's wrong?" We sat down again and began a deep conversation that lasted into the afternoon.

The man was blocked. His commitment to Christ had not involved a surrender of his old ways of using his own human power to achieve his goals. He needed to be clothed with Christ's power. But this required an honest confession of his dependence on his own power.

To do this, I led the man through the five steps to authentic power we've been talking about. It was not easy for him to confess his addiction to power, and his powerlessness when it came to the gigantic challenges of loving and forgiving, caring and serving. Up to this point in his Christian life, he had wanted Christ's power for his own problems rather than for Christ's greater purpose of ministry to others.

We talked at length about how the man could re-order his priorities to become a channel for true power. It was threatening at first, but eventually he got the picture for his marriage, family, friends, and his job. Because things were not going well for him in any of these areas of his life, he was willing to take an honest look at the difference between playing power games and receiving power for gracious living.

At the end of our time together, we had a deep time of prayer. I'm happy to say that my friend was filled with authentic power when he made a commitment to be a servant to others rather than struggle for power over them. His new freedom from feeling at loose ends is remarkable! He has superabundant power to equal his immense challenges.

And so, "Power to you!"

Christ is already at work in you, making it possible for you to expect and receive your power clothing—the clothing of His Spirit. *Anything* is possible for those committed to serve. All power is ours.

3.

YOU WERE MEANT TO SOAR

It was the middle of winter when the trapper ran out of what he called his "vittles," provisions for survival on the mountain. There was nothing to do but pack up and make the long journey down the mountain to the valley below. He had not sold his pelts yet, and he had only fifty dollars. With care, he could buy just enough staples to last the rest of the winter. Along with what he could catch in his traps and fish for by cutting holes in the ice of the river, he could make it to spring.

In the supply store, he cautiously checked the price of each item, gathered up exactly fifty dollars' worth, and presented his necessities for the storekeeper to ring up on an old, time-worn cash register.

While the storekeeper totaled his purchases, the trapper observed all the stuffed animals and birds on a shelf behind the counter. In the middle of the array of taxidermy was a cage with a great bald eagle in it. The trapper didn't like that—he loved to watch eagles soar. Upon closer observation, his indignation turned to anger. The eagle was alive!

On the front of the cage was a sign: "Price— $50.00." The trapper looked down on his vittles, now ready to be boxed. Then he looked back up to the poor, confined, caged eagle.

With consternation, the trapper voiced his complaint, "Them critters are meant to soar. Them ain't meant to be in cages!"

"Then buy it and do what you want with it," the storekeeper replied.

The trapper's fingers tightened on the fifty dollars he was clutching in his fist. He looked down at his provisions and once again to the caged eagle. With a decisive sweep, he pushed the supplies aside and threw down the fifty dollars.

"Gimme that critter!" he exclaimed. "Like I said, mister, them ain't meant for cages. Them's supposed ta soar—I'm gonna' set 'im free!"

With jaw set in determination, the trapper stomped out of the store, cage in hand. Out in the open under the "big sky" that was a magnificent cloudless blue, he opened the cage door and released the eagle. Laughing with glee, he watched the eagle fly away. It circled once, as if to express gratitude, and then flew higher and higher until it was caught up in the jet stream. With wings outstretched, it was effortlessly lifted to the lofts above the mountain from which the trapper had come.

Returning to the reality of facing half a winter ahead without money or supplies, the trapper was heard to mutter, "Don't care, just don't care. Eagles gotta soar!"

In order to survive the rest of the winter, the mountain man worked as a day laborer in the valley. Often while doing his menial chores, he would look up and see a soaring eagle and imagine it was the one he had set free. "Soar on, Baldy. Soar higher, ya free critter! Ya was never meant for a cage!"

You Too Were Meant To Soar

You and I were also created to soar. We were not meant for the cages that we and others have built. Christ has set us free at a far greater cost than the trapper gave for the eagle's freedom. The Savior gave His life on the cross to release us from the bondage of fear and worry, from our negative thinking about our potential, and from our limited vision of the power He has to help us soar to new heights of abundant living.

We have been equipped with soaring wings; we were not created for a cage, but to "mount up with wings like eagles" (Isa. 40:31). I've discovered something about eagles' wings that has given me an exciting secret of the power in our soaring wings.

On a cross-country flight, I was seated next to a pilot who was deadheading home to Los Angeles. When he noticed I was reading my Bible, he confided to me that he was a Christian. This gave me the chance to ask a question I'd wanted to ask a pilot for a long time.

So I said, "I've been studying the soaring ability of the eagle and understand there's a similarity in its wings to the wings of an airplane. What is it?"

The pilot smiled. "So, you're into eagles, too! I guess I'm a frustrated ornithologist or something. I'm fascinated by eagles, and I can sit for hours on a mountain watching them soar. Maybe that's why I enjoy flying these jets so much."

He went on to tell me about the power secret of eagles' wings. "It's all in the alulas," he said. He then took me on an imaginary flight of an eagle to explain what he meant. It was spellbinding.

The eagle leaves its perch and with its mighty wings climbs to great heights. Then, when it reaches the fast-moving air currents, the eagle spreads its wings to full extension and begins to soar. The air currents flow over the upper surface of the wings faster than the underside, creating lesser pressure on the top and greater pressure below. This forces the wings up. If the angle of the wings is too steep, the lift is lost. The air stream begins to break away, causing turbulence and possible stalling. That's why the alulas are so crucial. They keep the wings at just the right angle to produce gradual ascent.

The pilot explained that the alulas are two small feathers attached to the thumb or pollex, at the bend, or joint, farthest out on each of an eagle's wings. These tiny feathers control the airflow over the wings. Then he pointed out the window of the plane in which we were flying, showing me what are called the air slots on the wings. Like the eagle's alula feathers, the air slots direct the flow of air currents smoothly over the top of the wing. With its alulas, the eagle can also use the currents to rise higher and higher without moving its wings.

Isaiah must have been an eagle-watcher. Surely he too knew the power secret of the eagle's alulas. When he speaks of the eagle "mounting up," he's not talking about an energetic flapping of its wings, but about taking advantage of the airflow in ascending to ever-increasing altitude. My pilot friend and I talked all the way to Los Angeles about the control factor of the alulas and drew some analogies for our life in Christ.

How Are Your Alulas?

Without stretching the metaphor in the least, I want us to think about our spiritual alulas in our minds. We too have spiritual power-flow regulators to help us soar. Misused, they can distort the flow and cause turbulence, stalling, and even a plunge downward. Learning how to use our spiritual alulas is one of the secrets of allowing the Lord to control our lives so we can soar to new effectiveness. He is able!

Earlier I promised that we would consider the eight "He is able" scriptures in the epistles of the New Testament. They delineate the dimensions of Christ's power available to us by forcefully telling what He is able to do for us when we turn over the control of our lives to Him.

Now we are ready to claim the first one from Ephesians 3:20–21. Note carefully the phrase "according to the power that works in us" in this amazing promise: "Now to Him who is able to do exceedingly abundantly above all that we ask or think, *according to the power that works in us*, to Him be glory in the church by Christ Jesus through all ages, world without end. Amen" (emphasis mine).

What does that have to do with the alulas in our souls? Everything! Let me explain.

Remember that the Greek word for "able" comes from *dunamis*, "power." To say God is able is another way of saying that He has all power. He has chosen to release this power in and through Christ. Christ is the power of God with us (1 Cor. 1:24). Through Him, God is ready to do "exceedingly abundantly" way beyond what we would normally and humanly dare to envision for the loose ends of what is unfinished, unresolved, and unfulfilled in our lives.

A Little Power Word

"According to," *kata* in Greek, is the little but decisive word in Paul's promise. It means "to the measure or the extent" of something. So to the measure or extent of Christ's power at work *in us* we are able to realize how His superabundant power can work *in our outer lives*—in the potential of what we can dare to attempt in our responsibilities, relationships, problems, and perplexities. The reason Christ's power at work in us is so crucial is that we have a control factor within us as part of our entrusted freedom. It functions in the cerebral cortex of our brains to govern the faculties of perception, imagination, and will. Without Christ's inner liberation, our imagination is inhibited and clouded, and our will is crippled. We can't see what is possible for our loose ends or will to have it happen. Until Christ heals us, what we "think" (*nooumen* in Greek)—our ability to perceive, understand, and apprehend—is limited. As a result, what we "ask" (*aitoumetha*, middle voice in Greek, meaning "ask for ourselves") is stunted. Our prayers are constricted to something far less than Christ is able—has the power—to do.

I compare the control factor of our imagination and will to the alula feathers of the eagle's wings. The lifting currents of Christ's spirit are available to all, if only we would allow Him to teach us how to use them to soar. Just as the eagle has no power to soar without the wind currents, so we have no power to soar without the jet stream of Christ's Spirit. And as the young eagle is taught to soar by using its alulas, so, too, Christ teaches us how to imagine and ask for His superabundant plan and power and how to yield to the lifting currents of His Spirit. He wants us to face into the wind and go with His flow—to be elevated by the rising currents and updrafts of His power.

The Danger of Stalling

Soaring is not without risk. The dangerous possibility of stalling is ever-present. Earlier we noted that this happens when an eagle's alulas are not properly used to keep the airflow moving smoothly over the top of its wings. When the wings are slanted up too much, the airflow beneath the wings increases until the wings are positioned against the air currents. Speed is then decreased, and eventually, if the wing slant is resisting the wind, turbulence and the danger of stalling occur.

In our daily lives, few things more closely correspond to the feeling of being at loose ends than the image of stalling. Consistent misuse of our spiritual alulas, setting the slant of the wings of our soul against the flow of Christ's Spirit, will cause emotional turbulence and eventually stall our flight, keeping us from accomplishing our tasks and reaching our goals. We forget that we were meant to soar. And, of course, when the stall lasts too long, we crash.

The Worry Turbulence

When the loose ends of the unfinished, unresolved, and unfulfilled pile up, we begin to feel the turbulence of worry. Worry is the anxiety of trying to stay in flight by our own power and under our control. We frantically flap our wings to stay aloft rather than living in the jet stream of Christ's power, where we will be in a position to receive the thermal updrafts of His lifting grace. And the constant turbulence of worry over our loose ends easily becomes habit.

The Worry Habit

Recently, while traveling, I had breakfast in a hotel coffee shop. I couldn't help overhearing a conversation between two traveling salesmen.

"Well, how'd you sleep?" one asked.

"Terribly," the other replied. "I was worried whether my travel alarm clock would go off. It's been acting up lately. The batteries must be running down."

"Why not change the batteries?" his friend asked with a smile. Then his face darkened with concern. "You must like to worry. I've noticed that in you a lot lately. You worry about everything. Have you always had the worry habit?"

The man with run-down batteries in his alarm clock, and obviously in his whole life as well, changed the subject.

I'd like for us to stay on the subject. Do we sometimes *enjoy* worrying? "Enjoy" hardly expresses my emotions when I feel at loose ends. And yet, there's a bit of masochism in all of us. When it comes to persistently muddling in worry, it would almost appear that we enjoy punishing ourselves.

A little boy observed this in his grandmother. "Grandma is a really good worrier. It's what she does best!"

We become expert worriers when the loose ends within us pile up in a mountain of guilt over our not having handled life better. Add to that our self-incrimination for not keeping up to date. Life rushes on with dangling loose ends flopping behind us— important things we either failed to do or did badly.

Let me be very honest with you. Perhaps you can identify. (Perhaps? That was an unnecessary, solicitous aside—I know human nature well enough to be certain you can identify with what I'm going to say!)

The loose ends I worry about most of all are the missed opportunities to love. In a quiet moment at the end of the day, or in an unguarded moment during the rush of life, the sharp points of those loose ends stab me and wound my sense of well-being. Sometimes in one of my midnight muddles I'm awakened, tossing and turning with the loose end of some significant relationship twisting around my memory like baling wire around a gate. The "what if's" and "why didn't I's" prance about to cadences of "oughts" and "shoulds." I rehearse a long-term need to love some person in ways meaningful to him or her, or remember a more recent time when I ought to have prayed for lockjaw instead of blurting out an angry criticism or cutting remark.

Life under my own control leads to a denial of love. For me, the opposite of being a controlling person is being a loving person under Christ's control. On those occasions when I fail, I get stalled in flight. My life shakes with the turbulence of uncreative worry. I use the alulas of my spiritual wings to will a resistance, rather than a response, to Christ's love. Know what I mean? I know you do.

Worry is a sure sign we have taken imperious control of our lives again. And the things that worry us most are the problems we've *caused* by trying to control others and life itself. In our ego, we don't trust God to take care of things in the way we think is correct and perhaps don't really believe He is able. A controlling attitude is the belief that (sigh . . .) we still have to do everything ourselves. The cycle becomes habitual. No wonder we get stalled in flight!

The turbulence of worry rattles the fuselage of our composure. Sometimes, it actually makes us sick. Dr. George Mayo once said, "Worry affects circulation, the heart, glands, the whole nervous system. I have never known a man who died of overwork, but many who have died from worry."

Some people actually confuse worry with conscientiousness! The mother of a teenage boy thought if she worried a lot, it meant she was being a "good mother." But her son sees the worry as negativity, not concern—complaints, not caring. "And when she tries to keep everything 'under control,' " he said, "my blood pressure goes up!"

Shifting the blame to others, "conscientious worriers" exercise even greater control with their threat of having a minor nervous breakdown. Have you seen the T-shirts and coffee mugs that announce, "Very soon I'm going to have a nervous breakdown—I've worked for it, I've earned it, I deserve it—and nothing is going to keep me from it"? Talk about control! We laugh at the absurdity of the slogan but our laughter dies down as we remember a time when a slight case of the "flu" we said we had was really nothing more than exhaustion over trying to stay in control. And chances are that we enjoyed the extra edge of control we got by reminding our family or people at work how difficult it was to get along without us.

A Controlling Sister

Jesus' friend Martha is a good example of worrisome control (Luke 10:38–40). When the Master made one of His visits to her home, she set herself up with a problem on which to focus her floating worry syndrome. She just had to display her culinary artistry with a many-course dinner. After greeting her guest at the door, she rushed back to the kitchen to perfect her gourmet presentation. Meanwhile, her sister Mary seated herself at the feet of Jesus while He shared spiritual truth and love.

Martha continued to be distracted by her self-appointed duties. It's interesting to note that the Greek word for "distracted" in Luke's account is in the imperfect passive, meaning that her duties continued to *work on her, pulling her away* into busy, overburdened care. There was not only water boiling in the kettle over the fire; there was anger boiling inside Martha. She was angry at Mary for leaving her to prepare all the dishes of the meal that she, not Mary, insisted on serving. It almost seems as if she wanted to worry over the meal and be upset with herself and angry at Mary. Eventually, she was impatient even with Jesus.

Watch Martha, a controlling person, in action. She burst in on Jesus, interrupted His teaching, and blurted out, "Lord, do you not care that my sister has left me to serve alone? Therefore, tell her to help me!" Stop and think about the most recent time you made a power move like that.

Jesus didn't let Martha get away with her power game. "Martha, Martha, you are worried and troubled about many things. But one thing is needed, and Mary has chosen that good part, which will not be taken away from her."

Checking the exact wording of Jesus' rebuke in the Greek, I'm ready to agree with some scholars that there may have been some spiritualizing by the transcribers of His actual words. Jesus' response, when understood from the earliest manuscripts, really deals with the elaborate meal Martha was preparing. He also used the metaphor of a portion of a meal to confront Martha's overfastidiousness and to commend Mary's rapt attentiveness. A paraphrase goes something like this: "Martha, Martha, you are worried and troubled by preparing too elaborate a meal. One dish would have been enough, and the real portion is fellowship with me. Mary has chosen that, but the food you've prepared will pass away; my food can never be taken from you."

What Is The Real Worry?

Jesus knew that Martha's greatest concern was maintaining her control. She wanted to make the dinner a success and polish her reputation as a cook and hostess. Most important to Martha was what she could do for Jesus, rather than what He wanted to give her. She knew that Jesus' main interest would be to share His message of the Kingdom. Yet Martha purposely prepared a many-course meal. Could it be that she intentionally (or subconsciously) planned ahead to be overly busy?

Martha also tried to control Mary. As the older of the two sisters, she must have assumed that she was in charge of Jesus' visit and Mary should carry out her bidding. It's difficult for us controllers when people won't march to our drumbeat! Sometimes not even the guilt, shame, or criticism Martha used on Mary will get them cracking to our orders.

Most of all, Martha could not control Jesus. That was her biggest mistake—trying to use Him as her pawn to maneuver Mary into place. Instead He put His incisive finger on the worry habit that made Martha a manipulator in her brand of power games.

But as with most of us who are stalled by a worry habit, one confrontation with Jesus doesn't break the syndrome. Later, Martha tried to pull off another power move on the Master after the death of her brother, Lazarus (John, chapter 11). This time, when Jesus arrived at her home in Bethany, she used an old ploy: "If you had been here, my brother would not have died." She tried to transfer her grief by placing the guilt on Jesus. Ever done that with people? Or tried it on Christ?

Jesus dealt with Martha's controlling methods by revealing to her that He was in control. Patiently, the Master helped her reaffirm her belief in Him as the Messiah. Then He spoke one of His most powerful I-AM assertions: "I am the resurrection and the life." And to be sure she had transferred to Him her control of herself, her grief, and the impossible situation confronting her, Christ asked, "Do you believe this?" When Martha's trust was in Him alone, He raised Lazarus from the dead.

But Martha's full transformation did not take place until after Christ's crucifixion, resurrection, and return to baptize His followers with the Holy Spirit at Pentecost. Surely she and her sister Mary were among the women (Acts 1:14) in the upper room, along with the disciples and followers of Jesus, when He gave them the power suits we talked about in the previous chapter.

Freedom From Worry

Nothing less than the healing power of the Holy Spirit could have liberated Martha from her worry habit. We sometimes forget that there was no conversion of any of Jesus' followers until after Pentecost. We wistfully look back and wish we could have known Jesus in the flesh during his Palestinian ministry. Yet three minutes after Pentecost, the followers of Christ knew Him more intimately than they had during the three years of walking with Him in His earthly, incarnate ministry.

Now they were empowered by His indwelling power through the Holy Spirit. They burst out on Jerusalem, and subsequently the then-known world, with the triumphant confidence "He is able." Prior to Pentecost they were at loose ends. Afterward they trusted completely in the Lord of Loose Ends who helped them do His will on His timing. They discovered that the only loose end of any importance was a world that desperately needed Christ—a world addicted to human power.

Power At Work In Us

The same coercive, human power that resisted Jesus' ministry and impaled Him on the cross was soon turned in full fury on the church. The leader of that persecution was the most elitist power broker of the Sanhedrin, a Pharisee from Tarsus, named Saul.

The church might not have survived. But Christ had other plans. He personally confronted Saul on the road to Damascus. The militant Pharisee, whose god was human power, was blinded. For days, he stumbled about in a dark awareness of something he had never experienced before—powerlessness. Saul was at the mercy of the very people he was on his way to Damascus to arrest or kill. One of the Christians, named Ananias, exercised the authentic power of love and forgiveness, and baptized his feared persecutor in the name of Jesus Christ.

After fourteen years of secluded study and preparation, Paul began his ministry. But in those long years of waiting, he had sorted out the difference between manipulative, human power and the authentic power of Christ. When Paul began to preach the Gospel, his message was the power of God: servant-love in Christ, the power of the cross and resurrection, and the power of the indwelling Spirit of Christ in the believer.

Near the end of his ministry, during his first imprisonment in Rome, Paul wrote to his friends in the church in Ephesus to remind them of the true power that had been given to them. In his letter to the

Ephesians, the apostle penned the "He is able" ascription about authentic power we've been considering. It is the testimony of a transformed power broker who stopped saying "I am able" and constantly declared, "Christ is able!"

Paul describes the "power connection" in his prayer for the Ephesians. It precedes this mighty assurance that "He is able." It asks Christ's power

- that we may be strengthened with might through His Spirit in our inner person; that Christ may dwell in our hearts by faith;

- that we will be able to comprehend the width, length, depth, and height of the love of Christ, which passes knowledge; and

- that we may be filled with all the fullness of God!

All this explains the "power at work in us" that gives us the wondrous ability to imagine what the Lord will do within and around us with His superabundant power.

Life In Balance

The secret of experiencing this power is revealed in what Paul goes on to admonish in the first three verses of Ephesians 4: "I, therefore, the prisoner of the Lord, beseech you to walk worthy of the calling with which you were called, with all lowliness and gentleness, with longsuffering, bearing with one another in love, endeavoring to keep the unity of the Spirit in the bond of peace."

We are offered power to live without power games. The Greek word translated "worthy" *(axios)* has to do with weights and measures. Something which is *axios* balances the scales, is equal in weight to that which is being compared.

Picture an ancient scale with two containers, one on each side. On one is placed the object to be measured, on the other, the weights of measurement. The apostle communicates the idea that one side of the scale is loaded with the love and power of the Lord, the other with our empowered life. A life worthy of our calling is one equal to the resources available to us — one of humility, meekness, patience, love, and keeping the bond of peace with others, rather than bartering with them in the struggle for power.

The ultimate test of authentic power is that it brings peace, not competitive discord; that it produces unity, not division; and that it moves us forward in the goals of the kingdom, not in our selfish desire to dominate.

Paul's words were written to a diversified church of Jews and Greeks, the strong and the weak, the rich and the poor. They were challenged to live in the power of the Lord, rather than seeking to lord it over one another. High priority was given to unity and oneness so that the church could be the riverbed for the flow of superabundant, miraculous power to the pagan world around it. The same is true for all the relationships of life. Power from the Lord is given when we are humble, meek, patient, and free of efforts to control.

The people and churches I know that are experiencing superabundant power from the Spirit of Christ are committed to this qualification for the flow of power. No longer stalled in worry over whether or not they are able, all they need to know is "Christ is able."

To Soar Is To Adore

The more we stop trying to be able on our own and claim that Christ is able, has all power, the more we will adore Him for what He is doing with our concerns. Our worry stall will be changed to a willing stillness. With our alulas of imagination and will, we can think and ask for what the Lord has for us. The wings of our souls will be perfectly positioned to receive the lifting flow of His power. As the rising currents lift us, our song of adoration will echo beyond the mountain peaks. "He is able! He is able!"

We weren't meant for a cage of fear, a perch of uncertainty, or a stall of worry—we were meant to soar!

4.

THE JOY OF BEING HUMAN

Overcoming Our Personality Loose Ends

LILY TOMLIN, WHO ROSE TO FAME AS A TELEVISION COMEDIAN for her rib-slapping portrayal of Ernestine on "Laugh-In," made a stunning statement in an interview that appeared in the *San Francisco Chronicle.*

> In a world where so many things are brutalized and desensitizing, maybe we yearn to make something that fills us with a kind of elation, a sense of something joyful and lovely, a sense of inspiration. Anything to make us rise above this banal, animalistic, low-grade, diminished cockroach level.

Miss Tomlin expresses a universal longing. We all yearn for something to give life sparkle, zest, a gusto — what Rudolph Nureyev calls *"iziominka."* But what gave me pause in Tomlin's lines was the idea that we are able to produce something joyful. If we could make it, it would have been manufactured and marketed long ago.

The manufacturers of Joy perfume have tried. Last July, about the time I read Lily Tomlin's statement, I saw a billboard advertising Joy perfume. "A single whiff of Joy turns a rich man into a generous man." The copy writer could sense the transforming power of joy—but real joy is more than a scent.

I'm no rich man, but the advertisement did remind me that Joy perfume is a favorite of a lovely lady I know—my first-born. Over the years, every so often on special occasions, a little bottle of the fragrance has expressed my father's heart of love and admiration.

Some Joy, Please

So I headed into the department store. "I'd like some Joy, please," I said to the woman behind the counter.

"And who doesn't?" the clerk replied and then smiled, "You and everybody else—if we could only find it! I mean the real stuff, not just the scent of it."

You can imagine this comment began a long conversation. I learned the woman was a struggling Christian. We talked at length about our mutual quest for true, lasting joy, and what keeps us from it at times.

"What is it for you?" I asked.

"You're looking at her!" the woman said with what I have subsequently learned is her customary frankness. "It's me! I get so impatient with myself. There are things I know I should change, but I put them off. And you know what? I get so impatient with my family and friends because I can't seem to change them either."

This woman had just enough Christianity to give her a wistful longing for joy, but not the power to change the things in herself and others that were robbing them of the fullness of joy Jesus promised. Like so many of us, she's discovered that her most disturbing, dangling loose ends are inside herself—things she'd like to change if she only had the power. This woman needed the Lord of the Loose Ends who alone has the power to change us. I'm happy to say that she is discovering His transforming power by experiencing the secret of change I want to share in this chapter.

A "He Is Able" Shout Of Joy

This secret of Christ's transforming power is in another of Paul's triumphant shouts of joy that "He is able." The apostle wrote it in a letter to his friends in Philippi, also during his first imprisonment in Rome.

In the third chapter of his letter, he begins to soar with his description of the joy in knowing Christ. He explains the progressive experience of death to his old self and confides that the resiliency of Christ's resurrection power is making a new man out of the personality he surrendered to his indwelling Lord.

Paul expresses his desire to press on so that he may lay hold of that for which Christ has laid hold of him. He was determined to "press toward the goal for the prize of the upward call of God in Christ Jesus." He longs for his friends in Philippi to be of the same mind, and also exposes some false teachers who are trying to rob them of their joy.

Then the apostle bursts forth with the secret: "For our citizenship is in heaven, from which we also eagerly wait for the Savior, the Lord Jesus Christ, who will transform our lowly body that it may be conformed to His glorious body, according to the working by which He is able even to subdue all things to Himself" (Phil. 3:20–21).

We meet that little Greek power word again—*kata* ("according to, the measure, extent"). Here it is used to introduce the working energy *(energeia)* of Christ's power in order to subdue *(hupotasso,* to bring into submission) all things in us and in the world around us. Just as Christ has subdued the power of death, Satan, and the binding power of sin, so He is able—has all power—to transform and conform us into His own likeness. The "according to" serves as a link between the change in us which will be completed in heaven and the changes in our character and personality which "He is able" to make *now*.

Claim Your Citizenship

Paul challenges the Philippians to claim their citizenship in heaven and to start living in the joy of heaven now, in the present. His readers would understand the simile of citizenship in a faraway land. Philippi was part of a colony of Rome and the people there enjoyed the privileges and benefits of Roman citizenship. Though they had heard about the magnificent city all of their lives, most of the people would never see Rome. The difference for the Christians was that their true citizenship was in heaven and they *would* get there!

In fact, through Christ, they were already on the citizenship rolls of heaven and were called to live in Philippi as if they were living in the ambience of heavenly joy. The power that would accomplish their complete transformation in heaven was the same power already at work in them, enabling them to live with joy during the earthly portion of their eternal life.

Paul's concern is with those who are resisting Christ's transforming power in the present. If they resist His personality-repatterning character reorientation now, he asks them, have they claimed their true citizenship? They will be very uncomfortable in heaven if they refuse the power of the Lord on earth.

Without losing a beat in the flow of his thought, Paul presses on to share a taste of heaven that he is experiencing in his friends in Philippi. But he then gives a dishonorable mention of two in the fellowship who are anything but joyous in their relationship with the Lord or with each other. What the apostle has to say to these two believers is directly related to the "He is able" statement and is meant to startle them, and others like them, into realizing what Christ needed to subdue in them.

The paragraphing and chapter divisions of Paul's writing were a later addition. Often the imposed divisions of chapter numbers keep us from grasping the flow of a completed thought. The intrusion of the chapter heading between what is now chapter 3 and chapter 4 of Philippians causes this kind of interruption.

Allow me to review. At the end of chapter 3, Paul is talking about Christ's power to transform our lives by subduing all things to Himself, overcoming the impediments of our growth in being conformed into Christ's glorious likeness. Then follows a strong linking—"Therefore, my beloved and longed-for brethren, my joy and crown, so stand fast in the Lord, beloved" (4:1). As continuation of the flow of that thought, Paul arrives at the concern on his heart. "I implore Euodia and I implore Syntyche to be of the same mind in the Lord" (4:2).

Unlike Their Names

No two people could have contradicted their names by their behavior more forcibly than Euodia and Syntyche. Euodia means "pleasant journey"; Syntyche means "fortunate coincidence." Life with Euodia must have been anything but pleasant, and relationships with Syntyche unfortunate happenings.

The women were in some kind of competitive power struggle. What their "power issues" were, we are not told. But whether they were hidden behind doctrinal, theological, or personality differences, the problem between them had become a threat to the peace and unity of the church. Word of it had even reached Paul in Rome. Surely the reason Paul takes up space in a relatively short epistle to deal with the problem must be that there were probably others in the church who had personality proclivities keeping them from receiving Christ's joy.

It's a good thing that Paul doesn't tell us the nature of the conflict between Euodia and Syntyche. We are forced to think about the possible changes we need—in us and our relationships. Then the ridiculous incongruity hits us: if Christ has all power to subdue all things to Himself, He could certainly deal with the problems between these women if they would be willing. The same is true for our personality problems and interpersonal conflicts.

Check Your Personality Loose Ends

What are the loose ends in our personalities that make it difficult to enjoy life and prompt us to play power games to control others? Think of the relationships in which we have the most conflict and competition for power. What do we contribute to the battle for dominance and control? If we were to meet Christ face to face, what would He say He wants to change *in us?* Not in other people . . . in us.

Christ Subdues What We Submit

Christ is able to subdue what we submit to Him. As we have noted, the Greek word for "subdue" is *hupotasso*, a military term meaning to rank under (*hupo*, under; *tasso*, to arrange). When we accept Christ as our Lord, He becomes our commander-in-chief. We are to march to His commands, His cadences, His direction. Then He takes on the responsibility for our personality transformation. Christ begins a continuous, never-ending process of conforming our nature to His own.

It's amazing, but Christ seeks to make us more human! Life under His control is humanizing. All the inhuman things we do to ourselves and others are confronted. Everything that debilitates us and keeps us from being free, life-affirming human beings, able to receive and give love, is drawn to the surface so that Christ may deal with it. Just as He drew the demons out of the possessed, He draws out of us the memories that motivate our uncreative behavior; the relationships in the past that cause us to be imperious in reaction or cautious in fear; the insecurities that make us controlling people. Then He parades before our mind's eye the failures of the past that drive us to try to control every circumstance so we'll never fail again, along with the successes that worry us by making us afraid that we can't top our own record. Then, one by one, Christ tears off the epaulets of the assumed authority these things have over us.

That's the kind of commanding Lord we have. If we submit to Him what is troubling us, He moves in, takes it, and strips it of any power to dominate our lives. With Christ subduing what subdues our humanness, we become free to soar higher and higher with joy.

The Pocket Veto

In the light of this "He is able" promise, it is astounding how we continue to exercise a pocket veto to

Christ's liberation and transformation. A pocket veto is an unspoken but persistent "No!" of passive resistance, an inner resolve to stay the way we are. We refuse to give over to the Lord the hard, inner core of our egos.

How can we know if we are exercising a pocket veto? Here are some telling questions:

- Was our conversion a radical transformation from self-centered willfulness or an effort to recruit the Lord to help us accomplish our goals?

- What significant changes have occurred in us over the past year because we have submitted more and more of our personalities to Christ's control?

- Have the harrowing experiences of life broken our inner core of proud individualism, or are we essentially the same people we always were?

- After a crisis is past, are we more flexible and willing to discern and do the Lord's will?

- Is there anything the Lord has called us to be or do that has put us into a contest of wills with Him?

- What challenges of obedience in our inner spiritual formation or call to ministry have we resisted?

It's difficult on our own to ask and answer these questions honestly. We need a trusted Christian friend or counselor who will go through them with us. It is best that this person be someone outside our families or fellow workers, someone who has nothing to gain or lose by helping us see the hidden control items on our pocket veto. Then, at all costs, we should tear up our pocket veto and say "Yes!" to the Lord's control of our lives.

I get a yearly "pocket veto" check-up. It's as crucial to my spiritual life as my yearly physical examination is to my health. I look for the subtle ways I resist the Lord's control. And I've learned that, like most, when I resist in any way, I drift into the danger of my own self-generated efforts to control life and people. This danger is ever-present in all of us. The less we trust the Lord to control our personal lives, the more controlling we become in our relationships.

I suspect this is what happened to Euodia and Syntyche. And most serious of all, they did not see that their efforts to gain control of each other were causing a serious fracture in the leadership of the church. Paul clearly identifies them as leaders who labored with him in the gospel.

The church's message about a victorious Lord who is able to subdue all things was being contradicted by two leading women who would not submit their difficulties and hostilities to the Lord. They were prevented by unresolved control problems in their individual spiritual lives. Paul was alarmed and called on the whole church to be his "companion" in helping these leaders. He knew that the effectiveness and credibility of the church in Philippi was at stake. The flow of power through a church is dependent on unity and freedom from power battles within it.

The Power Principle

The basic principle of power for any unit of the kingdom of God—a family, a church, a movement—is that the principals must be under Christ's control and not seeking to gain control over one another. The forces of evil are waiting for a chance to undermine the Lord's work. We become open channels of destruction when our ego needs create a competitive quest for power. We can be so right about some matter of doctrine or organization and so wrong in our *motivation!*

When our unmet spiritual and psychological needs get focused on an issue of control, everyone loses. This is why it's so crucial to allow the Lord to subdue anything in us which is not consistent with His character and indwelling presence. And, when we do find ourselves in conflict with another Christian, it's very important to be sure it is not because we're jockeying for some position or recognition.

Among those who need to be sure of this are church leaders. Often pastoral staffs of churches face the potential danger of the Euodia-Syntyche syndrome. Senior pastors can become imperious in their control of staff and fail to utilize the creative gifts of those called to serve with them. Insecurity and ambition can prompt assistant and associate pastors to hide a lot of competition conflict behind a supposed love for the Lord, their perceptions of His truth, and their concept of the church's welfare.

A couple of years ago, the problem of associate pastors bucking for the boss's job became serious enough in the Presbyterian Church (U.S.A.) that it was ruled they could never succeed the senior pastor. How sad for everyone concerned!

I spend a lot of time at clergy conferences talking with pastors who are in crisis over personnel problems. Most often they are caused by personality loose ends in themselves or others. The joy in their church has diminished in proportion to the intensity of the conflict.

But even in churches where there is unity among clergy, disunity can fester in congregations. We need to confront the causes of this debilitating situation.

Factions In The Church

Factions in the church are usually centered in persons who need a power base. They have not grown through an experience of the Lord's subduing power in their personality problems. Often people who have not had sufficient recognition and success in the secular world gravitate to the church to satisfy their needs. Before long they run into others who also are working to secure their turf. Factions develop around power-hungry people and the secondary issues or causes they use to galvanize support for themselves.

Because local churches are not commonly therapeutic centers for the healing of personality disorders, members usually remain the same as when they joined. This is why it is so important to raise the questions we have in this chapter about our personality loose ends and the healing power of Christ who is able to subdue, bring under control, the things in us which debilitate our own joy, and make us ineffective in our relationships.

Preaching needs to include a clear presentation of spiritual maturity so that people can take an honest look at how they need to grow. The dynamics of personality growth in Christ and conflict management under His subduing control must be discussed in depth with church leaders.

A retreat on this theme, with adequate time to study the "He is able" passages, will refocus the leaders' attention on what Christ can do rather than what they must produce by human power and manipulation. But there must be time for process: periods for silent meditation, two-by-two reflection on the loose ends inventory questions, small groups to discuss the implications of what people are discovering, and then time for a whole board to spell out how to function more effectively as a church centered in the Lord of power.

Paul follows his personal challenge for the church to help Euodia and Syntyche with four specific steps to claim Christ's *hupotasso* power. These are applications for the healing of individual personality loose ends and for the loose ends of conflict in the church as a whole.

Rejoice!

The first step to realizing that Christ is able to subdue all things to Himself is to rejoice. Rejoicing is so important to the apostle that he repeats his admonition twice. "Rejoice in the Lord always. Again I say rejoice!" *Chairete,* the verb, in the present active imperative, gives emphasis: "Oh, please, be sure to rejoice!"

Don't start by focusing on the loose ends in yourself, in others, in the combatively competitive relationship, or in the church. Deliberately focus on Christ and His subduing power. Think of the cross and the defeat of the false power of sin. Savor the cosmic and personal reconciliation He has won for us. "Old things have passed away, behold all things are new." "Therefore, if anyone is in Christ, he is a new creation." Christ has done it by His subduing power. Think of the defeated enemies of pride, envy, selfishness, lust for power, aggrandizement, acquisitiveness, competition, and factionalization that He is able to subdue, to put into subjection by His power. Then think of the resurrection and Christ's victory over death. Claim again abundant and eternal life through Him. Go back to the upper room of Pentecost and receive again the fire to burn out the chaff and the wind to fill the sails of your soul.

Praise liberates! As I've said often in my writings, it is the thermostat that opens our minds and hearts to the power of Christ's Spirit. His joy liberates. Don't focus first on the problems; as an act of will, turn your attention to the One who is able.

Conspicuous Gentleness

We are to be known for a conspicuous gentleness. "Let your gentleness be known to all men. The Lord is at hand" (Phil. 4:5). Paul is not only talking about the second coming of Christ, but His present power in believers and the church. The outward evidence that He lives in us is "gentleness," *epieikes* in Greek. The word signifies an attitude of open reasonableness; moderation and graciousness are also implied. A consistent experience of the grace of the Lord Jesus frees us of defensiveness. We are open to grow, so we don't have to defend what we are; we are willing to change, so we can take creative criticism; we are yielded to the Lord, so we don't have to defend our turf; we are dependent on Christ's subduing power, so we don't have to face the battle with evil alone.

The startling thing about this second admonition is that carrying it out is to be conspicuous. *Make* your gentleness *known.* Model it, express it, tell others about it! Why? Because doing this destroys combative competition. Defensiveness puts out a scent that agitates the hound dogs around us. They have to trap and attack. When we pretend we know everything, people want to expose our lack of knowledge or experience in some area. Pious perfectionism baits people. They have to pull off the mask. Posturing strength is a sure way to get people to tell us about our weaknesses.

On the other hand, if we are open, receptive, teachable people whose only source of power is Christ, whose only purpose is to glorify Him, and whose only relational strategy is *affirmation* of others—then we can grow. This gentleness is quick to admit needs and constantly willing to receive Christ's remedial correction and molding power.

My granddaughters were playing the "what-are-you-going-to-be-when-you-grow-up?" game. After each had told what she wanted to be, they all turned to me, "How 'bout you, Papa—what are you going to be when you grow up?" Good question. I'll never be fully grown until I get to heaven and Christ totally conforms me to His nature. In the meantime, the old slogan will do: "I'm not what I used to be and I'm sure not what I'm going to be!"

"Letting our gentleness be known" is done by sharing with others what Christ has done to save us, changing us from inhumanity to humanness. Sometimes our self-aggrandizing witness about our Christian experience elevates us to the near status of *fourth person* of the Trinity! Instead, other people need to hear what Christ has done with our weaknesses, mistakes, and inadequacies. And when He has used the talents and spiritual gifts He has entrusted to us, it's important to focus on His intervention and not our performance.

Also, it is important to remember that the quality of gentleness cannot be faked. In fact, the lack of it may be our *greatest* personality loose end. If so, the pride-motivated defensiveness that denies gentleness is where we must begin, submitting ourselves to Christ who is able to subdue all things to Himself. This brings us to the third step.

Submit Your Needs

Being honest about our personality loose ends will lead to terrible discouragement unless we examine them and submit them in the context of intimate prayer. Paul gives us the key: "Be anxious for nothing, but in everything by prayer and supplication, with thanksgiving, let your requests be made known to God" (Phil. 4:6). I'm applying this verse directly to the discoveries we make about things we need to change in ourselves and in the relationships that become a tug-of-war for power. To see ourselves and do something about our personality loose ends requires the transforming power of Christ, the Lord of the Loose Ends. He has been delegated by the Father to be our High Priest. He helps us to plumb the depth of our needs, enables us to give thanks for what we are learning, and then relinquish them.

Don't miss how the "Subduer" works. He is the one who focuses in on the change we need, helps us to ask for it, takes it directly to the Father's heart, and then gives us the resolve, the will, and the enabling energy to follow through. He wants to eliminate what hinders our joy. "Until now you have asked nothing in My name. Ask, and you will receive, that your joy may be full" (John 16:24).

Guarding Peace

The process of submitting our personality loose ends to the subduing power of Christ and realizing lasting character reorientation is a lifetime calling. We need protection as it takes place. Paul speaks of the protective power of Christ's peace as our guard. The word "guard" means garrison, but it implies more than a wall around us. The Greek word is from the verb *phroureo*, "to see before, to look out." Christ's peace is like a sentinel who watches for invading enemies, not only alerting us to them but standing guard to subdue them before they storm the walls. Good thing. We can't take it alone.

When we allow Christ to begin His transformation of our personalities and relationships, we become the target of Satan's attack. He uses his arsenal of weapons: doubt that change is possible; uncertainty as to whether it's happening; discouragement over the time required; people's reluctance to accept the new person they see emerging in us; defeatism when we fall back into old patterns; and problems that gig our old self-reliant, combative, competitive style into action.

Few things have helped me personally more than to claim the wall around my mind with Christ, my peace, standing guard. Most of my problems happen in days when I don't constantly claim protection. When the pressure of a very demanding life mounts, I am vulnerable to attack. But most of all, when I am tired, my physical exhaustion can really take a toll on my emotions. I have learned that it's not necessary. Submitting my fatigue to Christ and getting rest reenergizes me within a few hours. Before I get rest, however, I especially have to claim the protection of Christ's peace. Without Him standing guard, I feel self-doubt, get edgy with people, and push with my old perfectionism.

For example, between two o'clock on Sunday afternoon and bedtime, I particularly need Christ's peace. Preaching two televised services, praying for people who respond to the invitation, personally greeting two large congregations with dozens of on-the-spot counseling sessions as people leave church, and some conversations with staff or church officers about programs, leave me physically drained.

By 2 P.M., I will have been up for ten hours with nonstop, energy-demanding prayer, study, preaching, and people concerns. If I don't claim Christ's peace protection, I repreach the sermon in my mind, thinking of ways it could have been better. If there have been goofs or mistakes, the memories of them strut about in my mind. And usually there is some encounter in which I must live out the aspect of the abundant life I have just articulated in the sermon. If I fail to meet the test, I can be very hard on myself.

But when I ask Christ's peace to guard me, I'm given a gift of freedom to accept my humanness, admit that I'm tired, and that my body must be replenished. I may go off to hit some golf balls, naming each one for some loose end I've submitted to Christ. Then I bash them down the fairway!

But most important, Christ reminds me I'm loved, accepted, forgiven, and *programmed for progress*—His in me. By Monday morning, I'm rarin' to go again! Joy indeed! In Paul's listing of the fruit of the Spirit, he puts peace after love and joy. Peace is a result of Christ's unqualified love and uncontainable joy.

In Hebrews, we are told that for the joy set before Him, Christ endured the cross (12:2). It was the joy of heaven and the joy He longed to impart to us. And to be sure we don't miss His full joy, He continues to work in us to subdue anything in us that debilitates and denies the abundant life in us and our relationships. That's why I call Christ the Lord of our personality loose ends. He is able to subdue all things to Himself!

To be sure, that is more than a whiff of joy that "changes a rich man into a generous man." It is an infilling of Christ's joy that makes an inhuman person gloriously human!

5.

THE FLOODGATE OF POWER

"Hey, mate, are you ready to move on?" I was roused from my nap by the sound of someone shouting over the side of a small old river lock in Canada.

My family and I were making our way through a succession of locks on a sailing adventure from New York Harbor to Quebec. We found the locks exciting and challenging. They were new to us and we had lots to learn. When we reached a lock on one level of the river, the door would open and we would glide in. Then the water of the upper river would rush in through conduits, lifting our craft up to the higher level of the waterway.

Having passed through dozens of locks, we were tired and decided to rest awhile in this particular one. We all fell asleep in the warm summer sun. A little more awake now, I realized it was the lock master who was shouting to me, repeating his question. "Hey, mate! You can't stay here forever. Now, tell me, are you ready to move on?"

I jumped to my feet, ran into the cabin, turned on the motor, and took a firm grip on the wheel. Looking out of the window of the cabin, up to the crusty old salt of a lock master, I saluted and shouted, "Yes, sir!"

When he saw that I was fully alert and really ready to move on, he started to turn the crank, opening the floodgate. Unlike more modern, sophisticated locks, this one was filled by opening the front door of the lock to let in the water from the higher level of the waterway. As the floodgate opened, a little at first, and then wider and wider, the water from the higher level flooded in with magnificent lifting power. Yes, we were ready to move on—at a higher level than before.

Motoring out of the lock, we waved good-by to the lock master. I thought to myself, "Now, that experience was a living parable of power. I'll save it and use it someday."

It's exactly what I need now to introduce the next of the "He is able" exclamations about the power of Christ to control our lives. In the previous chapter we claimed the power of the Lord of the Loose Ends to help us with the loose ends of our personalities. Now we are ready to deal with the loose ends of the problems we face.

The Locks of Life

Life is made up of locks—times when we've gone as far as we think we can on our own strength. The gate behind us closes, and we can't retreat back to stay on a lower level. The door to the future is closed, and it seems impossible to go forward. It's then that our eternal lock master of life says, "Are you ready to move on?" The moment we say we are ready, the floodgates of His power open and lift us, empower us, and enable us to move on in the next phase of our voyage.

One Word To Open The Floodgate

What is the secret of opening the floodgate? What is it that makes it possible for us to receive the power available to us? One word. *Power* is spelled with ten letters: c-o-m-m-i-t-m-e-n-t. It tells the Lord we are ready to move on; it opens the floodgate for the inrush of the rivers of living water; it lifts us and makes progress possible. Commitment is the key to beginning, growing in, and living victoriously in the Christian life. Without Christ, we can't; without us, He won't. Our Lord waits for us to desire what He inspires.

A Committed Apostle

The Apostle Paul was unreservedly committed to Christ. When he met the Savior personally, he experienced His unchanging, unlimited grace. He made a commitment. "For me to live is Christ" became the apostle's watchword. His explanation of what Christ meant to him was written in flaming words of gratitude in one of his earliest epistles, "I have been crucified with Christ; it is no longer I who live, but Christ lives in me, and the life which I now live in the flesh I live by faith in the Son of God, who loved me and gave Himself for me" (Gal. 2:20).

Paul could never shake the wonder of Christ's death for him or adequately praise Him for His presence with him. The apostle never boasted about his own adequacy, but Christ's triumphant adequacy. It was never "I am able," but always "He is able."

Each step of the way in his missionary journeys, in every problem he faced, in times of imprisonment, persecution, and difficulties, Paul committed his problems to the Lord, and that commitment opened the floodgate of the immense flow of Christ's power into his life.

If we are amazed by what Paul preached and wrote, the indefatigable energy he expended, and the miracles of changed and healed lives that surrounded his ministry, we must trace it all back to the commitment that made him a person the Lord could bless so abundantly.

Power Through Commitment

Near the end of Paul's life, while in prison in Rome, he opened his mind and heart to Timothy, his son in the faith. Paul gave him the formula for receiving power, whatever his surroundings or suffering. "For I know whom I have believed and am persuaded that *He is able* to keep what I have committed to Him until that Day" (2 Tim. 1:12b).

The Greek word translated as "commited," *paratheken*, means literally a deposit committed to another person's trust for safekeeping. In Paul's time there were no banks, so there was no more trusted duty than to accept the responsibility for another person's valuables. An equally high trust was to allow a person to invest your money for you and faithfully to return the interest earned. The word for "keep," *phulaxai*, means to guard against robbery or loss. It also implies investment with high return.

So here is this seasoned apostle, after years of experience with Christ, saying, "There's no doubt in my mind about Christ's reliability. In knowing Him personally and from all I've been through, I am totally convinced that He has all power to protect and guard, as well as multiply, the return on what I commit to Him."

Because Christ has all power, we can trust our problems to Him and, with Paul, make four unequivocal assertions: I know, I believe, I am persuaded, and I have committed. A closer look at Paul's life indicates that the progression occurred in a slightly different order: the apostle first believed in Christ after his Damascus road encounter with Him; then, during those long fourteen years of preparation for his ministry, he came to a complete commitment; and throughout his life in Christ, he became fully persuaded of His faithfulness and committed his daily needs to Him.

Paul's Loose Ends

And yet, near the end of his life we find the great apostle with loose ends! His triumphant "He is able" statement is set in the context of suffering, obvious concern over Timothy, disappointment over the wavering faith of some of the Christians, and longing for the continued growth of the churches he had founded. Would the infant movement of the followers of "the Way" survive? Would it sweep across the world until every knee bowed to Christ and every tongue confessed Him as Lord? What could the chained prisoner do?

Paul did the same thing he had done in every tough time he had been through all across the years. He committed his concerns to the Lord. And then, as always in difficult circumstances, he experienced the power of the risen Lord.

I'm thankful that this "He is able" exclamation was written in real life to life's problems. It gives a dimension of depth to our consideration of the opening of the floodgate of power when we commit our tough challenges and problems to Christ.

I Don't Know Where To Turn

When the loose ends of our unresolved problems pile up, we explode with frustration: "I don't know where to turn!" We've also heard those words said with a sigh of hopeless resignation, or with a cry of anguished grief. We hear them in hospital rooms, in deep conversations with friends, in times of calamity and adversity. These six words express loneliness, and the longing for direction and power to solve our problems.

We've all said these words. We get to the end of our endurance and don't know what to do. We face seemingly impossible challenges that stretch us beyond our understanding and our ability to cope. All the alternatives seem equally unacceptable and unworkable.

Sometimes physical illness brings us to the place where we don't know where to turn, but emotional pain can be just as excruciating. Failures, broken relationships, anxiety, and fear can paint us into a lonely corner.

Then there are times when these six words take on added intensity as dilemmas have to be shared by two or more persons. In a rocky marriage, a family facing a crisis, or a church that needs renewal, we cry out, "*We* don't know where to turn!"

Also, these words are drenched with dismay when we confront the monumental problems of our society, or allow ourselves to empathize with the suffering of the disadvantaged, the poor, and the hungry. And we wring our hands over the lack of morality and integrity around us.

Added to all this are all the loose ends of our loaded schedules and things we postponed in procrastination. We get behind and feel we'll never get caught up. There are decisions to be made and conflicts to resolve, and our personal problems are usually in a condition that renders us least capable of handling the big crises when they hit.

For many of us, the times when we do not know where to turn expose the fact that we have been living in two separate worlds that seldom meet. One world is our relationship with Christ which often lacks vitality because of (possibly) benign neglect, willful independence, or unconfessed sin. Our other world is the reality of daily life with its mixture of routines, pressures, and busy-ness pursued with far too little thought of Christ. Sometimes, this realm gets overloaded with disappointments, frustrations, and stress.

Today, there's a tendency to think that being a Christian should exclude us from the distresses of life. But shallow triumphalism does not help us in the depth of difficulties. If Christ is only for the up, successful, hurrah times of life, He is excluded from three-fourths of our lives.

It's in times of distress that our two realms have an opportunity to come together in a profound way. In those times, the vital connection can be made between what is happening to us or around us, and our supreme need for Christ. Then we can discover the prescription for perplexity: "When you don't know where to turn, return to the Lord."

Paul helps us bring our two worlds together when frustrating, painful, or heartbreaking things happen. He shows us through his experience that in tough times, when we are overcome with the feelings of being at loose ends, there is a place to turn. These are the times to return to Christ. He has power to help us. And our commitment is absolutely required.

Threefold Commitment

Commitment has three parts: repentance, relinquishment, and responsiveness.

REPENTANCE

Repentance may seem like a harsh word. You may be thinking, "Here I am up to my neck in loose ends and you give me another big one to make me feel even more down on myself!"

Not so. Repentance means to return to the Lord and to change our minds about one immense misconception: that we are alone and have to untangle and tie down our loose ends with our own strength. It's this "I've-got-to-fix-it-myself!" attitude that has gotten us into the fix we're in.

True repentance means to turn around, to deliberately turn from going in one direction and go in a new direction. It's to confess to the Lord that the big and little loose ends of our lives have gotten woven into one massive tourniquet around our souls and we don't know how we are going to survive. We cry out, "Lord of Loose Ends, help me!"

And it's important to repeat that to call Christ Lord of the Loose Ends does not mean He causes them or sends them to punish us. Rather, He will be Lord over them if we will surrender them to Him.

The Lord is wonderfully practical and specific. He first takes off the woven fabric of the intertwined loose ends of the tourniquet that is choking us. Then He unravels it. Patiently but persistently, He helps us look at each strand and see it for what it is. "Deliberately turn these over to me," He says strongly.

RELINQUISHMENT

Next, commitment is *relinquishment.* It's taking the loose ends individually and depositing them in the Lord's problem-solving grace. There we lose our control of them. And why not? Our control has either created them or made the ones we haven't created even worse. Relinquishment must be decisive if it is to be liberating.

Now the Lord helps us prioritize the loose ends. Some can be dealt with immediately; others will take longer; still others He will give us the courage to endure. But for all of them He gives us a practical strategy. Steps to take. Specific things to do. Solutions we could never have conjured up on our own.

At this point commitment shifts. In listening prayer, we are given guidance about what we are to be or do. Interestingly enough, Paul's assurance that "He is able to keep what I have committed to *Him* . . . " can also be translated "He is able to keep what He has committed to *me.*" This is certainly supported by Paul's further word to Timothy: "That good thing which was committed to you, keep by the Holy Spirit who dwells in us" (2 Tim. 1:14).

Actually, in the context of the broader meaning of *commitment* in Scripture, it is both trusting our problems to the Lord and also acting on what He guides. We commit our needs to the Lord and He commits to us what we are to do.

The wonderful result of relinquishment is twofold: we receive a release from the tension of trying to be in control of everything, and the Lord releases His power to help us. It is a law of the spiritual world that the Lord releases His power to those who give up their controlling power over their problems and perplexities. Only then does the floodgate open and His power lift us so we can move on.

How the Power Works

It's so important to understand how the Lord's power works. He strengthens us, and He intervenes for us in the problems we commit to Him. Our first need is to know that the Lord has heard our cry for help and will do what is best for our ultimate good.

This comes in the power of His grace. We are re-affirmed by the conviction that we are loved. Remember that this assurance was what motivated Paul's burst of strength expressed in this "He is able" claim we are considering. He brought his two worlds together: his relationship with Christ and the difficult problems of being a prisoner in Rome.

Driven To My Knees

Over the years of seeking to claim the power offered in this "He is able" assurance, I've tried to follow the apostle's lead by staying with a review of Christ's love on the cross for me and the thousands of times He's helped me in my tight places, until I can say again, "I'm persuaded that He is able to keep this present problem if I really commit it to Him."

I was driven to my knees to do that a few months ago, late one Thursday evening. The desk in my hideaway where I study and do my sermon preparation was piled high with unfinished projects; incomplete chapters for books that were close to or behind deadline; correspondence I had foolishly taken from my church office thinking I could catch up on it late that night; and stacks of research material I needed to read. On top of everything was a red folder (red alert!) containing crucial memos from staff in both my church and radio and television ministries. Every memo alerted me to some crisis that needed immediate attention. Loose ends!

I sat in my desk chair moving things around on the desk wondering what to do first. Usually on Thursday evenings I can wade into the pile and clean it off before midnight. Not that evening!

From early morning until late evening, the day had been nothing but continuous meetings with people. Concern over those people reverberated in my soul. There had been lots of phone calls, too. Some of them had dealt with profound concerns on my heart—a need that one of my children was facing, a friend who was near death, a fellow pastor across the country in real trouble. Serious loose ends!

And staring me in the face on my study desk was a two-page list of the calls I'd not been able to return. Just as I settled down to try to do something about the condition of my desk, the phone rang. It was my assistant calling to remind me of a speaking engagement the next morning which I had totally forgotten! Tangled loose ends!

My usual response to a jumbled mess of loose ends like that would have been to brew some coffee so I could stay awake, mentally chain myself to the desk, and with sheer grit and guts, grind out the work. It would have been foolhardy that night. There was a week's work piled on the desk. Yet, the problem was not on the desk, but in myself. Having been in a mood of exasperation like that before, I knew what I had to do.

I got out of my desk chair and onto my knees. It was another of what I call my "He is able" recovery times. As I mentioned earlier, years ago I memorized these potent statements about Christ's power and I go over them when I'm attacked by the awful, grim feeling of being at loose ends. I've learned that, for me, those are times when I will try to assume control and live on my own power.

But I've discovered that if I linger long enough in prayer about the goodness of the Lord, I renew my relationship with Him and reconfirm my basic conviction that He is able with His superabundant power to control my life, showing me what I am to do, based on what's on *His* agenda for me.

So, on my knees, I read my Bible, sang songs of praise, and delighted in the Lord for Himself—not for what He would do to help me with that wretched pile on my desk. Strangely enough, I lost track of time. When I was assured again that if my Lord could pull off Calvary and an open tomb, He was able to deal with my problems, I got up saying triumphantly, "He is able, He is able!"

With gusto, I waded into the few things that really needed to be done that night. The talk for the morning fell together quickly, and I left the rest of the problems for the next day. After turning off the lights, I went out to my car and drove home whistling. The floodgates of power had opened for me again as I made a commitment of the loose ends to the Lord.

Sure, the next day the desk was in the same condition, but *I* was different. And with the fresh flow of power from the renewal of my relationship with the Lord of the Loose Ends, I was given strength to work at top speed. But, of course, you've guessed it: in a few days the desk was full again. Loose ends don't go away—but neither does the Lord!

Timely Interventions

Unreserved commitment also opens the floodgate of Christ's power in timely interventions. By timely, I don't mean His interventions are always immediate or according to our timetable. Nor do I want to imply that Christ always gives us what we think we need. Over the years of seeking to learn the dynamics of commitment, I have often had to relearn this lesson: whatever the Lord grants or denies is intended to bring us closer to Him— for the working out of His greater plan for our lives. Looking back, I am as thankful for some of my prayers that were not answered in the way I wanted as I am for those that were. In reality, all prayer is answered. The misnomer "unanswered prayer" is a click phrase of controlling people who find they can't control the Lord.

And yet, when we do leave the timing and the nature of the intervention up to the Lord, trusting Him completely for the results, He does truly magnificent things for us. He delights in surprising us with what He can do with our loose ends if we completely commit them to Him.

You see, He does have all power to arrange situations, deploy people to help us, release blessings, and provide what we need to do His will. I find almost every day is filled with dozens of interventions, and in my years of trusting Christ, I've never lived a week in which there weren't at least several that rocked me on my heels.

RESPONSIVENESS

I've learned something else: start controlling and the interventions stop happening; assume the glory for them and glorious things are withheld. I'm so amazed that the Lord decided to call me, with all my inadequacies, and use me, that I look at life as one continuous succession of interventions in response to a consistent commitment. The only down days are those when I forget to commit each problem or challenge to the Lord.

The reason I have put an emphasis on continuous, hour-by-hour commitment in our daily round of responsibilities is that I find most people think of Christ's power only for the really big crises of life. What we all need is a consistent flow of power.

I have a friend who talks about committing his way through the day. Every decision, plan, problem, conversation, and challenge is committed to the Lord as it comes along. The beginning and end of each day are marked by special commitment. The result is a remarkable buoyancy and resiliency expressed in a very positive attitude. He doesn't store up problems or put off opportunities for a weekly time of commitment. Instead, he's constantly asking, "I wonder what the Lord has in store with this?" The man's life verse is Proverbs 3:5–6, "Trust in the Lord with all your heart, and lean not on your own understanding; in all your ways acknowledge Him, and He shall direct your paths." It's always a delight to talk with this man. I know that before we talk, he's committed our conversation and is praying to be used, even as our visit develops.

This quality of consistent commitment doesn't mean that we won't confront some big crisis that requires prolonged listening prayer. You may be facing one of those times right now as you read this. You don't feel able to take what's happening; you have a decision, and it's beyond your ability to make the right choice; someone has you on the ropes and you don't know what to do. Maybe your heart aches over a shattering disappointment.

But don't let me tell you what it is. Whatever it is, I understand. How do I? Because I've got some of my own.

So together we long to receive power. A lock in the waterway of life is before us. We yearn to get on with life, but solving our problems is higher than we can reach. We enter the lock and wait. Christ wants to know if we are ready to move on. Will we commit our need to Him?

"Yes! I believe, I am persuaded, and now I commit my way to Him."

See the floodgate open? Feel the lifting power? It's time to move on—with His power!

6.

STOP HUGGING CENTER STAGE!

AFTER A PLAY IN WHICH ONE OF MY CONGREGATION PLAYED the leading role, I was invited backstage to visit him. What I didn't know was that I was about to hear a word from the Lord from a most unexpected source and under very unusual circumstances.

While I stood talking to my friend, congratulating him on his performance, our conversation was interrupted by a sharp and loud reprimand. The director of the production was talking to a supporting actor in the play. He held the young man by the shoulders, looking him in the eye. They were chin to chin as the director blurted out in disgust, "Listen to me! You're not the leading man, so stop hugging center stage!"

I left the theater with the words ringing in my soul. Strange how the Lord sometimes puts an exclamation point to things He's been saying to us by actually articulating them through some person.

117

It just so happened that I'd been through a week of dealing with controlling types who were trying to hug center stage in the drama of their lives. By their attitudes, they were saying to the lighting man, "Hey, I'm here. Put the spotlight on me!" And I know the reason these people troubled me. It wasn't only what they were doing to preempt center stage, but also because I saw myself and so many of my friends in them.

It's one thing to admire an Orson Welles whose immense theatrical talents enabled him to write, produce, direct, and take the leading role in a play. It's quite a different thing to try to assume all these roles and responsibilities in the real drama of our lives.

And yet we try. We want to write the script, bankroll the production on our own strength, direct how everyone else should act as bit players in our drama, and take the starring role ourselves.

The purpose of this chapter is to say to myself and to those of you who need to hear it (and who doesn't?), "Stop hugging center stage! You're not the star—Christ is!"

The Big Temptation

All our temptations are but diminutive demonstrations of our desire to hug center stage. They are beguiling enticements to misuse power. To play God. King of the mountain. Lord of our own lives.

Try that on for size. Think of the temptations you've had in just the past year. Didn't they involve side-stepping some spiritual or moral law of God? Start with the basics. Begin with the first commandment, "You shall have no other gods." All the rest of the commandments focus on the danger of breaking that fundamental spiritual law. We can make a false god out of controlling our use of time, people, the family, truth, sex, or things.

Then reflect on the Sermon on the Mount and the absolutes Jesus gave us for living in the Kingdom of God in both thought and action. Which of these absolutes of Christian ethics have you been tempted to break? Are they not temptations to assume control over your own life or over someone else?

The temptation beneath all temptations is to make our theme song "I'll do it my way," sung at center stage, with all spotlights focused on us, and all the stagecraft, stagehands, and players organized to support our performance!

The Pretentious Director

The producer and director of that production is Satan. He's a fallen angel who tried to hug center stage. Having lost his place in glory, he's busy recruiting and casting power-hungry people in roles that usurp the spotlight in their life story. He delights in getting us to seek the glory rather than glorify Christ. But center stage is where we get the worst case of feeling at loose ends, because we cannot cope with the pressure. It's inevitable; we were never meant to be there in the first place.

Temptations to get and keep control are distracting loose ends. They keep pulling us away from our central purpose of glorifying God and doing what we know He has called us to do. And now the central question: Is Christ also Lord of these loose ends of temptation?

Christ Is Able To Help

There is no doubt in the mind of the author of Hebrews. For him, Christ is our High Priest who intercedes for us and imparts the power of God to us in our times of temptation. Since Christ has been through every temptation we face, He can understand and can give us exactly what we need to withstand and come through victorious. The author of Hebrews gives us another of the empowering "He is able" assertions to help us in tempting, testing times. "Therefore, in all things He [Christ] had to be made like His brethren, that He might be a merciful and faithful High Priest in things pertaining to God, to make propitiation for the sins of the people. For in that He Himself has suffered, being tempted, *He is able to aid those who are tempted*" (Heb. 2:17–18, emphasis added).

Ponder that little word "aid," *boethesai* in Greek. It's an old compound verb, *boetheo—boe*, a cry; *theo*, to run. Running at a cry for help! And that's exactly what Christ does—He runs to our side when we cry out for help in times of temptation.

How Jesus Was Tempted And How He Helps Us

To fully appreciate this "He is able" declaration, let's take a look at the times when Jesus was tempted and how these qualify Him to be the Lord of the loose ends of temptation in our lives today.

At the beginning of His ministry, Jesus had a "soul-on" encounter with Satan in the wilderness. It was an excruciating ordeal. The stakes were eternally high. Satan knew that Jesus was the Son of God sent to redeem and reconcile the world that he was trying to hold in his diabolical control. He also knew that if Christ succeeded in His mission, He would begin a new creation with new women and men under His control who would emulate His faithfulness to the Father!

Jesus Christ, the God-man in whose nature the divine and human were blended in perfect oneness, was the new Adam, the first completely obedient Man in the midst of a disobedient, fallen creation. "God was in Christ reconciling the world to Himself" (2 Cor. 5:19). The cross was His central purpose and passion.

Satan's attacks were to tempt Him to short-cut that awesome destiny of Calvary. So his attack had to be subtle: his temptations had to be beguiling substitutes that would attempt to dissuade the Savior from the cross. Instead of Calvary, Satan offered immediate success, expedient methods, and temporary results. All good things to keep Christ from the best—the salvation of the world!

Insidious "Ifs"

All of Satan's temptations had an insidious "if" in them. The first one, "*If* you are the Son of God, command these stones to become bread," was the temptation to be satisfied with the secondary. Jesus had been in the wilderness for forty days. He was famished and physically weak. The flat stones of the wilderness area looked like the loaves of unleavened bread of that time. And Jesus was acutely aware of the physical hungers of people. Yes, Christ could use His divine power to turn those stones into enough bread to feed thousands. And yes, it would make Him a renowned hero of the people.

But Christ also knew that He had been sent to be the true bread of life. Only the cross would enable Him to meet the deepest hungers of people. Christ's answer to Satan was a decisive quotation of Deuteronomy 8:3. "It is written," He said, "man shall not live by bread alone, but by every word that proceeds from the mouth of God" (Matt. 4:4). And Jesus knew that He was *the* Word of God.

The Second "If"

Having lost in his first try to tempt Jesus, Satan was ready with another "if" to try to undermine the Savior's true purpose. "If you are the Son of God, throw Yourself down from the pinnacle of the Temple." This second temptation was the substitute of the spectacular. What Satan had in mind was for Jesus to climb up to the pinnacle of the Temple in Jerusalem, to the corner of the plateau where Solomon's Porch and the Royal Porch met at Mount Zion. There was a sheer drop of 450 feet into the Kidron Valley.

Jesus, the Christ, could have pulled it off. He could have reversed the laws of gravity, jumped off, and with an intervention from the Father's angels, landed safely on His feet. This attention-getting feat would have won Him the absolute allegiance of His people—for a time. Jesus knew His powers were for healing the sick, exorcising the possessed, and to be the power of God in a cosmic redemption at Golgotha. Satan had used Scripture from Psalm 91:11–12, promising angelic intervention: "In their hands they shall bear you up, lest you dash your foot against a stone." Jesus' response was with another Scripture, "It is written, again, 'You shall not tempt the Lord your God'" (Deut. 6:16, in Matt. 4:6–7).

The Third "If"

Satan's third "if" was not like the previous two in trying to unsettle Jesus' authority. This was an attempt to assert his own. He described the kingdom of the world, human power, and might. "All these things I will give You if You will fall down and worship me." Quite an offer—all the kings, princes, empires bowing at Jesus' feet—if He would only bow down to worship Satan. It was the temptation of the substitution of success. Jesus knew that one day the kingdoms of this world would become His kingdoms! But only through the cross, resurrection, and the creation of a new, missionary people who would turn the world upside down. So Christ, flamed with divine indignation, said to the Devil, "Away with you, Satan! For it is written,

'You shall worship the Lord your God, and Him only you shall serve'" (Deut. 6:13, 10:20, in Matt. 4:10).

Before we consider some of the other times Jesus was tempted, let's pause to collect our thoughts about what these three temptations in the wilderness teach us about our temptations. First, there's nothing Satan can pull on us that Christ hasn't been through Himself. The One who runs to our cry for help has the power to defeat Satan's attempt to use these same basic temptations on us. Just as Satan tempted Jesus to evade the cross, so too, all our temptations are rooted in an attempt to by-pass what Jesus accomplished for us on the cross with the substitutes of the secondary, the spectacular, and the immediately successful.

Please Be Specific

I hear you saying, "Lloyd, please be specific!" Well, any time we are tempted to false pride, we are substituting security in ourselves for our security as people who already have been loved to the uttermost on the cross and through His presence as the risen Savior. Whenever we grandstand with self-aggrandizement, it's to gain the assurance of the worth only Christ can give us. When we justify ourselves, we act as if we had not been justified on Calvary. Stretching the truth or downright lying is either trying to be more than we are or an effort to cover our dirty tracks.

To be even more specific, whenever we use the gifts of God as a substitute for Him we give in to Satan's tactics. Food beautifully prepared is a delight, but if it's used to stuff an aching spiritual emptiness, it will not only make us overweight but block out our need for the Lord.

Sex is a wondrous gift for a married man and woman, but it's no substitute for prayer, or the lasting ego-fortification of Christ's love. Sexual satisfactions outside of marriage, in fantasy, flirtation, or actual adultery, end up in power struggles and are a subtle effort to grasp enjoyment without commitment and long-range responsibility.

An inordinate lust for things, clothes, possessions, or a fat bank account is a hungry suckling that's never satisfied. Professional success eventually will leave us with one question: "Is this all there is?"

We exercise our quest for control when we refuse to allow our status, security, and strength in Christ to be sufficient as the basic spiritual sustenance of our lives. Satan wins as Christ is edged out of first place. And then guess who's hugging center stage.

As part of the "me generation," we want immediate satisfaction of our wants while our real needs go unmet. We are willing to use expedient control methods of manipulation to get what we want from people—now! In an unguarded moment of honesty many contemporary Christians would admit that for them, Christ, His cross, His intervening power, and His indwelling Spirit are just not enough. But those unguarded moments of honesty are far too rare.

And so we dabble in syncretism—the worship of several gods while at the same time we still assert our belief in the Lord God. When we flash our pious "teeth-dry" perpetual smile at center stage, it is Satan who applauds loudest, as we continue our "gods-juggling" act. And he claps most enthusiastically when the god we drop for a time is the One we confidently assume will never drop us. We're right in that assumption, but one thing He won't do is support our self-appointed top billing. When our vaudevillian play flops because people have grown tired of our grabbing the spotlight, we cry out to Him to take charge of our lives. He still comes running to help us deal with our despair of being uncontrollably at loose ends.

Christ's Example

The opposite to the attitude of hugging center stage is humility. Christ helps us to learn that from His example. In His humanity, the incarnate Son of God revealed the true quality of glorifying the Father: He was quick to affirm that His power came from the Father; He attested that the Father did the mighty works through Him; He made it clear that He had come not to do His will but the Father's will.

Paul was profoundly affected by Christ's humility. He couldn't get it off his mind and returned to it repeatedly in His epistles. Christ was the apostle's example of how he longed to live, and the example Paul yearned for his friends to discover: "Let nothing be done through selfish ambition or conceit, but in lowliness of mind let each esteem others better than himself. Let each of you look out not only for his own interests, but also for the interests for others" (Phil. 2:3–4).

Paul was the first to admit that this attitude was not something achieved, but received. It is the result of Christ's indwelling power. "Let this mind [attitude] be in you which was also in Christ Jesus, who, being in the form of God, did not consider it robbery to be equal with God, but *made Himself of no reputation, taking the form of a servant, and coming in the likeness of men*" (Phil. 2:5–7, emphasis added).

As a servant of the Father and the people He came to save, Jesus gave Himself away, revealing that humility is really obedience to God. That's why Satan lost the battle in the wilderness. But he didn't give up! We are told that he left Christ to return at a more opportune time. Since a frontal attack did not work, Satan then tried to use people as his pawns and spokespersons. He uses the same strategy today.

Satan's Use Of People Pressure

Again, because Christ has been through the same kind of people pressure, He is willing and able to run to our aid when we cry out for help. But when we decide to give Christ center stage in our lives, not everyone is ready to handle our commitment. Sometimes our detractors are in our own families, among our friends, or even our religious leaders. Their problem? That they can't control us. But they try—and the temptation to water down our beliefs, tone down our enthusiasm, or adjust our priorities is ever present.

Jesus understands. His disciples tried to control Him, dissuade Him from the cross, and wanted to use

127

Him for their power agendas. The Master knew what was happening—He even identified Satan's use of Peter to discourage Him from His resolute purpose. How similar are Christ's words to Satan in the wilderness and His rebuke to Satan's manipulative use of the Big Fisherman: "Away with you, Satan!"; "Get you behind me, Satan!"

And Jesus' own family understood Him even less than His disciples. One of the most heartrending episodes in His life is recorded in John 7:1–13. At the time of the Feast of the Tabernacles, the Lord's brothers challenged Him to go up to Jerusalem. John tells us that Jesus had been ministering in Galilee because of the hostility against Him among the religious leaders in Jerusalem. Yet Jesus' brothers said, "Depart from here and go into Judea, that Your disciples also may see the works that You are doing. For no one does anything in secret while he himself seeks to be known openly. If You do these things, show Yourself to the world" (vv. 3–4). Then in verse 5 came John's stabbing reflection: "For even His brothers did not believe in Him."

What was behind Jesus' brothers' manipulative power move? At best, they were playing amateur publicists trying to manage Jesus' career. "If you are the Messiah, as You claim, You've got to make Your power connections in the power structure of Jerusalem! It's who you know in this world that matters."

An even less attractive possibility was that Jesus' brothers wanted to share in His fame. "Let's go up to Jerusalem together and when You are a success, we'll share the glory!"

But I suspect that the real motivation had a fes-
tering sliver of fraternal jealousy or even latent
fratricide in it. Could it be that Jesus' brothers realized
they could not control Him and their frustration was
turning to anger, even hatred?

How Jesus Dealt With Pressure

Note that Jesus did not bend to His brothers'
pressure. He simply refused to comply with their plan
for Him to go with them to the feast. But after they
had gone, He went anyway. Some see this as vacillation
on His part. I don't think so. Jesus wanted to go to
Jerusalem under the Father's guidance and timing. He
was not about to allow His brothers to orchestrate His
appearance in Jerusalem. He had to break with their
efforts to control Him and manage His ministry. He
went to Jerusalem leisurely, at His own pace. Once
there, He listened to what people were saying about
Him, and when He was ready, He spoke openly.

Jesus did not solidify His brothers' opposition with
a confrontation! He did not back them into a corner
from which they could never reverse their opinions.
The reason was twofold: He trusted the Father to
change their attitudes, and He had plans for them.
After Pentecost, James became the leader of the church
in Jerusalem and Jude a faithful disciple. Both wrote
epistles contained in the New Testament.

But the salient point for our discussion of temptation is that Jesus knows and understands when we
feel the excruciating pressure of people. He runs to

the aid of wives or husbands whose mates are seeking to control their faith; to children whose parents fear that their allegiance to Him has gone too far—"We didn't send you to church camp to become that spiritual"; to people whose friends pull back and want to limit their obedience to Him in their beliefs or social righteousness and justice.

A Controlling Preacher's Wife

An English preacher was holding meetings in Ireland. He returned to his lodging and as he stepped into the room, a hand grasped the locks at the back of his head and swung him around the room in anger. Now, his assailant was not a member of the IRA, but the preacher's termagant, shrewish wife. The year was not in the later twentieth century, but around 1771. The woman's name was Mary, but she went by the name Molly. And her husband's name was John Wesley!

Wesley's friend John Hampton happened in on that room when Molly was venting her spleen. He wrote, "Once, when I was in North Ireland, I went into a room and found Mrs. Wesley foaming with fury. Her husband was on the floor, where she had been trailing him by the hair of his head; and she was still holding in her hand venerable locks which she had plucked up by the roots . . . ."

Wesley's own journal entry about his wife's reluctance to share his calling reveals that all his patience was "put to the proof again and again; and all my efforts to please yet without success; . . . to hear at my ear fretting and murmuring at everything is like tearing the flesh off my bones."*

Life on the road with John Wesley, facing bad weather and constant preaching services, must not have been easy. Molly Vazeille, a wealthy widow of a Huguenot merchant, had nursed Wesley back to health after he'd had a bad fall on the London bridge. A courtship had ensued and they were married. It seems fairly clear that she had thought she would be able to control the lifestyle of the itinerant founder of Methodism. When she failed, she used other tactics. Not-so-dear Molly knew what she was getting into, and when she couldn't dominate her husband, she tried to limit his vision. Yet while she nagged and fumed, Wesley pressed on.

The account of the Wesleys made me appreciate all the more this pioneer of the faith, but also some of the truly great marriages of Christian leaders through the years. I praise God for my own, and I think of some clergy wives who far outdistance their husbands in both vision and prayer for the renewal of their churches.

This historical aside about the Wesleys is a re- minder that Christ does give strength, even when family or friends fail to understand, or when they try to limit our faithfulness.

Sometimes other Christians try to control us by pressing on us the customs, verbiage, and emphases

---

* Quoted in *John Wesley and His World* by John Pudney (New York: Charles Scribner's Sons, 1978), p. 101.

131

of their brand of Christianity. Acceptance is given or withheld depending on the extent to which we conform—whether it be to the traditional practices of a historic denomination, a charismatic movement, or a social action campaign. Issues also can be control factors. Often relationships are put on the line to make others conform. The fear of rejection makes acquiescence a real temptation.

Our Lord also understands those times of anguish when our faith calls us to costly obedience. We go through a Gethsemane of our own, and pray that the cup might be taken from us. Before we can say "Your will be done," we must be aware that everything hangs on that word "nevertheless," "in spite of everything" (v. 39). Christ's Gethsemane led to Calvary. And our willingness to take up our cross daily, in tough choices and difficult relationships, brings us to our repeated "nevertheless" times of decision. And when we cry out for help, Christ, who brought us to the choice, gives us the courage to make it.

Christ Delivers

In the final analysis, our confidence in overcoming temptation is in the faithfulness of the Lord of the Loose Ends to answer the petition He taught us to pray in the Disciples' Prayer: "Lead us not into temptation, but deliver us from evil." He has been sent by the Father to provide that answer.

Christ seeks to lead us out of patterns that will make us vulnerable to Satan's attack. That's why He confronts us about our preemptive hugging of center stage. He seeks to deliver us from habits of control because He knows we can't pull it off alone. When we try, and then find we need power, He knows that Satan will be ready to offer us false power.

Satan's power comes at very high cost: his methods and his control cause a frightening spiraling descent into power tactics. But at any point we can call, and Christ will deliver us.

Not only has our Lord been through all the temptations we face and not only does He know every device of the Tempter, He alone has power and authority over Satan. In the power struggle between good and evil in the spiritual world, Christ always wins. The Father has given that authority to Christ.

But we must call for aid. As we have stressed, He waits until we want His deliverance. His ongoing care to keep us out of temptation is freely given. He meets us at the pass erecting "Do not enter!" signs on certain paths. But even as we push His sign aside and get into trouble, He will help us even then in response to our cry for help.

A Way of Escape

The same Lord who erects "No Entry" signs also places "Only Way Out" signs in the jungle of defeat when we get lost. Christ's help is the expression of the faithfulness of God that Paul touted with such gratitude: "No temptation has overtaken you except as is common to man; but God is faithful, who will not allow you to be tempted beyond what you are able, but with the temptation will also provide a way of escape, that you may be able to bear it" (1 Cor. 10:13). The name of Christ is the way out.

Use My Name

Names have power. On a human level the name of a person in great authority will put fear into another person in lesser authority. The names of powerful, authoritative people open doors, cut red tape, clear channels. And Christ says, "Use my name." In the spiritual realm, the name Satan cannot resist is the name of Jesus Christ. Satan is a rebellious underling in the realm of power. A cry for help in the name of Jesus Christ sends him running away whimpering and brings us Christ's power over temptation.

The danger place for temptation is center stage. So stop hugging center stage. You are not the leading character. Christ is! "Therefore God has highly exalted Him and given Him the name which is above every name, that at the name of Jesus every knee should bow, of those in heaven, and those on earth, and of those under the earth, and that every tongue should confess that Jesus Christ is *Lord*, to the glory of God the Father" (Phil. 2:9–11, emphasis added).

7.

AN HONEST QUESTION

IT'S AN HONEST QUESTION. SOME ARE ASKING IT OPENLY. Others wish for an opportunity to ask it. Still others have the question lurking deep inside. I've discovered from experience that all three groups are present whenever I speak. Also, I've learned from letters and personal conversations with readers of my books that you are a part of one of these groups.

There are those who are undecided, openly inquiring about the Christian faith. Then, there are those who are uncertain, Christians longing to be sure of their faith. And finally, there are those who are unfulfilled, growing Christians, desiring the full measure of the joy and peace Christ promised.

All three groups are asking this same honest question from different perspectives. It's a very legitimate question and I dare not side-step it. Our answer will be all-important for receiving the power we've been talking about in this book.

The question is, simply, "Why be a Christian?"

Those of you in the first group of inquirers really want to know what difference being a Christian makes. Does it work? You in the second group of uncertain Christians are wondering whether it's worth it to try to keep on living the Christian life, struggling against the current of cultural values and the lure of self-satisfaction that dominates nine out of ten of the people around you. Is it worth it? And you in the third group are wondering if Christianity really has any power. You are not fulfilled by your Christian faith because you have not personally received the evidence of the abundant life you read about in the Bible, and which others talk about so glibly.

Beneath all these questions of all three groups— Does Christianity work? Is it worth it to be a Christian? and, Where's the power?—is the more fundamental question (yes, let's dare to ask it) "Why be a Christian at all?" Let's throw caution, propriety, and pretense aside and ask this question. Why not? It's on all of our minds!

A Powerful Answer To An Honest Question

The author of Hebrews gives us a powerful answer to our honest questions. It is in one of the most propitious and comforting of the Bible's "He is able" ascriptions about Christ. It is also the one that needs the most careful explanation. One thing all of us, in all the three groups I've mentioned, share is a unison groan over theological terminology. We want reality, not lifeless words. So I want to be as free of "preacher talk" as I can be in considering this exclamation about the enabling power of the Lord: "He is able to save to the uttermost." Remember that the words "He is able" mean that He, Christ, has all power.

Why be a Christian? Does it work? Is it worth it? Where is the power? Let's take a look at this stunning promise.

Christ Is Able To Save

Well, I've done it right off. In the subheading just above, I've used one of those theological words that set all of you on edge. We've all been pressed with the presumptuous question "Are you saved?" It's usually asked in a pious way, drenched with superiority, as if the questioner really knew all the many-splendored facets of a positive answer.

One Sunday, a new member of my congregation brought her parents to a Sunday morning service. While they sat in the sanctuary waiting for the service to begin, an usher, who was looking for places to seat people, noticed there were two empty seats in their pew.

"Are those two saved?" the usher asked, referring to the two seats.

"They sure are!" the young woman responded, thinking the usher was asking about her parents. When they all realized the question had been misunderstood, they joined in a good laugh. It would be less than effective to have an usher, or anybody else for that matter, going up and down the aisles checking peoples' spiritual pulses with the diagnostic inquiry "Are you saved?"

I can remember, as a lad of thirteen, being conscripted against my will to attend a children's evangelistic service. At the end of a long sermon that went straight over the heads and hearts of all the children (most of all, mine!) the preacher started to "draw the net"—a term used by some evangelists to describe gathering in the converts. (What fish was ever brought willingly into a boat in a net?) For hours (sigh), the preacher went on explaining salvation in terms most adults would find irrelevant, if not boring. To the children, it was frightening.

As this 1940s Jonathan Edwards fervently waxed on with his own rendition of "sinners in the hand of an angry God," I said to a pal next to me, "I want to get out of here!"

When the preacher said, "Those who want to be saved and washed in the blood of the Lamb, stand up," I remained resolutely seated, just long enough to establish that I was not responding to the speaker's invitation, and then I stood up and marched out, determined never to enter a church again. I remained faithful to my teenage promise until some years later when I really understood what it means to "be saved."

Perhaps this is why I'm sensitive to the three groups reading this chapter. You may be put off by the word "saved" because you have heard it used carelessly without an explanation of what it means. Or you may have used the word yourself without the music of its joy. And you may be saying, "Sure, I'm saved, but from what and for what? What difference has it made in the rough-and-tumble of life?"

An enthusiastic young woman who is a new Christian has had what sounds like an authentic experience. "The thing I like about Christ's salvation is that it's so down to earth. It's for me, it's for now, it's forever." She didn't leave anything out — her salvation was practical, it was working in her life now, and she had a peep at the last page and knew it included heaven.

What is said of some Christians could not be said of this young disciple. Ever hear it? "Some Christians are so heavenly-minded they are no earthly good!" Not so among genuine Christians. The assurance of heaven intensifies their living on earth.

Now back to you. I'm fully aware that the word "save" in "He is able to *save* to the uttermost" may be tarnished for you from overuse or dulled by familiarity. And yet, maybe our task is not to find new words but to put the red-blooded flesh of life on the old ones through an explanation in contemporary phrases. In any intimate conversation (I think of writing as a personal conversation with you), we must be sure we agree on the meaning of the words we use. So here goes.

"Save" is a power word. In fact, it's the most powerful verb in the Bible. The entire sweep of its use in both the Old and New Testaments means deliverance, healing, wholeness, new life now, and eternal life forever. This cornucopian word of the Scriptures overflows with matchless treasure. "Save" encapsulates all that Christ came to do, has done, is doing, and will do for us. Through His life, death on the cross, victorious resurrection from the dead, and present power, Christ is able to deliver us from the loneliness of separation from God (a helpful acrostic for *sin*—separation, *i*ndependence, *n*ihilism); is able to free us from guilt over past failures, able to repattern our minds with a new image of ourselves and our potential; able to liberate our emotions of debilitating fear, anxiety, and worry; and is able to make us whole, integrated, complete persons, altogether new in every way for this life and eternity.

Now I know that was a long, loaded sentence. I just had to put it all together so we can get our lives together. All of us. Christ has the power to save the inquirer in his or her sense of estrangement, the struggling Christian from discouragement, the unsatisfied, unfulfilled believer from dissatisfaction with his or her present stage of growth.

The Christian life is dynamic. (Reminder: the word comes from the Greek *dunamis*—power. So does dynamite!) It must have a definite beginning, it is constantly growing, and it is never fully complete until we reach heaven. It is a personal relationship with Christ. And as we've said repeatedly, the power He has to save is released in us by His indwelling presence.

We are permanently saved when we accept Christ as our Savior and Lord. Once and for all—our souls, minds, bodies. We have both the status of saints, people who belong to the Savior, and security that our standing will never change. Life's biggest insecurity is healed; we belong to God our Father.

142

What power this security gives us! It meets the deepest longings of our hearts, fills the empty void inside, gives confidence and courage. We are free from having to earn our status by competing with others or establish our worth by trying to be adequate. We have been elected to receive power, not continually to struggle for human control.

We are also saved persistently. This has been a major theme of this book. Let's review what we've claimed. When we admit our addiction to false, manipulative, and coercive human power, we are able to accept Christ's indwelling power. Dwelling in us, Christ continues the process of salvation, healing our character and personality, and consistently presses us on to what Paul calls the "fullness of the stature of Christ." We are people programmed for progress. Being saved is being made in the image of Christ. We have His inner power.

So to those asking, "Is it worth it to be a counter-cultural Christian?" my response is "Yes!" But it depends on what's really important to us. If we spend all our energies gaining the approval, accolades, and awards of human success, we'll probably get plenty of cheers from culture, though it may mean some costly compromises along the way. Each compromise cuts off Christ's power—stalls us in our soaring. Christ's power is not given to make us culturally successful, but to be His servants in our culture. If professional or monetary success comes our way without compromising our commitment to Christ, we can use our positions to forward the Kingdom and our money to support Christ's mission for the spiritually and physically hungry.

Last month I had the privilege of giving the invocation at two banquets, each honoring a personal friend who has risen to a position of human power without losing the flow of Christ's power. Both have eight things in common: they have put Christ first in their lives; they are filled with His indwelling power; they spend time in the Word and in prayer and consistently commit their decisions to Christ's guidance; they are husbands in long-term marriages and are caring fathers; they are dedicated to excellence in their work, with Christ as their real boss; they are involved in personally sharing their faith with individuals and are actively leading causes to alleviate social suffering and remove injustice. It just so happens that these two men work for the same company and one has succeeded the other.

The retirement banquet for George Moody, President and Chief Operating Officer of the Security Pacific Corporation, was a celebration I'll not forget. The important thing for me was to listen to the account of George's rise to being one of the truly great business and humanitarian leaders of our time, while never missing a day of growth in the depth of his salvation. He was saved at an early age and he is being saved as Christ continues His work in him, opening the floodgate of His power in response to George's commitment of his immense challenges as lay leader of the American Red Cross and countless other causes, including being chairman of the board of my radio and television ministry.

John Singleton, following in George's footsteps, is now Vice-Chairman of Security Pacific Corporation and Chairman and CEO of Security Pacific Automation Company. The banquet honoring him was in support of one of his primary ministries as a servant of Christ. He has on his heart the poor, homeless, hungry, and broken men and women on the streets of skid row in Los Angeles. He believes that, through the power of Christ, people can be redeemed, rehabilitated, and returned to a positive place in society. This has involved him in leadership of the Union Rescue Mission and as the stem-winder of a campaign to raise millions for the work and a new building to house the homeless. With equal zeal, John teaches an adult Sunday School class. Every time I visit with him, he's on fire about some new discovery he's made in his study and teaching of the Scriptures. Christ has him on the growing edge on all fronts, including developing a network of other top executives across the nation committed to servant ministry.

I see the same quality of growth in "being saved" among people in my congregation who are in the entertainment industry. I think of Clint Holmes, who is one of the rising singing stars in America. Music critic Bob Osborne calls him the new Sammy Davis, Jr., of the music world. As his pastor, I call him "a man on-the-grow with Christ" who is unwilling to compromise his faith or his commitment to excellence as an entertainer. Clint draws on his rich heritage from his mother, who was a British opera singer, and his father, a jazz singer, as well as on his immense talent, training, and discipline in rehearsing. I've seen him bring tears to the eyes of the most secular audience imaginable, and the same audience to their feet for a standing ovation. And then to top it off by singing them into the agape heart of God.

If you were to ask Clint and his lovely wife, Brenda, if it is worth it to hang in there against the cultural currents that could easily take their life in a very different direction, they would answer that there's no other way than to keep on growing in Christ who saved them and is saving them. They express this commitment to grow in their salvation by daily prayer and study, involvement in support groups with other Christians, and by sharing their faith with nonbelievers.

It's easy to be critical of a lot of what comes out of Hollywood. What many do not know is that there are a great number of actors and actresses, writers, producers, directors, and technical people who are deeply committed to Christ. At great cost to their careers at times, they take their stand for what they believe.

I'm thankful for Elders in my church like Rob Loos who helped organize a group called Inter-Mission in 1987. It's for Christians employed in Hollywood's television and film industry. Under the outstanding leadership of staff member and actor David Schall, the group meets periodically to provide a network of support and encouragement for hundreds of these hard-working professionals. Sponsored by our church and the Actor's Co-op, the nation's first professional (Actors Equity Approved) Christian repertory company,

146

Inter-Mission, has fast become a strong and viable organization of Christians in the entertainment industry.

Growing in "being saved," realizing the full measure of Christ's transforming, healing, repatterning power, is the goal of so many people whose stories I'd love to share. They are discovering that Christ saves in several *in* ways: *in*itially, *in*tensively in their inner lives, and *in*clusively in all phases of their relationships and responsibilities. And let me add another important *in:* their discipleship is *in*tentional. A spiritual awakening is taking place in our congregation because of those who are convinced that Christ is able to save to the uttermost.

Spiritual Formation

As a congregation, we are so convinced of our need to grow on in the experience of uttermost salvation that we have established on our pastoral team a position called Pastor of Spiritual Formation. Dr. Dorothy Cross, a national leader in the spiritual formation movement, has joined our team to work with people who want to experience a complete, thoroughgoing renewal of their total lives. Our prayer for ourselves and our congregation is the same as Paul's for the Galatians – that Christ may be formed in us (Gal. 4:19). We want to press on in being saved, so that our assurance of salvation is coupled with assimilation of Christian character. Bible study, prayer, classes, small groups, retreats, along with joyous worship, are the church's programmatical responsibility to encourage uttermost salvation.

Christ Saves Perpetually

Why be a Christian? Because Christ saves—perpetually and for perpetuity. It is a great comfort to know that the Father gave Him the assignment of watching over us—now, during the years after our conversion, and finally as He sees us through death and on to heaven. Does that sound a bit old-fashioned? If so—I'm guilty as charged. There's no other clever way to say it. As we stressed in the previous chapter, Christ does, in fact, take you and me on as His responsibility. He watches over us, ever attentive to our needs. But what about death?

The Frightening Loose End

One big, dangling loose end that twists about in so many of us is anxiety over death. We all want to live as long as we can here on earth. The thought of all that we will leave behind—unfinished, unexpressed—haunts us. Departure for the walk through the valley of death also means the anguish of leaving loved ones behind. But all of this is on the surface of our anxiety. Death really troubles us because we can't control it. With good health habits we may postpone its arrival, but eventually it will come. Our need to be in control of our lives, people, and circumstances is threatened each time we think of death, our own dying, or go through the death of a loved one or friend. We can't live to the fullest now until we are sure that we will live forever. Christ alone can put the fear of death

148

behind us—but not until we give up the need to control even this final scene in the last act of the drama of our life on earth.

Now pause for a moment. Be as honest with yourself as you can. Has the Lord of the Loose Ends tied down this final loose end for you once and for all? He is able to save to the uttermost: from death for heaven. Are you sure of that for yourself? Christ not only conquered death, but conquers *fear of death* in us—our own dying and the death of those we love. The only passport to heaven is faith in Christ. It's not what we've accomplished that will qualify us, and our failures will not disqualify us.

Why be a Christian? Because Christ is able to save us from a lifelong anguish over dying.

For Whom Is The Promise Given?

Now we are prepared to ask, for whom is this "He is able" exclamation given? Whom does Christ save to the uttermost? The author of Hebrews draws us on, telling us it is for "those who come to God through Him" (7:25). The Greek word for "those who come," *proserchomenous,* is from a verb meaning to come with consent. The idea is that we come in response to a call, an invitation. We could not come if we were not first called; we could not elect to respond if we were not elected. The Father is behind it all.

We turn to Jesus' promise to underline this astounding grace. "All that the Father gives Me will come to Me, and the one who comes to Me I will by no means cast out" (John 6:37). In the Greek, "no means" is a double negative for an unlimited positive: I will "no, no!" cast out. For you and me, Christ's invitation is initially and consistently "Come!" "Come to me all you who are weary and heavy laden."

The gift of faith is given to us so we can come to Him. Not even the ability to respond is our self-generated achievement. "Nothing in my hand I bring; simply to the cross I cling." The ultimate loss of control brings our lives under Christ's control—now and forever.

How does Christ do it? The last phrase of this "He is able" assurance in Hebrews 7:25 tells us: "since He always lives to make intercession for them." As our High Priest, Christ is constantly interceding for us. He is our link with the Father's heart, bringing our needs to Him and then bringing to us the Father's guidance, wisdom, and power.

Christ is our eternal cheerleader. He's for us, not against us. He desires His best for us and is working in and around us to accomplish it.

Why be a Christian? Christ Himself is the answer. A personal relationship with Him is life's greatest joy. He alone has the power to save us now, in the days to come, and when we face the transition we call death. He is pulling for us each step of the way. This is why we should be a Christian. It's the most powerful life, the most joyous life, the most exciting life, the most creative life, the most challenging life, and the most hopeful life! It's the only way to come alive and stay alive—now and forever.

150

8.

STUMBLING OVER OUR STUMBLES

LAST SUMMER MY WIFE, MARY JANE, PUT ME THROUGH A traumatic emotional experience. She did it out of love and for my good and growth.

After my study leave in Edinburgh, Scotland, she joined me for two weeks of leisurely touring the west coast of the Highlands and the western islands off the coast. The itinerary, accommodations, and route were completely left up to her excellent travel planning skills. However, the one place I told Mary Jane I did not want to go was back to where I'd had a near-fatal accident three years before.

Late one evening, while hiking alone on the rugged northern west coast, I had stumbled and fallen on some very treacherous rocks and crushed my left leg. It took me almost three hours, on my back, to inch myself over some very rugged territory to where someone could find me. Miraculously, I was rescued. Though I experienced a greater closeness to the Lord of hope in these lonely hours than I had ever known before, I still wanted to block out the memory of the physical pain and emotional anguish I'd been through.

But Mary Jane knows me very well. She could see that the experience and the long process of surgery and healing afterward had made me cautious. I lacked my usual gusto and daring. She also sensed my hidden worry that I might have exaggerated how frightening the harrowing experience had been. Was it all that bad? Had I been overly dramatic in recounting it?

One day on our carefree vacation last summer, Mary Jane was driving. At a crossroads she took a turn onto a road I knew all too well—I had traveled it in the middle of the night in an ambulance!

"Mary Jane, where are you going?" I said angrily. "I thought you agreed we would never go back to the place where I fell! That's exactly where we're headed!"

"Trust me, Lloyd" was all she said. Her tone was so drenched with love and tenderness (with a measure of firmness thrown in) that I felt I should not resist.

Sure enough, an hour later, we drove into the lane leading to the inn where I had been staying before I took the solitary hike that ended in catastrophe.

Inside the country hotel, I was greeted like a Lazarus out of the tomb. The son of the owner, who had carried and cared for me after I was found, gave me a big hug. He wanted to relive the experience and have me go over every gruesome detail of the accident. I groaned inside. Just what I had expected would happen and exactly what I didn't want to do.

154

But since Mary Jane and I were treated like royalty, and because of the delight the hotel staff expressed over my recovery, dinner went well. We went to bed, and I fully expected that in the morning we'd have breakfast and be on our way. Mary Jane had other plans.

Early in the morning she awakened me, and as I rubbed the sleep out of my eyes, I saw she had laid out all our rain gear and walking shoes. I knew what that meant! She wanted to hike to the very place of my accident!

"When it's all over, you'll thank me," she said confidently, with the same love and concern she'd expressed the day before. So I got up, dressed, and prepared for the hike. I looked out the window and saw that it was raining as hard as on the night I had fallen. "What if it happens again?" I said to myself, fearfully.

In the rain, we hiked the long way to the place of painful memories. When we reached the spot where I had crushed my leg between two rocks, I didn't stumble and fall again. Instead, Mary Jane and I sat silently for a long time, while I allowed the memories to flood back and be healed by the Lord.

Then we prayed. The Lord had saved me and enabled me to survive. My carelessness caused the accident, and yet He used it to deepen my relationship with Him during the long recovery. There, together, Mary Jane and I recommitted our lives to the Lord.

The long hike back gave Mary Jane a chance to see more closely the terrain over which I had dragged myself after the fall. She insisted on taking pictures to show the children. One shot I wanted for myself, though—the place, now hallowed in my memory, where I felt a direct encounter with the Lord before I lost consciousness.

When we arrived back near the hotel, Mary Jane stopped me and looked me in the eyes. "Lloyd," she said with encouragement, "what you went through was not as bad as you recounted it. It was worse! And you don't have to keep reliving it. You are free." I knew she was right.

Once again I was taught that until we learn from the past, we will repeat it. Until the hurting memories are healed, we will keep on recreating them in present actions and attitudes. Most of all, we'll limp along fearful of repeating past mistakes.

I have shared the account of that revisit last summer to a place of difficult memories because it illustrates what I think the Lord wants us to learn about our spiritual stumbles, *and* His power to keep us from stumbling.

Stumbling On The Fast Track

With all that we've discovered thus far about the Lord of the Loose Ends who is able, we should be ready to run on the fast track with freedom and joy.

We could, if it weren't for some other loose ends that flop around and trip us like untied laces on our jogging shoes.

We stumble over having stumbled. These loose ends are the memories of previous failures. If we could only get them off our minds! They are yet another reason we feel at loose ends, and further evidence of how desperately we need the Lord of the Loose Ends to get control over our lives.

Again, He is able. Once more, He has exactly the power we need. The Lord's own brother, Jude, sounds the trumpet note this time. What we hear seems too good to be true, but as we listen more closely, we realize that it is too true to be ignored.

"Now to Him who is able to keep you from stumbling and to present you faultless before the presence of His glory with exceeding joy, to God our Savior, who alone is wise, be glory and majesty, dominion and power, both now and forever. Amen" (Jude 24–25).

This explosion of praise at the end of Jude's 25-verse epistle makes an audacious claim. God's power is for now as well as at the end of our life when we get to heaven. And it's for the likes of you and me with our loose ends of past stumbles dangling around our ankles, making our steps limp with caution, fear, and restraint.

So let's go straight for the jugular. How do we stumble? Why do we keep on stumbling? And most important of all, how can Christ keep us from stumbling? Exactly how does Christ make us sure-footed for the race of life?

We All Stumble

We all have two things in common: spiritually, we have stumbled, and we do stumble. It's not a flat-out fall that we take, but a trip that throws us off balance.

These stumbles are our failures, our denials of our calling to be great by grace, our refusals to be to others what Christ has been to us. Oh, let's call them for what they are—sins. Some are what we've thought or fantasized; others have been committed in action; still others involve what we've said and done to people, or what we knew love demanded and yet we still refused either to say or do.

Then, too, we've stumbled over what people have said or done to us. We remember all too well the hurts and how we reacted—and continue to react as our memories parade the experiences and we feel the pain all over again. Most of all, we remember how we stumbled in our anger, retorts, or efforts to get even.

But that's not all. We stumble when our road is bumpy and strewn with obstacles. We trip far too easily when life gets difficult. We don't take things in stride. When the wind is against us, we grumble a lot. Interruptions that disturb our ordered plans unsettle us. And when the big crises hit, we wonder where all our talk about courage and patience has gotten us. We don't like to admit it, but we do stumble.

Why We Continue To Stumble

When I was a cub radio announcer, I discovered that making a "fluff," what we called stumbling over a word, often caused me a succession of them by the time I got off the air.

A senior announcer explained what was happening. "A 'fluff' is an announcer's nemesis. We allow our minds to focus on the mistake and lose concentration on what we're reading. So another one happens. Now we really get concerned and tighten up. Others follow. The rule to keep is: 'One fluff is enough—so forget it!' "

You're probably way ahead of me on the application of that illustration. I've thought about it often. Previous stumbles take our attention off where we are and where we're going. You guessed it. We stumble more and more. Mistakes become repetitive.

How Christ Keeps Us From Stumbling

Christ breaks into the syndrome of our repeated stumbling and deals with our obsession with our past stumbles. The Greek word translated "from stumbling" is a verbal that means sure-footed, in a positive sense.

The way the Lord helps us with this obsession is to transform our self-image into that of forgiven, forgiving people. Jude tells us that He is able, has all power, "to present [us] faultless before the presence of His glory with exceeding joy" and "to God our Savior . . . " (Jude 24–25).

A two-step process is implied. It is important to keep clear the double use of the pronoun "His." It is Christ the mediator who reaches us in our stumbling state. He reveals to us that through His atonement on the cross, we have been forgiven and now in His eyes are *faultless.* The word in Greek is the same as is used for an unblemished, sacrificial animal. Christ Himself was the faultless Lamb of God who took our faults, failures, and sins, and was sacrificed for us.

Don't miss the redemptive picture Jude is paint-ing. We are given a faultless status through the propitiation of Christ and in the presence of His glory.

Mind-boggling as it is, Christ presents us to God in His image, and the Father relates to us as to His Own Son! Our minds reel at the wonder. So the Fa-ther and the Son and all the company of heaven rejoice over us, not as stumblers, but as those totally exon-erated for our stumbles.

Too Glorious?

Well! Too glorious a vision? No. Either God has forgiven us or He hasn't. If Christ bore our sins on Calvary, then surely God is not still holding a grudge against us about them. Of course, we must ask for forgiveness. But it is not to change God's mind about us or placate Him for what we've done or been. We seek forgiveness not to be forgiven but to accept the forgiveness already offered to us. Confession is a change of our minds, not God's. We simply receive what has been there waiting for us all along.

God exists beyond the limits of time and space. And yet, at a point in time, He sent Christ to die for our sins. God had to be both the just and the justifier, as Paul puts it (Rom. 3:26). He had to judge sin and justify sinners. The inestimable cost of that action leaves us lost in wonder, love, and praise. When Jesus cried out on the cross, "It is finished," it was a shout of triumph and completion. The sins of the world before the cross, and for all time afterward, were forgiven. The cosmic atonement was completed.

Now let's ask the key question: did Calvary's finished reconciliation include the sins and failures of our times of stumbling? If so, then they have been forgiven, and our plea to be forgiven is to claim the accomplished reality of our forgiveness.

But are we willing to follow the thought to its glorious conclusion? If we know we were forgiven through the cross, and have accepted that, can we relate to ourselves as God does? Are we able to see ourselves as forgiven for our stumbles, or will we continue to ruminate over them, and as a result, live under the compulsion to stumble?

Don't get me wrong. I'm not suggesting that we might never stumble again. What I am saying is that the sheer wonder of already being forgiven breaks our bondage to the repetitive pattern. As we praise God for the forgiveness of our past stumbles and see ourselves as He sees us, we will stumble less and less. And Christ the Mediator has all power to present us as faultless as a result of forgiveness—not only to God, but to ourselves. That's the mystery of how He keeps us from stumbling. And when we do stumble, forgiveness and a new beginning is only a prayer of acceptance away. People who claim this awesome truth stumble less and less. They praise God more, are more gracious to themselves, and more forgiving of others.

More Than We Can Imagine?

Is this more than we can imagine or accept? It would seem so. We find it difficult because of our struggle for control. As I mentioned earlier, the ultimate loss of our control is to accept grace and stop trying to earn it. We maintain the control over ourselves and others when we continue to assume the authority to punish ourselves and others with lack of forgiveness.

Recently a man said to me, "Well, God may forgive but I'm having a hard time forgiving myself." Of course he is—the man has been controlling everything in his life for years. He was unsettled when I said, "That's the height of arrogance! You are pitting your opinion of yourself over and against God's." You might imagine that deepened the level of our conversation! The man had never been confronted with the extent of his addiction to control—he was willing to take on the responsibility of punishing himself rather than accept God's grace and control. When he realized the blasphemy of contradicting God, the man began a long process of dismantling his control structure.

A few Sundays ago, he came forward for prayer at the end of the 11:00 service. As he knelt he said, "I'm here to accept God's forgiveness and His power to forgive myself!" We both had tears in our eyes as we prayed together.

Is There Hope For Me?

On another Sunday morning, as I greeted the congregation streaming out of the sanctuary, a woman named Julie shook my hand and asked if she could stay to talk with me after I had finished. She sat waiting quietly with her head bowed. I knew Julie and wondered why she needed to talk so urgently.

You see, Julie is a recovering addict who had been one of Hollywood's peddlers of drugs. Months before she had wandered into a worship service. Christ got hold of her life and she became a Christian. The One who is able broke her addiction.

Eventually, Julie became involved in our Lord's Lighthouse ministry, a program on our campus for feeding the hungry and homeless on Sunday afternoons. Some of the men and women she served food to were those to whom she had formerly sold drugs.

"Hey, look who's here!" some of the street people would exclaim, amazed that Julie not only fed them, but witnessed to her new faith and freedom from drugs.

Other more sophisticated and closet drug users who came to the worship services, searching for a new life, were shocked to see Julie there, so obviously changed. She had a great impact on them and a growing ministry with them.

I knew something was wrong when I was finally able to talk with Julie that Sunday morning. She threw her arms around me and sobbed convulsively. Then I looked into her lovely face that drugs and hard living have plowed with furrows beyond her years. Her eyes were filled with pain.

"Lloyd, I stumbled! Is there hope for me?" Julie sobbed. She had slipped back into her addiction in a two-day stumble. Since then she had been staying away from church because she couldn't imagine that the Lord would forgive her, or that she would be accepted by her new Christian friends.

"Yes, Julie," I said, "there's hope for you, unless Christ is a vacillating Lord who changes His mind. But His love never changes. He has forgiven you and you must claim that again. Make a fresh start!" I'm glad to say that she did make that new beginning as we prayed together.

Julie had taken her eyes off Christ for a time. She had begun to think back over her life of stumbling and, rather than praise the Lord for His intervention to deliver her, she had been filled again with remorse. It was when she had started stumbling over her stumbles that she stumbled again. Julie knows the danger of that now.

It's through a consistent, daily, hourly experience of the presence of Christ's glory—the reassurance that through His shed blood we have been made faultless—that He keeps us from stumbling.

Not License

What I am saying is not license. I would be contradicting the whole thrust of the Epistle of Jude if I gave that impression. In fact, Jude wrote to the early Christians to counteract false teachers who were distorting the meaning and practice of grace by saying that if grace abounds it doesn't make any difference what you do. Jude asserts just the opposite: it is because of grace that we are free to fulfill the absolute requirements of holy living. Grace gives us the power to live the Ten Commandments and the ethical standards of the Sermon on the Mount. Our response to God's stunning love is that we desire not to go on stumbling.

The Real Test

The real test of whether or not we have accepted God's love in Christ is in our attitude toward people who have stumbled in their walk and hurt us. We stumble over the stumbles of others.

Earlier I talked about a man who stumbled in his arrogant unwillingness to forgive himself. There was no less a struggle for power going on inside a woman who recently spouted the old shibboleth, "I'll forgive, but I'll not forget!" She had been deeply hurt by a friend whose stumble had inflicted great emotional pain on her. And in lots of little ways she reminded her friend that she had not forgotten.

"You can understand how I feel, can't you?" she demanded of me. Yes, I could understand. But I also could empathize from past experiences that the woman was going to have a life of continual stumbling herself unless she stopped controlling the memory of her friend's stumble. She was holding a power club over her friend's head; she was in control over the relationship as long as her forgiveness did not include forgetting.

More serious, the woman was contradicting God, who said, "Do not remember the former things nor consider the things of old" (Isa. 43:18).

The more we visited, the more I realized the woman had others besides this friend on her relational hit list. Perhaps it was her use of the word "stumbling" that caught my attention. "I keep stumbling over the mistakes and failures of people these days. What's this

165

world coming to?" By "stumbling" she meant that she was aware of the weaknesses of people. She, in fact, was tripping over them and stumbling herself in unrighteous indignation, rather than showing compassion or willingness to help.

I asked the woman to write down a list of the people she had "stumbled" over. We talked at length about the power game she was playing as judge and punisher in her disdainful attitudes, and by withholding acceptance. "Are you willing to be as gracious in offering a second chance to others as Christ has been to you?" I asked. I suspected that failures of her own were being expressed in countertransference hidden behind her "Mrs. Adequate" façade.

In a subsequent visit, my friend was willing to tear up her hit list, and we set a match to it. The flames leaped up in the dish on my coffee table as we prayed in my study.

Slipping In The Shower

It so happened that a few days later I had to live the advice I had given to the woman. I slipped in the shower one morning and caught myself before I fell. It was an unmistakable signal to me of the potential slip I was in danger of having in my spiritual life.

I had awakened with a heavy heart. The day before I had stumbled across (more than discovered) some insidious divisiveness a friend was causing because of his own insecurity and competitiveness. "Why doesn't that guy just get on with what God has called him to do rather than criticizing the way I'm doing what He's given me to do?" I almost said it out loud in the shower. I was deeply hurt. The soap I was outwardly sudsing all over my body was what I needed the Lord to do inside to cleanse my soul. Then, in the suds that covered the floor of the shower, I slipped. "Careful, Lloyd," I said, "what's going on inside you will really cause a spiritual stumble."

As I toweled and shaved, I looked into the mirror. My face did not look very rested. Apparently, most of the night in my sleep I had worked the man over in a wrestling match.

By the time I got to my devotions, I was ready to listen to the Lord. My Bible study at that time was in the Psalms. Slated for this particular morning was Psalm 95: "O come, let us worship and bow down; let us kneel before the Lord our Maker." That's certainly what I needed to do.

Years of experience getting loose ends under the leadership of the Lord of the Loose Ends had taught me that feeling follows thought, and I knew I needed my thinking changed. So I read the rest of the psalm on my knees. In that more humble position of receptivity and openness to what the Lord had to say, I read on in the Psalm. Verse 8 hit me between the eyes: "Do not harden your hearts."

In jeopardy, I knew, was my ability to run with the Master that day without stumbling over either what my friend had done or my reaction to it. My prayer was, "Lord, help me! I'm ready to listen. I don't want this situation to produce a memory for me to stumble over constantly." The Lord's answer was to remind me that disappointments can make me bitter or better. "It all depends," the Lord seemed to be saying, "on whether you will express the forgiveness I have given you all through the years. Now go and forgive this man and act as if he had not hurt you. Leave it to me to deal with the deeper problems in him that have caused this." I did what the Lord told me to do, and fresh grace flooded both my heart and attitude. Once again the Lord kept me from stumbling over another person's stumble.

How To Become Sure-footed

Christ is able not only to keep us from stumbling by freeing us of our memories of previous stumbles and the stumbles of others that affect us; He is able to make us sure-footed for the race of life. In verses 20–21 of his epistle, before Jude makes his stirring "He is able" declaration (vv. 24–25), he gives us the dynamics of what we can do to cooperate with the Lord in His efforts to keep us from stumbling as we run the race of life.

Jude gives us some very strategic, daily, pre-run stretching exercises. Read over Jude 20–21; note that there are three participles and an imperative. Like fragments of metal, the participles are drawn to the magnet of the imperative, "*keep* yourself in the love of God." Jude tells us how to do that in the three participles: "*building* yourself up in your most holy faith"; then, "*praying* in the Holy Spirit"; and finally, "*looking for* the mercy of our Lord Jesus Christ unto eternal life."

The central issue of life is keeping ourselves in the love of God. This does not mean that we can earn His love by our own goodness or make Him stop loving us because of our failures. What it does mean is that we can choose to receive a consistent flow of His fresh grace. Jude gives us three ways to do it. They involve objectivity in our thinking, spirit-guided praying, and merciful living. Let's take a look at how these keep us in the love of God.

Objectivity In Our Thinking

What Jude calls "building yourselves up on your most holy faith" is the way to maintain objectivity in our thinking. For the first-century Christians, this meant building their thinking about God's grace, salvation through Christ, and the abundant life in the power of the indwelling Christ on the teaching of the apostles. For us, it means founding our convictions on the truth of the Bible. Our faith is a gift of the Spirit to respond to this objective truth. Then our character, personality, actions, reactions are shaped around this truth. We grow as women and men of faith; the structure of our lives becomes strong and can resist the winds of changing ideas in our culture about who God is and how we can know Him.

Consistent daily study of the Bible builds up our knowledge and experience of the love of God. And as we've seen in our discussion of how God relates to us in our failures, it's crucial that we base our thinking on the Bible. When does God forgive us? Before, during, after, or when we confess? Our faith is built on the objective, biblical truth that "God demonstrates His own love toward us, in that while we were still sinners Christ died for us" (Rom. 5:8). There need be no loose ends about what we believe about the love of God!

How firm a foundation, you saints of the Lord
Is laid for your faith in His excellent Word.
What more can He say than to you He has said,
To you who for refuge to Jesus have fled.

Prayer In The Spirit

Keeping ourselves in the love of God really means being kept there by the Holy Spirit. Prayer in the Spirit is prayer that is motivated, clarified, and liberated by the Spirit, who lifts us to heights of unrestrained praise. And, as we have observed, praise opens us to experience more of God's love for us. We yield our minds to the Spirit and He prays through us—sometimes in a yearning for more of God that is too deep for words. Other times we burst into words beyond rationality, and then, with the Spirit's gift of interpretation, the meaning is given to us. We realize wisdom, discernment, and knowledge previously beyond our human ability to understand.

God cares about us so much that He wants to free us to experience life's greatest joy—to be engulfed by His love. Through His Spirit, He keeps us in His love.

Everlasting Mercy

Further, we are kept in the love of God by "looking for the mercy of our Lord Jesus Christ unto eternal life"! Our stumbles need not keep us out of heaven or from beginning the joy of heaven now. We look for Christ's second coming, but we must not be so busy reading the signs of the times in order to set a date by human calculation that we miss His presence with us now.

His gift is mercy. That, above all else, keeps us in the love of God. Jude would have used *mercy* with the thought of the Hebrew meaning. The root word in Hebrew signifies the quality of a mother and father's love for an unborn child in the womb, who is helpless to earn or deserve their love. And that's how Christ relates when we stumble over having stumbled.

Help For The Helpless And Those In A Bind
Healing For The Broken In Body, Soul And Mind

And the mercy we receive now is to be given, in His name, to other stumblers. "Blessed are the merciful for they shall obtain mercy" (Matt. 5:7). Christ is able to keep us in the love of God, keep us from stumbling, and keep us from the memory of previous stumbles. I know it's true — by the stumbles over my own stumbles — whether physically on the treacherous rocks of the northwestern coast of Scotland, or spiritually, in my own or another's human failures.

9.

MONEY TALKS

Money talks,
*   That I'll not deny,*
I heard it once,
*   It said, "Good-by."*

As MONEY SLIPS THROUGH OUR FINGERS, MOST OF US WOULD agree it says "good-by" all too soon. And while it's slipping through our fingers, we realize how good it feels. Sooner or later we learn how to put those fingers closer together so less slips through. With careful planning, we can even hang onto a little of it; using both hands, we can clutch a great deal more of it; getting our arms involved, we can even clutch it to our hearts.

Money talks. We use that phrase in a critical way when someone uses money to get what he or she wants. But it talks in lots of other ways. The way we use it tells us and the people around us what's really important to us.

Bob Dylan said, "Money doesn't talk. It screams!"

Well, at the very least, it's a megaphone shout about who's in control of our lives.

Money is congealed power. It gives us a sense of control over our own lives, over other people, over circumstances. But not without a lot of worry over earning enough. Saving some for a rainy day is getting harder. The rainy day is now, and the monsoon doesn't ever seem to end. The possessions money can buy all too soon have a way of possessing us. Our real estate can bring real concerns.

Few things can cause the feeling of being at loose ends more than fretting over money. The loose ends of worries over money are not the exclusive problem of any one stratum of society. While one person struggles to pay his bills, another person suffers from quivering hands and a racing heart when he checks the condition of his investments in the business section of the morning paper. Both of these persons at opposite ends of the financial scale have money loose ends twining around their hearts.

People stand before a slot machine with a paper cupful of quarters, feeding a "one-armed bandit," hoping for a pot-of-gold "fix" for their money problems. They have a lot in common with the wealthy man or woman who never got a tan on an expensive vacation because the days were spent in one of those plush stock exchange offices watching a closed-circuit teledisplay of the market fluctuations.

And in between those extremes are all the rest of us who have money loose ends of our own. Funny thing about money—we never get enough. Our desires for what money can provide us and what we can do when we have some of it are seldom satisfied. Guess that's not really funny at all. It's more tragic than humorous, and advertisers know how to motivate a gnawing dissatisfaction with what we have and the desire for a new something-or-other. To play on an old English line from World War II: people with money loose ends are overstimulated, overacquisitive, over budget, overextended and over here, on the street where we live, in your house and mine.

Oh, I'm not down on money. I've heard it said too often, "You preachers talk like you're down on money until you want to raise some of it from those of us who have it!" That's probably true; some spiritual leaders do sound high-and-mighty when they so eloquently hold forth about the pitfalls of wealth, and then grovel and snivel with hat in hand (twisting it nervously) when they go to the people they've castigated, asking for a fat check for the church budget or an elegant sanctuary in which to preach.

So, I guess I have to tell you—writing this chapter on the loose ends of money worries is a relief. My purpose is not to raise money. I'm going for higher stakes than that. A bigger burden. I'm really troubled about what frustration over money does to us. Let me say it flat out: I'm aware of the illicit love affair many of us have with money. It would make eighth-century-B.C. Hosea, who confronted ancient Israel with its spiritual adultery, blush.

Also, I'm concerned about what money wrangles and financial competition do to marriages, families, and friends. When someone says, "It's not the money, it's the principle . . . ," you can be sure of one thing—it's really the money! The principal of the money usually clouds the principles in a dispute.

It's alarming how much time we all spend thinking about money. We seldom spend as much time praying as in trying to tie down the loose ends of money matters. The Lord can become a last-item addendum to our full agendas. Oh, we wouldn't dare take Him off, for we suspect His blessing is mysteriously involved with our material security. It's just that we get obsessed with what we possess.

Your Money Or Your Life

The highwayman of old used the menacing threat: "Your money or your life!" when demanding the purse of some unfortunate traveler. It may be closer to the central issue than we'd like to think at times. Jack Benny played the line out to the fullest advantage with his inimitable delivery and timing. I still laugh when I remember the routine. The robber demands persistently, "Your money or your life!" *Long pause. . . .* Benny would finally respond, "Don't rush me!" *Another pause. . . .* "I'm thinking, I'm thinking."

In this chapter we are thinking about that awesome alternative. It's certainly a choice we face in living the abundant life. Jesus said, "For what is a man profited if he gains the whole world, and loses his soul?" (Matt. 16:26). Our concern isn't gaining the whole world; we just want control over our little world. And one of the ways we think we can get it is with our money. With its congealed power we try to maintain our diminutive autocracy by controlling others and denying the Lord's authority. Strange thing about money: we think we own it; soon it owns us.

A single mother who was managing financially with the Lord's help but thought she was only surviving, found herself a contestant on a television game show. In the course of events, she won a veritable fortune and quickly discovered what real money worries are. First, she was losing sleep over the money she now had and for which she was responsible; next, she was trusting in wealth to solve her problems and experiencing the frustration of wasting money in the process; third, she was suffering the alienation of some friends who thought they knew best what she should do; and finally, she was missing the former freedom she had known when she was trusting the Lord with her lack of money. Suddenly, her life was not her own — she felt as if the new money had come to own her. How very soon it becomes obvious that money can buy anything except people's real love, true joy, or the Lord's power for abundant living and eternal life!

Money talks, but it develops a stammer in life's big crises, a lisp in deep communication, and becomes tongue-tied when what it wants to buy is not for sale!

We really do not give Christ control of our lives until our commitment includes our money and the material possessions it provides.

Money is our commodity of control. We can use it to manipulate others with controlling statements like "This is what I've done for you lately" and "This is what I'm willing to do *if* . . . ." We use money, or what we can do for people with it, to cover our guilt, get a desired response, or make sure that we will not be opposed. We use it to "sweeten deals" and "grease the skids." It works to control almost everyone—except the Lord. And when money loose ends mount into a feeling of being at loose ends overall, the Lord won't snap to attention and march for us. He will be Lord of money loose ends only when we give Him complete control of our total lives.

Martin Luther said we need two conversions—one of the heart, the other of our pocketbooks. In reality, the first never truly happens until the second is included.

A Baptist pastor friend of mine loves to tell Presbyterians the story of a man who came up to the baptismal tank. He pulled his wallet out from under his baptismal robe and laid it on the side of the tank. He had been afraid to leave it in the robing room because he was afraid someone would steal it. The pastor said, "It's probably best not to get your money and credit cards wet, but I want you to be thinking about your money and possessions, as well as your soul, as I immerse you. You'd better include them in your commitment to Christ or your baptism will have little lasting effect on your life."

The man smiled. He had gotten the full impact of what his pastor said. Playfully, without breaking the mood of the moment, he whispered to his pastor, "Could you just sprinkle the wallet lightly like the Presbyterians do?"

Whether our outward symbol is sprinkling, pouring, or immersion, our baptism must include our money.

Historians record the fact that when non-Christian soldiers were recruited for the Crusades, they had to be baptized. Whole groups of them would be marched across a river. As some of them waded in, they were careful to hold their swords above the water. They were not about to have what they did with their swords brought under the waters of baptismal dedication. Many of us feel the same way about our money.

Some of you may be thinking, "Why all the fuss about money control? I don't have enough to be all that disturbed about." But unless I miss my guess, you're troubled about making ends meet and you spend time worrying about finances like everybody else.

We all do, whether we're trying to get enough money or keep what little we've acquired. And most are anxious about having enough set aside for the long pull after retirement. A woman confided, "I'm in absolute panic about our retirement plans. Will Social Security, our pension, and what we've been able to save be enough? With the cost of living skyrocketing every year, what we've saved is worth less and less. I feel so out of control of our future." And a father of a daughter in her twenties who was no longer covered by the family medical insurance plan shared this concern: "My daughter wants to be independent and doesn't see why medical insurance is necessary. She refuses my help, but if anything happens to her the medical bills would wipe me out!" Money worries—the not-so-hidden inner turmoil in all of us.

The line from the popular musical *Cabaret* that says "Money makes the world go 'round" is wrong.

Sometimes fears about it grind the happy merry-go-round to a slow turn. The music at half speed is not very pleasant.

Only the Lord makes the world go around. He is the Lord of the loose ends of our money. Jesus was concerned about how we relate to money and possessions. Seventeen of His thirty-eight parables, and one-fifth of the New Testament, deal with the theme.

Nestled in the middle of Paul's message to the Corinthians about giving is one of the most liberating of the "He is able" promises of the Bible. It's one of my favorite verses because I have claimed it in times of financial need and also in times of abundance, when I needed to remember that I am accountable for how I use whatever resources I have been given. This verse brought me to a commitment of my loose ends of constant anxiety over money.

Like many, I had the hidden scar of being raised during the Depression and a deeper need to trust the Lord of the Loose Ends with my financial concerns. Even as I quote this verse now, I get a lump in my throat thinking about how its promise has been fulfilled in my personal life and ministry: "And God is able to make all grace abound toward you, that you, always having all sufficiency in all things, have an abundance for every good work" (2 Cor. 9:8).

In this verse the word "able" is in a slightly different form in the Greek than in the other "He is able" exclamations we've been considering. Here it is *dunatei*, "to be able," a Pauline word made from *dunatos,* "able." Though closely related to *dunamis,* "power," the emphasis here is on "mighty," the ability to show oneself powerful. Paul also uses the same word when reminding the Corinthians that Christ is mighty in them (2 Cor. 13:3).

The Lord of the Loose Ends of money worries is mighty. Paul tells us in this key verse (2 Cor. 9:8) that God through Christ is mighty in His abounding grace that brings us to trust all our affairs to Him, mighty in giving us sufficiency in our needs, and mighty to provide an abundance to give away for His work in the world.

Mighty Grace

Like all the other loose ends we've considered, the loose ends of money and material concerns confront us with the truth that we can't make it alone. Loose ends have a way of bringing us to the limit of our ability to run our own lives. No loose end can do that more quickly than money problems. I'm not only talking about a lack of money, but all the related anxieties about it as well—however little or much we have. The great need, beneath all our surface needs, is for grace—the assurance of unchanging love. When the loose end of financial trouble hits, we need to be sure that our Lord knows and cares. And more than needing a solution to our problems, we need Him, and the relationship with Him for which we were created. Sometimes He waits to unveil the solution until we long, most of all, to rest in His love.

It may surprise us to know that our Lord does not have everything. He has given us the one thing He will not force—our love and faithfulness. This is what we can offer to Him in response to His grace. Turning our unsolved needs over to Him is where a solution begins.

Mighty Sufficiency

Paul borrows a Greek philosophical term to describe the result of trusting the Lord completely— *autarkeia*, meaning "contentment with exactly enough." Of course, our concept of "enough" may need to be altered. Sometimes we establish our lifestyle with all its expenses, and then, when we face difficulties, we want the Lord to bolster a level of living that may not be good for us or glorifying to Him. There are times when His guidance is to simplify our lives, cut out some extravagant luxuries, and not live at a level beyond our earning ability.

Recently we have been through a period of Christian history in which the "name-it-and-claim-it" and "prosperity-is-your-divine-right" philosophies have had an impact on people's expectations. Two important things are left out: the concept that the Lord can use our financial problems to bring us to Him in a deeper way, and the further concept that our idea of prosperity and what we should claim must be carefully sorted out in prayer. My motto is, "The Lord provides what He guides." Our task is to seek His guidance in what we ask for and claim. His grace abounds; His sufficiency is to meet our needs.

Mighty Abundance

The Lord's mighty abundance is for the purpose of making us channels for the support of His work in the world. Often we think of abundance as a further expansion of our own brand of luxurious living. Our giving must keep pace with our increased resources, or the Lord may taper our resources to our limited willingness to give. The Lord has chosen to do His work of evangelism and mission in the world through the resource of those who have received His grace. He does not rain down money from heaven; He entrusts it to people like you and me to distribute.

Two questions inevitably arise: What part of my income belongs to God? How much am I supposed to give away for His work? Both questions are based on the fallacious assumption that what we have is ours. Everything we have, and are, belongs to God.

Tithing and Giving

The biblical mandate is that the tithe, the first tenth of what we earn in any year, is to be returned for the Lord's work. Giving doesn't even start until the tithe is distributed. The exciting thing is that the Lord provides us with extra resources to give generously beyond the tithe.

We have come to the control factor of the loose end of money problems. Tithing and giving are the ways we say to the Lord we love Him—that we deliberately and specifically turn over to Him the control of our financial and material resources as part of a total commitment of our lives.

Most people facing financial problems can't imagine returning the first tenth to the Lord's work. It seems absurd and surely will only compound their problems. And yet the experience of God's people through the ages back to Abraham is living proof that just the opposite is true.

Release From The "Debt Set"

I began to tithe when I was part of the "debt set." Mary Jane and I were in seminary and serving in what was then a small church. We had two babies and each week got further behind in bills. I believed in Christ as the Lord of my life and was preparing to serve Him. I thought the least He could do was help pay the bills. I had not committed the financial part of my life to Him.

One day I poured out my spiritual needs to a seasoned old saint, but out of embarrassment I did not tell him about my money loose ends. "Tell me about your life," he said kindly. I told him about my zeal for Christ, the people I had won to Him, the Scriptures I had memorized, and all the hard work I was doing for Him.

The man's only response was, "Do you tithe?" I reminded him I was a student with very little income. "Are you in debt?" he asked, incisively. Finally, I poured out my tale of financial woe and told him I had planned to start tithing after I finished seminary and had a full-time salary. "Oh, no!" the old man exclaimed.

"The time to start tithing is now. The place is right where you are! Your problem isn't anything more than financial disobedience."

I was stunned. Then, after that teeth-rattling confrontation, I talked with Mary Jane about what he had said. We poured over the Scriptures to learn all we could about tithing. Malachi 3:8 was particularly shocking: "Will a man rob God? Yet you have robbed Me! But you say, 'In what way have we robbed You?' In tithes and offerings." After talking at length about that, we read on in verses 9–10 about the potentially positive results of tithing and giving: "Bring all the tithes into the storehouse, that there may be food in My house, and prove Me now in this. . . . If I will not open for you the windows of heaven and pour out for you such blessing that there will not be room enough to receive it."

After a few days of pondering that immense promise, we made a commitment to tithe, and to give beyond that, as the Lord provided the funds.

Of course, it was difficult at first, but each month it got easier. Then unexpected serendipities started happening. Extra funds were provided to finish seminary, and an interest-free loan was given by a friend who "just happened" to call when I was about to give up hope of going to postgraduate school.

I'm glad I learned how the Lord of Loose Ends ties down the loose end of financial frustration under the most difficult of circumstances, when from a human analysis, I was the least prepared to tithe and give beyond that to the Lord's work.

It was then I discovered that money does indeed talk. As it was distributed and given, it said to the Lord that we were serious about leaving all the pages of the Bible intact and were not going to tear out those pages that made challenging demands for obedience. It also freed me from a feeling of equivocation, and I felt a new boldness to follow the Lord in other areas. Money under the Lord's control now talked to me. For the first time, I was able to hear the truth that it all belonged to Him.

I don't want to give the impression that there haven't been really tough financial times through the years. Mary Jane and I have known all the same challenges everyone faces in raising and educating three children, sometimes wondering if the ends would meet. Looking back, the toughest times came either when our wants exceeded our needs and we got into unguided expenditures, or when we faltered for a brief time in our resolve to distribute our tithe from off the top of our income.

Of course, there have been detractors along the way. Some have said, "You're bound to the law and not grace. Christ has set us free from the law, including the tithe. How can you be a free man in Christ and feel obligated to tithe?"

My response has been that Christ set us free to fulfill the law, not evade it. He plainly told us that He did not come to destroy the law, and He took tithing and giving for granted, as a part of the responsibility of the people of God. What He did warn against is thinking that tithing could give us license to neglect the weightier responsibilities of glorifying God and being His servant. Tithing is never a substitute for knowledge of God nurtured in prayer, personal caring for people, or social obedience. If a person feels that tithing is slavish obedience to the law, and gives *way beyond* the tenth to the Lord's work, that's fine. My experience, however, is that those who object to tithing are giving far less. The real issue is: does the Lord have control of all our money and do we give cheerfully? The Greek word translated as "cheerful" is *hilaros* "propitious," and our word "hilarious," as in "abandoned, free, happy," comes from it.

The sure test of whether the loose end of money worry has been surrendered to the Lord of the Loose Ends is whether we are joyous in managing the resources He gives us, and whether we delight in giving to meet the spiritual and physical needs of others.

When it comes to tithing and giving, I want to turn the exclamation of the blind man whom Jesus healed: "Once I was blind but now I see." My witness is: "Once I was bound by the loose end of money; now I'm free."

The Message Of Our Money

Earlier I said our money talks to the people around us about our relationship to God and our values. If we go out to eat and spend $75.00, and then give $5.00 to God's work, our money has spoken about what we think is important. If we make our monthly payments on an expensive car, but haven't given at least the tithe off the top of our paycheck, our checkbooks are speaking. If we spend $50.00 for a coiffeur and manicure, and turn our adorned head away from the poor or don't lift our polished hand to help, our expenditures are exclaiming something about what we believe.

But in a very positive way, our money can talk to people in need about God's love. It can say we care. Our money can spread words of compassion and hope. And what a joy it is to be a partner with God in deciding where our tithe and giving should be distributed. For me, evangelism to introduce people to Christ and missions to meet their physical needs are top priorities. But I promised this would not be a fund-raising chapter, so I'll not go any farther in identifying specific causes where our money needs to talk.

Yes, money talks. It tells us, the people around us, and those in need, what we've allowed the Lord of the Loose Ends to do about the loose ends of money worries.

Remember the margarine commercials on television in which a person would say, "Tastes like butter," and the yellow pat of margarine would say, "Parkay!"? The animation made for good advertising.

We take a dollar bill and say, "Mine!" and the bill talks back, "God's!"

10.

GOOD NEWS FOR LOOSE ENDS

UNLESS I MISS MY GUESS, SOME OF OUR MOST DISTURBING loose ends are other people with the problem of loose ends! Their constant worry over the loose ends in their lives actually makes them loose ends to add to our own bundle.

We're so troubled about them because we can see ourselves in them. Often the people who frustrate us most are those who have problems similar to our own. And sometimes after we've made a certain amount of progress in dealing with those problems, we can be very impatient with others who have yet to discover the freedom we have found.

Oh, we readily sympathize. But that's caring at a distance. In our better moments, we actually empathize with an identifying "Yeah, I know how you're feeling— I've certainly been there!"

If we have experienced for ourselves the wretched anxiety of those nine dangerous words of the '90s, "I've just got to get control of my life," we can feel what others are going through. We can spot people who are addicted to control and can see the results of the "I've got to run everything" compulsion—like icy fingers gripping their souls.

Eagles stalled in flight, unable to soar, are easy to identify. People deadlocked in a lock of life, because of their lack of commitment to open the floodgate of power, are obvious. We can see those who are hugging center stage, and those who are stumbling over their previous stumbles. Oh, we can readily sympathize and even empathize with people with loose ends. But is that all we have to offer?

Not if we personally know the Lord of the Loose Ends. If we've admitted our addiction to false, manipulative, coercive power games, with Him and with the people in our lives, we now have power to help others who are addicted. When we overcome the temptation to live at center stage, when we really begin to soar by the Lord's power, when we know that we have been, and are being, delivered from the tension of running our own lives, we are ready to be recruited as a very special breed of the Lord's people!

We become loose-ends liberators. A sure sign that we are being set free is the new, powerful desire we feel to join the Lord in helping to remove the tourniquet of twined loose ends from around the souls of others. When we've experienced the power in the many-splendored "He is able" exclamations that we've discussed, and have accepted for ourselves the power offered to us, we want everyone in the grip of feeling at loose ends to know the same freedom we are enjoying.

Good News

We have good news for people who are caught in the entangling web of feeling at loose ends. We can say with Paul, "The grace of the Lord Jesus Christ be with you all. Amen. Now to Him *who is able* to establish you according to my gospel . . . " (Rom. 16:24–25, emphasis added).

I have kept this "He is able" promise and assurance expressed by the Apostle Paul for this concluding chapter because it summarizes all the others we have claimed in this book. It presses us to wonder if we, too, have a gospel—good news—for sufferers in the doldrums of being at loose ends.

At the conclusion of Paul's comprehensive statement to the Christians at Rome about the power of God in Jesus Christ (Romans 1–11), and the call to discipleship (chaps. 12–16), Paul sums up all he has written with a benediction of the grace of the Lord Jesus Christ *and* a reminder of His power to *establish* the believers. The Greek word translated here as "establish" is from the verb *sterizo*, "to fix, make fast, stabilize, strengthen." Christ is able, has all power, to create stability in our lives. He makes us secure.

Paul opened his letter to the Romans by saying that he looked forward to visiting them personally. "For I long to see you, that I may impart to you some spiritual gift, so that you may be *established* — that is, that I may be encouraged together with you by the mutual faith both of you and me" (Rom. 1:11–12, italics added). He wanted to help the Roman Christians to be solid and secure in their faith. Note how he uses the same word, "establish," at the end of his epistle. Everything Paul wrote between verses 1:11–12 and 16:24–25 was to make the Christians stable believers in an unstable world.

In my own way, everything I have written about Christ who is able has been to enable you and me to accept our security in His power. The questions that remain for both of us to answer are: Has it happened? Have these "He is able" exclamations about Christ's power become our own exuberant shouts of joy?

To put it even more directly: Have we experienced Christ's antidote to feeling at loose ends? Are we secure in His control of our lives? Can we trust Him to guide us in what we do with the details and duties of life because we are no longer at loose ends inside?

The Gospel According To You

How can we be sure? Well, I believe that happens only when we can say with Paul, "according to my gospel." You wonder, *isn't it a bit presumptuous to say "my gospel"?* We know about the Gospels of Matthew, Mark, Luke and John, and with a stretch, can appreciate Paul writing about his gospel, but it seems like quite an audacious leap for us to talk about our own gospel.

The basic word in Greek for "gospel" is *euangelion*. In secular Greek it was used both for an announcement of good news and for the one who brought the message. The writers of the New Testament used it as a synonym for the truth of Christ's life, message, death, resurrection, and His living presence as Lord of all life. It is the good news of the power of Christ written in the accounts of His life, the preaching of the apostles and the epistles of Paul, John, James, Jude, Titus, and the author of Hebrews.

You and I also have a gospel of power! It is the biblical good news according to you and me. Our gospel is expressed in what we say and do. It's written in our attitudes, values, actions, and relationships. People around us are reading our gospel about power every day—not only in what we say we believe about power, but how we use power. Our convictions, character, and countenance are preaching our gospel all the time. Our credo of power is communicated to the extent that Christ has transformed our feeling of being at loose ends. Our gospel is the evidence of stability we communicate when the unfinished, unresolved, unfulfilled, and unexpected present us with a new set of loose ends.

If you were to take an 8½" x 11" piece of paper and write out the gospel of power according to you, what would you write? What would you say about Christ who is able, if you had to limit what you wrote to only what you have personally experienced and want to express in action? What have you learned about false power and the authentic power of Christ?

In other words, what is your own good news about loose ends and the feeling of being at loose ends?

Of course, the litmus test of our gospel is what other people discern as our essential, lived-out convictions—expressed in how we use human power or depend on Christ's power. What would our families, friends, and people at work say is our gospel of power, our own good news? What has the power of Christ done to give us stability and lasting security? I wonder about what others would write as "the gospel according to Lloyd." How about the people around you?

The Objective and Subjective Gospel

To be sure, I'm not suggesting that the irreducible, absolute, objective, biblical gospel can be changed in its unshakable truth by our personal expression of it, or by the subjective opinions of others about how we have lived it. All I am saying is that the biblical gospel must become our own gospel in order for it to be good news to those who have not read the Bible, or to those who are familiar with the Christian faith and still yearn to know that it works.

Most of the people around us long for power. Many are living by the established competitive rubrics of human power and are failing either to get or to keep control of their lives. Everyone desperately wants to know what to do about the anguish, the constant muddle, the anxiety of feeling at loose ends. Now, do we have a gospel, some good news, for them? Or, more pointedly, are you and I a living gospel for the people we meet?

A Living Letter

Now shift the metaphor slightly. Paul reminded the Corinthians that they were living letters of Christ: "You are manifestly an epistle of Christ, . . . written not with ink but by the Spirit of the living God. . . . And we have such trust through Christ toward God, . . . who also made us. . . sufficient as ministers of the new covenant . . . " (2 Cor. 3:3, 4, 6). We are to be a letter written by the Lord to the world, saying, "Here is a powerful person who has given Me control, who ex-emplifies what I am able to do to make a person truly secure in My love and free to love and serve as the expression of My indwelling power." I suspect you and I are of one heart in wanting to be that kind of letter.

What is required is that we have a gospel of power that's truly good news and not merely general views. There's a great difference between a person who has only theories about Christ's power and one who is actually experiencing His power. We can have a cor-rect understanding of what Scripture declares about Christ as the power of God (1 Cor. 1:24), about the power of Christ's resurrection (Phil. 3:10), and about the power of the Spirit (Rom. 15:13), and still be a garbled letter because we continue to depend on our own strength, using manipulative ways to control our own lives and others. To turn Emerson's phrase— how we use human power speaks so loudly that people can't hear what we say we believe about Christ's power.

Specific Application

Let's think specifically about our gospel of power in the context of the "He is able" promise we're considering from Romans 15:25, "He is able to establish"—stabilize, make secure. Has Christ's power made us secure people? Can we trust that He is at work in us and in our problems? How is that communicated to the people around us?

Take the simple, daily frustration of getting what we want. Here we are with our desires, hopes, even vision, for what we think is good for our lives, for other people, and for various situations. Does our gospel of power tell us how to get from where we are to the accomplishment of our deepest longings?

Let me pitch our reflection about this on a higher level. Suppose we really want the Lord's best and feel all the more convinced that what we envision is the highest possible goal for us and for all concerned. Are we established (fixed, secure) in the assurance that the Lord will help us move toward the goals we have set? Will He create a responsiveness in people? Will He open doors that seem shut?

A Gospel For The Interface

In the interface between what we want and how we get it is where our personal gospel of power is expressed. In this space, what we really believe about Christ's power, and whether we truly know that He is able, will be shown.

You see, it's in this interface that we display our real colors. If we have to wait, we are tempted to become impatient and fall back into old power struggles. Once again, our game plan often emulates what seems to be the only game in town—a power game to get what we desire by whatever method works.

In marriage, we repeat old patterns of bartering by giving or withholding affection and approval to get our way. As parents, we threaten; as friends, we coerce. On the job, if we're managers, we use the club of authority; if we're employees, we exercise our pocket veto of passive resistance, criticism, or whatever gets the boss's attention and puts him or her on edge.

Strange as it may seem, it's insecure people who lust for control. The more secure we are, the less we have to dominate others and manipulate situations. Again, the greater our invisible means of power in Christ, the less we will resort to visible tactics of trying to get the upper hand.

All the while, remember, people around us are reading the gospel according to you and me. If we're still struggling for control, it may not be good news at all. In fact, it may be very bad news. More than likely, they are hoping that with all we believe, we might be different in the way we exercise power. However, it usually comes as a shock to us when one of our children or a friend emulates our methods of getting or keeping control.

Christ Never Gives Up

But Christ does not give up on us! He keeps working to heal our insecurities so that our gospel will be an expression of the true Gospel. The confidence He has in our potential is amazing—"You did not choose Me, but I chose you and appointed you that you should go and bear fruit, and that your fruit should remain, that whatever you ask the Father in My name He may give you. These things I command you, that you love one another" (John 15:16–17). We have been chosen to be loved so that we can love by Christ's power.

Yet, rather than blasting our misuse of human power, Christ blesses us with the only cure for the insecurities that are causing our dependence on controlling methods. He knows we do the things we do because of what we are inside. He also knows we cannot change what we do until He changes what we are. And Christ's method of changing us is to love us. Insecurity is simply the absence of knowing we are "loved to the uttermost." Christ is able to establish us, make us stable and secure—by loving us.

How does He do it? If we are willing, He leads us back over the painful memories of experiences that contribute to our feelings of insecurity. He heals the wounds others have inflicted, and forgives our own failures. All the loose ends—sins of commission and omission—over all the years are exposed. Then He says, "You are forgiven."

The biblical gospel of what Christ did for us on the cross becomes our own gospel of what He is doing in our lives, now. Instead of simply saying, "Christ died for the sins of the world," we can say, "He died for me; He gave Himself for me!" It is Christ's sacrificial love that woos and wins us. We are willing to give Him control of our lives because we have been, and are being, loved. There is no greater power in all the world than His unqualified love!

Only The Beginning

But this is only the beginning of the healing of our insecurity. Next, Christ graciously tells us that we have been chosen to receive His Spirit. He knows that we will not experience lasting security until we are sure that we have adequate resources to meet the challenges of life. He develops our trust by showing us what He can do in us, and then, through us. Each time we yield our needs to Him, He gives us supernatural wisdom, knowledge, and discernment. Our gospel now includes our own personal assurance of what He is able to do to guide and strengthen us. William Law said, "A Christ not in us is a Christ not ours." When He lives in us, our insecurity is healed at the tap root.

Secure in the power of Christ's indwelling love, we are ready to "bear fruit." We are given power to love others as He has loved us. Love is the secret of true power. In fact, love *is* power. We are given a steady supply of Christ's love so that He can reproduce in our relationships His methods of dealing with us. Instead of playing power games, we become communicators of grace.

Five Aspects Of Our Power Gospel

Here's how it works in that distance between what people are and what we long for them to become. Below are five vital steps using Christ's power methods for our relationships. As we live them out, our personal gospel gives vital evidence of His power.

1. *Pray with openness.* Prolonged prayer for a person enables us to love him or her unselfishly. We surrender our wish dreams and personal desires for that person to Christ's greater vision. In place of our plans, we are given a picture of how He wants to love through us. Only after that image is set firmly in our minds should we dare to exercise any influence on another person.

2. *Communicate with acceptance and affirmation.* Remember Christ began with us as we were. In the same way, we are not called to love people in order to change them, but to communicate that they are *valued* and *esteemed* by us. Changing people is the Lord's job! If we truly believe He is able, we will not have to gig people with nagging or pressure them to measure up to our standards. People need to know that we *enjoy* them.

3. *Listen with sensitivity.* The lost art of love is listening. We are so used to straightening people out or giving unrequested advice! Listening to people seems far too passive, especially for those of us who tend to manipulate people by telling them what they ought to be or should do. It is an act of love to ask people how they are feeling, or how things are going for them. If we listen attentively, we'll soon discover what's important to others. Once we do, we have the privilege of entering their world. And after we have listened, we find natural openings for further conversation about

their interests. Little by little, the door is opened to a deeper relationship. It's then that people will share their concerns and problems.

4. *Care with specific actions.* People long to know that they are special to us. We express this by showing them. Having listened, we can respond by doing something for them that indicates we understand their priorities and problems. A good question to ask ourselves is: what could I do that would say to this person that I really care?

Do you remember middle-aged Joe Saul, John Steinbeck's character in *Burning Bright?* He had to find some way to express his delight in his wife who had just shared with him the news of an expected child. "I want to bring a present to her . . . something like a ceremony, something like a golden sacrament, some pearl like a prayer or a red flaming ruby of thanks. That's the compulsion on me . . . I must get this thing. My joy requires a symbol."

Our joy in people also requires a symbol. The delight we experience in them needs a focused expression of our caring. Sometimes it's an unexpected gift; other times, an act of kindness. Or it's spending time doing what the person enjoys, writing a timely note, or making a phone call. And, of course, everybody faces times when he or she needs someone to lift a burden with practical, down-to-earth help.

You may be thinking, *These first four aspects you've mentioned are nothing more than the basics of friendship.* You are right. And yet, these are the very qualities often missing in our relationships with our mates, children, friends, people at work. Without them, we must rely on the shortcuts of raw authority, manipulative methods, or the dominance of our personalities.

Instead, our goal is to become bonded to others by communicating that we are for them and believe in them. This makes us the kind of person they will turn to when they feel their lives are out of control. In the context of caring friendships, we will live our gospel of power. They will read that gospel in our security and stability, and our faithfulness to them. All this leads to the fifth aspect of the creative use of power.

5. *Be personal with vulnerability.* Mutual trust will be nurtured as we have followed the first four steps of bonding ourselves to a person who is suffering from the anxiety of being at loose ends. Eventually, we will have an opportunity to share personally our own gospel, our good news, for loose ends. Instead of confronting a person with an abrasive analysis of her or his loose ends, we can talk honestly about what the Lord of the Loose Ends has done, and is doing, in our own lives. There's creative power in being personal.

We do not say, "I've been watching you. Your life is out of control. You're at loose ends and you need to admit it!" Rather, with vulnerability, we communicate how we came from weakness to how the Lord's strength is making us secure. We can laugh at ourselves as we reveal, from personal experience, how the Lord is taking control of our lives. It's the "show, not tell" use of personal illustrations from our lives that will get through to others. I've tried to exemplify this throughout our discussion of our loose ends in this book.

And quite frankly, being honest about what I've gone through with my own loose ends and what Christ has done to help me was not easy. An impersonal exposition of Scripture or expounding doctrine is far less demanding—and much less effective. At a certain point in every sermon I preach or chapter I write, I'm tempted to be impersonal—preaching or writing ideas and theories without sharing the agony and ecstasy of my own pilgrimage in living the objective truth I'm trying to communicate. People want to know how the truth has worked for me. They want my gospel. And the people in your life want nothing less than *the gospel according to you.*

But let me stress again, Christ is the subject of our gospel! We do not preach or teach or share ourselves as the answer. To keep our heads and hearts straight about that, we need to repeat frequently 2 Corinthians 4:5–7: "For we do not preach ourselves, but Christ Jesus the Lord, and ourselves your servants for Jesus' sake. For it is God who commanded light to shine out of darkness, who has shown in our hearts to give the light of the knowledge of the glory of God in the face of Jesus Christ. But we hold this treasure in earthen vessels, that the excellence of the power may be of God and not of us."

It is the honest admission of the cracked, imperfect earthen vessel of our humanity that helps people to identify with us so that we can then reveal Christ as the true treasure. Pretending to be perfect earthen vessels, when we are really cracked pots, will deny the "excellence of the power" working in and through us. And the pretended adequacy will set up barriers between us and the very people we want to help.

One day in 1940, Leslie D. Weatherhead, for many years a great preacher at City Temple in London, leaned over his pulpit and said to his war-weary listeners, "I know now that what for years I thought was faith in God, which I should have described as a radiantly happy experience of Him, was partly health, youthful high spirits, and success. When the first two went, and the last was seen to be unimportant and even paltry, I found I had precious little faith or trust in God, for faith had never been required. Now, slowly and humbly, I'm trying to build up a faith and trust in God. It isn't much yet, but I'm preaching something that's mine in a new way. Religion so often seems to have little power about it for ourselves, and makes little appeal to others, because it has never been geared into our need. It isn't our gospel. An engine is running and it is an engine with power, but we do not know how to let in the clutch and link the power up with our troubles."*

Weatherhead identified with what many of his listeners were also feeling in those dark days of 1940, but he didn't stop there. He went on to describe the biblical gospel and what it meant to him as it became his gospel, his own good news, about what Christ was doing to transform his life.

In my congregation, the most effective communicators of the power of the Lord of the Loose Ends are

---

* From a sermon by Leslie D. Weatherhead in *The Eternal Voice* (New York; Nashville: Abingdon-Cokesbury Press, 1940), p. 34.

those who are willing to share the truth with others—
that they, too, had lived in the miserable anxiety of
feeling at loose ends, out of control. But they also have
a gospel to communicate about how Christ was able
to "establish" them, making their lives stable and secure. And because the loose-ends syndrome is
spreading in epidemic proportions today, they don't
have to look far for people who need the authentic
power they are receiving. People at loose ends are
among their friends, at work, and in their own homes.
Also, they are discovering that all of the above five aspects of communicating their gospel are absolutely
essential. Whenever they skip one of them, they are
back into using old human power methods.

I've listed these five dynamics for sharing our
good news for loose ends because they help to bring
congruity between our message and method of authentic power. To be effective, we cannot talk about Christ's
power and, at the same time, play power games. It's very
important after we confess our addiction to false power
that the vacuum be filled by a new way of using power—
Christ's way of love and servanthood.

We *are* the gospel we communicate. Our walk in
the Lord's power must be consistent with our talk about
His power. Keeping the two together is a never-ending
challenge!

Daily Inventory

At the conclusion of each day, it is important to
review both what we said and how we acted. Then

we can thank the Lord for the times we claimed our security in Him and depended on His power. We also can confess ways we side-stepped His requirements for receiving authentic power, and fell back into the patterns of false manipulations with human power.

Our evening evaluation needs to include questions like these: What was the gospel of power I lived today? What kind of witness did I give about Christ's gospel according to me? In my desire to influence others, did I pray for guidance, communicate acceptance and affirmation, listen with sensitivity, care specifically, and when I had the opportunity, did I share what Christ is doing in my own life?

New Beginning

Each new day gives us a fresh new beginning. Christ offers His power to establish us, make us stable and secure, for the day ahead. We can claim Moses' promise to the tribe of Asher, "Your sandals shall be iron and bronze; as your days, so shall your strength be" (Deut. 33:25). Christ who is able will make us able to stand (Eph. 6:11, 13, 16). The Lord's mercies are new every morning (Lam. 3:22–23).

Annie Johnson Flint discovered this and wrote a poem that could well be a daily prayer for trusting the Lord of the Loose Ends with the challenges on the day ahead. Note the kinds of loose ends that are tied down as we claim God's mercy through the ever-present Christ.

Yea, "new every morning," though we may awake,
    Our hearts with old sorrow beginning to ache,
With old work unfinished when night stayed our hand,
    With new duties waiting, unknown and unplanned,
With old care still pressing, to fret and to vex,
    With new problems rising, our minds to perplex,
In ways long familiar, in paths yet untrod,
    Oh, new every morning, the mercies of God!

His faithfulness fails not; it meets each new day,
    With guidance for every step of the way;
New grace for new trials, new trust for old fears,
    New patience for bearing the wrongs of the years,
New strength for new burdens, new courage for old,
    New faith for whatever the day may unfold;
As fresh for each need as the dew on the sod;
    Oh, new every morning, the mercies of God!

With that kind of stable security we can face any day. We can be assured that every time a loose end springs up, the Lord will be able to tie it down. More than that, the new confidence in His power will add data and dynamics to our personal gospel. Whatever we go through will be used to deepen our relationship with the Lord and prepare us to help others with the same loose ends.

We'll always have loose ends. The unfinished, the unresolved, the unexpected—but no longer the unfulfilled. With the Lord of the Loose Ends in charge, we'll be free of feeling at loose ends. Never again do we need to say the dangerous, desperate words of the '90s, "I've just got to get control of my life!" The *last* thing we want is to be in control. Rather, our daily motto will be, "I trust Christ's control of my life." And He is able!

Those who love most and serve best have the greatest power. Lasting, liberating power. The power of the Lord of Life's Loose Ends.

LANGUAGE FOR DAILY USE
HARBRACE EDITION — REVISED

HARBRACE EDITION – REVISED

MILDRED A. DAWSON · ERIC W. JOHNSON

1. N^P V^be
2. Adj. Ad
3. Adj. Ad
4. Adj. N

New York   Chicago   San Francisco   Atlanta   Dallas   *and*   London

7

LANGUAGE FOR DAILY USE

MARIAN ZOLLINGER · M. ARDELL ELWELL

HARCOURT BRACE JOVANOVICH

ACKNOWLEDGMENTS: For permission to reprint copyrighted material, grateful acknowledgment is made to the following publishers, authors, and agents:

Gustav Davidson: "Essential Delight" from *Moment of Visitation* by Gustav Davidson. Published by Alan Swallow, 1950.

Dodd, Mead & Company, Inc.: Two verses from "The Skater of Ghost Lake" from *Golden Fleece* by William Rose Benét, copyright 1933, 1935 by Dodd, Mead & Company, Inc.

Doubleday & Company, Inc.: First stanza from "The Overland Mail" from *Departmental Ditties and Ballads* by Rudyard Kipling.

E. P. Dutton & Co., Inc.: From "Daniel Boone" from *I Sing the Pioneer* by Arthur Guiterman, copyright 1926 by E. P. Dutton & Co., Inc., renewal 1954 by Vida Lindo Guiterman.

Harcourt Brace Jovanovich, Inc.: From *Through the Frozen Frontier* by George Dufek. From *Mama's Bank Account* by Kathryn Forbes.

Harper & Row, Publishers, Incorporated: From *The Adventures of Tom Sawyer* by Mark Twain.

Holiday House, Inc.: From *Outlaw Red* by Jim Kjelgaard.

Holt, Rinehart and Winston, Inc.: "Steam Shovel" from *Upper Pasture* by Charles Malam, copyright 1930, copyright renewed © 1958 by Charles Malam. "Fog" from *Chicago Poems* by Carl Sandburg, copyright 1916 by Holt, Rinehart and Winston, Inc., copyright renewed 1944 by Carl Sandburg. Last stanza from "The Road Not Taken" from *Complete Poems of Robert Frost*, copyright 1916, 1921 by Holt, Rinehart and Winston, Inc., copyright renewed 1944 by Robert Frost.

Houghton Mifflin Company: From *Shane* by Jack Schaefer.

J. B. Lippincott Company: "Felicia Ropps" from *The Goop Directory* by Gelett Burgess, copyright 1913, 1941 by Gelett Burgess.

Little, Brown and Company: "Celery" (page 358) and "The Fly" (page 422) from *Verses from 1929 On* by Ogden Nash, copyright 1941, 1942 by Ogden Nash. "The Centipede" from *Verses from 1929 On* by Ogden Nash, copyright 1935 by The Curtis Publishing Company.

The Macmillan Company: "The Coin" from *Flame and Shadow* by Sara Teasdale, copyright 1920 by The Macmillan Company, renewed 1948 by Mamie T. Wheless. From *The Call of the Wild* by Jack London.

Julian Messner, Division of Simon & Schuster, Inc.: From *The Great Houdini* by Beryl Williams and Samuel Epstein.

Juanita J. Miller: From "Byron" from *Selections from Joaquin Miller*, copyright 1945 by C. H. Miller.

Harold Ober Associates, Incorporated: From "A Stolen Day" by Sherwood Anderson, first published in *This Week*, April 27, 1941, copyright © 1941 by Eleanor Anderson, renewed.

A. D. Peters & Co.: One stanza from "A Dedicatory Ode" from *Sonnets and Verse* by Hilaire Belloc.

Frances Rodman: "Spring Cricket" by Frances Rodman, first published in the American Junior Red Cross *News*, copyright 1947 by Frances Rodman.

Mrs. Lew Sarett: "The Wolf Cry" from *Many, Many Moons* by Lew Sarett, copyright 1920 by Henry Holt and Company, Inc., copyright renewed 1948 by Lew Sarett.

Scott, Foresman and Company: From *Thorndike-Barnhart Advanced Junior Dictionary*, edited by E. L. Thorndike and Clarence L. Barnhart, copyright © 1962 by Scott, Foresman and Company, Chicago.

The Literary Trustees of Walter de la Mare and The Society of Authors as their representative: "All But Blind" by Walter de la Mare.

Helen W. Thurber: From "Snapshot of a Dog" from *The Middle-Aged Man on the Flying Trapeze* by James Thurber, copyright © 1935 by James Thurber, copyright renewed © 1963 by Helen W. Thurber and Rosemary Thurber Sauers. Published by Harper & Row, Publishers.

The Viking Press, Inc.: Excerpt from *The Red Pony* by John Steinbeck.

James T. White & Company: From "Not by Bread Alone" by James Terry White.

For use of photographs by courtesy of the following:

Page 28, David Rhinelander; page 49, Bettmann Archive; page 107, Metropolitan Museum of Art, Gift of Alfred Stieglitz; page 145, British Crown Copyright; page 171, National Portrait Gallery, London; page 193, Metropolitan Museum of Art, Rogers Fund, 1921; page 239, California Historical Society, San Francisco; page 271, Museum of Fine Arts. Boston; page 297, The Macmillan Company; page 335, George Eastman House; page 348, Prints and Photographs Division, Library of Congress; page 372, The Poetry Society of America.

For use of illustrative material from the following:

THESE HAPPY GOLDEN YEARS: Copyright 1953 by Garth Williams. Reproduced by permission of Harper and Row.

IT'S LIKE THIS CAT: Copyright © 1963 by Emil Weiss. Reproduced by permission of Harper and Row.

NIGHT OF THE WALL: Copyright © 1964 by Denny McMains. Reproduced by permission of G. P. Putnam's Sons.

NORTH TOWN: Copyright © 1965 by Ernest Crichlow. Reproduced by permission of Thomas Y. Crowell.

JOHN F. KENNEDY AND PT-109. Copyright © 1962. U.S. Navy photo by Wide World. Reproduced by permission of Random House.

ISBN 0-15-317500-1

CONTENTS

12   How to Study More Efficiently   311

13   Listening: Receiving Ideas   343

14   Reading   363

15   Making Sentence Diagrams (Optional)   387

PART III: REVIEW HANDBOOK

How Your Language Grew

English is one of the great languages of the world. In some ways, perhaps, it is the greatest. When you and your parents and your grandparents learned English, it had long been an established language with a literature and a long history. But it has not always been so. Modern English has existed only about 450 years, and the "Modern English" spoken in 1500 was quite different from the English you speak today. It will help you to understand your language if you learn something of its fascinating history.

How English Has Changed

Every language used daily by ordinary people is constantly changing. English is no exception. One of the best ways to observe the change in our language is to read a passage which has been translated into English at different periods over the centuries. Here are four versions of part of the "Twenty-third Psalm." Read them and then discuss how English has changed over the past thousand years. Answer the questions which follow the Biblical quotation.

1. *Old English (Anglo-Saxon), about 900*
   Yeotudlice ond theah the ic gonge in midle scuan deathes, ne ondredu ic yfel, forthon thu mid me erth; geird thin ond crycc thin hie me froefrends werun.

2. *Middle English, about 1300*
   For gif that ich haue bon amiddes of the shadowe of deth, y shal nought douten iuels, for thou are wyth me; thy discipline and thyn amendying conforted me.

◄ *Many invasions of the land that is now England helped form the English language we speak today.*

◄ *The farmers and laborers continued to speak Anglo-Saxon even after the Norman invasion in 1066, and thus many Germanic words remained in our language.*

1

3. *Modern English, about 1600 (King James Version of the Bible)*
Yea, though I walk through the valley of the shadow of death,
I will fear no evil: for thou art with me; thy rod and thy staff
they comfort me.

4. *Present-day English, Revised Standard Version, 1952*
Even though I walk through the valley of the shadow of death,
I fear no evil; for thou art with me; thy rod and thy staff, they
comfort me.

To discuss

Study closely the four samples of English given above and see if
you can answer these questions about them:

1. How many years passed between the first translation given
   and the most recent one?
2. If you were not already familiar with the meaning of the
   passage, do you think you could translate either the Old
   English or the Middle English version into present-day English? Try translating it word for word into present-day English without changing the order of the words as they are in
   the old versions.
3. About 400 years elapsed between translations (1) and (2)
   and between translations (3) and (4). Judging solely from
   these brief passages, in which of these 400-year periods do
   you think English changed more?
4. Even in the 1952 translation there are three words that you
   yourself would not ordinarily use. What are they? What
   modern words do they stand for?
5. Read the following paragraph and then see if you can explain
   one reason why the rate of change of English slowed down
   after 1600:

   In 1476 William Caxton set up the first printing press in England. Before that time, books in English had to be copied by
   hand. After that time, many copies could be printed without
   any new errors entering in, or without changes. By 1600 the
   printing of books had almost completely replaced hand copying.

6. What important fact about the English language have you
   learned from this discussion?

How Did Language Start?

No one really knows how or when language first started. The best that historians and experts can do is to make intelligent guesses. A little over 2,000 years ago, the Greek philosopher Plato supposed that "names belong to things by nature." He thought that in the very beginning there was a perfect language made by a great "lawgiver," and that it was the task of man to rediscover the original perfect language. His theory on the origin of language is only one of many.

The "bow-wow" theory

One modern theory is that language began when man started to imitate natural sounds. This is sometimes called the "bow-wow" theory, after the sound a dog supposedly makes. In English, such words as *murmur, pop, purr, whiz, squelch,* and *swish* are clearly imitations of natural sounds. Dictionaries sometimes call them *imitative* or *echoic* words. However, only a very small part of the words of any known language can be traced back to an imitation of natural sounds. This theory, at best, then, only slightly explains the beginnings of language. Most English words seem to have no relationship to the sounds of nature.

The "pooh-pooh" theory

Still another modern theory holds that man has always made certain noises when faced with certain situations and that our languages are based on these instinctive responses. Examples of such sounds might be "Ugh!" "Hey!" "Ouch!" "Humph!" The theory is sometimes called the "pooh-pooh" theory. It comes partly from the observation that babies everywhere, whether in Tokyo, New York, or Moscow, cry, gurgle, and babble in the same way during the first few months of their lives. There may be some truth in the theory, but until now it has been able to explain only a few of our words.

To discuss

1. How many English words can you list on the board which imitate, or seem to imitate, natural sounds? Give the meaning of each word you think of. Use your dictionary.

2. How many words can you list on the board that might support the "pooh-pooh," or instinctive, theory of language origin? List them, giving each a definition.

Words are symbols

How language started is an interesting subject to think about. Although there are many theories, no one is able to say for certain which of the theories is the correct one, because there are no written records from those early days. The best that language specialists can do is to make educated guesses. No single simple theory can ever explain satisfactorily the origins of language. All we know is that language seems to be an *artificial* thing, something that was made, certainly very gradually. Different sounds (words) stand for different things, actions, and ideas. Words have histories, of course, that can be traced to other earlier words. But finally they are traced back to a place where we no longer know how they started. All we can do is to suppose that some men agreed somehow that a certain sound would stand for—symbolize—a certain thing or action or idea. Gradually the symbol spread among more people, more symbols became agreed upon, and thus a language got started.

We cannot explain why certain sounds got attached to certain things, actions, or ideas. For instance, the following sounds would be totally meaningless to you:

shou	yu	ssu	chih	yi	ta	chih
(hand)	(has)	(four)	(fingers)	(one)	(large)	(finger)

The literal translation of each word is in parentheses. A free translation of this statement from Chinese to English is, "The hand has four fingers and a thumb." To the Chinese, *shou* means "hand." To you, *hand* means "hand." Who is to say that the sound *hand* is more "handish" than the sound *shou?* It just depends on what we agree upon as a sound to mean "hand."

Chinese is used as a first language by more people than any other language in the world. English is second. What you have been reading shows that the Chinese have entirely different symbols for the same things and ideas.

You might find it interesting to make up the beginnings of an artificial language and to demonstrate that you can use it perfectly well. For example, if you agree with a partner that *yuk* means "go," *ipp* means "you," and *glorishoo* means "quickly," you could say or write: "Ipp yuk glorishoo," and your partner would know that you mean "You go quickly." Now try your hand with the exercises on the next page.

4

1. Divide the class into pairs (or small groups) and develop with your partner a fifteen-word vocabulary, agreeing on the meanings of certain sounds. Use a very simple vocabulary, as follows:

VERBS	NOUNS OR PRONOUNS	ADJECTIVES	ADVERBS
go	you	black	quickly
come	myself	white	slowly
give	thing	large	not
take	book	small	

Now demonstrate to the class that you can use your made-up language to communicate with another person who agrees with you about the meanings of the sounds. Hold a short conversation with your partner in front of the class, first in your made-up language and then translated into English. Have your conversation include some command which is to be obeyed by an action, for example: "Give me my book." Then it will be easy for the class to observe that you have actually communicated an idea through your artificial language.

2. See if you can state in your own words an important fact about language that the preceding exercise illustrates.

The Origins of English

Although no one really knows how language, in general, originated because there are no written records, we do have a good idea of how English got started. English is only one of two or three dozen languages which seem to have a common ancestor. The language from which English developed is called *Indo-European*, and the languages that came from it are called *The Indo-European Family of Languages*. On the next page you will see a chart showing this family of languages.

No one now alive has ever heard or read Indo-European. We merely *suppose* it must have existed because of the resemblance of the languages that we think must have come from it. However, there are hundreds of languages currently spoken on earth which have no resemblance to any members of the Indo-European family.

The Indo-European Family of Languages   (Simplified)

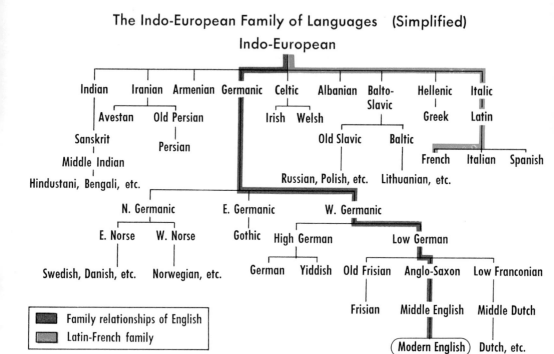

Look now at the resemblance of these five languages, all of which
are members of the Indo-European family:

> ENGLISH: The hand has four fingers and a thumb.
> FRENCH: La main a quatre doigts et un pouce.
> ITALIAN: La mano ha quattro dita e un pollice.
> SPANISH: La mano tiene cuatro dedos y un pulgar.
> GERMAN: Die Hand hat vier Finger und einen Daumen.

All members of the Indo-European family of languages do not have
similarities as obvious as the five languages given above.   There are
enough resemblances and common ancestors, however, to make language experts sure that they all belong to the same family.

To discuss

Look now at the chart above and answer the following questions:

1. Can you trace the origins of modern English?
2. From which main member of the family does English come?
3. Did English originate from Latin?
4. From which branch of the Indo-European family does Latin
   come?

6

German and English

The first recorded event in the history of English occurred in the fifth century A.D. (from about 450 to 550 A.D.). Certain Germanic tribes, the *Angles*, the *Saxons*, and the *Jutes*, invaded the territory that is now England and brought their Germanic language with them. They conquered the *Celts*, who were then living there and whose language has now almost entirely disappeared, except in certain small sections of England, such as Wales.

Gradually, the Germanic language of the Angles, Saxons, and Jutes spread over England and became the principal language. By about the year 1000, most of the people who inhabited England were speaking what we now call *Anglo-Saxon*, or *Old English*. To see an example of this language, look back at the first page of this chapter.

It is easy to see even today the resemblance between modern English and modern German, both of which have their origin in a Germanic language.

Exercise: German and English

Here are twelve modern German words. You probably can guess their English meaning. It will be easier if you know that the letter *d* in German is often used where *th* is used in English. On your paper, make a list of the German words and beside each word, write your guess as to its English meaning.

1. Bruder	5. Finger	9. musst
2. danke	6. Garten	10. Mutter
3. Ding	7. Hand	11. Nacht
4. eins, zwei, drei	8. Kirche	12. Wasser

After you have made your guesses, ask your teacher or someone else who knows German to give you the actual English translations. You may want to look them up in a German-English dictionary, if one is available.

To discuss

1. What does the preceding exercise show you about English and German?

2. Which tribes brought the Germanic language into England?

3. Can you give another name for *Old English?*

French and English

The Anglo-Saxons lived largely undisturbed in Angle-land (England) until William the Conqueror crossed the Channel from Normandy (part of present-day France) in 1066. He defeated the Anglo-Saxons and set up a permanent kingdom in England. For several hundred years after that, England and large parts of France were divisions of the same kingdom. The language of the rulers (the nobles and those who cooperated with them) was French.

However, English, the language of the Anglo-Saxons, did not die. It was spoken mainly by plain people. Many of its difficult words were forgotten, since plain people—farmers and laborers—did not need them. This explains the fact that the German and English words that resemble each other are plain, simple words like these:

GERMAN	ENGLISH	GERMAN	ENGLISH
Hand	hand	Welt	world
Bruder	brother	Wort	word
Kuh	cow	Wille	will

French remained the language of the rulers from 1066 until about 1500. The rulers were usually well-educated people and tended to use a large and elegant vocabulary. Many French words gradually entered the English language during this period. By 1500, when

BATTLE OF HASTINGS

▲ *In 1066, Duke William of Normandy and his army crossed the English Channel from France to England and camped near Hastings.* (See opposite.)

Harold, the King of England, led his army to meet William. In the battle that followed, Harold was killed and his army routed. Duke William became King William I of England. The Battle of Hastings is said to be one of the fifteen battles in history that changed the course of history. (See above.)

English started coming into its own again as a respectable language used by educated people as well as the uneducated, our language had come to contain a mixture of French and German words.

Exercise: French and English

Here are twelve modern French words. Despite the fact that both English and French have changed greatly since the period 1066–1500, you will probably be able to guess the meanings of the words. Write each French word together with its English meaning.

1. activité	5. félicitation	9. parlement
2. association	6. institution	10. politesse
3. brillant	7. liberté	11. ridicule
4. constitution	8. magnifique	12. triomphe

To discuss

Are the French words above more elegant and complicated than the German words on page 7? How do you explain this fact?

Latin and English

Many English words are similar to Latin words. Although English did not come mainly from Latin, Latin has had a tremendous influence on our language. If you look at the chart of The Indo-European Family of Languages, you can see that French descends directly from Latin. When English borrowed words from French, it indirectly borrowed them from Latin. These words which come from the Latin through French plus the words which come directly from Latin make up a large group of the words we presently use in English. This is why a knowledge of Latin is useful in increasing your English vocabulary.

However, do not forget that the English language originated mainly from the Germanic branch of Indo-European, not from the Italic or Latin branch. If you do not understand this clearly, look again at the Indo-European language chart.

Exercise: Latin and English

Here are fourteen Latin words. List them, and next to each word write its English translation, if you can guess it. This will help to demonstrate the close relationship between the present-day English vocabulary and the Latin vocabulary. If possible, check your guesses by referring to someone who knows Latin or to a Latin-English dictionary.

1. absolutus	8. masculinus
2. accusator	9. specialis
3. consequentia	10. superstitiosus
4. elegantia	11. operatus
5. hospitium	12. stipulatus
6. inexcusabilis	13. penetratus
7. insanitas	14. obligatus

To discuss

1. Do the words above seem to you to be the plain, simple words that have derived from the Germanic?

2. What kinds of people would be likely to use these words?

3. Where would they be more useful—in a conversation about ideas or the talk necessary to carry on the routine work of a farm or village?

The two main streams in English

There have come to be two streams, then, in English—the Germanic stream and the Latin-French stream. As a result of this, English words very often seem to come in pairs, each member of the pair having a similar meaning. There is a plain, short word which comes from the Germanic stream: *house*; and there is a more elaborate, formal word which comes from the Latin-French stream: *residence*. Words like these, with meanings that are almost the same, are called **synonyms.**

Exercise: Synonyms

Here are more pairs of synonyms. Can you tell from which stream each word comes? List the words in two columns, one headed *Germanic* and one headed *Latin-French*.

amity	friendship
brotherhood	fraternity
bovine	cowlike
canine	doglike
liberate	free
hall	vestibule
deliberate	think

How English Has Borrowed

English has probably borrowed more words from other languages than has any other language. This is one of the reasons it is such a rich, varied, and beautiful language. You have already learned how it borrowed—or had injected into it—thousands of words from French and Latin. The borrowing continues today. For example, modern science tends to use Latin and especially Greek to develop scientific vocabulary, as in *antibiotic, electronics, extrasensory, hydroponics,* and *television.* A recent addition from another language is *sputnik,* which means "artificial satellite," and which was borrowed from Russian.

In this lesson you will consider only words that have been borrowed by English during the past 400 years, that is, since Modern English has been established as an important, stable language, worthy of use by the best speakers and writers.

Borrowings from American Indian

When the English colonists came to America in the seventeenth and eighteenth centuries, they encountered tribes of Indians speaking many different languages. Some interesting words have entered the English language from our contacts with the American Indians. Here are a few:

chipmunk	moccasin	opossum	raccoon	succotash
hickory	moose	powwow	skunk	wampum

It may interest you to look up these words in the dictionary to see where they came from. For example, according to *Webster's New World Dictionary of the American Language,* the word *succotash* derives from the Narragansett Indian word *misickquatash,* meaning "ear of corn."

Borrowings from Spanish

American English has been enriched by our contacts with the Spanish-speaking peoples of the Southwest and by other contacts with the Spanish during our history. Here is a list of a few of the words that have entered the English language from the Spanish:

adobe	cigar	mustang	mosquito	rodeo
bronco	corral	Negro	ranch	vamoose (slang)
arroyo	desperado	matador	renegade	vanilla
cargo	lariat	cafeteria	armada	patio

To discuss

In class, discuss the meanings of the words above. Check your answers with a dictionary.

Borrowings from German-Dutch

Here are a few of the words taken into English from the German language. They are recent borrowings from the German language group, not English words that have come to us from Anglo-Saxon.

frankfurter	noodle	kindergarten	quartz
schnorkel	waltz	delicatessen	sauerkraut
blitz	stein	hamburger	pretzel

There are also some words which have been borrowed from the German-Dutch colonial settlers in New York and Pennsylvania.

boss	coleslaw	cruller	Santa Claus	snoop	spook

Borrowings from Arabic

A minor but interesting group of words borrowed by English are those which came from contacts with the Arab world. Here are a few. If you do not know what they mean, look them up.

emir   fakir   harem   sheik

There are many other borrowings into English, but there is neither time nor space to discuss them here. The main point you should learn from the information you have read is that English is a great language for borrowing. This is one of the principal ways that our language has expanded and become the fine, varied language it is.

Exercise: Origin of English words

Here is a list of twenty English words. Copy the list and then write beside each word how it came into English. All the information you will need in order to do this exercise is found in this chapter. Doing the exercise will help you to review the facts of the chapter.

EXAMPLES: 1. *hickory*—from American Indian
                2. *water*—from Anglo-Saxon
                3. *corral*—from Spanish

1. chipmunk	6. association	11. special	16. brother
2. mother	7. masculine	12. thing	17. moose
3. institution	8. cigar	13. three	18. spook
4. elegant	9. cow	14. politeness	19. harem
5. thanks	10. liberty	15. ranch	20. hand

GOING AHEAD

1. See if you can list five or ten pairs of synonyms—words with meanings that are almost the same. Each pair should contain a word from the Germanic stream and a word from the Latin-French stream. Be sure to check the origin of your words with a good dictionary.

2. Using charts, maps, posters, and diagrams, make a bulletin-board exhibit showing how English has amassed its store of words. Use the information from this chapter and supplement it with references from dictionaries and encyclopedias.

3. Form a committee to plan and present an assembly program based on this chapter.

PART I

Speaking and Writing Our Language

CHAPTER 1

The Grammar of Sentences

If you own a bicycle or a model train or a hair dryer, you will use it better if you know how it works and what to do if it does not work well. The same thing can be said of language. You should know how it works and how to improve it. You should know what parts go into it and the different ways they can be put together for various purposes. Fortunately, language does not wear out with use as does a bicycle, train, or hair dryer. The more you use it, the better it serves you.

Identifying Sentences

One way to recognize a sentence is to *hear* whether it *sounds* like a sentence. This is what most of us do every day as we listen to people speaking. We recognize sentences without worrying about what they are.

Listen now while someone reads the following paragraph aloud, naturally but slowly. What happens to the reader's voice at the end of each sentence? As you listen, look at the pictures on the opposite page.

The first books were printed from wooden blocks. Words were carved on a block of wood so that a whole page could be printed from a block. It was an expensive method because it took a great deal of time. Printers worked their presses entirely by hand.

Did you notice how the voice of the reader marked the end of each sentence? Did you hear a *drop in pitch* (a lowering of the voice) and a *pause*? Listen for the pitch drop and pause as the sentences are read again.

Now try this method with another paragraph or two from one of your textbooks. Listen carefully as each paragraph is read aloud.

Most of the thoughts you express through the use of language, you express in sentences. Indeed, a sentence is often defined as *a group of words expressing a complete thought* or *a group of words that makes sense by itself*.

Read the ten groups of words below, five sentences and five non-sentences:

1. Aunt Frieda likes apple tarts.
2. Likes apple tarts.
3. When we see that boy.
4. We are glad when we see that boy.
5. Dogs chase cats.
6. After I spoke for an hour.
7. Speaking to the candidates.
8. I am not leaving.
9. The balloons floated to the ceiling.
10. Under the old rickety table in the corner.

Do you see that the thoughts in groups 2, 3, 6, 7, and 10 do not make sense? In 2, you do not know *who* likes tarts. In 3 and 6, you feel like asking, "What about it?"

What is missing in the other nonsentences above? Add words of your own so that each of these word groups makes sense to you.

Of course, in many conversations, people often speak in fragments of sentences:

JOHN: Where's Mary?   (sentence)
JIM: Mary who?   (fragment)
JOHN: Mary Smith.   (fragment)
JIM: Oh, Mary Smith.   (fragment)
        She's in the house.   (sentence)
JOHN: Which house?   (fragment)
JIM: The Jones house down the street.   (fragment)

In this conversation, the sentence fragments make good sense, because the hearer connects them with the words that came just before them. However, in written paragraphs, complete sentences should be used, unless you are writing dialogue for a play, as shown above, or a story.

If you wish to test whether a group of words is a sentence, read it aloud and listen to it.

Exercises: Recognizing sentences

1. Here are eight word groups. Decide whether or not each is a sentence by seeing whether it makes sense by itself. Write *sentence* or *fragment* beside the appropriate numeral on your paper.

1. My uncle imitates a monkey very well.
2. Under the bed an old slipper.
3. Coming down the garden path.
4. Fido was trotting down the garden path.
5. I shiver when the weather is cold and damp.
6. At twelve o'clock George Snell and Peter Chenery.
7. Every man on the pier.
8. We wash dishes after dinner.

2. Listen carefully to the paragraph your teacher will read. See if you can tell, just from the sound, how many sentences it contains. Listen for pauses *and* pitch drops. One alone does not mark the end of a sentence, but both together do.

✓ Check Test 1: Punctuation marks

Take this test to see whether you need to review the use of punctuation marks.

A. Copy the following sentences, inserting punctuation marks where they are needed:

1. Jerry look at these model ships
2. They are models of the *Pinta* the *Niña* and the *Santa Maria*
3. Didnt Columbus buy the original ships with Queen Isabellas money
4. Yes she wasnt afraid to finance his brave venture
5. Columbus sailed from Palos Spain on Aug 3 1492
6. What a long and extremely difficult trip it was

B. Copy the following conversation, punctuating it correctly:

Who built these model ships Mrs Sel asked
I did replied Dr James Its my hobby
Jerry exclaimed Wow That is an interesting hobby sir

If you need study and practice on punctuation, turn to the Review Handbook and study the rules on pages 423–30. Then do the practice which follows the rules. You will find the rules listed alphabetically according to the name of the punctuation mark.

The Subject and Predicate of a Sentence

Examine the following sentences:

1. A small turtle | bit my sister's finger.
2. George | found a tack on his chair.

A sentence has two main parts. One part, the **subject,** names something: *A small turtle,* in sentence 1 above. The other part of the sentence, the **predicate,** tells something about the subject: *bit my sister's finger.* These two parts together form a sentence.

What is the subject in sentence 2? What is the predicate? Find the subject and predicate in each of these sentences:

3. That girl in the next house eats too much.
4. Our relatives visit us each summer.

■ The **subject** of a sentence names what the sentence is about.

■ The **predicate** tells something about the subject.

Exercises: Adding subjects and predicates

1. Here are six groups of words that can be used as subjects in sentences. Copy each one on your paper and form a sentence by adding a predicate.

1. All the books in the boy's desk . . .
2. That flea . . .
3. Automobiles . . .
4. Several teachers at Central High School . . .
5. Meg's father, a famous track star, . . .
6. The main entrance to the auditorium . . .

2. Here are six groups of words that can be used as predicates in sentences. Write sentences using these predicates. You will need to add a subject to each one.

1. . . . cooked the best breakfasts in town.
2. . . . chased the fish downstream.
3. . . . are lovely.
4. . . . wants two free passes to the game.
5. . . . was covered with large rocks.
6. . . . have been waiting for a signal.

The simple subject

There is one word in the subject which is the main, or key, part of the subject. In the sentences below, the subject is underlined and a circle is drawn around its main part:

1. The (furnace) in that house exploded last night.
2. Fourteen little (mice) crawled around the nest.
3. (He) whispered the password to the man at the gate.

Furnace, mice, and *He* are called the **simple subjects** of their sentences.

The simple subject plus the words that cluster with it is called the **complete subject.** What are the complete subjects in sentences 1 and 2 above? Why is the complete subject in sentence 3 the same as the simple subject?

The simple subject sometimes consists of more than one word. Proper names such as *Mary Krewson* and *North Carolina* are examples.

■ The **simple subject** is the key word (or words) in the complete subject of a sentence.

Exercises: The simple subject

1. Copy the complete subject from each of the sentences below. Then circle the simple subject.

1. Our small friend at school saw the automobile accident.
2. That weasel annoys all the barnyard animals.
3. The handsomest boy in the class has black hair and freckles.
4. He finally threw his old snowshoes away.
5. Laura Bell became president of her class.
6. Those books on the first shelf are rare volumes.

2. Supply a simple subject for each blank space below:

1. A __?__ fell on the floor.
2. The __?__ always appeals to me.
3. Our __?__ ate up all the fish.
4. The __?__ is more attractive on the outside.
5. His __?__ lay in the attic for many years.

The simple predicate

Just as there is a key word in the complete subject, so there is in the complete predicate. Here are four sentences with the complete predicates underlined:

1. The ducklings (swam) across the brook.
2. The traffic on Penn Street (sped) past our door all morning.
3. A good dictionary is a key to school success.
4. The school sports program aroused our enthusiasm.

In sentences 1 and 2 the key word is circled. Can you tell which word should be circled in sentence 3? in sentence 4?

The key word in each predicate is called the **simple predicate.** Since the simple predicate is always a **verb,** that is the term we use for it in this book.

Sometimes the verb can be more than one word.

5. The island women (are diving) for sponges.
6. We (have been watching) them for hours.

(You may want to study and practice diagraming. If so, turn to Chapter 15, "Making Sentence Diagrams," pages 387–88.)

▪ The **simple predicate** is the key word (or words) in the complete predicate of a sentence. The simple predicate is always a **verb.**

Exercises: The simple subject and verb

1. Copy the complete predicate for each of the sentences below. Then circle the verb, or simple predicate.

1. My schoolbooks fell to the floor during class.
2. Frostbite is a painful experience.
3. Recent storms have flooded the stream.
4. The subway rattles the windows of our house.
5. Medicine for bee bites is sold widely in our town.

2. Supply a verb for each of the sentences below:

1. Those boys __?__ automobiles this afternoon.
2. The English language __?__ difficult for her to pronounce.
3. The feathery snow __?__ all during Christmas Day.
4. That ugly hound dog __?__ at my friends.
5. The players __?__ through the long afternoon.

▲ *Ichabod rained a shower of kicks and blows upon his horse Gunpowder, hoping to escape from the mysterious headless horseman.*

3. Name the simple subject and verb in each of these sentences:

1. Our class read "The Legend of Sleepy Hollow."
2. The author of this story is Washington Irving.
3. The story tells of the rivalry between Ichabod Crane and Brom Bones.
4. Both men sought the hand of Katrina Van Tassel.
5. Brom Bones was a strong, young, handsome man.
6. In contrast, Ichabod looked ridiculous.
7. His head resembled a weathercock.
8. Baggy clothes fluttered about his tall, lanky frame.
9. His hands dangled out of his sleeves.
10. The people of Sleepy Hollow believed in ghosts.
11. They told stories of the headless horseman.
12. Each night this ghost would arise from his grave.
13. He haunted the glen and nearby roads.
14. Ichabod's rival had devised a plan.
15. The contest between the two men ended with a ghostly ride.

Verbs of Action

Notice the verbs circled in the sentences below:

	SUBJECT	PREDICATE
1.	Harrie Price	(walked) into camp.
2.	His old aunt	(kissed) him on the cheek.
3.	We	(doubted) his sincerity.
4.	Mary	(wonders) about that noise outside.

The easiest kind of verb to recognize is the verb which expresses the action of a sentence. *Kick, cough, run, strangle, erase,* and *grumble* are **verbs of action.** Read aloud the verbs of action in the four sentences above.

A verb of action often tells what the subject of the sentence *does.* In sentences 1 and 2, the verbs *walked* and *kissed* express **physical action**—action that you can see or hear. Verbs can also express **mental action**—action that you cannot see or hear—such as *think, consider, dream, imagine,* and *hate.* Which verbs in the sentences above express mental action?

Exercises: Action verbs

1. Pick out the verbs in the sentences below. For each verb, give the simple subject, which you find by asking *who* or *what* did the action.

1. Thirty bats flew out of the attic.
2. My elderly friend chewed her food eagerly.
3. The shortstop threw the ball to first base.
4. The teachers remembered him.
5. The class thought about the problem all day.
6. After the storm we knew about the strength of the wind.
7. He considered all the facts.
8. The whole audience applauded the announcement.
9. Mary wrote a note to the school librarian.
10. A frightened elephant stamped into the arena.

2. Separate the verbs in the sentences above into two lists. In one list, write all the verbs that express action you can see or hear. In the second list, write all the verbs that express action you cannot see or hear.

3. Supply an action verb for each of the blanks below. Be sure to make good sense. Use only *one* word for each blank.

1. Last night we __?__ to the movies and __?__ a short on Alaska.
2. The photographer __?__ some beautiful pictures.
3. I __?__ the short better than the main feature.
4. In one scene a polar bear __?__ majestically on a piece of ice.
5. Before the ice __?__ too far from shore, the bear __?__ to another piece of ice.

Verbs of Being

A few very common verbs do not express action. They are called **verbs of being.** They are frequently used in sentences which tell what or where the subject *is* or what it *is like.* The most common of them is the verb *be.* Here are five sentences using different forms of the verb *be*:

1. My horse *is* lame.
2. Those pots *are* useless.
3. That animal *was* a raccoon.
4. My matches *were* in a waterproof can.
5. I *am* king.

What does each predicate above tell about the subject? Notice that no action, physical or mental, is expressed by the verb.

You should memorize these forms of the verb *be*:

am	**are**	**is**	**was**	**were**

There are a few other words commonly used as verbs of being. Here are three of them, each used in a sentence:

1. Some boys *become* heroes.
2. My hands *feel* rough.
3. Their actions *seem* ridiculous to me.

Notice that none of these verbs of being expresses action in the sentence. Any one of them could be replaced by a form of the verb *be.* Try replacing each of them with the verb *are* or *were.*

■ **A verb** expresses action or being.

Exercises: Verbs of action or being

1. Find the verbs of being in the sentences below. For each verb, pick out the simple subject.

1. The name of my book is *Stranger on Big Hickory.*
2. Stephen W. Meader is the author.
3. Skip Rollins became a member of the 4-H Club.
4. Photography of wild animals became his special project.
5. The mysterious stranger seemed unhappy about Skip's hobby.
6. The pictures of the playful otter were excellent.
7. A few days later the otter was the victim of a trap.
8. In a few moments the little animal was free once more.
9. Skip felt certain of the identity of the trapper.
10. This deed was surely the work of the mystery man.

2. Supply a verb of being for each of the blanks below. Then write the sentences on your paper. Be sure they make good sense. Use only one word for each blank and do not use any word more than twice in the exercise.

1. Skip ___?___ curious about the tracks.
2. The wind ___?___ bitingly cold.
3. The snow ___?___ too deep for small animals.
4. Away from the cliff the snowshoe tracks ___?___ sharp.
5. Near the cliff the surface of the snow ___?___ unbroken.
6. The elusive stranger ___?___ too smart for him.

3. The sentences listed below contain action verbs and verbs of being. On your paper, write the verb from each sentence. Then tell whether it is a verb of action or a verb of being.

1. This side of Big Hickory is the short way up the hill.
2. The caves of the bears are behind the trees.
3. The cries of the bluejays suddenly became raucous.
4. A little brown ball of fur tumbled across Skip's path.
5. The boy snapped a picture of the bear cub.
6. Just then a huge black shape charged toward him.
7. The mother bear seemed enormous to Skip.
8. The boy scrambled up the trunk of a birch tree.
9. The bear rocked the tree with her terrible paws.
10. Skip felt terribly afraid.

26

Order of Subject and Predicate

Read these two sentences:

SUBJECT	PREDICATE
1. A severe thunderstorm	started during the night.
2. The column of soldiers	marched down the deep valley.

In each of the two sentences above, the subject comes first, followed by the predicate. This is the *usual order* of an English sentence. The typical sentence first names something:

That warty old toad

and second tells something about it:

hopped under my bed.

However, you can get variety into your writing by occasionally changing the usual order of the sentence. You can put the predicate first and the subject second, as, "Under my bed hopped that warty old toad." This is called *inverted order*.

(You may want to study and practice diagraming. If so, turn to Chapter 15, "Making Sentence Diagrams," pages 388–89.)

Exercises: Order of subject and predicate

1. Pick out the simple subject and the verb in the following sentences. Write them on your paper after the appropriate numeral. Underline the subject once and the verb twice.

EXAMPLES: 1. Into my life came Jane.
           2. The muskrat scurried into his hole.

YOU WRITE: 1. *Jane   came*
             2. *muskrat   scurried*

1. Over that hill marched three thousand young boys.
2. The dust flew into the room.
3. The field of science research always needs able young men.
4. Far above the clouds the astrojet sped toward its destination.
5. Under the blankets snuggled the lost hamster.
6. Down the river chugged a noisy motorboat.
7. On the bookshelf stood a hundred unread books.
8. At the corner appeared a gas station.

2. Five of the sentences below are in natural order and five in inverted order. Rewrite each sentence, reversing the order. In parentheses after each sentence you have rewritten, write *natural* or *inverted*. Draw a line between subject and predicate.

EXAMPLE: 1. Up the street marched the band.
YOU WRITE: *1. Up the street marched/the band. (inverted)*

1. Out of the frying pan leapt the trout.
2. Between the two girls stood Miss Ostler.
3. My noisy alarm clock sits on the bureau.
4. In his house is a policeman.
5. Across the screen flashed the announcement.
6. The president stood in front of the stockholders.
7. Crowds of tourists gathered outside the building.
8. Beautiful buttons are in the wooden box.
9. Hundreds of priceless paintings hung on the walls of his home.
10. On the shelves of nearly every good library in the country stands a set of the *Encyclopædia Britannica*.

3. On your paper, write first the simple subject from each sentence above. Then, next to the subject, write the verb.

TO MEMORIZE

FROM *The Road Not Taken*

I shall be telling this with a sigh
Somewhere ages and ages hence:
Two roads diverged in a wood, and I—
I took the one less traveled by,
And that has made all the difference.

ROBERT FROST

Robert Frost, one of America's greatest poets, loved his country and his New England home. His poems can be read and appreciated simply for the beauty of his descriptions of nature and life on a New England farm. A closer look, however, will reveal another layer of meaning: for instance, if you substitute the word *life* for *wood* in line 3, you will see that the word *roads* also takes on another meaning. What do you think this meaning is? What new meaning do these five lines have for you now?

Four Types of Sentences

Discuss in class what you think the purpose of the speaker was in each sentence below—that is, why did he speak the sentence?

1. A thousand bats live in those caves.
2. How can I get from here to the park?
3. Please speak softly.
4. What a terrible temper he has!

In your discussion you may have suggested many purposes. For example, the speaker of the first sentence may have wanted to amaze the hearer or to frighten him away or to persuade him to get the exterminator. You cannot know for sure. Here, though, are four rather general purposes:

1. To make a statement giving information.
2. To ask a question in order to obtain information. A response is expected.
3. To make a request. Appropriate action is expected.
4. To express feelings.

Your discussion may have led you to see that there are four types of English sentences.

1. A **declarative sentence** makes a statement. It ends with a period.
   Many mushrooms are poisonous.
2. An **interrogative sentence** asks a question. It ends with a question mark.
   Is this mushroom good to eat?
3. An **imperative sentence** makes a request or gives a command. It ends with a period.
   Please eat your mushrooms.
4. An **exclamatory sentence** expresses emotion or strong feeling. It ends with an exclamation point.
   How strange-looking this mushroom is!

Exclamatory sentences can take several forms. Most sentences—declarative, interrogative, or imperative—can be made to show emotion or strong feeling by putting an exclamation point at the end.

The firemen are here!   Do you want to get hurt!
Watch out for that snake!

Exercise: Four types of sentences

On your paper, copy the following sentences, punctuating them correctly. Then indicate in parentheses what kind of sentence each one is.

1. What a nerve that young girl has , declar .
2. How long will you need for the project ? interog
3. A stitch in time saves nine , declar.
4. Come into the kitchen, Margaret , imper.
5. How large the peonies are this year. exclam
6. Please do not eat the apples . impar.
7. They are not ripe , exclam
8. What time will the boat leave ? interog
9. Please buy our tickets for tonight , imper.
10. What a narrow escape that was ! exclam

Interrogative sentences; order of subject and predicate

In many interrogative sentences, the subject and predicate are in usual order. Name the simple subject and the verb in this sentence:

Who killed Cock Robin?

More often, however, there is a special order of subject and predicate in questions:

1. What did Cock Robin say?
2. Where has Mary Jane gone now?
3. When was John giving that talk?

Once you find the verb in the predicate of a sentence, it is easy to find the simple subject. In sentence 1, the verb is *did say*. Ask yourself, "Who or what *did say*?" The answer is *Cock Robin*, so *Cock Robin* is the subject. Name the simple subjects and verbs in sentences 2 and 3.

Do you see how *in an interrogative sentence the subject often comes between two parts of the verb*?

If you have difficulty finding the simple subjects and verbs in questions, turn the sentence around, following the natural order of the subject and predicate in a statement. For example, you can rearrange the words in sentence 1 this way:

Cock Robin did say what?

Imperative sentences; where is the subject?

Notice that each of the following imperative sentences begins with a verb:

    Go over to the door.   Stay in your seats.

What and where is the subject in each? It is *you*, the person or persons to whom the command is addressed. In commands or requests, the subject *you* does not usually appear in the sentence. It is *understood* to be there, but not expressed. We call it "*you* understood."

    (you) Go over to the door.   (you) Stay in your seats.

Sometimes the command is softened by a "please" or "kindly" before the verb, as in, "Please stay in your seats."

There are some commands, however, in which the subject *you* is stated, as in, "*You* help her."

(You may want to study and practice diagraming. If so, turn to Chapter 15, "Making Sentence Diagrams," page 390.)

■ The subject **you** is often not stated in requests and commands.

Exercise: Finding the subject and verb

Find the simple subject and the verb in the following sentences. Write them on your paper after the appropriate numeral. If the subject is understood, write it in parentheses. Underline the subject once and the verb twice.

1. Who knows their new address?
2. Where did you buy that hat?
3. How long will the cat keep the kittens?
4. You will pick up those books now, please.
5. What does Sue eat for breakfast?
6. Who was running down the hall last night?
7. Remove all those empty cans from the doorstep.
8. To whom shall I give this broken egg?
9. Kindly sweep the street in front of the tenement.
10. Why were you laughing?
11. Set a few rat traps in the hallways.
12. Speak louder, please.
13. Who spoke so rudely to Mrs. Corwin?
14. How do people like our new pool?

Sentence Patterns

Are these word groups sentences?

1. Grumbled mightily this afternoon the boy upstairs.
2. In spite of my cold severe, I be will studying most of the night.
3. Woodsman the trees down chopped tall all the winter long through that sturdy.

On your paper, rearrange the words in the three items above so that they will make good sense and sound like normal English sentences. Do not add or omit any words.

You can see how important *word order* is to English grammar. Fortunately, you have learned to put your words together in the right order without even thinking about it. You learned it very young and by imitation.

It does not take any study to know that it is good normal English to say,

Alice will be going downtown on Saturday.

It is not normal English to say,

Alice be will going downtown on Saturday.

● Rearrange the words in each word group below to make a good English sentence. You may think of more than one acceptable order for some of the sentences you write. Do not add or subtract any words.

1. A fire blazing feels after skiing good.
2. Never John was able to climb that mountain.
3. Those swimming there fish are over not normally.
4. The coach John's high jump accurately will measure.
5. That kitchen blue broken chair bought was by my grandmother.
6. There rolling were down her cheek sparkling several tears.
7. Headaches the Mother doctor for visits her.
8. He threw the horse over the fence some hay for.
9. Brave boys two that drowning man saved.
10. Me before see practice afternoon football this.

32

Avoiding Sentence Fragments and Run-ons

You can use what you have learned in this chapter to improve your writing. You know, for example, that a written sentence *sounds* complete when read aloud. You know that most sentences have a subject and a predicate and that neither one written alone makes a sentence (except a verb in a command or request). This knowledge should help you avoid two of the most common sentence errors.

Sentence fragments

What is wrong with the word groups below?

1. Uncle John always returned from his voyages. *With unusual presents for all of us.*
2. Up Shooter's Hill struggled the horse. *Covered with mud and sweat.*

Each group is punctuated as if it were two sentences, whereas it should be punctuated as one sentence. Read aloud the italicized portions of 1 and 2 above. Do they sound complete? Does each have both a subject and a predicate?

You see, do you not, that a final punctuation mark was used before each thought was really complete? The word groups *With unusual presents for all of us* and *Covered with mud and sweat* are only pieces of sentences, called **sentence fragments.** Thus, example 1 should have been written: "Uncle John always returned from his voyages with unusual presents for all of us." How should example 2 be written?

Run-on sentences

Now consider another common sentence error. Read this paragraph:

The left engine was on fire and the fuel tank was leaking there was only one thing to do, the pilot had to try for a crash landing.

What is wrong with the paragraph you have just read? Read it aloud and see if you can tell where the periods should be put to punctuate the ends of the sentences. There are three sentences in the paragraph.

When two sentences are run together as if they were one, separated by a comma or not separated at all, the result is a **run-on sentence.**

> *Remember:* A sentence has a subject and a predicate and sounds complete; it makes sense by itself.
>
> A sentence begins with a capital letter and ends with a period, question mark, or exclamation point.

Do not punctuate a sentence fragment as a sentence.
Separate two sentences from each other with a period, a question mark, or an exclamation point.

Exercises: Correcting fragments and run-ons

1. Below are six run-on sentences. Read each one aloud and decide where each sentence begins and ends. Write the sentences correctly on your paper. Be sure to use the correct end punctuation for each one.

1. That parachutist barely missed the trees in the orchard he finally landed safely in the wheat field nearby
2. George lived with his family in Cairo, Egypt there his interest in archeology was born
3. That is mine it's not yours would you like to borrow it
4. Between me and my supper is a two-mile hike two miles is too far
5. John, that person over there is your uncle, speak politely to him
6. After school, my brother works at a very interesting job he assists the professors in the university laboratory what a lucky boy he is

2. There are sentence fragments and run-on sentences in the paragraphs on the next page. Read the paragraphs and decide where each sentence begins and ends. Then write the paragraphs, punctuating them correctly. Watch for one sentence that is not a declarative sentence.

The Panama Canal can run through land of various levels. Because it has locks, The lock chamber has concrete walls as high as the canal level, they are as high as a six-story apartment house.

At the ends of the locks are watertight gates, the gates are worked by electricity. The locks are really twin locks they are similar to a double-track railway. Ships can pass in both directions at the same time. Each lock is 1,000 feet in length and 110 feet in height. The concrete and cement in the locks of the canal. Would cover a road around the earth, Twenty feet wide to a depth of six inches. What a lot of concrete that is!

✓ Check Test 2: Capital letters

Take this test to see whether you need to review the use of capital letters.

Write the following sentences correctly on your paper. Supply capital letters wherever they are needed.

1. the vast land mass of europe and asia is called eurasia.
2. the continent of africa is bounded by the mediterranean sea, gulf of aden, red sea, indian ocean, and atlantic ocean.
3. the colorado river flows through the grand canyon across the northwest corner of arizona.
4. the american pioneer families in the south and midwest welcomed the arrival of the yankee peddler.
5. he would buy fabrics, kitchen equipment, bibles, clocks, and gadgets from factories in the east and from english sea captains on the boston docks.
6. he often followed the unmapped indian trails through the appalachian mountains, carrying wares and news from the seacoast cities to the lonely settlers.

If you made mistakes in the Check Test above, turn to the Review Handbook and study the rules for capitalization on pages 419–22.

Sentence Patterns

The order of the words in an English sentence is very important if the sentence is to make any sense at all. Examine the following lists of words and their arrangements below:

the   corral
cowboys   train
that   wild
near   these
will   horses

Near that will cowboys train horses the corral these wild.
Cowboys that near horses will train these wild the corral.

Words strung together without any particular order, as shown above, make little or no sense. Here are these same words re-arranged:

1. The cowboys near that corral will train these wild horses.

The sentence above is a good English sentence. Yet even this sentence is useless unless it expresses exactly what you want to say. Simply by rearranging these words, you can express different meanings:

2. The cowboys near that train will corral these wild horses.
3. These wild cowboys will train the horses near that corral.

We arrange words in a certain order not only *to make sense* but also *to express our exact meaning*.

● Rearrange the words in each numbered group listed below to produce sentences that make sense. Remember what you learned about subjects and predicates. Write several sentences for each group.

1. Librarian, stories, some, tell, children, to, the
2. A, asked, minstrel, wandering, the, three, bold, questions, knights
3. Have, two, scientists, helped, famous, professor, the, young
4. My, baby-sitting, sister, is, Mrs. Hall's, with, daughter, little
5. Bank, the, for, guards, the, men, are, those, watching, two

A Book to Read

Island of the Blue Dolphins
by Scott O'Dell
Houghton Mifflin Company

Far off the coast of California there rises from the ocean depths a rocky island, the Island of San Nicholas. Blue dolphins play around the island, and sea elephants sun themselves on its stony beaches.

Here, in the early 1800's, an Indian girl lived alone for eighteen years after warriors had killed most of the men of the island village and, later, the other villagers had gone far away to the mainland. How she tames and makes a wild dog her faithful companion, maintains her food supply, cures illness with herbs, and builds a satisfactory life in spite of loneliness and terrifying dangers makes a dramatic story. Then, the day comes when kindly people visit the island and take Karana home with them.

About the author

Scott O'Dell comes from the family of the great Scottish novelist Sir Walter Scott. He is an authority on California history, in which state he was born and lives. *Island of the Blue Dolphins* is a historical novel, Karana was a real girl, and this story is a true one.

38

Test I

Here are ten groups of words. Write *sentence* or *fragment* beside each numeral on your paper, depending on whether each group makes sense by itself.

1. His best friend for the past two years.
2. My brother sent me a ticket to the ball game.
3. Unless the sun doesn't come up tomorrow morning.
4. Each boat in the Panama Canal.
5. After dinner, when the news is on TV, my father wants absolute quiet.
6. It's too hot.
7. Singing in the shower, Greg didn't hear the telephone.
8. That kind but unpopular dentist.
9. The wailing of the hoot owl in the church tower is an eerie sound at midnight.
10. Over the mantelpiece on a golden chain.

Test II

Copy each of the following sentences. Underline the simple subject once and the verb twice.

1. The queen of Brobdingnag chewed upon the wings of a lark nine times the size of a turkey.
2. The bread in her mouth was as big as two huge loaves.
3. A mouthful seemed enough food for a dozen English farmers.
4. She used knives twice as long as scythes.
5. The other instruments appeared in the same proportion.

Test III

1. Separate the verbs below into two lists, headed *Physical Action* and *Mental Action*:

believe	throw	crash	cry
choke	doubt	yell	expect
suppose	hope	chew	agree
write	fold	think	call
shout	consider	imagine	wonder

39

2. Copy the verbs in the following sentences. Beside each one, write *verb of action* or *verb of being*.

1. Herman always was a pessimist.
2. We tripped on the stairs.
3. The envelope fell into a puddle.
4. Your ideas are quite unusual.
5. The fabric feels smooth.

Test IV

Some of the subjects and predicates below are in usual order; some are inverted. Pick out the simple subject and the verb and write them on your paper after the appropriate numeral. Then underline the simple subject once and the verb twice.

EXAMPLE: 1. Into the room sailed the teacher.
YOU WRITE: *1. teacher sailed*

1. In the hall stood Horace Alphonso.
2. In his eyes were unshed tears.
3. Under the bed is dust.
4. The unhappy baby crawled directly to his mother.
5. Out of the cave dashed the thieves.
6. My first poem was about tall city buildings.
7. The two barrels of pickles crashed into the wall.
8. On the top shelf in the toy shop sat the blue and white zebra.
9. Over the roar of the falls came the sound of howling wolves.
10. Out of the dark the rockets exploded.

Test V

1. Copy the following sentences, punctuating each one correctly. Then write the kind of sentence it is—declarative, interrogative, imperative, or exclamatory.

1. How beautiful that dog is
2. What kind of dog is he
3. The dog is a collie
4. Stop growling, Rascal
5. Keep out of that dog's way

2. Copy each of the following sentences. Underline the simple subject once and the verb twice. If the subject is understood, write it in parentheses.

1. Finish your homework first.
2. Please be quiet.
3. Call the police!
4. When did your money disappear?
5. Why do you shout?

Test VI

1. Examine the two word groups beside each numeral below. In some, both word groups in each pair are complete sentences; in others, one of the word groups is a fragment. On your paper, copy each fragment and connect it to the sentence in which it belongs. Do not copy the correct pairs of sentences.

1. Hercules stole toward the sleeping figure. He grasped the Old Man of the Sea.
2. Suddenly he found himself. Holding a stag by the legs.
3. What an amazing happening that was! Still he held fast.
4. The stag disappeared. In its stead was a seabird.
5. Hercules held tight. It fluttered and screamed in vain.
6. When he then clutched an ugly three-headed dog. It growled and barked and snapped fiercely.
7. Next a six-legged man-monster appeared. Which kicked Hercules with its legs.
8. Then there was a snake. Of immense size and strength.
9. As it twined about the hero's body. It opened its deadly jaws to devour Hercules outright.
10. Hercules held on. He was no whit disheartened.

2. The following paragraph is incorrect because it contains fragments and run-ons. Write the paragraph correctly on your paper.

The strange-looking insect attracted attention. Outside of the scouts' tent. The boys had never seen one like it before, they followed its movements with great interest. No one knew how dangerous this poisonous creature was the youngest boy Johnny stepped forward to pick it up. Just at that moment the scoutleader returned. And saved the day by grabbing Johnny. Before he could touch the poisonous tarantula.

Exercise I

1. Review "Identifying Sentences" on pages 17–18.

2. Some of the groups of words below are sentences, and others are fragments. Copy each fragment and add words of your own to make it a complete sentence.

    1. When the bell rang, the students.
    2. Shot the wolves that had eaten his chickens.
    3. At first I did not see him.
    4. Wore boots over his shoes.
    5. All of the guests became sleepy after dinner.
    6. At the station door the mob of passengers.
    7. Blushed at the remark.
    8. These monkeys do not like bananas.
    9. We refused.
   10. After the salesman spoke.

Exercise II

1. Review "The Subject and Predicate of a Sentence" on pages 20–22.

2. Find the simple subjects and verbs in the following sentences and write them on your paper. Underline the simple subject once and the verb twice.

    1. Two men with binoculars walked up and down the bridge.
    2. At one o'clock, the bells in the steeple rang.
    3. We watched a special TV science program.
    4. The funny-looking penguins waddled over to the water.
    5. A change in seasons often finds me with a cold.

Exercise III

1. Review "Verbs of Action" and "Verbs of Being" on pages 24 and 25.

2. Write five sentences with five different verbs that express physical action—action that you can see or hear. Write five sentences with five different verbs that express mental action.

3. Write five sentences with five different verbs of being that tell what or where the subject is or what it is like.

42

Exercise IV

1. Review "Order of Subject and Predicate" on page 27.

2. The subjects and predicates in the following sentences are in usual order. Rewrite each one so that the subject and predicate are in inverted order. When you have rewritten the sentence, underline the simple subject once and the verb twice.

1. The tractor came across the wheat field.
2. The worm lives under the earth.
3. The smoke billowed around the stacks.
4. The airplane rose into the sky.
5. The boys jumped into the shallow brook.
6. The kite crashed into a field of corn.
7. The sailboats glided across the harbor.
8. The sound of whispers traveled through the keyhole.

Exercise V

1. Review "Four Types of Sentences" on pages 29–31.

2. Write two examples each of declarative and exclamatory sentences.

3. Write two interrogative sentences in which the subject comes between two parts of the verb.

4. Write two imperative sentences.

5. For each of the sentences you wrote for parts 2, 3, and 4 of this exercise, underline the simple subject once and the verb twice.

Exercise VI

1. Review "Avoiding Sentence Fragments and Run-ons" on pages 33–34.

2. Read the following paragraph. It is incorrect because it contains fragments and run-ons. Copy the paragraph on your paper, correcting these errors.

In the beginning of the story. The author said that Cecil wasn't completely at fault, it was partly Frank's fault. At least, if Frank had not sniffed the artificial flower, the water wouldn't have squirted in his face Frank's father happened to be passing by he saw what happened. Boys often play that kind of prank. He was glad his son was a good sport, Frank was laughing. Right along with Cecil.

43

CHAPTER 2

Speaking: Expressing Ideas

Speaking is a highly personal activity, and each of us does it his own way. Fortunately, there is not just one single right way to speak; life would be quite dull if this were so. There are certain characteristics of good voice and speech production, however, which you should try to learn and to apply. It is important to pronounce correctly and to try to improve your voice and speech by listening to yourself and your classmates.

Your Voice and Speech

Voices differ; no two voices sound exactly the same. It is usually quite easy to recognize the voice of a person you know. You need not see him. In some ways, your voice *is* you, and a very flexible instrument it is.

We have many sounds in English—consonant sounds and vowel sounds. In order to make these sounds, we use the organs of voice and speech, shown in the chart at the top of the next page.

Our speech consists of many kinds of sounds made by the different parts of the vocal apparatus. Did you know that a human being can make hundreds of sounds with the organs used for speech, but that the English language uses only about forty-five main sounds?

Exercise: Your voice

To demonstrate how easy it is to identify a person by voice alone, have six members of the class—all boys or all girls—go to the back of the room. Number your paper from 1 to 6 and, one at a time, have each person in the back of the room say the same sentences in a natural voice: "Who am I? Do you know?" Guess who each speaker is and write his name on your paper beside the appropriate numeral. Check to see how many pupils were able to guess all six correctly.

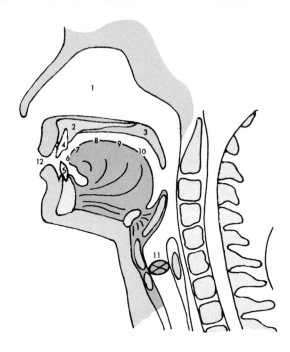

Organs of Speech

1. Nasal Cavity
2. Hard Palate
3. Soft Palate
4. Upper Teeth
5. Lower Teeth
6. Tip of Tongue
7. Blade of Tongue
8. Front of Tongue
9. Middle of Tongue
10. Back of Tongue
11. Vocal Cords (Larynx)
12. Lips

Voice Characteristics

What is the first thing you notice about a stranger's speech? Your initial reaction is to the *sound of his voice.* You either enjoy listening to it or you find it unpleasant. You have often heard the expression "his voice gets on my nerves." In addition to causing an unfavorable reaction, a sharp, shrill voice, for example, or a slow, muffled, weak voice will detract from what is being said. Perhaps the most important single characteristic of effective speech is *good voice quality.* There are four qualities of voice that you might think about:

Pitch

The pitch of your voice is determined by the length, thickness, and tightness of your vocal cords. You have no control over the length and thickness, but you can control the tension. When the vocal cords are too tense, they may produce unpleasantly high tones. Try to speak easily and without strain.

Volume

Straining the ears to listen to a voice that is too weak or soft is tiring. It is annoying to hear a voice that is too loud. Your control of volume should be such that you can adjust the volume to suit your purpose and the place where you are speaking.

Tone

The tone of your voice is the way your voice sounds. Ask a good friend to listen to you and react to the sound of your voice. If your friend says that you sound as though you talk through your nose, you have the problem of nasality. There are only three nasal sounds in English: *m, n,* and *ng.* No other sound should be produced through the nose. Try this sentence which has no nasal sounds:

Ted is outdoors.

Block your nostrils and say the sentence again. If you are *not* nasal, you should feel no pressure of air through the nose. All breath should be coming through the mouth.

Inflection or flexibility

Your voice should help to express the meaning of words and sentences. An expressive voice adds life and interest to what you say through inflection. That is, your voice is flexible, not static and monotonous. You make your voice expressive by the way you change pitch, speed, and volume. Different words and sentences need to be said in different ways to make their meaning clear.

To discuss

1. Ask the following questions of your classmates:

   1. *Pitch:* Is my voice too high or shrill? Is it too low?
   2. *Volume:* Does my voice sound thin and weak? Is it too loud or too soft?
   3. *Tone:* Does my voice have a nasal tone? Is it harsh and rasping? Is it clear and pleasing?
   4. *Inflection:* Is my voice flat and colorless? Is it monotonous?

2. Try to think of as many situations as you can where your speech could count for or against you in an important way. Telephoning someone to ask for an appointment and trying to make friends with somebody are two examples. Discuss these situations in class.

3. Think of the individuals whose speech pleases you. What qualities of their speech do you like? Are there special differences in their ways of speaking which interest you?

The way your voice sounds depends on the four characteristics of *pitch, volume, tone,* and *inflection.*

Exercises: Practicing voice control

1. Prepare a short story to tell before the class, or choose from literature a passage of three or four paragraphs to read aloud. Ask your classmates to judge your voice by the questions on page 47.

2. Repeat these italicized expressions or sentences to reflect the different moods suggested:

1. *No*
   (a) doubt; (b) fear; (c) disgust; (d) pleasure; (e) excitement
2. *All right*
   (a) impatience; (b) understanding; (c) certainty; (d) hesitation; (e) sarcasm
3. *Sit down, Gene, you're rocking the boat.*
   (a) terror; (b) authority; (c) entreaty; (d) anger; (e) ridicule
4. *Which one?*
   (a) impatience; (b) amazement; (c) puzzlement; (d) indifference; (e) exhaustion

3. Read the following sentences aloud, making your voice reflect the feelings suggested at the left.

interest; *boredom*	1. Are they antiques, Mr. Bell?
	2. Dave, did you have a good trip?
	3. Did he really win the race?
pleasure; *sarcasm*	4. Of course, I'll help serve refreshments.
	5. What a beautiful summer day this is!
	6. How kind of you to volunteer your help!
gratitude; *disgust*	7. Thank you for interrupting that conversation.
	8. You are always so helpful, Miss Walker.
	9. I'm so glad you gave me your permission.
excitement; *relief*	10. We can go home now, Larry!
	11. How that rocket can travel!
	12. The game is over! We won!
worry; *eagerness*	13. Did you find the tickets, Kitty?
	14. That puppy may not have an owner.
	15. Florence hasn't visited us for a week.

Taking turns, read each of the following italicized sentences aloud three times. For each reading, vary the emphasis in your voice so as to express the meaning given after letters *a*, *b*, and *c*.

1. *I did not like the movie.*
   a. The others liked the movie, but I did not.
   b. I enjoyed the original play, but I did not like the movie.
   c. I wasted my time because the movie was dull.
2. *Paul walked out.*
   a. Paul, not I, walked out.
   b. Paul did not run or sneak out.
   c. Guess what Paul did!
3. *How much money do we need?*
   a. Do you really think we need all that money?
   b. I know we need some money, but how much?
   c. You have listed everything else we need, but you have not told us how much money we need.

TO MEMORIZE

There Is No Frigate Like a Book

There is no frigate like a book
    To take us lands away,
Nor any coursers like a page
    Of prancing poetry.

This traverse may the poorest take
    Without oppress of toll;
How frugal is the chariot
    That bears a human soul!

EMILY DICKINSON

A great English poet named Coleridge once said, "Prose—words in their best order; poetry—the best words in their best order." Emily Dickinson used precise and carefully chosen words to create the beautiful and memorable poem above. Each word contributes to the overall idea—the comparison between travel and reading books.

What do the words *frigate, coursers, traverse,* and *frugal* mean?

How does "prancing poetry" contribute to the comparison in the poem? What does the line "Without oppress of toll" mean?

Articulation

In general, most of us are rather lazy in forming speech sounds and do not make vigorous enough use of our *organs of articulation,* mainly the tongue. Remember, the more carefully you articulate, the more likely you are to be understood.

Of course, no one expects you to give full weight to each vowel and consonant of each word you speak. Your speech would then be colorless and stilted. It would sound false. Speakers of every language, English included, blend sounds and words together, such as "Maryisgoing home." This elision is correct. However, "Havyeetnyet?" is sloppy and incorrect for "Have you eaten yet?"

Here are some exercises to give you practice in speaking carefully. Let your classmates decide whether you say the words clearly.

Exercises: Practicing careful articulation

1. Read aloud these words and make an effort to sound the italicized consonants clearly:

(b) *b*un, *b*i*b*, *b*uy, *b*ill, *b*oy, ru*b*, ri*b* *b*o*b*, clu*b*, *b*ean
(c) *c*ub, *c*ap, *c*ame, *c*ab, *c*ar, *c*ube, pi*c*nic, ar*c*tic, *c*ubi*c*, antic
(d) *d*ie*d*, *d*en, *d*ay, *d*ine, *d*oll, bu*d*, *d*oor, re*d*, playe*d*, *d*i*d*
(g) *g*a*g*, *g*ame, *g*un, *g*oose, *g*irl, ba*g*, hu*g*, e*gg*, fla*g*, sa*g*
(l) *l*i*l*y, *l*ow, *l*ie, *l*u*ll*aby, *l*ap, *l*id, unti*l*, ai*l*, *l*u*ll*, mi*ll*
(m) *m*ay, *m*y, *m*ole, *m*ine, *m*ore, ra*m*, ai*m*, *m*ai*m*, ta*m*e, sa*m*e
(n) *n*or, *n*ice, *n*o, *n*ame, *n*ail, *n*ot, ta*n*, *N*a*n*, *n*i*n*e, *n*o*n*e
(p) *p*ie, *p*ear, *p*an, *p*ale, *p*art, ma*p*, li*p*, *p*u*p*, *p*o*p*, soa*p*
(s) *s*o, *s*ee, *s*ay, *s*ap, *s*ame, *s*led, atla*s*, thu*s*, Elli*s*, dres*s*
(t) *t*ake, ma*t*, *t*ie, *t*ear, *t*ale, an*t*, ea*t*, *t*o*t*, *t*oo*t*, most
(v) *v*eil, *v*ote, *v*est, *v*im, *v*oice, *v*i*v*id, *v*iper, *v*iew, *v*ein, *v*ault

2. The italicized letters below are often sounded carelessly. Practice saying them aloud carefully.

1. Say the *u* as if pronounced *yoo* or *yə*. Be sure the *y* part of the sound is pronounced.

circ*u*lar	reg*u*lar	ed*u*cation	circ*u*lation
form*u*la	partic*u*lar	ridic*u*lous	pop*u*lation
tab*u*late	rep*u*tation	sec*u*lar	man*u*facture

2. Do not pronounce the italicized letters like a *u*.

           per*c*olate   es*c*alate

3. Say the long *o* (ō).

  mead*ow*   shall*ow*   yell*ow*   pill*ow*

4. Say the *ng*. Do not omit the sound of *g*.

doi*ng*	seei*ng*	havi*ng*	goi*ng*	studyi*ng*
helpi*ng*	sayi*ng*	maki*ng*	sewi*ng*	leavi*ng*

5. Say the *t*.

me*t*al	*ti*tle	bo*tt*le	tur*t*le
be*tt*er	li*tt*le	ba*tt*le	le*tt*er

3. Say these expressions. Be careful to pronounce the *t* in *to* and the *th* in *them*. (In normal rapid speech, *to* may be pronounced *tuh* and *them* may be pronounced *th'm*.)

                 ought ***to***   saw ***them***
                 had ***to***   try ***them***
                 going ***to***   take ***them***
                 trying ***to***   call ***them***

4. Say the *t* and the *d*. (In normal rapid speech the *t* and *y* in expressions like *don't you* is slurred to *ch*, as in *donchoo*; and the *d* and *y* in *would you* to *j*, as in *wuhjoo*. To omit the *d* or *t* altogether, as *don'you* or *foun'you*, is substandard, and you should try to avoid it.)

don'***t you***	woul***d you***	tol***d*** you	di***d you***
haven'***t you***	can'***t you***	sen***d*** you	foun***d you***

If you think some of your speech habits are careless, test yourself daily for a while. Carefully read aloud a stanza from a poem or a paragraph and ask someone to criticize your speech. Each time you read aloud, try to improve on the points that need improvement.

If you can obtain a tape recorder, you may be able to make great improvements in your voice and speech by working alone. Listen to the pitch, volume, tone, inflection, and articulation. After a while you will develop the ability to hear your mistakes even without a recorder.

Form a committee and listen very carefully to the speech of your class members, both in and out of class. Take notes of examples of poor articulation immediately after hearing them.

EXAMPLES: The words *"gonna go"* should be *"going to* go."
"Mary *hadda* stay after school" should be "Mary *had to . . ."*

After you have gathered evidence for several days, get together with the other committee members to pool your findings. Weed out any duplications. Then report to the class by writing these examples of articulation faults on the board. Each class member should write in his English notebook those faults which he needs to work on.

Check Test 3: Verbs and pronouns

Take this test to find out whether you know how to use certain verbs and pronouns correctly.

A. Write these sentences, choosing the correct verb in each:

1. There (is, are) bananas all over the shipping platform.
2. There (is, are) my uncle and aunt near the entrance.
3. We (could have, could of) helped you with the packing.
4. There (was, were) no dark clouds in the sky.
5. I (says, said), "Please join us next Saturday."
6. Yesterday Jim (says, said), "Let's go fishing this weekend."
7. I always (says, say), "She is my best friend."
8. There (was, were) apple pie and ice cream for dessert.

B. Copy these sentences, choosing the correct pronoun from each pair in parentheses:

1. Yesterday Ned and (I, me) played Scrabble.
2. The scout leaders are Harry and (he, him).
3. Were you and (she, her) planning to join us?
4. The bus driver did not see (she, her) and (I, me).
5. Did anyone leave a package for Jessie and (I, me)?
6. The first one there was (he, him).

If you did not make a perfect score in Check Test 3 above, study the lessons you need on pages 443, 452, 454, and 455–56 in the Review Handbook.

Pronunciation

You have been reading about articulation—speaking clearly. Now consider the problems of pronunciation. Pronunciation requires knowing *what* sounds to utter when you say a word aloud. If you mispronounce a difficult or unusual word, you are not likely to be criticized. If you mispronounce common words you ought to know, you make a bad impression. At times you even fail to get across your meaning.

If you do not know how to pronounce a word, look it up in a good dictionary. Sometimes, though, when you look up a word, you will find there are two or more ways to pronounce it. The first pronunciation is often the one the dictionary-makers consider is used more by educated people. Choose the one that is considered acceptable by careful speakers in your locality.

Exercises: Pronouncing words correctly

Here is a sampling of words very commonly mispronounced in various parts of the United States. Say each word aloud. Refer to the pronunciation key at the bottom of this page if you need to.

1. Say *all* the syllables as you pronounce each word. Do not omit a syllable.

poem (pō′əm)	finally (fī′nəl i)
champion (cham′pi ən)	geography (ji og′rə fi)
governor (guv′ər nər)	generally (jen′ər əl i)

2. Do not reverse the order of the italicized letters in each of the following words:

ap*ro*n	hund*r*ed	pe*r*spiration
int*ro*duce	p*r*oduce	p*r*onunciation
child*r*en	p*r*onounce	p*r*oposal

---

hat, āge, cãre, fär; let, ēqual, tėrm; it, īce; hot, ōpen, ôrder; oil, out; cup, pút, rüle, ūse; ch, child; ng, long; th, thin; ~~TH~~, then; zh, measure; ə represents *a* in about, *e* in taken, *i* in pencil, *o* in lemon, *u* in circus.

---

3. Do not add a letter at the end of these words:

once (wuns)   somewhere (sum′hwãr)
across (ə krôs′)   draw (drô)

4. The vowels in these words are sometimes mispronounced:

catch (kach)   Do not say "kich."
genuine (jen′ū ən)   Do not say "jen′ū īn."
America (ə mer′ə kə)   Do not say "ə mur′ə kə."
get (get)   Do not say "git."
maybe (mā′bi)   Do not say "mebbe."
wrestling (res′ling)   Do not say "ras′ling."

5. Say only the syllables that are a part of each word. Do not
add a syllable.

athlete (ath′lēt)   said (sed)   Do not say "see ed."
athletics (ath let′iks)   friend (frend)   Do not say "free end."
attacked (ə takt′)   masonry (mā′sən ri)
drowned (dround)   grown (grōn)
burglar (bėr′glər)   mischievous (mis′chə vəs)
film (film)   elm (elm)

6. Be sure to accent the italicized syllable in each word below:

*the*ater   ce*ment*   ga*rage*
*mem*orable   po*lice*   *for*midable

7. Be sure to say the italicized letter in each word below:

recognize   congra*t*ulations   lib*r*ary   represen*t*ative

■■■■■ **GOING AHEAD** ■■■■■■■■■■■■■■■■■■■■■■■■■■■■■■■■■

1. Look up each of the following words in a high school dictionary and decide which one of the given pronunciations is most
frequently used by careful speakers in your section of the country:

apricot   pecan   pianist   blouse   adult
root   either   tomato   forehead   juvenile
roof   iodine   forest   creek   greasy

2. Follow the directions for the "Going Ahead" exercise on page
52, but this time, list some of the major pronunciation mistakes that
are made by your classmates.

Conversation

Conversation is the most common and informal type of speaking you do. It is the talking you do mostly with friends, acquaintances, and family members. The fact that conversation is informal and that it is an activity which you engage in all the time may lead you to think that there are no guides to follow. Certainly there is a great difference between speech-making, which has many formal rules, and conversation. However, good conversation, at its best, can be an art. As with any art form, there are qualities which make it good and others which make it poor. To be a good conversationalist, try to follow these three general guides which can help you: (1) talk about a subject which interests you and your listeners, (2) express yourself in a lively manner, and (3) be a good listener.

Getting conversation started

Starting a conversation with a good friend is easy. It almost starts itself. However, when you have to carry on a conversation with someone you do not know very well, thinking of a topic sometimes seems difficult. If you begin by taking it for granted that the person is interested in many of the things that interest you, you will find yourself talking as easily as with a friend. If the other person does not start the topic of conversation, you start it. Mention or ask a question about something that has happened in school, a current movie, a television program, a book you have just read, or the chances of your basketball team winning the next game.

If you fail to get a conversation going with the first few topics you introduce, keep trying. Sooner or later you will hit upon something that will get the other person talking. Most people want to be friendly, but some of them are shy. Perhaps you are shy yourself. If so, you know how much you appreciate someone who can draw you out.

In conversations, especially in a group, you have a responsibility not only to contribute but also to listen carefully while the other members of the group are talking. To talk well, you must listen well.

Conversations should take place naturally, helped by the thoughtfulness and interest of those who take part. During the next two or three days, be alert in the conversations you engage in. Try to judge whether or not you think they were good conversations.

To discuss

On the board, make a list of things that made some of your recent conversations good and a list of those that made others poor. Discuss these lists in class.

Guides for conversation

1. Be friendly.
2. Choose interesting subjects to talk about.
3. Let your manner be easy and informal.
4. Listen carefully and intelligently to others.
5. Contribute your ideas. Encourage others to contribute their ideas.
6. If you disagree, do it pleasantly. Differences of opinion are stimulating.
7. Be polite and wait your turn to talk.
8. Develop a sense of humor.

Exercises: Judging yourself

1. It will be helpful for you to judge yourself as a conversationalist and, if you can arrange it, to have someone else judge you. There are eight guides above for being a good conversationalist. Rate yourself on each item: *1* for excellent, *2* for good, *3* for fair, and *4* for poor. Try not to be over-modest or too self-satisfied. Just be objective and state frankly your strengths and weaknesses. It might be interesting to get two or three people who know you well to rate you independently and to compare their ratings.

Use this scoring guide: 8–12, Excellent; 13–20, Good; 21–28, Fair; 29–32, Poor.

2. After you have studied the ratings, write a brief paper on the topic: "My Strengths and Weaknesses as a Conversationalist."

Joseph Banks, Grade 7

Guides	Ratings
1	2
2	3
3	1
4	1
5	2
6	3
7	2
8	4
	18—Good

Sample Score Card

Introductions

Sometimes, before a conversation can start, you will need to introduce people to each other. Since this is such a natural and courteous thing to do, you should try not to be embarrassed either by making introductions or by receiving them. The main thing is to be friendly, natural, and courteous.

Making introductions

Introductions are not difficult to make. Actually, there are only a few rules to remember.

1. Introduce a boy to a girl by mentioning the girl's name first.

   EXAMPLE: Linda, this is Al Carelton.
   Al, this is my best friend, Linda Schmidt.

2. Introduce a younger person to an older person by mentioning the older person's name first.

   EXAMPLE: Miss Morley, this is Clara Chapman, who has just entered our school. She is interested in trying out for the class play.
   Clara, this is our English teacher, Miss Morley. Miss Morley is directing our play this year.

   EXAMPLE: Mother, I'd like you to meet Donald White. He and I are working on the science project together.

3. Introduce a boy to a boy or a girl to a girl by mentioning either name first, if they are about the same age.

Avoid expressions like "Meet Glenn Barker" or "Shake hands with Glenn Barker" or "Say hello to Glenn Barker." It is better to say simply, "This is Glenn Barker" or "I'd like you to meet Glenn Barker."

For a group introduction, you may say: "Emma, I'd like you to meet Ted Anthony, Bob Short, and Charles Lockhart. Fellows, this is my cousin, Emma Norris."

Do not hesitate to introduce yourself if you are the only stranger in a group or if the one person you know is busy. You can make your introduction simply and naturally, telling something about yourself, for example, "I am Pauline Roberts. We just moved into the gray house on the corner."

Acknowledging introductions

"Hello, Gene" or "Hi, Grace" is correct to say when acknowledging an introduction, if the person being introduced is your own age. If the person is an adult, it is probably better to say, "How do you do, Mr. Smith?" You may add, "I am very glad to meet you." Avoid the worn-out expression, "Pleased to meet you."

A girl who is seated should stand if one of the persons being introduced is an adult. A girl does not have to rise when she is introduced to a boy who is standing. If a boy is seated, he should *always* rise, no matter who is being introduced.

Usually, girls do not shake hands, as men and boys always do when being introduced. However, it is courteous to shake hands with anyone who extends his hand to you in an introduction.

Introducing a topic of conversation

When you introduce two people to each other, you can be helpful by adding a friendly "icebreaker" to your introduction. An icebreaker is a topic that helps to start people off on a conversation.

> EXAMPLE: (*Introduction*) Diana, I'd like you to meet Bob Kane. This is Diana Dewees, Bob. (*Icebreaker*) Bob has just moved here from Oregon, Diana. I know you visited in Oregon last summer.

To discuss

Answer the following questions about introductions:

1. If a boy is being introduced to a girl, whose name is mentioned first? If a younger person is introduced to an older person, whose name is mentioned first?
2. Do boys stand up to be introduced? Do they shake hands?
3. Do girls stand up for an introduction? Explain. Do girls usually shake hands? When should they shake hands?
4. Why is the person who is making the introduction usually responsible for starting a conversation?
5. What topics do you think would make good icebreakers?

Introduce a boy to a girl and a younger person to an older person, mentioning the girl's or older person's name first.

Exercises: Practicing introductions

1. Act out a few introductions with icebreakers by dramatizing some of the following introductions:

1. A girl to a boy
2. Several students to one other student
3. Yourself to a group
4. Yourself to another person
5. A student to a teacher
6. A parent to your teacher
7. A schoolmate to your mother

2. Discuss the dramatizations above. How successful were the icebreakers as springboards to further conversation?

Telling a Story or Anecdote

Telling humorous or exciting stories or anecdotes about experiences you have had or know about can often contribute to a conversation. Such stories are best if they entertain the group and illustrate a point at the same time. Telling stories is an art, and an old one. Everyone enjoys listening to good stories.

Here is an example of a personal-experience story. In this story the teller tries to build some suspense. He wants his listeners to be curious about the final outcome of his experience.

I guess I have a tendency to leap into things before I think about them enough. A good example of this was the summer my family and I were camping on a saddle in Glacier National Park, Montana. The first night out, while everyone else was getting ready for bed, I decided to slip away from camp and climb—by myself—a small peak just north of the saddle.

I streaked to the top quite easily. After a quick look east and west at the magnificent scenery, I began a rapid descent. I was letting myself down a narrow crevice between two big rock surfaces when I realized that this wasn't the way down. I tried to crawl back up the crevice, but it was too steep. Below me was a narrow ledge, and I slid down onto it.

At the right end of the ledge was a sheer drop to a boulder field and, to the left, an equally dangerous drop. I was rim-rocked! All around the ledge was death—if I should fall. If I spent the night on the ledge, I'd probably freeze to death.

Then I noticed at the far left a smooth rock, leading up to the top of the peak. To get onto this rock, I would have to go beyond the ledge I was on. If I slipped, I'd fall to certain death.

Lying flat on the ledge, I gradually edged outward and upward onto the rock. I grabbed at a grass tuft but couldn't quite reach it. Just then, a pebble dislodged under the toe of my shoe. I began to slide down—slowly but surely toward the edge. I felt my feet go over, and I tried desperately to brake myself with my hands. It was no use.

Just then I noticed a little sapling growing out of a crack in the rock. I grasped it carefully to find out if it was enough to stop me. It was! I lay panting and trembling a few seconds and then started to work my way up again. This time I made it. I heaved myself over the top edge and raced down to the saddle just before dark. Never before had I been so thankful for life.

To discuss

1. What is the conflict or main problem that had to be solved in the story on page 60?

2. How does the storyteller build suspense?

3. Does the story have action? Read some sentences to illustrate your answer. Does the action lead to a *climax*, or high point of suspense?

4. Which sentences show that the storyteller has tied in his story with a conversation about rushing into something without considering the consequences? What point does he illustrate?

Guides for storytelling

1. Tie a story in with the subject of the conversation.
2. Start off quickly with an interesting sentence.
3. Avoid giving details of happenings which do not help to make the point or to set the mood of the story.
4. Use dialogue (conversation) to increase interest.
5. Build suspense, if the story allows it. Once you have the interest of the listener, then you can tell details to make the situation come alive.
6. Do not keep laughing before you tell the story. Avoid expressions such as "It was very funny" or "It was very exciting."
7. Do not interrupt your story with a repetition of *uh*'s and *and*'s.
8. When you get to the end of the story, stop.

Exercises: Telling stories

1. Come to class prepared to tell a funny story that might come up in a conversation. Show the class how the story might fit into a conversation and make clear what point it illustrates. You can practice telling your story beforehand, but do not memorize it word for word. Keep the atmosphere informal and tell your story from your seat.

2. Come to class prepared to tell a serious experience that might be used as part of a conversation. Be sure you show how it would fit into what is being discussed. For example, the story on page 60 fitted into a conversation about boats and safety.

3. Judge your own stories and those told by your classmates, using the guides listed above.

Giving a Talk

One of the most useful skills you can learn is that of giving a brief talk, or speech. An occasion when this skill might be useful to you is during election time when you have to elect club or class officers. The talks you make at election time are constructed mainly to persuade your listeners to vote for your candidate. At other times, you may be asked to give talks in class. Then your purpose will usually be to inform or to entertain. Can you think of other occasions when knowing how to give a talk might help you?

The essential thing to remember in giving a talk is to interest your listeners. If you cannot interest them, your speech will be a failure, no matter how hard you may work on it. Once you catch the interest of your listeners, you are well on your way toward achieving your purpose—*to persuade, to inform,* or *to entertain.*

There are many different ways of giving a good talk. As you consider the suggestions on the following pages, try to find the way to give a talk that works best for you.

Choosing a topic

If you have not been assigned a topic, choose one about which you have something definite to say. You will probably do best if you speak from your own experience. Do not make your topic so broad that you could not possibly cover it in the few minutes you will have for your talk. For example, "Food" or "Democracy" would probably be poor topics. Why? "My Favorite Chinese Restaurant" or "How to Improve Elections in the Seventh Grade" would probably be good ones. Why?

Getting ideas and organizing your speech

Once you have your topic, you will then need to collect ideas and information for it. If your talk is based on your own experience, your job will be to note down the ideas and happenings you want to tell. If you are speaking on a topic about which you will need to do some reading, take careful notes. (Taking notes is discussed in detail on pages 327–30.)

After you have gathered your material, you will need to organize it. The best way to do this is to make a rough outline first. Decide what the main topics are under which you wish to group your ideas.

For example, if you are giving a talk on "Living in a Small Family," perhaps you will have only two main topics:

I. Disadvantages
II. Advantages

Or perhaps you will have several, for instance:

I. Attention from Parents
II. Friendships Outside the Family
III. Birthdays and Gift-giving Holidays
IV. Mealtimes
V. Space in the House
VI. Chores

Around each of these topics you might compare the situation in a small family with that in a large family. (For more about outlining, see pages 330–31.)

The best way to proceed is to write your final outline notes on 3″ x 5″ or 5″ x 8″ cards, which can be held easily in your hand. It is a good idea to write out and memorize the first and last sentence of your talk.

You should choose the exact wording of the rest of the talk while you are speaking. Then you won't need to keep your eyes glued to your notes, and your talk will sound lively and spontaneous.

Exercise: Preparing a talk

You are now ready to begin work on a short three- or five-minute talk. Choose a topic, if you are not assigned one, and gather material for it. (The list of subjects on pages 122–24 may suggest a topic you like.) Organize your ideas in outline form.

Presenting your talk

Certainly the key to making a good speech is to have something interesting to say and to say it well and naturally. If you are nervous, you should first practice saying your talk *aloud* at home. Then when you are giving it, imagine that you are conversing with a friend. In this way, you will probably make a good talk.

As you present your talk, keep in mind that you must be heard. *If you speak to the people in the back of the room or auditorium,* your voice will be heard.

Sometimes, as you are talking, you may find yourself stuck for a word or thought. If this happens, just wait until it comes. Do not fill in the time with "uh, uh . . ." A pause is much less objectionable to a listener than a repetitious, meaningless noise.

Your body. Inexperienced speakers allow body movements and gestures to detract from what they are saying. Here are examples:

> Meaningless, repeated gestures
> Scratching your head
> Pacing back and forth or rocking from foot to foot
> Leaning against things
> Fussing with your clothes, tie, etc.

It is best, when your turn to speak comes, to walk quickly to the front of the room and wait quietly for everyone's attention before you start. Then stand firmly on both feet and deliver your talk. Use no gestures except those which will help the listeners grasp your meaning.

Your eyes. Look mainly at your listeners, not out the window, up at the ceiling, or down at the floor. Glance only occasionally at your notes. Pick out four or five people in different parts of the room and speak to them, shifting your eyes from one to another.

Exhibits and illustrations. It may help you to get your ideas across if you bring something to show: a picture or an object you are describing. If you are speaking before a chalkboard, you may wish to sketch or write some things on the board. Be sure, though, not to overdo the exhibits or they will detract from your speech.

Exercises: Giving and judging talks

1. Prepare and deliver a three- to five-minute talk on any subject.

2. Evaluate the talks you hear, judging each talk on the basis of the questions in the Check list on the next page.

Give a mark for each of the questions under the four categories. Use the following system: *1* for excellent, *2* for good, *3* for fair, and *4* for poor.

Keep a record of the name, subject, and marks of each speaker. When all the speeches have been given, gather into several small groups and discuss frankly the speech of each person in the group. Present your criticism courteously.

Check list for judging a talk

1. *Interest*
   Did the speaker know his subject?
   Did he make use of specific details?
   Did he hold your attention?
2. *Organization*
   Was the plan of the talk easy to follow?
   Did the talk have a good beginning and a good ending?
3. *Speech*
   Did the speaker articulate clearly?
   Was his pronunciation correct?
   Did his voice show variety and maintain a pleasant tone?
   Could the speaker be heard easily by all in the room?
4. *Poise*
   Did the speaker look at his audience?
   Did he avoid useless gestures and body movements?

Conducting Club Meetings

Club meetings can give you good practice in participating in group discussions. In Mrs. Shelton's class, the boys and girls wanted to form a dramatics club. Here is what happened at their first meeting—an organization meeting. Read carefully, and be prepared to discuss some questions about the meeting.

LEONARD (*acting as temporary chairman*): All of us think it would be a good idea to have a dramatics club. At this meeting the first thing to do in planning our organization is to elect a chairman.

Mrs. Shelton has asked me to take charge as temporary chairman until a chairman is elected. I will ask Miriam Stone to serve as a temporary secretary.

Nominations for chairman are in order. Miriam, will you put down the names as they are given.

PAT (*rising and addressing the chair, that is, the person in charge of the meeting*): Mr. Chairman.

LEONARD (*recognizing the speaker*): Pat.

PAT: I nominate Calvin Marks. (*The secretary records Calvin's name.*)

FRIEDA: Mr. Chairman.

LEONARD: Frieda.

FRIEDA: I nominate Jerry Ryan.

DONALD *and* PAUL (*both rising*):   Mr. Chairman.

LEONARD: Don may have the floor. (*Don had risen just a second before Paul.*)

DONALD: I nominate Betty Stark.

PAUL (*rising again*):   Mr. Chairman.

LEONARD: Paul.

PAUL: I move that nominations be closed.

LEONARD: Paul has moved that nominations be closed. Is there a second to that motion?

MARK (*after rising and addressing the chair*):   I second the motion.

LEONARD: It has been moved and seconded that nominations for chairman be closed. Is there any discussion? (*No response.*) If not, all in favor of the motion please say "Aye." (*All respond.*) All those opposed to the motion say "No." (*No response.*) The motion is carried. We'll proceed with the voting.

Our candidates for chairman are Calvin, Jerry, and Betty. Please write your choice on the ballot to be given you by Donald and Helena, who will act as tellers.

(*Tellers pass and collect ballots and count the votes, and the chair calls for their report.*)

DONALD (*rising and addressing the chair*):   The tellers submit this report. (*He hands the paper to the chairman.*)

Calvin Marks	14
Betty Stark	12
Jerry Ryan	8
Total votes cast	34

LEONARD: Calvin Marks received the most votes, so he is our chairman. Will you come and take the chair now, Calvin.

CALVIN (*coming forward and taking the chair*):   Thank you very much. I'm glad to help get the club started.

I'll ask Miriam to continue as secretary to record today's meeting.

Next in order is the appointment of a committee to draw up a constitution. I appoint Jerry, Alice, and Marion to serve as a committee to draft a simple constitution for our club.

At our next meeting, one week from today, we hope the committee will have the draft of the constitution ready for us to discuss. We'll meet in Room 104 at 3:45 P.M. The meeting is adjourned.

To discuss

1. How does a club member *address the chair?*
2. What happens if two members rise to address the chair at the same or nearly the same time?
3. How does the chairman *recognize a speaker?*
4. What is a *motion?* What words are used to *make a motion?* Must a motion be *seconded?* Must a nomination be seconded?
5. After a motion is seconded, what must the chairman ask before a vote is taken?
6. What do *tellers* do?
7. Who appoints club members to a committee?
8. Explain these terms: *meeting adjourned, have the floor, draft a constitution.*

Learn the points of procedure listed below for all club meetings. If you need to do so, first discuss them in class to be sure that everyone understands them.

Points of procedure

1. Before speaking, you should first rise, address the chair, and be recognized by the presiding officer.
2. The presiding officer is addressed as *Mr. Chairman, Mr. President, Madam Chairman,* or *Madam President.*
3. If two or more rise at the same time, the chairman usually recognizes the person who has not yet had the floor or who has not spoken for some time.
4. Nominations do not need to be seconded.
5. A motion, a proposal to do something, must be seconded before it can be discussed. Otherwise, the motion is dead.
6. The chairman repeats the motion before he calls for a second. If discussion of the motion is long, he repeats it again before calling for a vote on it.
7. If someone wants to change part of a motion, he does so by offering an *amendment,* like this: "I would like to amend the motion to read 'one play instead of two.'" The amendment must be seconded and passed by vote before the original motion is voted on. It then becomes part of the original motion.
8. The chairman does not vote unless there is a tie vote.

Keeping minutes

The secretary is the record keeper of the club. She will take notes of all that occurs in any regular or called meeting. Later she should prepare a report of the meeting from these notes. These are called the *minutes of a meeting*.

Read the following minutes:

March 16, 19__

The weekly meeting of the Drama Club was called to order Tuesday, March 16, at 3:00 P.M., by President Calvin Marks.

The minutes of the previous meeting were read and approved.

Old Business: Pam Taylor, Chairman of the Properties Committee, reported that all the animals borrowed for the recent production of Skippy's Family have been returned to their homes. The secretary read the letter of thanks to be sent to Jack Smith's brother Jerry for the use of his car and his help in returning the animals.

New Business: Brian McLean made a motion that a collection be taken to buy Jerry Smith a pair of trousers to replace those damaged by Mr. Rufus Scott's spaniel Alphonse. The motion was carried. The president appointed Martha Reeves of the Flower and Gift Committee to make the arrangements.

The meeting was adjourned at 3:45 P.M.

Respectfully submitted,

Miriam Stone

Miriam Stone, Secretary

If the secretary is a secretary-treasurer, she also keeps the financial records, either filing them in a separate treasurer's book or in her secretary's book.

Order of a meeting

In order for a club meeting to accomplish its purpose in an orderly and democratic way, it must follow a certain plan. Such a plan has been the result of many years of experience in conducting meetings of all kinds. It is known as the *order of a meeting*, or *parliamentary procedure*.

1. The chairman calls the meeting to order.
2. The secretary records absences.
3. The secretary reads the minutes of the last meeting. This is followed by correction or approval of them.
4. Old business: unfinished business and reports of committees appointed earlier.
5. New business: motions to consider new problems, followed by discussion and vote; appointment of new committees.
6. Adjournment.

The chairman may declare a member *out of order* if there is a departure from this procedure.

Opening the meeting

Certain words and expressions have come into common use, and the chairman and members of a group learn to use the accepted language.

Read this sample of the way a meeting is opened and be prepared to discuss it:

CHAIRMAN: The meeting will please come to order. (*In a small group, the secretary then records the number present and absent. In a formal organization, the chairman may ask for a roll call.*)

CHAIRMAN: The secretary will please read the minutes of the last meeting. (*The secretary reads the minutes.*)

Are there any corrections? (*Pause for response.*)

If there are no corrections, the minutes stand approved as read. (*If corrections are suggested, the secretary makes them, and the chairman proceeds.*)

The minutes stand approved as corrected.

Is there any unfinished business to be brought before the meeting?

SAM (*after being given the floor*): The committee on play selection is ready to make its report.

Discussing a motion

The following section of a club meeting shows how to handle discussion:

CHAIRMAN: The motion has been made and seconded that the program committee plan a one-act play for our final meeting, Tuesday, May 29. Is there any discussion of that motion?

DAVID (*after being given the floor*): Isn't our last meeting a business meeting? How can we invite an audience to a business meeting? How can we give a play?

(*The speakers are given the floor one by one as they rise. This means that the chairman must recognize each speaker before he can take part in the discussion.*)

ALBERT: There's no reason why we can't have a called meeting [*special meeting*] to take care of any final business.

LISA: I don't see how we'll have time to get up a play, with all the final exams. There's so much work to do!

FRED: Well, what if there is some extra work? We ought to be willing to do a little extra work in order to give the club a bang-up final meeting. Anyway, it'll be up to the members of the cast to decide.

CHAIRMAN: If there is no further discussion, I'll *put the motion*. It has been moved and seconded that the program committee plan a one-act play for our last meeting, Tuesday, May 29. All in favor of this motion please say "Aye." (*A chorus of "Aye."*) All opposed say "No." (*Pause.*) The ayes have it; the motion is carried.

To discuss

Answer the following questions:

1. Does a motion need a second?
2. How does a member get the attention of the chair?
3. As a member of a club, how can you propose some action?
4. When is discussion permissible?
5. What does each of the following expressions mean?

address the chair	make an amendment
given the floor	minutes approved as read
put a motion	minutes approved as corrected
called meeting	declared out of order
old business	new business

You need to know your responsibilities if you become chairman, if you get up to speak, or if you are merely a listener and voter.

Points to remember

The presiding officer . . .

1. Presents the topic or problem clearly.
2. Decides who is to have the floor.
3. Takes no part in the actual discussion.
4. Conceals his own feelings or opinions.
5. Keeps the discussion directed toward a decision.
6. Summarizes the main points at the close. If the discussion concerned a motion, he puts the question to a vote.

A club member . . .

1. Listens with courtesy to each speaker.
2. Weighs the facts and opinions expressed.
3. Speaks only when he has been given the floor.
4. Speaks only when he has an idea to contribute.
5. Raises intelligent questions to clear up misunderstanding or brings out new angles of the problem.
6. Takes only his fair share of time and attention.
7. Avoids a personal argument with another member.
8. Sticks to the topic or problem.

Exercise: Practicing parliamentary procedure

Take turns dramatizing the following, with your teacher acting as chairman for the first three items:

1. Make and discuss a motion to invite parents to a program you are planning.
2. Make and discuss a motion to rent costumes and props for the club play.
3. Make a motion that your class have monthly dues for minor expenses in presenting a play. Carry through the steps of making the motion, seconding it, discussing it, and voting on it.
4. Carry through the steps of opening a meeting, approving and passing the minutes of the last meeting, and asking for a committee report.

A Book to Read

These Happy Golden Years
by Laura Ingalls Wilder
Illustrated by Garth Williams
Harper & Row, Publishers

How would you like to be only fifteen years old and on your way to teach school in an abandoned shanty in a strange community? Not only that, what if you did not know *how* to teach school? That is the situation that confronted Laura, the oldest girl in a pioneer family in the Dakota Territory many years ago. But Laura, in the true pioneer spirit, conquered homesickness, mischievous pupils, a schoolhouse with cracks so wide the snow blew in, and weather so cold she once almost froze to death.

The next year, Laura taught in a bright new schoolhouse, Almanzo Wilder became her "best beau," and sleigh rides, picnics, singing lessons, and, best of all, helping Almanzo "break in" a pair of wild colts provided fun and excitement. Then Laura and Almanzo fall in love. What happens next you will learn when you read this story of a hardy, happy pioneer family.

About the author

Laura Ingalls Wilder began life in a log house in Wisconsin and later traveled West, where she married. You will enjoy all the stories she wrote about life on the prairies in the early days of our country.

Mastery Tests

Test I

Match the words on the left with the words related to them on the right. On your paper, write the letter of each item beside the correct numeral.

1. pitch
2. volume
3. tone
4. inflection
5. good articulation
6. good pronunciation

a. expressiveness
b. highness or lowness
c. clear consonant sounds
d. harshness or smoothness
e. loudness or softness
f. correct sounds

Test II

Number your paper from 1 to 5. In introducing the following people to each other, whose name do you mention first?

1. A boy and a girl of about the same age
2. A teacher and a girl
3. A girl to another girl
4. Your father to Miss Curtis, your English teacher
5. Yourself to a group

Test III

Answer each of the following questions in one or two sentences. Write the answers next to the appropriate numerals on your paper.

1. What does telling a story have to do with conversation?
2. How do you start a good story?
3. What kind of details do you include in a good story?
4. How does dialogue help to make a story interesting?

Test IV

Answer each of the following questions in one or two sentences. Write the answers next to the appropriate numerals on your paper.

1. What are three general purposes for giving talks?
2. What are two things to remember in choosing a topic for a talk?
3. What are two ways of collecting information for talks?
4. What should you memorize before presenting your talk?

Review and Practice

Exercise I

1. Review the lessons on voice and speech on pages 45–47.

2. Name four important characteristics of voice.

3. In class, take turns reading aloud each sentence below in one of four strongly expressive ways: *doubt, anger, astonishment, enjoyment.* First announce to the class which feeling you want to express; then read the sentence.

1. Did we win the argument?
2. They printed it in the newspaper.
3. Have you come back again?
4. I would like to believe you.

Exercise II

1. Review the section on "Introductions" on pages 57–59.

2. On your paper, list only the items below which apply to making and acknowledging introductions correctly.

1. A boy should always rise when being introduced.
2. Avoid expressions such as "Meet Joe Short."
3. A girl should always rise when being introduced.
4. Girls never shake hands.
5. Boys usually shake hands when being introduced to another boy or man.
6. Say the girl's name first when introducing a boy to a girl.
7. Mention the older person's name first when introducing a younger person to an older person.
8. It is courteous to shake hands with anyone who extends his hand to you in an introduction.

Exercise III

1. Review "Telling a Story or Anecdote" on pages 60 and 62.
2. List five guides for telling a good story.
3. Prepare and tell a story or anecdote in class.

Exercise IV

1. Review "Giving a Talk" on pages 63–66.
2. List the similarities between giving a good talk and telling a good story. List the differences.

CHAPTER 3

Nouns: What They Are and What They Do

Any subject can be studied more easily if the elements that go into it are organized and classified. This is true of electricity, carpentry, sewing, or cooking. It is also true of language.

For convenience, linguists (experts on language) have traditionally organized words into eight main *classes* called **parts of speech.** A word, *when it is used in a sentence,* can be assigned to one of these parts of speech. Their names are **noun, pronoun, verb, adjective, adverb, preposition, conjunction,** and **interjection.**

To see how much you remember from previous study of grammar, look at the eight short lists below. Each is made up of words belonging to only one of the parts of speech. Can you identify them?

1. do, believe, terrify
2. into, from, at
3. quickly, now, always
4. zoo, animal, kindness
5. Oh! Aha! Ouch!
6. you, I, theirs
7. big, beautiful, good
8. and, or, because

Nouns

There are more nouns in our language than any other part of speech. Here are four sentences, each with a missing noun. Can you suggest a noun for each blank?

1. The sporting goods store is next to a football __?__.
2. __?__, the owner, is interested in all our games.
3. He says that a good athlete must have a lot of __?__.
4. He gave our team the money for some new __?__.

A noun is a word that names a *person,* a *place,* or a *thing.* How many nouns can you give for the persons, places, and things in the picture on the opposite page?

Of course, the word *thing* has a rather broad and indefinite meaning, for almost anything could be considered a "thing." If you use the sentence: "(A) __?__ is a thing I know about," any word that will go in the blank is a noun.

Nouns can name things you can see and touch: *box, brick, bison, ball, bat.* These are called **concrete nouns.** They also can name things you cannot touch or see: ideas, qualities, or amounts. Examples are *imagination, silence, thought, sound, week, quantity, love.* These are called **abstract nouns.**

■ A **noun** is a word that names.

Exercises: Recognizing nouns

1. Make a list of twelve concrete nouns that you can see now. In another list, give six abstract nouns that you can think of.

2. Name the nouns in the following sentences. There are twenty-one of them.

1. Molly opened her heavy purse and took out four coins.
2. "Imagination and faith are needed to do this job," said John to his mother.
3. Too many cooks spoil the broth.
4. George and Margaret were in costume.
5. Pennsylvania is a state full of history, culture, and politics.
6. George Washington was the father of his country.

3. Here are ten sentences with blanks where nouns are required. Copy each sentence, supplying a noun for each of the twenty-four blanks.

1. My __?__ won the __?__.
2. __?__ is my favorite __?__.
3. Under the __?__, we saw four __?__.
4. Four __?__ rushed into his __?__.
5. __?__, __?__, and __?__ were seen on the __?__.
6. It requires great __?__ to defeat a __?__.
7. Down the __?__ and into the __?__ came __?__, followed by his __?__.
8. Those __?__ make so much __?__ that we cannot hear you.
9. The __?__ are causing great __?__.
10. While staying at __?__, I met __?__.

Two Characteristics of Nouns

There are two facts about nouns which can help you to recognize a noun when you see one.

1. Most nouns can be changed from *singular* (one) to *plural* (two or more) by adding *s* or *es* to the singular form.

> SINGULAR: book   glass
>
> PLURAL: books   glasses

Look at this list of ten words. Only six of the words are nouns which can be made plural by adding *s*. Can you tell which ones they are? Try each word in the blank of this sentence: "There are two ___?___." If the word fits, it is a noun.

said	dog	writer	spaceship	sad
tall	rabbit	rapidly	astronaut	language

2. Many nouns can be made to *show possession* by adding an apostrophe and *s* or an apostrophe alone.

NOUN	SHOWS POSSESSION
Jack	*Jack's* shoelace
ladies	*ladies'* hairdresser

Jack's and *ladies'* are called **possessive nouns**.

The two numbered statements above are true only of nouns. No other part of speech has these characteristics.

Exercises: Recognizing nouns

1. Here is a list of twelve words. On the basis of whether or not a word can be made plural by adding *s* or *es*, decide which words can be used as nouns.

1. stone	4. blade	7. flood	10. between
2. box	5. thought	8. stupid	11. obvious
3. beautifully	6. think	9. heater	12. plate

2. Here are twelve more words. On the basis of whether or not a word can show possession, decide which words are nouns.

1. Bob	4. always	7. glorify	10. explorer
2. monkey	5. pretty	8. dogs	11. cruel
3. book	6. they	9. soldiers	12. chicken

Forming the Plural of Nouns

Even though most nouns form the plural simply by adding *s* or *es*, the nouns which form the plural in other ways can sometimes cause some spelling problems. Such nouns as *man—men, goose—geese, mouse—mice* are exceptions to the general rule. Perhaps the only way to be sure of how a noun forms its plural is to look it up in a dictionary. If it forms the plural simply by adding *s* or *es*, no plural will be shown. If the plural is formed irregularly, it will be shown in the dictionary entry.

Since you will not always have time to consult a dictionary, here are a few useful *rules for the formation of plurals*:

1. Most nouns form the plural by adding *s.*

   playground—playground**s**   magazine—magazine**s**

2. Nouns that end in *s, ss, sh, ch,* and *x* add *es:*

   fox—fox**es**   gas—gas**es**
   church—church**es**   pass—pass**es**
   bush—bush**es**

3. Nouns that end in *y* preceded by a consonant, change *y* to *i* and add *es:*

   fly—fl**ies**   pansy—pans**ies**
   courtesy—courtes**ies**   entry—entr**ies**

4. Nouns that end in *y* preceded by a vowel, simply add *s:*

   toy—toy**s**   donkey—donkey**s**
   valley—valley**s**   day—day**s**

5. Some nouns ending in *o* add only *s:*

   radio—radio**s**   rodeo—rodeo**s**   soprano—soprano**s**

   Some add *es:*

   echo—echo**es**   tomato—tomato**es**   potato—potato**es**

   Others add *s* or *es:*

   cargo—cargo**s**, cargo**es**
   volcano—volcano**s**, volcano**es**

6. Many nouns ending in *f* or *fe* change *f* to *v* and add *es*:

loaf—loa*ves*	thief—thie*ves*
life—li*ves*	wolf—wol*ves*

There are a few exceptions. Some merely add *s*:

belief—belief**s**	safe—safe**s**
dwarf—dwarf**s**	roof—roof**s**

7. In addition, there are a few common and highly irregular plurals:

ox—ox*en*	tooth—t*ee*th
woman—wom*en*	man—m*en*
child—child*ren*	mouse—m*ice*

8. Further, there are a few nouns that have the same form for the singular and plural:

sheep—sheep	deer—deer
moose—moose	

9. It is sometimes difficult to know how to form the plural of compound words written either hyphenated or as two words. The safest thing to do is to consult a dictionary. However, here are a few of the most common types. Notice that the most important word takes the plural ending.

father**s**-in-law	passer**s**-by
looker**s**-on	tap-dancer**s**
old-timer**s**	

Exercise: Writing the plural of nouns

Write the plural of the following nouns. If in doubt, consult a dictionary.

1. box	9. piano	17. mother-in-law
2. reply	10. shelf	18. constitution
3. play	11. library	19. pigeon
4. echo	12. dish	20. assembly
5. wolf	13. tray	21. patch
6. roof	14. hero	22. glass
7. deer	15. thief	23. foot
8. cushion	16. louse	24. child

Forming the Possessive of Nouns

The rules for forming the possessive of nouns are simple, but they can sometimes cause trouble. When two nouns come next to each other and the first ends in **s,** it is probably a possessive:

Bob's hat   a cat's claws

Sometimes an adjective or two may come between the possessive noun and the noun possessed:

Bob's queer hat   a cat's sharp claws

To form the possessive:

1. If the noun does not end in **s,** add an apostrophe and an **s:**

that girl's dress   the children's sleigh

Note: The noun *children* is plural without an **s.** The noun *men* (men's) and *women* (women's) are plural also.

2. If the noun ends in **s,** add only an apostrophe:

the students' committee   the animals' trainers

Note: Most nouns that end in **s** are plural nouns. However, there are a few that are singular, for example: *lass, waitress,* and *Charles,* and they form their possessive with an apostrophe and **s:** *the lass's bonnet, the waitress's wages, Charles's speech.*

A singular noun which shows possession is called the **singular possessive** form.

A plural noun which shows possession is called the **plural possessive** form.

Exercises: *Writing the possessive of nouns*

1. Write the singular possessive and plural possessive for each noun below. Use each in a phrase to show what is possessed.

EXAMPLE: 1. pirate

YOU WRITE: *1. the pirate's dagger*
                 the pirates' ship

1. dog	3. rabbit	5. teacher	7. policeman
2. man	4. cousin	6. child	8. government

2. Write the singular possessive of the following proper nouns, using each in a phrase:

1. Bob	4. Mildred
2. Alice	5. Francis
3. James	6. Phyllis

3. Copy and punctuate correctly the nouns in parentheses, making each one possessive. If a noun ends in *s,* be sure to notice whether it is singular or plural.

1. (George) goldfish died.
2. An (author) typewriter is an important tool to him.
3. Those four (horses) bits are too loose.
4. The (geese) pond dried up during last (summer) drought.
5. The (children) toys are scattered around (Charles) garden.
6. (Napoleon) dictatorial habits aroused the (citizens) anger.
7. The (women) cakes won the (judges) approval.
8. The (students) desks were arranged according to (Mrs. Jones) wishes.
9. Who knows that (waitress) address?
10. The (astronaut) message reached millions of people.

Noun Signals

A red light at a traffic intersection signals *stop.* The gesture of a baseball coach may signal a runner to steal a base or a batter to bunt. A pitch drop and pause in speech are the signal for the end of a sentence. Life and language are filled with signals.

Frequently in English, certain words signal that a noun is coming. Read the following two items. Notice the words that come before the italicized nouns.

1. For want of a *nail,* the *shoe* was lost;
   For want of the *shoe,* the *horse* was lost;
   For want of the *horse,* the *rider* was lost.

ANONYMOUS

2. An *apple* thrown by a jealous *goddess* caused the famous *Trojan War.*

All of the italicized nouns in the passages above are introduced or signaled by one of three words. What are the three?

You will never see *the, an,* or *a* in a sentence without finding a noun following immediately, or after a word or two. In item 1 on page 83 the nouns come immediately after the *a* and *the.* In item 2 an adjective comes between the signal and two of the nouns. Can you name the adjectives?

A, an, and *the* are commonly called **articles,** which are a special kind of adjective.

Of course, nouns frequently are not preceded by *a, an,* or *the,* as in this sentence: *"Cats* eat *mice* and *rats* for *breakfast, lunch,* and *dinner."* However, whenever you do see *a, an,* or *the* in a sentence, you can be sure a noun will follow. Therefore, these words are called **noun signals.** They signal that a noun is coming.

■ The articles *a, an,* and *the* are **noun signals.**

Exercises: Noun signals

1. Test the following list of words by trying them with the noun signals *a, an,* or *the* and tell which of them can be used as nouns. Your ear will help you decide.

treaty	~~suggest~~
automobile	imagination
~~absolutely~~	suggestion
~~stewed~~	~~honorable~~
painting	Arab

2. Name the noun signals below. Put in parentheses after each one the noun it signals. Do not list any words that come between the noun signal and the noun.

1. The lightning struck a tall tree and the barn next to it.
2. A customer entered the small shop and bought an antique.
3. The entire family and a governess will arrive tomorrow on the four o'clock plane.
4. A small group of farmers got together and devised a plan to save the crops.
5. On Saturday we gave her a complicated puzzle, an interesting game, and a frightening-looking stuffed animal.

3. There are two nouns in the sentences above that do not have the noun signals *a, an,* or *the.* Which two are they?

FROM *The Village Blacksmith*

Each morning sees some task begin,
  Each evening sees it close;
Something attempted, something done,
  Has earned a night's repose.

HENRY WADSWORTH LONGFELLOW

This famous American poet once said that he was "better pleased with those pieces [of literature] which touch the feelings and improve the heart." Much of his poetry reflects this feeling. Many of his poems are romantic stories that are also designed to instruct and inspire the reader. What is he telling you in the four lines above? You may want to find and read the entire poem.

85

Common and Proper Nouns

Read the two lists below:

building   Chrysler Building
person   William Shakespeare
organization   National Association of Manufacturers
event   World War II
city   Tallahassee
nation   Finland

The nouns in the first list are **common nouns;** those in the second list are **proper nouns.** By studying the two lists, can you tell the difference between proper and common nouns?

You see that the noun *building* names any object that could be defined as a building. However, the noun *Chrysler Building* is the name of a particular building. The common noun *person* names any person; the proper noun *William Shakespeare* names a particular person.

Did you notice that some nouns contain more than one word?

■ A **proper noun** names a particular person, place, or thing; it is always capitalized. Any other noun is a **common noun.**

Exercises: Common and proper nouns

1. Under the headings *Common Nouns* and *Proper Nouns*, list the nouns in the following sentences:

1. The state of Louisiana is shaped like a boot, with its toe in the waters of the Gulf of Mexico.
2. It lies at the lower end of the Mississippi Valley.
3. One newspaper, the *Monitor*, was established before 1803, the year of the Louisiana Purchase.
4. By the state constitution, legislative power is vested in a General Assembly.
5. Mardi Gras occurs in late February or early March.
6. It expresses the carnival spirit of the Louisianians.
7. Tulane University is located in New Orleans.
8. During the War of 1812, Andrew Jackson turned back the British invasion of Louisiana at the Battle of New Orleans.

2. For each common noun below, write a proper noun.

EXAMPLE: 1. dog

YOU WRITE: *1. Lassie*

     1. river   6. book
     2. ship   7. day
     3. city   8. language
     4. person   9. organization
     5. school   10. trade name

3. For each proper noun below, write a common noun that tells what it is.

EXAMPLE: 1. the Declaration of Independence

YOU WRITE: *1. document*

     1. Oklahoma   6. the Mississippi
     2. Chevrolet   7. the *Queen Mary*
     3. Sahara   8. December
     4. *The Swiss Family Robinson*   9. the Constitution
     5. Central Junior High School   10. Africa

GOING AHEAD

Rewrite the following sentences, changing each common noun to a proper noun and each proper noun to a common noun.

EXAMPLE: 1. Miss Perkins read that poem to us.

YOU WRITE: *1. The teacher read "The Highwayman" to us.*

1. Our horse fell on the street and injured Dr. Southern.
2. Mrs. Jones told her son to stop reading that adventure story and go to the store.
3. The river flooded the city and destroyed Mike Hatch's old car.
4. In the hospital Sally Spencer met her aunt, who gave her a book and a game.
5. Dr. Smithers lives in Custer House beside the Columbia River and seldom sees his friends.

Mother, father, uncle, aunt

Pupils often have difficulty deciding whether or not to capitalize *mother, father, uncle, aunt,* or other words describing family relationship. The words should be capitalized when they are used as the *name* of the person, for example, "I love *Mother*, but I'm not fond of *Uncle* Jack." They should not be capitalized when they are merely naming the relationship, "I love my *mother*, but I'm not fond of my *uncle*." In the first sentence, *Mother* is the name you are calling her; in the second, the word merely shows the relationship.

For more examples, study the capitalization in these sentences:

NAME: Please, *Dad*, let me go.
RELATIONSHIP: I asked my *dad* to let me go.

NAME: I always love to see *Aunt Martha*.
RELATIONSHIP: I always love to see my *aunt*.

Note: Usually words such as *mother* and *father* are not capitalized when they follow the articles *a, an,* or *the* or the words *my, your, our, their, her,* and *his.*

Capitalize the words **mother, father,** and other words showing relationship only if they are used as the name or part of the name you are calling the person.

Exercise: Capitalizing correctly

Copy correctly the sentences below which need changes in capitalization. Write *correct* beside the numerals of those which do not.

1. I am glad to see you, Uncle.
2. He asked my mother to let him go.
3. Come here, father.
4. Oh, aunt Emily, look at this!
5. George loved his mother and father.
6. I shall give mother a present on her birthday and then go bowling with my Father.
7. There is uncle Harry talking with father and mother.
8. To me, lots of uncles and aunts make for a jolly life.
9. "Where are Auntie, Uncle, and Mamma?" asked my father.
10. All the fathers gathered to honor uncle Jack.

Nouns As Subjects and Direct Objects

Earlier, you have studied simple subjects of sentences. In this lesson, you will see that these simple subjects are often nouns. You will also learn about another use of nouns.

Here are three sentences in each of which the action of the verb is complete. The simple subject noun is underlined once and the verb twice.

1. The <u>students</u> <u>gathered</u>.   2. The <u>tide</u> <u>rose</u>.
3. Those <u>actors</u> <u>rehearsed</u>.

Notice that no other word is needed in each sentence above to complete its meaning. In many sentences, however, the subject noun and verb alone do not make much sense. Something more is needed to tell *who* or *what* received the action of the verb. For example, if you write, "<u>John</u> <u>makes</u>," you need another part of the sentence to complete the meaning. Otherwise, you think, "John makes *what?*" So your sentence would read:

John makes *candy*. (or) John makes too much *noise*.

In the two sentences above, *candy* and *noise* are nouns which are called the objects of the verb, or the **direct objects.** In each sentence we have a *doer* (John), an *action* (makes), and a *receiver* of the action (candy, noise).

Now study these examples:

SUBJECT (doer)	VERB (action)	DIRECT OBJECT (receiver)
1. That <u>girl</u>	<u>sewed</u>	a <u>seam</u>.
2. <u>Thrushes</u>	<u>sing</u>	<u>songs</u>.
3. The <u>comedian</u>	<u>told</u>	many funny <u>stories</u>.

Direct objects may or may not have modifiers. Can you name the modifiers of the direct object in sentence 3 above?

(For study and practice in diagraming, turn to page 391.)

■ A noun that follows a verb of action and receives the action expressed by the verb is called a **direct object.**
■ A noun can be used as **simple subject** or **direct object.**

Exercises: Uses of nouns

1. Name the direct objects (receivers of the action) in the following sentences. Do not include the modifiers.

1. The teacher scolded the boys.
2. A terrible fog stopped traffic.
3. Underneath his coat, Joe wore red coveralls.
4. The cook quickly prepared our dinner.
5. The students elected my best friend.
6. Her uncle bounced the baby on his knee.
7. The caretaker buried the dead squirrels.
8. The mother lion called her cubs.

2. Name the simple subject noun in each sentence above.

3. For each blank, a sentence element is needed. Supply the element and tell whether it is a subject, verb, or direct object.

1. Their pitcher threw a fast __?__.
2. Larry __?__ the ball into left field.
3. The __?__ of the crowd excited our mascot.
4. Zeke caught the __?__ between his jaws.
5. He __?__ three bases before reaching home plate.
6. Our __?__ lost the last __?__ of the season.

Sentence Patterns

All English sentences are built upon a very few basic patterns which are repeated over and over with different words and meanings. These sentence patterns can be seen more easily if we substitute certain symbols for the parts of speech. Since you have now studied two parts of speech, *nouns* and *verbs*, learn the following symbols for them:

N = Noun

V = Action verb

These symbols are combined below to show two typical English sentence patterns. They are put together in the same order in which nouns and verbs often appear in sentences.

SENTENCE PATTERN 1: N V

SENTENCE PATTERN 2: N V N

In the sample sentences below, notice that in a Pattern 1 sentence there is a subject and a verb. In a Pattern 2 sentence there is a subject, a verb, and a direct object.

SENTENCE PATTERN 1	SENTENCE PATTERN 2
Parakeets fly.	Jerry likes hash.
An officer arrived.	Mom watched the program.
Pauline fell.	The comedian told a joke.

The noun signals *a*, *an*, and *the* have been added to some of the sentences above. These words do not change the basic pattern of a sentence.

● Write these two headings at the top of your paper: *Sentence Pattern 1, Sentence Pattern 2.* Under each heading, write ten sentences that follow the pattern. You may use the noun signals *a*, *an*, and *the* in some of your sentences. Remember that noun signals do not change the basic pattern of a sentence.

● Write additional sentences of your own, following the groups of symbols below. After each sentence, write which pattern the sentence follows, *Pattern 1* or *Pattern 2.*

1. A N V
2. The N V N
3. The N V
4. A N V the N
5. The N V an N
6. N V a N

Subject Complements

A noun often follows a verb of being. Study the following example sentences:

1. My uncle was the president.
2. The building next to ours is a church.
3. Our little dog is a dachshund.
4. The clown in our circus will be Paul.

Each verb of being above *links* two nouns together that mean the same person or thing. That is why verbs of being are called **linking verbs** in sentences such as these.

Notice that the word *president* is the same person as the subject *uncle* in sentence 1. In sentence 2, the word *church* means the same thing as *building*.

The nouns *president* and *church* are called **subject complements** because they mean the same person or thing as the subject. Another name for these nouns is **predicate noun.**

What are the subject complements in sentences 3 and 4?

(You may want to study and practice diagraming. If so, turn to Chapter 15, "Making Sentence Diagrams," pages 392–93.)

▪ A noun that follows a verb of being and means the same person or thing as the subject is called a **subject complement.**

Exercise: Naming subject complements

Name the subject complements (or predicate nouns) in the sentences listed below:

1. The bus driver was Mr. Perkins.
2. The largest vehicle on the lot was the bus.
3. This package is a present for Annie.
4. That boy will be a leader.
5. The campers on the other side are boy scouts.
6. The contents of the bottle is poison.
7. Patricia has been champion for two years.
8. On stage Lester is a good actor.
9. My favorite book is *Treasure Island.*
10. After the show the only ones in the auditorium were the ushers.

Appositive Nouns

Nouns are frequently used in expressions that explain someone or something, as in the following sentences:

1. We invited our next-door neighbor, _Mrs. Patton._
2. Hans Christian Andersen, _a famous Danish writer,_ is the author of these fairy tales.

The expression _a famous Danish writer_ explains who Hans Christian Andersen is just as _Mrs. Patton_ explains who the next-door neighbor is. These expressions are called **appositives;** they consist of an **appositive noun,** underlined in the examples above, which may or may not have modifiers.

Which appositive noun in the examples above has modifiers? Which words are the modifiers?

The word _apposition_ means "placed next to." Appositives are placed next to the nouns they explain. Can you tell how they are set off from the rest of the sentence?

■ An **appositive noun** is placed next to another noun in a sentence to explain it.

Separate the appositive, plus any modifiers, from the rest of the sentence with one or two commas, as needed.

Exercise: Punctuating appositives

Copy the following sentences on your paper, punctuating each sentence correctly. Underline the appositive noun in each sentence.

1. There is Mr. Miller our superintendent.
2. The plane a new jet liner streaked across the sky.
3. The redcap an elderly gentleman offered to carry our bags.
4. Poochie Clara's little dog ran through our garden.
5. We received a pep talk from Charlie our team captain.
6. My favorite uncle Uncle Joe is now living with us.
7. I plan to invite Dorothy Banks the new girl in school.
8. The first speaker a doctor looked quite uncomfortable.
9. On Sunday we listened to _La Traviata_ my favorite opera.
10. The clothes costumes for our play were at the cleaner's.

Sentence Patterns

You have studied the symbols for nouns and for action verbs. A third symbol is **V^be**, which stands for verbs of being when they are used to connect a subject with a subject complement; that is, when they are used as *linking verbs*.

$$N = \text{Noun}$$
$$V = \text{Action verb}$$
$$V^{be} = \text{Verb of being (linking verb)}$$

With the symbol **V^be**, we can introduce a third sentence pattern. You have already worked with the first two listed below:

SENTENCE PATTERN 1:   N V   Warren giggles.

SENTENCE PATTERN 2:   N V N   Clara Green married Frank.

SENTENCE PATTERN 3:   N V^be N   Pyramids are tombs.

In Pattern 3, notice that a verb of being links the subject with a noun that means the same thing as the subject. This pattern always contains a subject complement.

Here are other examples of Pattern 3 sentences. Remember, the addition of noun signals does not change the pattern.

SENTENCE PATTERN 3:   N V^be N

A fireman was the hero.

The building is a monument.

The teachers were chaperones.

● Write five sentences following Sentence Pattern 3. Each sentence should have a subject, a verb, and a subject complement noun.

● Here are fifteen groups of symbols based on the three sentence patterns above. For each one, write an interesting sentence that makes sense. Except for the noun signals, do not use the same word more than once in this exercise. Next to each sentence, write *1, 2,* or *3* to show whether the sentence follows *Pattern 1, 2,* or *3*.

1. *The* N V N
2. *The* N V
3. N V *a* N
4. *A* N V
5. N V^be *a* N
6. N V^be *the* N
7. N V *the* N
8. N V^be *an* N
9. *A* N V *a* N
10. *The* N V^be *a* N
11. *A* N V^be *the* N
12. *An* N V *the* N
13. *The* N V^be *an* N
14. *A* N V *the* N
15. *The* N V *a* N

✓ Check Test 4: Capitalization and punctuation

Take this test to see whether you need to review the rules for using capital letters and punctuation marks in letters and outlines.

A. Write this letter correctly:

9 glenwood terrace arden montana october 5 19—
dear michael i am giving a columbus day party on tuesday october 12 can you be here for the party at 3 o clock we have missed you since you moved across town your friend james

B. Copy the following section of an outline. Use punctuation marks and capital letters where they are needed.

I   columbus's journey to america
   a   financial backing
   b   preparation for the trip
   c   hardships of the trip
II   the discovery of america

If you made any mistakes in the Check Test above, you will find the rules for capitalization and punctuation with practice exercises on pages 419–28 in the Review Handbook.

Test I

On your paper, copy the nouns from the following paragraph. There are twenty nouns in all.

Captain Lewis and Captain Clark were natives of Virginia. They were firm friends, able scouts, and fearless explorers. Their famous expedition consisted of two captains and twenty-seven men. The whole party left St. Louis in three boats and traveled slowly up the Missouri River. Sometimes they left the boats and made inland trips. Finally the explorers reached the Pacific Ocean, where the roaring breakers were a welcome sound.

Test II

1. On your paper, write each of these nouns and form its plural:

1. automobile	8. roof	15. kiss
2. brother-in-law	9. crutch	16. tooth
3. valley	10. glass	17. potato
4. echo	11. city	18. porch
5. deer	12. ox	19. woman
6. house	13. foot	20. monkey
7. knife	14. soprano	

2. Write the singular possessive and the plural possessive for each of the nouns below:

1. bed	6. Negro
2. mouse	7. church
3. cow	8. car
4. class	9. sheep
5. woman	10. day

Test III

Copy each article below and the noun that it signals. Do not copy any words that come between the article and the noun.

1. The best time of the day is the hour before dinner.
2. The alarm clock that wakes me up has a horrible sound.
3. An enormous cake greeted the wedding couple.
4. The guests cheered, and a huge white balloon soared off into the sky.

Test IV

1. Below you will find a list of nouns; some are proper nouns and some are common nouns. On your paper, make two columns headed *Common Nouns* and *Proper Nouns*. Put each of the words in its correct column.

1. June	6. brand name
2. school	7. politician
3. England	8. Rockies
4. store	9. Asia
5. astronaut	10. World War II

2. The words *mother, father, uncle,* and *aunt* are in some instances used as proper nouns in the following sentences and should be capitalized. Copy the sentences on your paper, capitalizing these words only when they are used as proper nouns.

1. Please, mother, may I go with uncle Matthew?
2. My mother said that aunt Beatrice will visit us today.
3. Larry's father called dad on the telephone.
4. Oh, father, let's hurry, or we'll miss seeing your uncle.

Test V

On your paper, copy the nouns in the following sentences. Tell how each one is used in the sentence by writing one of these basic sentence parts next to it: *simple subject, direct object,* or *subject complement.*

1. These campers are new members.
2. My neighbors have bought an old house.
3. Our little puppy won't eat his dinner.
4. His behavior has been a problem.
5. Their only protection was a small fire.

Test VI

Copy the following sentences on your paper, punctuating each one correctly. Underline the appositive noun in each sentence.

1. Did you see Mrs. Farmer our new landlady?
2. Lassie the dog on TV is a beautiful animal.
3. The jet a new design in aeronautics looks like a bird.
4. Take this card to Mr. Helman your new supervisor.

Review and Practice

Exercise I

1. Review the lessons on nouns on pages 77–79.

2. Write the headings *Concrete Nouns* and *Abstract Nouns* on your paper. Write each of the following nouns under the proper heading:

1. idea	7. dime	13. meal
2. hate	8. coat	14. suggestion
3. grass	9. paper	15. axes
4. people	10. thoughts	16. protection
5. day	11. mountain	17. woods
6. affection	12. fire	18. month

3. Write five sentences of your own with at least two nouns in each sentence. Underline all the nouns.

Exercise II

1. Review "Forming the Plural of Nouns" and "Forming the Possessive of Nouns" on pages 80–81 and 82.

2. Copy the nouns listed below. Next to each one, write its plural.

1. child	6. roof	11. mother-in-law
2. box	7. ax	12. deer
3. wife	8. pass	13. Negro
4. ox	9. spy	14. tray
5. foot	10. monkey	15. church

3. Copy the following phrases and make each noun in parentheses show possession:

1. the (radio) racket	6. a (cup) handle
2. the (lady) smile	7. (James) book
3. our (parents) devotion	8. a (boy) brains
4. the (book) ending	9. the (song) melody
5. the (thieves) hideout	10. the (child) toy

Exercise III

1. Review "Noun Signals" on pages 83–84.

2. Write the articles *a, an,* and *the* three times, using them with different nouns. Then rewrite each article and noun, adding words that come between them.

Exercise IV

1. Review "Common and Proper Nouns" on pages 86 and 88.

2. Look back at the paragraph in Test I on page 96. Separate the nouns into two lists, one headed *Common Nouns* and the other, *Proper Nouns*.

3. Use each of the following words in two sentences—first as a common noun, then as a proper noun.

EXAMPLE: 1. father

YOU WRITE: *1. My father and I like chocolate cookies.*

I would like to go, Father.

1. mother	4. niece
2. grandfather	5. dad
3. mom	6. brother

Exercise V

1. Review "Subjects and Direct Objects" and "Subject Complements" on pages 89 and 92.

2. Copy the following sentences, using a noun in place of each blank space. In parentheses on your paper, label the noun as a subject, a direct object, or a subject complement.

1. That ___?___ bit the frightened woman.
2. The director of the play is ___?___.
3. Our reward was a ___?___.
4. My friend borrowed some ___?___.
5. Lenny put the ___?___ on the shelf.

3. Use each of these nouns as a direct object in a sentence:

     fire engine   bridge   ball   bell   field

4. Use each of these nouns as a subject complement in a sentence:

     champion   teacher   fireman   Mr. Smith   friend   enemy

Exercise VI

1. Review "Appositive Nouns" on page 93.

2. Write five original sentences, each of which contains an appositive noun. Be sure to punctuate your sentences correctly.

CHAPTER 4

A Start on the Year's Writing

Much of the writing you will do in your English course this year will be "creative" writing. By that we mean that you will create the material out of your own mind. The writers of the books and stories that you enjoy are creative writers. Some are experts at creating exciting plots and swift action. Others describe a scene in such vivid language that you seem to be there in person.

These favorite authors may be expert now, but you can be sure they worked long and hard at developing their writing craftsmanship. They began by putting sentences and paragraphs together with words that they selected carefully, studied critically, and perhaps threw out to start all over again.

You are not at this point learning to write in order to earn your living. But some of you may enjoy your attempts at writing creatively so much that you may be starting, in your way, to become the novelists, reporters, columnists, and playwrights of tomorrow.

Describing an Action

You know how much you enjoy reading a story or an article in which there is heavy action. Well, action not only is fun to read; it also can be fun to write. One of the marks of a good writer is the ability to write clear, accurate, vigorous action passages.

The illustration on the facing page shows the action described in a paragraph from Sir Arthur Conan Doyle's story *The White Company*. Read this paragraph and one by Robert Louis Stevenson on the following page. Be prepared to discuss them.

◄ *Three hundred years after the Battle of Hastings, England was again in a struggle with France. In the service of England was a group of chivalrous men known as the White Company.*

On the facing page, the fair-haired young squire, Alleyne Edricson, is seen protecting himself from another young squire, a bully named John Tranter.

As Alleyne walked toward Tranter, Tranter suddenly bounded forward and sent in a whistling cut that would have severed Alleyne in twain had he not sprung lightly back from it. So close was it that the point ripped a gash in the jutting edge of his linen cyclas. Quick as a panther, Alleyne sprang in with a thrust, but Tranter, who was as active as he was strong, had already recovered himself and turned it aside with a movement of his heavy blade. Again he whizzed in a blow which made the spectators hold their breath, and again Alleyne very quickly and swiftly slipped from under it and sent back two lightning thrusts which the other could scarce parry.

from *The White Company* by Sir Arthur Conan Doyle

He had risen from his position to his hands and knees; and though his leg obviously hurt him pretty sharply when he moved—for I could hear him stifle a groan—yet it was at a good rattling rate that he trailed himself across the deck. In half a minute he reached the port scuppers and picked out a coil of rope, a long knife, or rather a short dirk, discolored to the hilt with blood. He looked upon it for a moment, thrusting forth his underjaw, tried the point upon his hand, and then, hastily concealing it in the bosom of his jacket, trundled back again to his old place against the bulwark.

from *Treasure Island* by Robert Louis Stevenson

To discuss

A very good way to improve your work in any field is to observe closely how an expert does it. The authors above were master story-tellers and experts at describing action. It may help you to appreciate the two passages more if you spend a few minutes looking at them closely.

1. Read the two passages aloud in class so that you can *hear* the action. Did the authors use vigorous verbs? Which verbs did the authors use to describe action?
2. Have someone read the Doyle passage aloud while a pair of actors try acting it out. The acting need not be carefully prepared. Discuss the dramatization. Does it demonstrate how vigorous the passage is?
3. Try the same thing with the Stevenson passage. However, this time only one actor is needed.

It does not always take a paragraph to express action. It can be done in a sentence. Here are some examples from expert writers.

Read them aloud and observe closely how the action is expressed. Then try your hand with the exercises that follow.

Jimmy's pet drill was biting smoothly into the steel door.   O. HENRY

She brushed a cloud of hair out of her eyes with the back of her glove and left a smudge of earth on her cheek in doing it.
JOHN STEINBECK

The bulldog had managed to roll him over on his back and, still hanging onto his throat, was on top of him.   JACK LONDON

To discuss

1. Can you see in your mind's eye the action expressed in the sentences above?

2. Which words help describe the actions vividly?

Exercises: Describing action

1. In class, have someone, your teacher or a pupil, perform a brief, specific action. Watch closely and then describe it in one or two sentences. Perform five or six of these actions.

EXAMPLES: 1. John picked up the history text in his left hand and laid it gently on Joe's head.
2. Bursting into the room, Miss Smith eyed us severely. Then her frown dissolved into a broad smile.

Compare and discuss your descriptions. Write a few of the best ones on the board. Tell why you think they are good descriptions.

2. Describe clearly and accurately five examples of action you imagine or action you have seen. Write about actions which take place in a few seconds or a minute of time. Use only one or two sentences for each description. Keep your sentences for later use.

EXAMPLE: 1. George grabbed the silver coin and flung it at the man. It missed, bounced on the asphalt, and then rolled easily into the gutter.

GOING AHEAD

Write a longer action passage of one or two paragraphs. You may describe action you have observed, or you may make up the events you describe.

Describing a Place, Object, or Person

You have been describing action. Writers must also be able to describe places, things, and people. Your first task in such description is to *observe* carefully with all your senses: sight, hearing, taste, touch, and smell. Your second task is to *select* what you will tell in your description. Tell only those things which will add to the picture of what you are describing.

Read the following two descriptions of the same boy and be prepared to discuss them:

1. The boy had hair on the top of his head, and on his face one could see two eyes, a nose, a mouth, and coal smudges. He stood on two feet and looked nice in his shirt, trousers, socks, and shoes.

2. John's black hair was tangled, and his pale, smiling face was covered with coal smudges. However, the sports shirt he wore was clean, his khakis were pressed, and even his white sneakers were spotless.

To discuss

1. Read and discuss the following pairs of words and expressions taken from the two descriptions above. Tell which ones give a more vivid picture of the boy. Explain why.

1. The boy had hair on the top of his head
   John's black hair was tangled
2. two eyes, a nose, a mouth, and coal smudges
   his pale, smiling face was covered with coal smudges
3. shirt   trousers
   sports shirt   khakis
        shoes
        white sneakers

2. In the light of your discussion, which is the better description of the boy, description 1 or description 2 at the top of the page?

Before you write some brief descriptions of your own, read the following descriptive passages by expert writers. Notice that the authors do not try to tell everything. They select only what makes the description more vivid. Be prepared to discuss the passages.

The walls and ceiling [of Scrooge's sitting room] were so hung with living green that it looked a perfect grove. The leaves of holly, mistletoe, and ivy reflected back the light, as if so many little mirrors had been scattered there; and such a mighty blaze went roaring up the chimney as that . . . hearth had never known in Scrooge's time. . . .

from A Christmas Carol, by Charles Dickens

He was clean-shaven and his face was lean and hard and burned from high forehead to firm, tapering chin. His eyes seemed hooded in the shadow of the hat's brim. He came closer, and I could see that this was because the brows were drawn in a frown of fixed and habitual alertness. Beneath them the eyes were endlessly searching from side to side and forward, checking off every item in view, missing nothing.

from Shane, by Jack Schaefer

"An American bull terrier," we used to say proudly; none of your English bulls. He had one brindle eye that sometimes made him look like a clown and sometimes reminded you of a politician with derby hat and cigar. The rest of him was white except for a brindle saddle that always seemed to be slipping off and a brindle stocking on a hind leg. Nevertheless, there was a nobility about him. He was big and muscular and beautifully made. He never lost his dignity even when trying to accomplish the extravagant tasks my brothers and myself used to set for him.

from "Snapshot of a Dog," by James Thurber

To discuss

The authors of the three passages on page 105 are known for their skill in describing people, animals, and things. In class, have each of these passages read aloud. Then discuss the following questions about each one:

1. Does the passage create a vivid picture in your mind?
2. If you were an artist, could you draw the man, the terrier, and the room described? (If you can draw, try it.)
3. What specific details does each author use to make his subject come alive?
4. Do any of the authors use comparisons to make clear what they are describing to the reader? Point out examples. Explain what the comparisons are.
5. Which phrases—word groups—in the descriptions do you think are especially effective?

Guides for writing descriptions

1. Using your senses, observe carefully what you want to describe.
2. Write specific details to make the subject come alive for the reader.
3. Select only those details which will add to the picture. Do not try to tell everything.
4. Use comparisons with familiar objects if they will make clear what you are describing. (Point out similarities or differences.)
5. In describing action, be sure to use vigorous verbs.

Exercise: Describing objects, places, and persons

Keep the sentences you write for this exercise. You may use them again later.

1. *Describe an object.* Bring an object to school which can be concealed in your desk or locker. Describe it in two or three written sentences. Read your description to the class, and then show the object. Ask your classmates to tell whether they think your description was interesting and accurate.

EXAMPLE: The torn, wrinkled shirt had once been white. Now it was gray, with smudges of grease on it. Most of the buttons had come off.

106

2. *Describe a place.* Think of a place that you and your class-mates know well and describe it in a sentence or two. Do not give the name of the place. Read your description to the class. Ask your listeners to guess what place you are describing. Remember, you have only a sentence or two, so choose your words and details carefully.

3. *Describe a person.* Think of a person you know well and describe him in a brief paragraph. It might be interesting to choose a member of your class and to see whether anyone can guess whom you are describing. (*Caution*: Be careful not to hurt anyone's feelings or embarrass him in any way.)

GOING AHEAD

1. Try writing two descriptions of a house, automobile, piece of furniture, or other common object. Let one description demonstrate the same weaknesses shown by description 1 of the boy on page 104; let the other demonstrate the strength of description 2. If there is time, read your pair of descriptions to the class. See if they agree with you on which description is the better one and why.

2. You have been writing short descriptions. Perhaps some of them have suggested an idea to you for a longer composition or story. If so, write it.

TO MEMORIZE

FROM *Andrea del Sarto*

Ah, but a man's reach should exceed his grasp,
Or what's a heaven for?

ROBERT BROWNING

This famous English poet had a great love and understanding of people. Many of his poems are conversations in which one person is speaking to another. They are called dramatic monologues because the speech of only one person is given.

Browning's poem "Andrea del Sarto" is based upon the character of an actual person, an artist whose real name is not known. Although this artist's paintings are admired for their technical skill, he somehow missed the mark of greatness. In the poem, he is talking to his wife and explaining why he thinks he is a failure. Can you tell in your own words what he is saying in the quotation above? Is this quotation true only of artistic ambitions?

Writing Paragraphs

In most writing situations, it is not enough to write only one sentence or two, as you have been doing for practice in the preceding exercises. You need to develop your ideas at greater length. After the sentence, the next step in developing an idea is the *paragraph*. Almost all good writing is organized into paragraphs.

What is a paragraph?

You have studied the paragraph before, but it will be well to review now some of the things which make a good one.

Do you remember how to signal the beginning of a new paragraph? If you do not remember, look at the paragraphs on this page. Notice that the first word of each paragraph is indented.

Many paragraphs have a **topic sentence**; that is, a sentence which tells what the paragraph is about. Often the topic sentence is the first sentence in the paragraph, and the other sentences develop the idea given in the topic sentence. In some paragraphs the topic sentence is not the first sentence.

Keeping to the topic

A paragraph which develops one topic or idea has **unity**. One of the most important things about writing a good paragraph is *to keep to one topic*. For example, if you are writing a paragraph on the topic "Homework," you should not suddenly throw in a sentence about your teacher's voice.

Another common way to go astray in paragraphing is to start out on one subject and end up on another. Do not allow your thinking to get off the track. If your topic is "Colonial Costumes," do not get sidetracked on Paul Revere's ride.

Read the following paragraph and be prepared to discuss it:

Keynote to being a good hostess is consideration of your guests. Find out what they really enjoy, then make your plans. In your Camp Fire group you have so many good times together that you should have no trouble at all in giving your guests a good time when you are having a party or entertaining at home. Store up a good stock of games and ideas for things to do, make your friends feel welcome and at home, give them a chance to talk about what interests them, and they will enjoy themselves and think of you as a wonderful hostess.

from *The Book of the Camp Fire Girls*, 1959 edition

To discuss

1. Which sentence is the topic sentence in the paragraph you have just read?

2. Do the other sentences in the paragraph develop the idea stated in the topic sentence? Discuss the ideas which support the topic.

■ A **paragraph** is a series of sentences which develop one topic or one idea.

Exercises: Paragraph unity

1. Read each of the following paragraphs. Then copy the topic sentence on your paper, giving it the same numeral as the paragraph.

1. He [Houdini, a great American magician, 1874–1926] was in many ways a contradictory figure. Volatile and quick-tempered, he was at the same time cold-bloodedly unswerving in the furtherance of his career. He was selfish and suspicious as an artist—but his devotion to his mother was deep and real; his private and unknown philanthropies were as numerous as those the press reported. He was generous to young performers—and bitter, sometimes cruel, to those who threatened his own position.

from *The Great Houdini*, by Beryl Williams and Samuel Epstein

2. Buck's first day on the Dyea beach was like a nightmare. Every hour was filled with shock and surprise. He had been suddenly jerked from the heart of civilization and flung into the heart of things primordial. No lazy, sun-kissed life was this, with nothing to do but loaf and be bored. Here was neither peace nor rest, nor a moment's safety. All was confusion and action, and every moment life and limb were in peril. There was imperative need to be constantly alert; for these dogs and men were not town dogs and men. They were savages, all of them, who knew no law but the law of club and fang.

from *The Call of the Wild*, by Jack London

2. Each paragraph below contains one sentence that does not keep to the topic. For each paragraph, write the topic sentence and underline it. Then write the sentence which is off the topic.

1. Using an electric chain saw is an efficient method of felling trees and cutting them into lengths. It is lighter than a gasoline saw and more certain to start. Its chain bites through the trunk and branches easily and quickly. Always keep some antiseptic in the house to put on cuts and scratches. Compared to the old-fashioned handsaw, an electric chain saw is a powerful, fast-working tool.

2. Regular exercise is often a key to good health. It improves the appetite and at the same time helps remove excess fat. The summer is usually too hot for me to exercise, but I find it enjoyable on beautiful autumn days. It strengthens the heart and keeps the muscles in good condition. Doctors tell us that a person's life expectancy will be longer if he plans his life so as to include regular exercise. Those who sit around the house or office all day and all evening are less likely to enjoy a healthy old age.

3. I am opposed to trying to force everyone into being well adjusted and having friends. There is certainly a place for the creative lone wolf, happy in his own thoughts and projects. Perhaps he will have one or two close friends who will share his activities, but that will be all. Hobbies help, too, and every young person should develop one. Some of the most successful, happy, and useful people that I know were never very popular in school. Therefore, parents should not worry if their child spends a good deal of time alone, especially if he does not seem unhappy.

3. In the following paragraphs the writer starts off well, but then he gets off the track. On your paper, write down the sentence where you think the writer has first wandered from his original topic. Be prepared to explain and defend your choice.

1. Reading is the best way of increasing your vocabulary. This is especially true if you pay attention when you read so that you notice new words. When you come across a new word, you can often make an intelligent guess about its meaning. Otherwise, you will need to look it up in the dictionary. The dictionary is the most useful of all books. It is a combination speller, pronouncer, word definer, encyclopedia, and set of tables. No home should be without one, and most homes should have two or three. There is a very large dictionary in the school library, if you don't have one at home.

2. There is probably no higher pitch of excitement than that reached during a close basketball game played in a packed gymnasium. The game itself is a thrilling one, full of action and quick change. And the crowded conditions, with hundreds of strong young vocal cords in a small space, tend to exaggerate the emotions. You must be careful not to engage in poor sportsmanship at a basketball game. This is one of the quickest ways to ruin the reputation of a school. Think what happened to Central High last year after that game against Bismarck. Seldom has public opinion switched so rapidly against a student body.

GOING AHEAD

There are many good paragraphs that do not start with topic sentences. Look at several paragraphs in a number of books. Try to find examples of paragraphs in which the author leads up to the topic sentence which he places at or near the end of the paragraph. If there is time, share your findings with the class.

Developing paragraphs

You are now ready to write some paragraphs of your own. As you write, keep in mind the importance of paragraph unity; that is, stay on the subject. But staying on the subject is not enough. You must go further. You must give information to support your main idea. Any good paragraph develops its topic.

Here are two ways of developing paragraphs:

1. *By details*
2. *By explanation*

Read the following paragraph. It illustrates one of the methods of development. Notice that the topic sentence is italicized.

From the top of the tower, the city looked like a toy village. Directly below, antlike people were swarming on the sidewalks. The automobiles moved slowly and neatly, and I felt as if I could reach down and push them around with my fingers. A church steeple in the distance didn't seem more than six inches tall, and even the river running through the west part of town looked as if a child's paintbrush had drawn it across a piece of art paper.

In the paragraph above, the writer mentioned a number of specific details as he described the scene.

The writer developed the following paragraph by explaining how the canal lock works:

A canal lock uses very simple principles to raise boats over an elevation. The principles are that boats float and that the level of water can be raised or lowered by pumps and by inlets and outlets. A boat enters a lock at the lowest level, and the gates are closed so that the boat is in a watertight section. Water is pumped or allowed to flow into the section, thus raising the boat to the next level. Then the upper gates are opened, and the boat is towed into the next section. Again the gates are closed, and the boat rises with the rising water. This process is continued, sometimes through several locks, until the boat is as high as necessary to cross over the elevation. At the other side, it may be lowered again by another series of locks.

Guides for writing paragraphs

1. State the main idea in a topic sentence. This sentence often appears as the first sentence in a paragraph.
2. Develop the main idea (explanation or details) in your other sentences.
3. Give your paragraph unity by keeping to the topic.

Exercises: Writing paragraphs

1. Here is a list of topic sentences. Choose two of them and write two paragraphs of about 100 words each. Choose the way you will develop your paragraphs—by details or by explanation.

1. Summer would be perfect were it not for weeds.
2. My mother has definite ideas about discipline.
3. It is not difficult to tie a square knot.
4. Traffic jams are the curse of modern cities.
5. Every boy and girl should learn the essentials of first aid.
6. Juvenile delinquency often begins in school.
7. Giving clear directions seems to be a lost art.
8. Nothing helps a child grow up more than being responsible for his own pet.

2. Take any of the sentences which you wrote for the exercises on page 103 and pages 106–07 and develop them into paragraphs. Do as many of these as you have time to do well.

You may now want to put a number of paragraphs together into a longer paper. Remember, though, that the principles of paragraph construction do not change whether you write a paper of one paragraph or several. Choose any subject that appeals to you. The exercises you have already done or the list of topics on pages 122–24 may suggest a subject to you.

✓ Check Test 5: Capital letters

Take this test to see whether you need to review the use of capital letters.

Write the following paragraph, supplying capital letters wherever they are needed:

The thirteen English colonies on the eastern coast of North America fought England in a struggle for independence. As a result they became an independent nation called the United States of America. The first bloodshed of the American Revolution occurred on April 19, 1775, at Lexington, Massachusetts. The British were on their way from Boston to the town of Concord, where the colonists forced them to retreat to Boston. At Philadelphia on May 10, the second Continental Congress met and declared war against Great Britain. They appointed George Washington as Commander in Chief of the Army. Six years later, after many battles, the Revolution was won on October 19, 1781, with an American victory at Yorktown, Virginia.

If you made any mistakes in the Check Test above, turn to the Review Handbook, pages 419–22.

Writing a Story

If you enjoy telling and hearing stories, you will want to try your hand at writing some. Turn back now to page 62 and review the "Guides for storytelling."

Many stories are composed of these parts: *the opening, the development, the climax*, and *the closing*.

The opening

A written story should capture the interest of the reader at once. Read the following story beginnings written by experts.

1. It must be that all children are actors. The whole thing started with a boy on our street named Walter, who had inflammatory rheumatism. That's what they called it. He didn't have to go to school.

from "Stolen Day," by Sherwood Anderson

2. He came into the room to shut the windows while we were still in bed, and I saw he looked ill. He was shivering, his face was white, and he walked slowly as though it ached to move.

from "A Day's Wait," by Ernest Hemingway

3. He began life as a red cub. As he grew older, his coat became darker, until it was the exact shade of a well-polished mahogany table, and gained him his name. By the time Old Mahogany had reached his full growth, he was the largest, the handsomest, and the wiliest fox in all that hill country of Litchfield County.

from "The Mahogany Fox," by Samuel Scoville, Jr.

To discuss

Do you think each of the openings above is a good one? Does each opening arouse your interest? Does it make you want to read on? Why, or why not?

Exercises: Writing story beginnings

1. In your literature books or in magazines, find examples of interesting story beginnings. Read aloud and discuss some of them in class to see if your classmates agree that each story opening arouses interest.

2. In not more than fifty words, write the beginning of an original story. In some way you must make your reader want to read on. You may present a problem, describe a character who is about to do something, or create a situation which makes the reader curious.

The development

Having started your story, your job is to hold the interest of the reader by *selecting* or *creating* those details and events which will make it come alive. A good way *not* to do this is simply to give a bare summary of the facts of the story. For example, "Stolen Day" written by a poor writer might have continued thus:

One day, however, I saw that Walter had walked down to the fishing pool. Then I decided to get inflammatory rheumatism, too. The teacher let me go home, but my mother just put me to bed and ignored me until I thought she didn't care if I died. So I got up and went down and caught a big carp at the pool. When I got home, everyone thought I was a hero because the fish was so big, but they all just laughed when I said I had inflammatory rheumatism. I felt ashamed.

This is merely telling *about* the story. Sherwood Anderson, on the other hand, really *showed* us, his readers, what happened by careful choice of details, by use of dialogue, and by keeping us in suspense about how the story was going to come out. Reread his beginning paragraph, numeral 1 on page 114, and then read the following fourteen paragraphs. Notice *how* Anderson develops his story.

Still, he could walk about. He could go fishing in the creek or the waterworks pond. There was a place up at the pond where in the spring the water came tumbling over the dam and formed a deep pool. It was a good place. Sometimes you could get some good big ones there.

I went down that way on my way to school one spring morning. It was out of my way, but I wanted to see if Walter was there.

He was, inflammatory rheumatism and all. There he was, sitting with a fish pole in his hand. He had been able to walk down there all right.

It was then that my own legs began to hurt. My back, too. I went on to school but, at the recess time, I began to cry. I did it when the teacher, Sarah Suggett, had come out into the schoolhouse yard.

She came right over to me.

"I ache all over," I said. I did, too.

I kept on crying and it worked all right.

"You'd better go home," she said.

So I went. I limped painfully away. I kept on limping until I got out of the schoolhouse street.

Then I felt better. I still had inflammatory rheumatism pretty bad, but I could get along better.

I must have done some thinking on the way home.

"I'd better not say I have inflammatory rheumatism," I decided. "Maybe if you've got that you swell up."

I thought I'd better go around to where Walter was and ask him about that, so I did—but he wasn't there.

"They mustn't be biting today," I thought.

The climax

The climax of the story is the high point of interest, and usually it comes near the end. The climax of "Stolen Day" comes after the hero catches the tremendous carp and gets it back home. His mother puts it in a tank, the neighbors come in to look, and he is a hero:

I got into dry clothes and went down to supper—and then I made the break that spoiled my day.

There we were, all of us, at the table, and suddenly Father asked me what had been the matter with me at school. He had met the teacher, Sarah Suggett, on the street, and she had told him how I had become ill.

"What was the matter with you?" Father asked, and before I thought what I was saying, I let it out.

"I had the inflammatory rheumatism," I said—and a shout went up. It made me sick to hear them, the way they all laughed.

It brought back all the aching again and, like a fool, I began to cry.

"Well, I *have* got it—I *have*, I *have*," I cried, and I got up from the table and ran upstairs.

The closing

Sometimes a story closes at its climax, but more often a paragraph or two are needed to finish it off to the reader's satisfaction. Be careful, though, not to ramble on after the climax is passed. Keep up interest to the very last. Here is the paragraph from "Stolen Day," following immediately after the paragraphs of climax:

> I stayed there until Mother came up. I knew it would be a long time before I heard the last of the inflammatory rheumatism. I was sick all right, but the aching I now had wasn't in my legs or in my back.

Exercise: Writing a story

Plan and then write a story. Keep in mind what you have learned about the structure of a story. After you have written your first draft, ask yourself the questions listed below. Revise your work if you are not satisfied with the answers.

Check list for writing stories

1. Will the opening arouse the reader's interest?
2. Will the development hold the reader's interest once I have captured it? Do the details strengthen the story and make it come alive? Do the characters and setting seem real?
3. Does the story have a climax?
4. Does the story have a good ending? Does it close rather quickly, without dragging on, and yet not so abruptly as to seem to be left hanging?

Writing Dialogue

You know how much more interesting a story is when it has plenty of conversation, or dialogue, in it. Readers like dialogue; they find it entertaining. Notice how the writer O. Henry uses dialogue in his famous story "The Ransom of Red Chief."

As I was about to start, the kid comes up to me and says, "Aw, Snake-eye, you said I could play the Black Scout while you was gone."

"Play it, of course," says I. "Mr. Bill will play with you. What kind of game is it?"

"I'm the Black Scout," says Red Chief, "and I have to ride to the stockade to warn the settlers that the Indians are coming. I'm tired of playing Indian myself. I want to be the Black Scout."

"All right," says I. "It sounds harmless to me. I guess Mr. Bill will help you foil the pesky savages."

"What am I to do?" asks Bill, looking at the kid suspiciously.

"You are the hoss," says Black Scout. "Get down on your hands and knees. How can I ride to the stockade without a hoss?"

"You'd better keep him interested," says I, "till we get the scheme going. Loosen up."

Bill gets down on his all fours, and a look comes into his eye like a rabbit's when you catch it in a trap.

Punctuating dialogue

In your own writing you will frequently want to have the characters talk to each other to increase the interest of the reader. Probably you have already studied the rules for punctuating dialogue, but it would be well now to review them.

To discuss

Using the passage of dialogue from "The Ransom of Red Chief," answer the following questions with a rule about the correct way to punctuate dialogue. If you have forgotten the rule, refer to the "Guides for punctuating dialogue" just below.

1. Why are there eight separate paragraphs?
2. Why do quotation marks enclose only part of paragraph 1?
3. In the third paragraph, why does the second part of the quotation begin with a small letter ("and . . .")?
4. In the sixth paragraph, why does the second part of Black Scout's words begin with a capital letter ("Get . . .")?
5. Is there always a punctuation mark to separate a quotation from the rest of the sentence? Answer with examples from four of the paragraphs.

Guides for punctuating dialogue

1. Use a new paragraph for each speaker.
2. Enclose quoted words in quotation marks. ("No!" cried Ed.)
3. If a quoted sentence is divided, do not begin the second part with a capital letter. ("I think," said Joe, "that you are right.")
4. Begin the first word of each quoted sentence with a capital letter. ("Come to dinner," said Mother. "Don't be late.")
5. Separate quoted words from the rest of the sentence by a comma, a question mark, or an exclamation point.
6. The quotation mark almost always follows other punctuation. ("Where are you?" asked Bill.)

Exercises: Writing dialogue

1. Copy and punctuate the following passage of dialogue:

Dad, where did you go to college asked young John I didn't go to college, Son replied Mr. Smith You didn't exclaimed John well, where did you graduate from high school Well, Son, said Mr. Smith unfortunately, I never graduated from high school either you might say I'm a self-made man That's what I like about you, Pop said John you're always ready to take the blame for everything

2. Write a typical conversation that might take place in your homeroom or English classroom before the class actually starts.

1. Find several examples of dialogue in stories or novels you have read or are reading. See if they follow the rules for the punctuation of dialogue. Be prepared to copy a few lines on the board and to explain the punctuation to the class.

2. Dialogue should be written to sound as much as possible like the people who are quoted. Notice that in the dialogue from "The Ransom of Red Chief," the words quoted are not always entirely grammatical or correct. Is this because O. Henry does not know how to write correctly?

If you have picked out some passages of dialogue for the first part of this exercise, observe them carefully to see if you think the author has made a successful effort to imitate the actual speech of the people he is quoting.

3. Write some dialogue between two people who talk in an unusual or distinctive way. Try to reproduce the way they pronounce their words and to imitate any unusual words or phrases they might use.

For a short example of such dialogue, look at the selection from *Mama's Bank Account* on page 363.

✓ Check Test 6: Using words correctly

Take this test to see how much you remember about using certain modifiers.

Write the following sentences, choosing the correct words from the ones in parentheses:

1. (That, That there) tree was struck by lightning.
2. (Its, It's) the only tree on the block.
3. (Its, It's) branches covered my bedroom window.
4. (Those, Them) tourists are looking at the building.
5. (Its, It's) a very old but beautiful building.
6. (Its, It's) hallways are long and spacious.
7. (This, This here) cornerstone will give us the date.
8. (Those, Them) apartment houses on the other side are new.

If you made any mistakes in the Check Test above, find the lesson or lessons you need to study on page 449 and page 456 in the Review Handbook at the back of this book. The usage items in the Handbook are arranged alphabetically.

Choosing a Topic for a Paper

Sometimes your teacher will assign you a topic for a paper. Frequently, however, you will have to think up your own topic. The following section will give you some suggestions for choosing topics which will be useful for the rest of the year. Whenever you have a paper to write, you will find it helpful to refer to these pages.

Here are two questions to ask yourself about a topic you have chosen:

1. *Do I really know the subject?* You should always choose a subject which you know about. Otherwise, there is really little reason for anyone to read what you have written. Your subject can be based on your own experience or on reading you have done to obtain information. Sometimes, you may know more about the subject than the reader or listener. At other times, your subject may be a common, everyday one, but what you have to say about it may be new and interesting.

2. *Have I chosen a subject of manageable size?* You should be able to treat your subject interestingly in a paper of reasonable length. A topic like "The World" is obviously too large and general in such an assignment. However, "The World as Seen from Our Back Yard" would be a topic worth tackling.

To discuss

1. Here is a list of ten titles for papers which might have been written by a seventh-grader. Decide which subjects are familiar to you either through personal experience or through reading about them. There is no one correct answer to this exercise, but be prepared to defend your choice of topics in a class discussion.

1. Should the United Nations Be Abolished?
2. A Typical Breakfast in Our Family
3. The Advantages and Disadvantages of Regular Homework
4. Should Team Sports Be Required of All Students?
5. Is There Life on Other Planets?
6. The Battle of Iwo Jima
7. How to Prevent Forest Fires
8. My Philosophy of Life
9. Modern Architecture
10. How Modern Architecture Impresses Me

2. Here is a list of fifteen titles for papers. Discuss in class which ones you think would be suitable for a paper of about 100 to 200 words and which ones are too broad and general. Be prepared to defend your choices.

1. Archaeology	8. My Problems
2. A Hike	9. My Sister
3. Saturday Night at Our House	10. My Ideal Bedroom
4. Parents	11. Friends
5. Agriculture	12. Movies
6. Stamps	13. Baby-sitting
7. How I Found a Rare Stamp	14. I Like Jazz

15. Our Car Is an Antique

Exercise: Writing suitable topics

Recall your class discussion above and list the titles which you thought were unsuitable either because you did not know enough about the subject or because they were too broad and general. Then after each unsuitable title, write a revision of it that would make it suitable.

EXAMPLE: 1. Agriculture   My Summer Growing Vegetables

Some suggestions for things to write about

You have learned two general principles for choosing a topic for a paper. Here is a rather long list of subjects which may stimulate your thinking or give you ideas of things to write about. The subjects are not all usable as titles; most of them are too general. They are presented merely to help you throughout the year, in case you get "stuck" for an idea. Use the list if you need to, but do not let it limit you in any way. Sometimes you may find that topics suggested on the list make you think of entirely different topics which you'd like to write about. Fine. That's one good use for the list.

1. ANIMALS

Dogs	Other pets	Farm animals
Horses	Zoo animals	Birds
Cats	Wild animals	

(You may describe or tell experiences with any of these animals.)

2. COMPARISONS

Home and school

Adults and children

Advantages and disadvantages
of ___?___

The present and the past

The present and the future

Good and bad habits

(These topics are rather general and broad. You will need to
narrow them and make them more specific before you write.)

3. DAYDREAMS AND FANTASIES

If I had a million dollars

The car of the future

What I want to be

The perfect day

The perfect party

If I had one wish

If I lived in ___?___ (any place
or time)

My ideal ___?___ (parent, girl,
boy, pet, hobby, house, etc.)

4. EXPLANATIONS

Hobby

Sports

Care of pets, gardens,
babies, etc.

Safety or other rules

How to ___?___ (swim, get somewhere, do something you
know how to do)

5. HAPPENINGS OR EVENTS

Adventures

Daily routines

Accidents

Embarrassing experiences

Funny experiences

A major event in my life

A news event

6. HOME AND FAMILY

What it's like in my family (or
someone else's)

Parents, brothers, sisters, babies

Relatives

Rules and regulations

Conflicts

Special family pleasures

Vacations

7. OCCASIONS

Parties

Athletic events

Holidays

Trips

Festivals

Birthdays

8. TV AND RADIO

Favorite programs or characters
Most disliked programs or characters
Commercials
What makes a good (or bad) program?
Effect of TV on family life

9. OPINIONS AND FEELINGS

Laughter	Advice
Art	Rules
Growing up	Ideals
Food	Studying
Behavior	What bores me

10. PEOPLE

Myself	Authors	Storekeeper
Parents	Characters in	Neighborhood
Friends	books	character
Teachers	Dentist	A person I'd like
TV personalities	Doctor	to know better

11. PLACES

Favorite places	Buildings
Most disliked places	Cities
Seashore	Farms
Mountains	Lakes
Caves	Camps

12. SCHOOL

Fads	Suggestions for change
Subjects you like	The best things about my school
Subjects you dislike	School rules
School spirit	Clubs

13. THINGS

Cars	Things that should be
Possessions	thrown away
Family treasures	Things that should be
Description of something	invented
rare	

Checking and Revising Your Writing

There is only one way to learn to write, and that is to write, to have your writing criticized by a knowledgeable person (like your teacher), and then to write some more. You cannot learn to write merely by learning rules, although they may help. Checking and revising your work are a vital part of the learning process.

Before handing in your paper

Consider the following suggestions each time you write a paper:

1. *Check the appearance of your paper.* If your teacher or school requires a standard arrangement for written work, be sure to follow it exactly. If there are no definite school or class standards, use the form given in the sample on the next page. Note the centered title, the placement of the heading (your name, class, and date), and the even margins.

2. *Check your paper for capitalization and punctuation.* Capitalization and punctuation require two things: a knowledge of the rules and care in applying them. Whenever you are in doubt about a point, check the rules in the Review Handbook on pages 419–30.

3. *Check your spelling.* If you are in doubt about the spelling of a word, always look it up in the dictionary.

4. *Check your paragraphs.* Did you indent the first word of each paragraph? Does each paragraph have a topic sentence? Does each sentence in a paragraph stick to the topic?

After getting back your paper

Some students merely glance at the mark on a paper and never look at the paper itself after it is returned. This is not the smart thing to do. The time your teacher spends on correcting and commenting on your paper is time spent for *you*. Note carefully everything your teacher writes on your papers. Correcting mistakes and revising poor writing are very important. If a player made a poor tackle in football practice, the coach would tell him what was wrong and then say, "Now do it again right!" So it should be with writing. Do it again. That is the best way to learn.

In most cases it will help you to write better if you have a chance to read your paper to someone. Ask any person whose comments you would value to listen as you read your paper aloud.

Your teacher may have a system for filing papers. In that case, follow it carefully. One good method is to keep your papers in a separate English folder. From time to time, look back over your work to see what progress you are making and in what ways you need to improve. Keeping your papers also provides a good opportunity for an occasional individual conference with your teacher about your written work.

Summary

Before you write the final draft, ask yourself these questions:

1. Is it punctuated properly?
2. Is the capitalization correct?
3. Is it paragraphed logically?
4. Is my spelling correct?

Especially on the final draft, ask yourself:

5. Is it arranged according to the class standards for written work?
6. Is my paper dated and headed properly?
7. Is it neat and legible?

Grade 7

Mary Jones
October 3, 19-

Tying a Square Knot

It is not difficult to tie a square knot...

When you get your paper back:

8. Note carefully all the teacher's comments and markings.
9. Correct the paper and have your teacher check it.
10. Share the paper by reading it to a person or group.
11. File the paper for future reference.

Exercise: Writing a paper

Choose any subject and write a paper from 100 to 200 words in length. Try to make it a paper that will entertain the class. Remember the various things about good writing that you have learned in this chapter.

It's Like This, Cat
by Emily Neville
Illustrated by Emil Weiss
Harper and Row

Fourteen-year-old David Mitchell is growing up in the midst of the excitement and variety of New York City. He has a lot of home problems even before he brings a tiger-striped tomcat into the family. "My father," he says, "is always talking about how a dog can be very educational for a boy. This is one reason I got a cat."

This humorous, exciting book is not mainly an "animal story." It's a realistic tale about people, about Dave's comradeship with a troubled nineteen-year-old, his first shy friendship with a girl, and his growing understanding of his father as a human being and not just as a parent.

About the author

It's Like This, Cat is Emily Neville's first novel, although she has written many stories about young people. Mrs. Neville, mother of five children, was born in Connecticut, graduated from Bryn Mawr College, Pennsylvania, and worked in New York as a newspaper copy girl before marrying. In 1964, her book won the John Newbery Medal of the American Library Association as the "most distinguished contribution to American literature for children" for that year.

Test I

1. Read the following pairs of sentences. Beside the appropriate numeral on your paper, write the letter *A* or *B* of the sentence that gives a more vivid description.

    1. A. The ship is worth a lot of money.
       B. This thirty-foot fishing vessel is worth $5000.
    2. A. At that distance, my green and yellow kite glided and dipped like a sea gull riding on air currents.
       B. My colorful kite went high up into the air.
    3. A. The large boxes fell over, and the dishes broke with a loud sound.
       B. The gigantic boxes of Wedgwood teacups toppled over and crashed with the shattering sound of broken china.

2. Complete the following statements about the descriptive sentences above:

    1. In one sentence, there is a comparison which suggests that a __?__ is like a __?__.
    2. Four vivid action verbs in the sentences above are __?__, __?__, __?__, and __?__.
    3. Description __?__ appeals to the sense of sight. (Write the numeral and letter.)
    4. Description __?__ appeals to the sense of sound. (Write the numeral and letter.)
    5. The use of specific __?__ makes a description come alive for the reader.

Test II

Read the following paragraphs and answer the questions printed below each one:

    A. The final game of the year was so exciting! In the last of the ninth, our team was one run behind. There were two outs and two men on base. Our best hitter, Gray, came up and hit the ball right to the second baseman, and we thought the game was completely lost. But their second baseman tripped on his shoelace. Baseball players should keep their shoes tied. The ball was going so fast it took their center fielder by surprise. Before he got the ball back to the infield, two of our men were home, and even though Gray was put out at third, he was the hero of the day.

1. Which is the topic sentence of the paragraph? Write the sentence on your paper.
2. Which sentence does not keep to the topic? Copy it on your paper.
3. Is the paragraph developed by details or by explanation?

B. My small dog Tiny looked very unhappy. He hadn't had a bone for exactly seven weeks, and I was certain his teeth would fall out without exercise. I started worrying when the coach told me that a dog's teeth need care and exercise just as much as his body does. As a matter of fact, he said that everyone should exercise. After a day at school, I'm too tired to do anything.

4. Which is the topic sentence of the paragraph? Copy the sentence on your paper.
5. Which sentence gets the paragraph off the topic and onto another topic? Copy it on your paper.
6. Is the paragraph developed by details or by explanation?

Test III

Complete the following statements about writing stories. Write your answers next to the appropriate numerals on your paper.

1. Keeping readers interested means keeping them in __?__.
2. The highest point of interest in a story is its __?__.
3. Writers often use __?__ to show their readers what the characters in a story say to each other.

Test IV

Copy the following dialogue on your paper, punctuating and paragraphing it correctly:

Do you really think Mrs. Hollis won't come in today I asked hopefully Yes said Joey That means we won't have that exam I said, grinning Did you study for it Sure he said Why I asked him, worried again He said somebody else may give us the test I didn't study I'll never pass I groaned

Review and Practice

1. Review "Describing an Action" and "Describing a Place, Object, or Person" on pages 101–03 and 104–06.

2. Remembering the importance of observing carefully with all your senses in order to write good descriptions, choose a vivid describing word in place of each blank below. The word should fit the sense suggested in parentheses.

EXAMPLE: 1. __?__ water (touch)
           2. __?__ wind (hearing)

YOU WRITE: 1. *icy*
           2. *howling*

1. __?__ brakes (hearing)   6. __?__ rain (hearing)
2. __?__ peacock (sight)   7. __?__ snow (touch)
3. __?__ mud (touch)   8. __?__ student (sight)
4. __?__ garbage (smell)   9. __?__ marble (touch)
5. __?__ pizza pie (taste)   10. __?__ bakery (smell)

3. Write a vividly descriptive phrase or sentence for each of these comparisons:

1. Wind to the sound of a train whistle
2. Roomful of students talking to the sound of an engine
3. Hot pavement to a frying pan
4. French-fried potatoes to pieces of wood

4. Describe a boy, girl, place, or object in two or three sentences. Referring to your senses, give specific details.

Exercise II

1. Review "Writing Paragraphs" on pages 108–12.

2. In the following paragraph, there is one sentence that does not keep to the topic. Write the sentence on your paper.

Walking in the rain is wonderful. It's much more exciting than a sunny day. Sometimes, when there's a lot of wind, the rain stings your face and soaks your hair. You should always cover your head in the rain, or you may get a cold. Sometimes, in the spring the rain is so gentle you hardly know it's raining except for soft cool spots on your face.

3. Printed below is a dull paragraph. Rewrite it, making it as interesting as you can by adding specific details. Begin with a good topic sentence. Then develop the topic by details. You may use the hints listed below.

> This morning I got up late. I put on my clothes, ate breakfast, and went to school. The bell rang when I walked in the door. The teacher said I was almost late for school. I was glad I got there on time.

Hints:

How late did you get up?
How did you put on your clothes? What did you wear?
How quickly did you eat breakfast? What did you eat? How
  did your stomach feel afterward?
How were you moving when the bell rang?
What was the teacher's tone of voice when she spoke to you?
How did you show you were glad you were on time?

4. Choose one of these paragraph topics and develop it into a paragraph by using details or by explanation:

1. This is a brave and helpful dog.
2. It is easy to keep a good neat notebook.
3. That man is not a fair referee.

Exercise III

1. Review "Writing a Story" on pages 114–17.
2. Many stories have four major parts. Name them.
3. Explain in a sentence or two the meaning of each of these terms: *suspense, climax, dialogue.*

Exercise IV

1. Review "Writing Dialogue" on pages 118–19.
2. Copy the following dialogue on your paper, punctuating and paragraphing it correctly:

> No you may not eat that cake his mother said I made it for a party tonight But Mom he pleaded Make a cake for yourself she said and smiled I will he retorted if you promise to eat half of it no matter how it turns out If those are your terms she decided maybe I should let you have some after all

CHAPTER 5

Verbs: What They Are and What They Do

By now, *verbs* may be an old story to you, but this year you will learn more about them than you ever have before. You remember from Chapter 1 that the verb of a sentence often expresses *action*; for example:

John *threw* the ball.   My bicycle *crashed* into a tree.

Other verbs express what is called *being;* for example:

My mother *is* a loving person.   Those insects *were* beautiful.

You know, too, that the key word in the predicate of a sentence is the verb. If you try reading any sentence without the verb, you will notice that it is the verb which makes the sentence go and that no group of words can be a sentence unless it contains one.

Transitive and Intransitive Verbs

When a verb is followed by a direct object, it is called a **transitive verb.** You can remember this word more easily if you know that the prefix *trans–* means "across." A transitive verb carries action *across* to a receiver of the action; for example:

Helen *knitted* some socks.   Mr. Jones *mowed* his lawn.

Which word receives the action of the verb in each sentence above? The answer is *socks* and *lawn.* These words are direct objects.

In the following examples, note that the meaning of each sentence is complete without a receiver of the action. The verbs in these sentences are **intransitive verbs:**

The thunderstorm *raged.*   A fierce wind *blew.*

Some verbs can be either transitive or intransitive. For example:

1. TRANSITIVE: The cowboy *sang* a sad song.
   INTRANSITIVE: The cowboy *sang* to the cattle.

2. TRANSITIVE: The trail boss *prepared* a list of instructions.
   INTRANSITIVE: The trail boss *prepared* for a difficult afternoon.

■ A **transitive verb** always has a receiver of its action.

■ An **intransitive verb** does not have a receiver of an action.

Exercise: Transitive or intransitive verb?

Name each verb below. Identify it as *transitive* or *intransitive*.

1. I love the life of the cowboys.
2. We usually hunted the wild cattle on moonlight nights.
3. The longhorns filed rapidly into the open.
4. The horses trembled with excitement.
5. Quickly the riders slipped into their saddles.
6. The leader of the group gave the signal.
7. Like an arrow, each eager vaquero dashed after a longhorn.
8. We threw a noose around the animal's horns.
9. Then we tied the other end of the rope to the saddlehorn.
10. Sometimes a collision between horses occurred.

Use each of the following verbs in two sentences, once as a transitive verb and once as an intransitive verb. Label each sentence *transitive* or *intransitive*.

1. spread   2. grow   3. sweep   4. pound   5. chop

Linking verbs

Verbs, as you know, express action or being. You have just worked with intransitive verbs that express action. Another type of intransitive verb is the verb that does not express action.

1. I *am* a cheerleader.   2. That star *is* a planet.
3. They *are* firemen.

In each sentence above, the verb is followed by a noun that means the same person or thing as the subject. *Cheerleader, planet,* and *firemen* are subject complement nouns. The verb *links* the noun, a subject complement, to the subject. Such a verb is called a *linking verb.* All the forms of the verb *be* can be used as linking verbs.

■ **Linking verbs** are intransitive verbs that do not express action.

Exercise: Transitive and intransitive verbs

The verbs in the sentences below are either transitive or intransitive. Copy each one and label it correctly. Four of the intransitive verbs are linking verbs. Next to these, write *Intransitive, Linking.*

1. My best friend bought new ice skates.
2. The icicles on the roof melted.
3. The lost child cried for an hour.
4. Our play last night was a comedy.
5. The instructor shouted his commands at the top of his voice.
6. The papers in his brief case are important documents.
7. These bees are great producers of honey.
8. Johnny is a very ambitious boy.
9. The boys hopped onto the stones in the creek.
10. We sent the invitations to our parents yesterday.

Verb Phrases

You have probably noticed that some verbs contain more than one word. Here are some sentences containing examples of these verbs. The verbs are italicized.

1. John *has eaten* supper.
2. The ruffians *have been breaking* the law.
3. Those diplomats *will travel* for two weeks.
4. New cars *are arriving* daily.
5. That meat *should have been eaten* on Tuesday.

Verbs that contain more than one word are called **verb phrases**. The last word in a verb phrase is the *main verb*; the others are called **helping verbs** or **auxiliary verbs**. Read the verb phrases italicized in the sentences above. What is the main verb in each one? What is the helping verb or verbs?

■ A **verb phrase** consists of a main verb and one, two, or three helping verbs.

Exercise: Verb phrases

From the ten sentences below, pick out the helping verbs and the main verbs. Write them in two columns.

EXAMPLES:
1. The butter was melting rapidly.
2. My watch has been gaining ten minutes each day.

YOU WRITE:

	Helping Verbs	*Main Verbs*
1.	*was*	*melting*
2.	*has been*	*gaining*

1. The island has been enchanted by Sycorax, a wicked witch.
2. Sycorax has imprisoned many good spirits inside trees.
3. Now Prospero and Miranda have come to the island.
4. Prospero is freeing the gentle spirits from the trees.
5. They will be obeying his will ever after.
6. Ariel is acting as chief of the gentle spirits.
7. Caliban, an ugly monster, has been found in the woods.
8. He has inherited a bad nature from his mother, Sycorax.
9. Prospero will be kind to him.
10. However, Caliban will learn nothing good or useful.

Words that separate parts of the verb; another question of word order

You have seen that the usual order in a sentence is subject first, verb following, but that in some cases the usual order is inverted. Now here are examples of yet another situation: the parts of the verb phrase are separated, sometimes by the subject.

VERB PHRASE TOGETHER:	1. The teacher *will praise* the class.
VERB PHRASE SEPARATED:	2. *Will* the teacher *praise* the class?
VERB PHRASE TOGETHER:	3. We *shall return* the flag.
VERB PHRASE SEPARATED:	4. We *shall* not *return* the flag.
VERB PHRASE TOGETHER:	5. He *should have noticed* the signal.
VERB PHRASE SEPARATED:	6. *Should* he *have noticed* the signal?
VERB PHRASE TOGETHER:	7. I *shall jump* onto the dock.
VERB PHRASE SEPARATED:	8. I *shall* now *jump* onto the dock.
VERB PHRASE TOGETHER:	9. It *is stalking* a mouse.
VERB PHRASE SEPARATED:	10. It *is* quietly *stalking* a mouse.

Study the ten examples above. What do sentences 2 and 6 have in common? They are interrogative sentences (questions). Very often interrogative sentences are formed by putting the subject of the sentence between parts of the verb.

In sentence 4, which word separates the parts of the verb?

What do sentences 8 and 10 have in common? In each of them, a word that tells *when* or *how* separates the parts of the verb. In sentence 8, *now* tells when; in sentence 10, *quietly* tells how.

Remember: The word *not* and words that tell *when* and *how* are not parts of the verb.

Exercises: Interrupted verb phrases

1. Write out the verbs in the following sentences. Do not include any words that separate the parts of the verb.

EXAMPLE: 1. How did you learn about flatboats?
YOU WRITE: *1. did learn*

1. Did you really paint this picture of a flatboat?
2. Yes, I have always been interested in early methods of travel.
3. The pioneers did not have the railroad or steamboat.

136

4. Trail breakers had originally carved new paths on foot.
5. The homesteaders would slowly follow by wagon or boat.
6. This type of slow, heavy boat was often seen on the Mississippi River.
7. The lumber from it would sometimes be used for a homesteader's first frontier cabin.

2. Write ten sentences of your own in such a way that the parts of the verb phrase will be separated. Put a double line under each part of the verb phrase.

Contractions

Do not be confused by verbs in *contractions.* In the contraction *aren't* the verb is *are;* in *didn't* the verb is *did.* The *n't* (*not*) is not a part of the verb. In contractions such as *he's* or *you'll,* the verb is *is* or *will.* Study the sentences listed below:

1. She's not giving the true facts.
2. We'll meet you at the ticket office.

What is the verb phrase in sentence 1? in sentence 2?

Exercise: Verbs in contractions

Name the verbs in the following sentences:

1. They'll wait.
2. He's leaving.
3. I don't understand.
4. Haven't they called?
5. We've heard from them.
6. Didn't you know?
7. Hasn't she a costume?
8. I've eaten dinner.
9. You'll see them soon.
10. Can't you hear it?

Sentence Patterns

Add the following new symbol to your list:

$$V^h = \text{Helping verb (Auxiliary verb)}$$

With helping verbs, you can now vary the sentences you are building. Although the group of symbols over each sample sentence below may look more complicated, the basic pattern of the sentence does not change when the verb contains more than one word. The sentence still follows an **N V**, **N V N**, or **N V^be N** pattern.

PATTERN 1:   **N V** (Subject—Verb)

          N   V^h   V
1. The boys will eat.

          N   V^h   V^h   V
2. The boys may have eaten.

PATTERN 2:   **N V N** (Subject—Verb—Direct Object)

   N   V^h   V   N
3. John will give a signal.

  V^h   N   V   N
4. Does John know the signal?

  V^h   N   V   N
5. Is John giving the signal?

PATTERN 3:   **N V^be N** (Subject—Linking Verb—Subject Complement Noun)

   N   V^h   V^be   N
6. Ronnie has been the coach.

  V^h   N   V^h   V^be   N
7. Would Ronnie have become the coach?

● See if you can write two different sentences for each group of symbols given below. Vary the ideas in your sentences.

1. N V^h V	7. V^h N V *the* N?
2. *A* N V^h V^h V	8. N V^h V^h V *the* N
3. N V^h V^be *a* N	9. *The* N V^h V^be N
4. *The* N V^h V *a* N	10. V^h N V^be *the* N?
5. V^h *the* N V?	11. *The* N V^h V^h V^be *a* N
6. N V^h V *the* N	12. *The* N V^h V^h V *the* N

138

● At the top of a sheet of paper, write *Pattern 1;* one third of the way down, write *Pattern 2;* two thirds of the way down, write *Pattern 3.* Then write each of the sentences below under its proper heading.

1. Pamela has opened the windows.
2. Have the windows broken?
3. Tornadoes are storms.
4. An officer will arrest the thief.
5. Does Marty sell newspapers?
6. The apples will fall.
7. The people have elected Mr. Hodges.
8. Valerie could have been a champion.
9. The answer was a mystery.
10. The New York Yankees have arrived.

Helping verb or main verb?

You have seen that with helping verbs we form verbs of more than one word—verb phrases. You should keep in mind, however, that most helping verbs can be used both as helping verbs and by themselves as main verbs. The most common of these are the forms of *have, be,* and *do.* Here are examples:

	USED AS MAIN VERBS	USED AS HELPING VERBS
have	He has three cents.	She has spent three cents.
be	You are very polite.	You are winning the game.
do	Sam did exercises for an hour.	Did Oscar ask a question?

Exercises: Helping verb or main verb?

1. Tell whether each italicized word below is used as a helping verb or a main verb. If it is a helping verb, name the complete verb.

1. Caliban *did* only the lowest of chores.
2. Why *did* he neglect his work?
3. He *was* one of the laziest beings alive.
4. Ariel *was* always teasing the monster.
5. Caliban *had* great fear of Ariel's mischief.
6. Many times Ariel *had* tumbled him into the mire.
7. Caliban *will* never change his bad nature.
8. Ariel *will* always have trouble with him.

2. Use each of the verbs below in two sentences, once as a helping verb, once as a main verb. Underline all verbs.

EXAMPLE: 1. did

YOU WRITE:

1. have
2. do
3. did
4. has
5. am

6. is
7. are
8. does
9. was
10. had

✓ Check Test 7: Irregular verbs

Take this test to find out whether you use correctly certain irregular verbs which you have studied in earlier grades.

Copy the following sentences on your paper. In place of each blank, use the correct form of the verb in parentheses. *Do not use the present tense.*

(choose)   1. Have you __?__ a partner yet?

(sing)   2. Have they __?__ the old school songs?

(ring)   3. The bell in the church steeple had __?__ for two minutes.

(drink)   4. Has the parakeet __?__ all the water?

(break)   5. That screen door has been __?__ all summer.

(choose)   6. Last night we __?__ Ronnie to be the spokesman.

(ring)   7. The telephone has __?__ five times in the past hour.

(choose)   8. Roberta has __?__ to stay at her cousin's house.

(drink)   9. Who has __?__ all the soda?

(sing)   10. Has Sarah __?__ the new song for our show?

(break)   11. Yesterday we accidentally __?__ the mirror.

(break)   12. The crates of melons have __?__ on the way to the market.

(drink)   13. Dad __?__ three cups of coffee this morning.

(ring)   14. Yesterday Jessica __?__ the wrong doorbell.

(sing)   15. At the end of the evening, I __?__ a solo.

If you made any mistakes in the test above, turn to pages 446–48 in the Review Handbook. Find the verb or verbs you need to study.

The Tenses of Verbs

When you express your ideas, you need to be able to tell whether something is happening now (in the *present*), happened earlier (in the *past*), or is going to happen (in the *future*). Verbs enable you to do this because *verbs express time*.

Tense: past, present, and future

In grammar we divide time into three main categories, called **tenses**. These are *present tense*, *past tense*, and *future tense*.

PRESENT TENSE (now)	John *likes* Mary.
	This apple *is* rotten.
PAST TENSE (in the past)	John *liked* Mary.
	This apple *was* rotten.
FUTURE TENSE (in the future)	John *will like* Mary.
	This apple *will be* rotten.

Exercises: Forming verb tenses

1. Name the verb in each sentence below and give its tense. To find the tense, ask yourself: "Did it happen in the past? Is it happening now in the present? Will it happen in the future?"

1. The cats howl all night in the alley.
2. Someone threw a shoe at them.
3. One woman called the police.
4. Soon the police will come.
5. The orchestra played my favorite song.

2. Rewrite each of these sentences, changing the tense of the verb to that named in parentheses after the sentence.

EXAMPLE:　　1. John looks at his toes. (past)
YOU WRITE:　*1. John looked at his toes.*

1. I felt ill. (present)
2. They will be rich. (past)
3. That ox was stubborn. (future)
4. The team plays hard. (past)
5. This summer will be very wet. (past)
6. The lemmings tumbled into the sea. (present)

The Principal Parts of Verbs

Verbs have different forms that are called the **principal parts.** They are *present, past,* and *past participle.*

PRESENT TENSE	PAST TENSE	PAST PARTICIPLE
cook, cooks	cooked	(have, has, had) cooked
use, uses	used	(have, has, had) used

With the three principal parts, we can form any tense we need.

Notice that the *present* includes a form with an **s** and one without an **s.** The subject of the sentence determines which form to use.

Verbs are flexible words and can express time—tense—in several ways. Examine these sentences:

PRESENT TENSE	PAST TENSE
They *cook* today.	They *cooked* yesterday.
She *cooks* today.	She *cooked* yesterday.

Notice that the verb *cook* in the sentences above expresses past tense by *changing form.* Verbs are the only part of speech that can show a change in time with a change in form.

Now look at another way that verbs show a change in time.

> She *has cooked* today.   They *will cook* tomorrow.

How does the verb in each sentence above show tense?

Verbs, then, can express tense *by changing form* and *by adding helping verbs.*

Regular verbs

Verbs that form their past tense by adding **d** or **ed** are called **regular verbs.** The verbs *cook* and *use* above are regular verbs.

Exercise: Writing regular verbs

Use each of the following verbs in two sentences, once using the *past tense* and once using the *past participle* with a helping verb (*have, has,* or *had*). The simple subjects for each sentence are given.

1. *call*: he, we
2. *test*: they, you
3. *resist*: I, people
4. *liberate*: man, it
5. *wait*: boy, birds
6. *rehearse*: she, actors
7. *want*: teachers, I
8. *advance*: fireman, we

Irregular verbs

Most verbs form their past tense regularly by adding *d* or *ed*. However, a few verbs are **irregular.** The formation of their principal parts goes far back into the history of the English language. The grammatical forms of these verbs were once much more complicated than they are today. Here are some examples of irregular verbs. You may have studied them last year.

PRESENT	PAST	PAST PARTICIPLE
freeze	froze	(have, has, had) frozen
ride	rode	(have, has, had) ridden
speak	spoke	(have, has, had) spoken
steal	stole	(have, has, had) stolen
teach	taught	(have, has, had) taught

There is no way to know the principal parts of irregular verbs except to memorize them. Fortunately, most people who hear them correctly spoken have no trouble learning them by ear. Are you making mistakes with some of these irregular verbs, saying, for example, "he speaked" instead of *he spoke,* or "I teached" instead of *I taught?* If so, practice saying the principal parts over and over until you get the correct form well established in your mind.

Here is a list of the principal parts of some irregular verbs you may not have studied:

PRESENT	PAST	PAST PARTICIPLE
beat	beat	(have, has, had) beaten
burst	burst	(have, has, had) burst
shake	shook	(have, has, had) shaken
shrink	shrank	(have, has, had) shrunk
sink	sank	(have, has, had) sunk
spring	sprang	(have, has, had) sprung
swim	swam	(have, has, had) swum
swear	swore	(have, has, had) sworn

As you study the verbs above, keep these two things in mind:

1. The past tense is always used without a helping verb.
2. The past participle is always used with a helping verb.

Notice that the verb *burst* has only one form for all three principal parts.

Using the dictionary to check principal parts

Whenever you are in doubt about the principal parts of a verb, consult a dictionary. Study the following entry from the *Thorndike-Barnhart Advanced Junior Dictionary:*

> **steal** (stēl), **1.** take (something) that does not belong to one; take dishonestly: *steal money.* **2.** take, get, or do secretly: *steal a look at someone.* **3.** take, get, or win by art, charm, or gradual means: *She steals all hearts.* **4.** move secretly or quietly: *She stole out of the house.* **5.** move slowly or gently: *the years steal by.* **6.** *Informal.* act of stealing. **7.** *Informal.* the thing stolen. **8.** run to (a base) in baseball without being helped by a hit or error. 1-5,8 *v.*, stole, sto len, steal ing; 6,7 *n.*

Exercises: Using irregular verbs

1. Read aloud the principal parts of the irregular verbs on page 143. Cover the middle and right-hand columns with a card and see if you can recite the principal parts correctly and without hesitation. If any verb gives you trouble, copy its principal parts into your English notebook. During the next week, memorize them by constant oral drill. Work with a friend, if you wish. Recite each part in a sentence, thus:

Today I *go.*
Yesterday I *went.*
Always I *have gone.*

2. Read each sentence aloud, using the correct form of the verb in parentheses. *Do not use the present tense.*

(steal)	1. After that I __?__ a few hours' sleep.
(burst)	2. The audience had __?__ into cheers.
(ride)	3. I had never __?__ a horse before.
(speak)	4. "I have __?__," said the sultan.
(teach)	5. Yesterday I __?__ Angie the new game.
(freeze)	6. The tenants __?__ until the furnace was repaired.
(beat)	7. The tennis team had __?__ their out-of-town opponents.
(swear)	8. He had __?__ allegiance to the flag.
(swim)	9. Yesterday we __?__ across the lake.

(shake) 10. Aldo had __?__ some apples off the tree.

(shrink) 11. I washed the sweater, and it __?__.

(spring) 12. The boat __?__ a small leak yesterday noon.

(sink) 13. It had __?__ before George could repair it.

3. For each verb below, write two original sentences. In one, use the verb in the past tense. In the other, use the past participle of the verb. Remember, with the past participle you will need to use the helping verb. Underline the verbs in your sentences.

EXAMPLE: 1. know

YOU WRITE: *1. She knew him quite well.*
She had always known him.

beat   burst   shake   shrink   sink   spring   swim   swear

Poets often write simple statements that contain a deeper, more important meaning than appears on the surface. Is De la Mare concerned with the eyesight of the Mole, Bat, and Barn-Owl? Or does he use their poor eyesight as a symbol to suggest a more important kind of blindness? What do you think De la Mare is saying? Who do you think Some-one is in the last stanza?

TO MEMORIZE

All but Blind

All but blind
  In his chambered hole
Gropes for worms
  The four-clawed Mole.

All but blind
  In the evening sky,
The hooded Bat
  Twirls softly by.

All but blind
  In the burning day,
The Barn-Owl blunders
  On her way.

And blind as are
  These three to me,
So, blind to Some-one
  I must be.

WALTER DE LA MARE

Some Confusing Verbs

There are a number of verbs in English which can sometimes be confusing. If you master the explanations below, you should not have any trouble with them.

Lie–lay

The verb *lie* means "to rest or to recline." Here are its principal parts:

PRESENT	PAST	PAST PARTICIPLE
lie, lies	lay	(have, has, had) lain

Study these sentences showing the correct use of *lie*. Notice that the *–ing* form *lying* is included. It is called the **present participle** form of the verb and is always used with a helping verb.

1. Those lazy people *lie* around all day.
2. The baby *lay* on the porch floor yesterday.
3. That rock *has lain* there for centuries.
4. His wallet *is lying* on the front steps.

The verb *lay* means "to put or to place." It is a verb which takes an object: "a person lays *something* somewhere; Joe *laid* the newspaper on the stoop." Its principal parts are:

PRESENT	PAST	PAST PARTICIPLE
lay, lays	laid	(have, has, had) laid

Study these sentences showing the correct use of *lay*. The present participle of *lay* is *laying*.

1. I now *lay* all my money on the table.
2. Yesterday our geese *laid* six eggs.
3. Oscar *has laid* his arm on the counter.
4. The workmen *are laying* the bricks slowly.

The most common error in the use of the verbs *lie* and *lay* is to use the verb *lay* when you should use *lie*.

WRONG: My book was laying on the table.
RIGHT: My book *was lying* on the table.

WRONG: The old man laid down on the couch.
RIGHT: The old man *lay* down on the couch.

Exercises: Using lie and lay

1. Decide which is the correct form of the verb *lie* to fill in each blank in the sentences below. Write it after the appropriate numeral on your paper. If you become confused, refer to the sample sentences on page 146.

1. Each night the queen __?__ on her bed and weeps.
2. The autumn leaves were __?__ all over the lawn.
3. After the picnic we __?__ around on the beach and talked.
4. A week later the money was __?__ exactly where it was left.
5. Our teacher has __?__ quietly in bed for three days.
6. Last summer I __?__ in my hammock and read good books.

2. Follow the same directions as in the first part of this exercise, this time for the verb *lay*.

1. My father __?__ down the law when he comes home.
2. The girls were __?__ embroidered mats on the table.
3. Two years ago they __?__ a new pipeline between here and Texas.
4. He is always __?__ his books down where he cannot find them.
5. Right here is where we have __?__ all those flat rocks.
6. Earlier in the day John __?__ four pies on the windowsill.

3. Choose the correct verb from the two in parentheses. Write your choice after the appropriate numeral on your paper. After your paper has been corrected, practice saying these sentences aloud several times.

1. Before we (lie, lay) down, let's take one more swim.
2. My little sister was (lying, laying) the newspaper on the ground.
3. The old dog (lay, laid) on the cool bricks and panted.
4. The boy has (laid, lain) on the hot sand for over two hours.
5. Singapore (lies, lays) south of China.
6. The chef was (lying, laying) slabs of ham on the skillet.
7. Dinosaurs had (lain, laid) eggs that were immense.
8. (Lay, Lie) those books on the top of the bookcase.
9. The woodsman (lay, laid) his ax on the ground.
10. Please do not (lie, lay) so close to the edge.

Ought

The verb *ought* causes trouble only because people try to make it more complicated than it really is.

Ought is almost always used with *to* and another verb, for example:

1. I *ought to* stop eating.
2. Last year he *ought to* have gone.
3. They *ought* not *to* have eaten that pie.
4. *Oughtn't* we *to* leave now?

Remember: The word *ought* has only one form for all tenses. Never use a helping verb with *ought*.

Exercise: Using ought correctly

Complete the following sentences, using *ought, ought not,* or *oughtn't*:

1. George . . .
2. In the future, those children . . .
3. Last year my brother . . .
4. I know we . . .
5. . . . to salute the flag?
6. Yesterday my sister . . .
7. Next week the newspaper boy . . .
8. . . . we to leave a note?

Bring–take

Use *bring* when the action is *toward* the person who is speaking:

"*Bring* me an apple, please," said Sally. (present)
"She *brought* the package to me," Father chuckled. (past)
He *has brought* me a magazine. (past participle)

Use *take* when the action is *away from* the person speaking:

"*Take* an apple to Grandmother, please," said Joan. (present)
"She *took* him from me!" cried Sue. (past)
He *has taken* my camp equipment away with him. (past participle)

You see that the action of *bring* and *take* is the same. It is the direction that is important. Just remember: take (*away* from the speaker); bring (*to* the speaker).

Teach–learn

Use the verb *teach* when you mean "to instruct or inform someone."

Use the verb *learn* when you mean "to gain knowledge or to receive instruction."

Study the uses of these two verbs in the sentences below:

1. The teacher *teaches* the student.
2. The student *learns* from the teacher.
3. My sister *taught* me to knit.
4. I *learned* to knit easily.
5. He *is teaching* us to make model jets.
6. We *are learning* quickly.

Exercises: Bring, take; teach, learn

1. In place of the blanks in the following sentences, use the correct form of *bring* or *take*.

1. Mother asked, "Did you __?__ any books to school today?" I answered, "No, I __?__ them home last night, but I have not __?__ them back."
2. The year he went to the YMCA camp, he __?__ my sleeping bag with him.
3. Herbert has __?__ away my electric trains and has __?__ me nothing in return.
4. "__?__ me some flowers," said Aunt Kate.
5. __?__ your brother to the movies.

2. For the blank in each of the following sentences, use the correct form of *teach* or *learn.*

1. Will you __?__ me to ski?
2. Mr. Small is __?__ us a new game.
3. I have __?__ you to be polite.
4. He has __?__ them to drive carefully.
5. My dog has never __?__ to sit up and beg.

✓ Check Test 8: Using set–sit and leave–let

Take this test to find out whether you know how to use the verbs *let* and *leave* and *set* and *sit.*

Write these sentences, choosing the correct verb from each pair in parentheses:

1. Will you (leave, let) me read you my theme?
2. Please (sit, set) down beside me for a moment.
3. (Let, Leave) your sister help you.
4. (Sit, Set) your bundles on this bench.
5. Valerie (sits, sets) her umbrella in the bathtub to dry.
6. Please (leave, let) David borrow your tools.

If you made mistakes on the sentences above, turn to the lesson you need to study in the Review Handbook on pages 450 and 452.

Sentence Patterns

The patterns of sentences are a key to the correct use of the verbs *to lie* and *to lay.* The verb *to lie*, which means "to rest or recline," is generally used in sentences that follow PATTERN 1: N V; that is, the pattern without a direct object. The verb *to lay*, which means "to put or place," is generally used in sentences that follow PATTERN 2: N V N; that is, the pattern containing a direct object. The exceptions to these uses are so few that you need not concern yourselves with them here.

Study the following examples. Keep in mind that the helping verbs in verb phrases do not change the basic pattern of a sentence. For example, if a sentence follows the symbols N Vʰ V, as in sentences 3 and 4 on the next page, the sentence is still considered a Pattern 1 sentence: N V.

PATTERN 1:   N V (Subject—Verb)

    N   **V**
1. <u>Jay</u> always <u>lies</u> on this couch.

             N   **V**
2. Yesterday, the <u>dog</u> <u>lay</u> under the tree.

     N **Vh**   **V**
3. The <u>man</u> <u>is</u> <u>lying</u> in the truck.

   N **Vh**   **V**
4. <u>Pat</u> <u>had</u> <u>lain</u> there for an hour.

PATTERN 2:   N V N (Subject—Verb—Direct Object)

          N   **V**   **N**
5. Each day the <u>boy</u> <u>lays</u> a <u>newspaper</u> on the windowsill.

  N   **V**   **N**
6. <u>Allen</u> <u>laid</u> the <u>hammer</u> here.

     N   **Vh** **V**   **N**
7. The <u>children</u> <u>are</u> <u>laying</u> their <u>toys</u> aside.

    N   **Vh** **V**   **N**
8. Mr. <u>Joels</u> <u>has</u> <u>laid</u> his <u>brush</u> down.

The words above which are not labeled with symbols are modifiers; they are not a part of the basic pattern.

● Number your paper from 1 to 6. Decide what pattern each sentence follows and write *Pattern 1: N V* or *Pattern 2: N V N* beside the appropriate numeral.

1. The workmen have laid the tiles unevenly.
2. Larry lay on the porch all afternoon.
3. Norma has lain down for an hour.
4. Mother laid the presents under the tree.
5. Our dog often lies under this table.
6. My brother is lying down.

● Write sentences, following the groups of symbols below. Choose the correct form of the verbs *to lie* or *to lay* for each sentence. Modifiers have been written out for you.

1. *The* **N** *always* **V** *next to the window.*
2. *Yesterday* **N** **V** *the* **N** *in the shed.*
3. **N** **Vh** **V** *your* **N** *on the shelf.*
4. *The* **N** **V** *their* **N** *down ten minutes ago.*
5. *Yesterday* **N** **V** *on the beach all morning.*
6. **N** **Vh** **V** *there all day.*

Agreement of Subject and Verb

When we say *number* in speaking of nouns, we refer to whether they are singular or plural. When we say *person* in speaking of verbs, we refer to their subjects and the question of whether they are first person (*I, we*), second person (*you*), or third person (*he, she, it, they*).

It is correct to use a singular subject with the singular form of the verb and a plural subject with the plural form of the verb. When this is done, we say that the subject and verb *agree*.

RIGHT: One cat drinks milk.   WRONG: One cat drink milk.

RIGHT: Three cats drink milk.   WRONG: Three cats drinks milk.

With a subject in the third person singular, the present tense form of the verb ends in *s*. With the third person plural, it does not.

RIGHT: He goes.   RIGHT: She goes.   RIGHT: They go.

WRONG: He go.   WRONG: She go.   WRONG: They goes.

The pronouns *I* and *you* always take the plural form of the verb.

RIGHT: I go.   RIGHT: You go.

WRONG: I goes.   WRONG: You goes.

Subject and verb must agree in person and number.

Exercise: Subject and verb agreement

Choose the correct form of the verb in parentheses to agree with the subject.

1. Those boys (go, goes) to town early.
2. That boy (go, goes) to town early.
3. We always (feel, feels) grateful for rain.
4. He never (need, needs) help in tying his shoelaces.
5. The ladies (feel, feels) happy about the agreement.
6. His black hair and shining eyes (was, were) attractive.
7. This little pig (has, have) always gone to market.
8. A large policeman (was, were) arresting the skinny thief.
9. He said to them, "You (was, were) my dearest friends."
10. I (has, have) only one dollar left to spend.

Test I

1. Copy the verb from each of these sentences and label it *transitive* or *intransitive*.

1. He spread butter on his bread.
2. The rumor spread rapidly through the village.
3. The waves break against the rocks.
4. The waves break the driftwood into splinters.
5. My favorite vegetable is the cherry tomato.

2. Now go back over the sentences in part 1 and copy the numeral of each sentence that has a transitive verb. Beside the numeral, write the word which receives the action of the verb (the direct object).

Test II

Each of the following sentences has a verb phrase. Number your paper from 1 to 5. Then copy the verb phrase from each sentence.

1. When will the teacher return the papers?
2. Didn't you do your homework carefully?
3. He shouldn't have laughed.
4. We had been impatiently waiting for that message.
5. He will not allow visitors.

Test III

Number your paper from 1 to 20. For each sentence below and at the top of page 154, write the correct form of the verb in parentheses. *Do not use the present tense.*

(freeze) 1. The bottles of milk have __?__ on the doorstep.
(ride) 2. The cavalry __?__ into the stockade at great speed.
(speak) 3. My mother has __?__ to the landlord about the heat.
(steal) 4. Bobbie __?__ home and scored the winning run.
(teach) 5. He __?__ at that school for ten years.
(beat) 6. Had they __?__ their opponents?
(shake) 7. That child __?__ all the berries off the bushes.
(shrink) 8. The grapes on the ground __?__ under the hot sun.
(sink) 9. My fishing pole __?__ to the bottom of the lake.
(spring) 10. The circus bears __?__ onto their bicycles.

(swim) 11. I have __?__ the width of this river.

(swear) 12. Has the new member been __?__ in?

(beat) 13. Yesterday I __?__ him at tennis.

(shrink) 14. Either I have grown bigger or my sweater has __?__.

(swim) 15. The boys __?__ in the pond all afternoon.

(swear) 16. He __?__ that he had told the truth.

(spring) 17. The monkey had __?__ from branch to branch.

(shake) 18. I have already __?__ the package, and it rattles.

(sink) 19. Our boat has __?__ into the seaweed.

(freeze) 20. My toes __?__ on the ski slope this morning.

Test IV

Choose between the verbs in parentheses. On your paper next to the appropriate numeral, write the verb which completes each sentence correctly.

1. Those lazy people have (laid, lain) around all day.
2. Please (bring, take) that pile of books out of here.
3. He is (teaching, learning) me to handle a sailboat.
4. The boy (lay, laid) his paper on the teacher's desk.
5. Alex has (brought, taken) the lost spaniel back to its owner.
6. The wedding dress has (lain, laid) in that trunk for years.
7. I'll (teach, learn) you to use the right verb.
8. The boys were (lying, laying) on the beach near the pier.
9. Please don't (lie, lay) on the floor.
10. Your cat (lay, laid) its kittens in the middle of my flower bed.

Test V

Copy each sentence on your paper, choosing the correct verb.

1. These girls (go, goes) to the sewing club once a week.
2. We always (go, goes) with them.
3. You (was, were) riding the bike carelessly.
4. Those boys (has, have) no help.
5. He never (walk, walks) the dog.
6. It (don't, doesn't) impress me.
7. I (is, am) feeling miserable.
8. She never (complete, completes) her assignment.
9. (Is, Are) you a genius?
10. He (go, goes) to the game every Saturday.

Exercise I

1. Review "Transitive and Intransitive Verbs" on pages 132–34.
2. Copy the verb from each of these sentences and label it *transitive* or *intransitive*:

1. The wind *blew* all night.
2. The wind *blew* the papers off the desk.
3. My mother *has been cooking* stew.
4. My mother *has been* a girl scout leader.
5. I *slipped* on the ice.
6. I *slipped* the letter into the mailbox.

3. Write five sentences using these verbs as transitive verbs. Make sure you include a direct object in each sentence.

ride   shout   beat   write   play

Exercise II

1. Review "Verb Phrases" on pages 135–39.
2. Copy the verb phrases from each of the sentences below:

1. I can never sing high enough.
2. Jeremy had always wanted a dragonfly.
3. The baby has not been crying.
4. Doesn't he answer your letters?
5. Is the sun shining this morning?

3. Use each of the following verb phrases in a sentence. Note the specific instructions for each pair of phrases:

1. have been eating	(Include the word "not" between
2. will go	parts of these verb phrases.)
3. should have asked	(Write interrogative sentences with
4. have complained	the subject between parts of these verb phrases.)
5. had barked	(Use a word that tells *when* or *how* in
6. will insist	the middle of each verb phrase.)
7. do not want	(Make contractions of the first two
8. have not been hearing	words in each of these verb phrases. Then use the phrases in sentences.)

4. Copy the italicized verbs from the following sentences. Beside each one, write *helping verb* or *main verb*, depending on how it is used in the sentence.

1. I *did* the dishes eleven times last week.
2. The car *was* zooming around the curves.
3. Why *does* Henry like that girl?
4. *Am* I on time?
5. You *are* shouting into the telephone.
6. The chairman *has* an assistant.
7. We *have* increased the dues.
8. He *is* an excellent speaker.

5. Write two sentences for each of the following verbs. In the first sentence, use the verb as the *main verb*. In the second sentence, use the verb as a *helping verb*.

1. had	5. has
2. was	6. does
3. were	7. have
4. is	8. are

Exercise III

1. Review "The Principal Parts of Verbs" on pages 142–44.

2. Below you are given the present tense of some regular and some irregular verbs. Copy the verbs in a list on your paper. Opposite each one, in parallel columns, write the past tense and the past participle forms. Use a helping verb with each past participle form.

1. sink	11. speak
2. swear	12. steal
3. learn	13. ride
4. bake	14. live
5. walk	15. cover
6. beat	16. cook
7. hope	17. practice
8. shake	18. swim
9. shrink	19. freeze
10. spring	20. play

3. Use each of the irregular verbs in part 2 of this exercise in a sentence. Use the verb in the past or the past participle form.

Exercise IV

1. Review "Some Confusing Verbs" on pages 146–49.

2. Copy the following sentences, using the correct form of the verb *lay* in place of each blank.

    1. Please do not __?__ your wet raincoats on this chair.
    2. Yesterday, she __?__ her knitting down near the cat.
    3. The speaker has __?__ his note cards on the podium.
    4. The men are __?__ the rug now.

3. Copy the following sentences, using the correct form of the verb *lie* in place of each blank.

    1. He is __?__ on some beach in the South Pacific.
    2. Please don't __?__ on the table.
    3. The dusty shirt had __?__ in the corner for months.
    4. Yesterday she __?__ on her bed and cried.

4. Choose the correct verb from each pair in parentheses.

    1. (Bring, Take) this book to the library and (bring, take) me another one by the same author.
    2. I'll (teach, learn) you how to play the guitar.
    3. Doug has (brought, taken) his paintings to an art dealer.
    4. He is (teaching, learning) me how to ski.

5. Use *ought* in three sentences, using *present*, *past*, and *past participle* forms once each.

Exercise V

1. Review "Agreement of Subject and Verb" on page 152.

2. Write ten sentences of your own, using the following subjects. Choose verbs from the list on the right.

SUBJECTS		VERBS	
1. I	6. Henry	want	offer
2. you	7. teacher	wants	offers
3. they	8. he	is	do
4. we	9. she	are	does
5. pilots	10. it	was	has
		were	have
		am	go
			goes

CHAPTER 6

Developing Your Vocabulary

A vocabulary is a stock of words. The average seventh-grader knows about 25,000 words. This is about one twentieth of all the words listed in the larger dictionaries of the English language. You will never know all of these words. You will always be challenged by new ones.

New words enter your vocabulary from many sources, mostly from your everyday reading and listening. They also enter through the many hobbies or special fields of activity which may interest you and which require specialized vocabularies. Music, for example, has its own specialized vocabulary. Do you know some of the words which the students in the picture on the opposite page must know and use?

The Importance of a Good Vocabulary

If you train yourself to notice new words, to find out what they mean, and to use them, your stock of words will increase. The richer your vocabulary is, the easier it will be to understand and appreciate the thoughts of others and to express your thoughts clearly to them.

To discuss

1. Take time now to consider and discuss the ways in which a good vocabulary would be helpful to you in the following situations:

Getting promoted	Appreciating a good book
Taking a science trip	Reading directions
Writing a history paper	Writing a letter
Applying for a job	Getting into college
Holding a job	Winning a class office

2. Can you name other situations where a good vocabulary would be helpful?

Keeping a Record

A good way to keep track of the new words you want to learn is to list them alphabetically in a section of your English notebook or in a special vocabulary notebook. Set aside a page, or part of a page, for each letter of the alphabet. If you make a thumb index, you can turn quickly to the letter you want. The illustration above shows how to do this.

You may find it convenient to combine your vocabulary notebook with a spelling notebook (see pages 332–33). You can use the top of each page for vocabulary words and the bottom for spelling words.

Always take your notebook with you to all classes—not just English classes. Then, when a new word comes up, you can write it down immediately. It will be helpful, once you have listed a word, to use it several times in the next few days in order to fix it in your mind. Try to review the words in your notebook about once a week.

Here are some sample entries:

> *gusto: hearty enjoyment*
> *He beats the drum with gusto.*
> *gratify: give pleasure to*
> *The boy's good marks gratified his parents.*

1. Write a new word in your vocabulary notebook.
2. Write a definition beside it.
3. Write a sentence in which the word is used correctly.

The dictionary can be your most useful tool for increasing vocabulary. Keep a dictionary at home near the place where you do your homework or your reading. Whenever possible, if you come across a word you do not know, look it up. A word often has several meanings given for it in the dictionary, but usually only one of these is the meaning you want.

Exercise: Starting a vocabulary notebook

Within the next week, write down in your vocabulary notebook at least ten unfamiliar words you come across in reading or listening which you think would be helpful to learn. Use a dictionary to look up the definition of each one.

Learning Words from Context

You can sometimes learn new words by making intelligent guesses about their meanings. If the words, sentences, or paragraphs that surround a new word are familiar to you, they will often reveal the meaning of the new word. This way of learning word meanings is called **getting the meaning from context.**

Suppose, for example, you are reading a science book and you come across this sentence:

> The mouth of the river was clogged with *detritus* the river had brought down from the hills.

To discuss

1. Examine the context of the word *detritus* in the sentence above and answer these questions about it:

   1. What is a stream likely to wash down from higher land?
   2. What is your guess as to the meaning of the word *detritus*?
   3. Check your answer with the dictionary definition. Did you guess the meaning correctly?

2. From the context of this lesson, can you give a meaning for the word *context?*

3. After you guess the meanings of words from context, how do you make the words your own?

Getting word meaning from context is a very useful skill, and one that can be developed with practice. If you want to move these new words over from your vocabulary of understanding to your speaking and writing vocabulary, learn their meanings, spelling, and pronunciation and then use them frequently.

■ The **context** of a word is its surrounding words, sentences, or paragraphs.

Exercise: Getting word meanings from context

Read the following sentences. Guess the meaning of each italicized word from its context. If you are doing this exercise in class, compare the various guesses of class members and decide which meaning of the word is probably the correct one. Then check with your dictionary.

1. Those who *procrastinate* never get things done on time.
2. The mountain lion *emitted* a cry, half *bestial,* half human.
3. Our team was *demoralized* by the fast playing of our opponents, and defeat was *imminent.*
4. With such a *meager* vocabulary, you should work *diligently* at learning new words.
5. Do not light a match in this room, for these cans contain *combustible* materials.
6. Scrooge *remonstrated* angrily with his nephew over his custom of making merry at Christmas.
7. The old house was *reminiscent* of our childhood.
8. We all had a feeling of *impending* danger.
9. The mountaineer hung *precariously* to the ledge.
10. In early summer the trees are in their fullest *foliage* and brightest *verdure.*
11. Susan *intercepted* the postman at the gate and told him about the new watchdog in the yard.
12. Jonathan will never *comprehend* algebra if he doesn't do his homework regularly each night.

How Words Are Built

Many words are composed of two or more parts. Often, if you know the meaning of the parts, you can make a good guess about the meaning of the whole word. Take, for example, the word *inaction*, a word you might occasionally use. It has three parts: *in-act-ion*. **Act** is the *root*, or foundation, of the word. It means "do." **In–** is the *prefix* which goes before the root and means "not"; *–ion* is the *suffix* which follows the root and means "condition or state of." If you put *in* and *act* and *ion* together, you get the meaning "condition of not doing." This is close to the dictionary meaning of the word.

By learning certain common prefixes, suffixes, and roots, you will have the keys for unlocking the meanings of many words.

Prefixes

The word *prefix* is built from the familiar root *fix*, which means "to place or fasten." *Pre–* means "before." A **prefix,** then, is a syllable or syllables joined to the beginning of a word to change its meaning. Do you see how a knowledge of the meaning of parts of the word can give you a good clue to the meaning of the word?

Examine these common prefixes:

PREFIX	MEANING	EXAMPLE
bi–	*two, twice*	*bi*annual
co–	*with*	*co*operate
dis–	*reverse of*	*dis*continue
ex–	*former, out*	*ex*-president, *ex*hale
im– in–	*not*	*im*possible, *in*expensive
inter–	*between, among*	*inter*state
mis–	*bad, wrong*	*mis*conduct, *mis*spell
non–	*not*	*non*stop
pre–	*before*	*pre*caution
re–	*again, back*	*re*trace
sub–	*under*	*sub*marine
super–	*above*	*super*highway
trans–	*across*	*trans*continental
un–	*not*	*un*welcome

Spelling note: When a prefix is added to a root word, the spelling of the root word does not change.

Exercises: Prefixes

1. Choosing among the prefixes listed above, add a prefix to each of the following words. Use each word you have formed in a short sentence. Check the words with the dictionary to be sure you have used them correctly.

1. place	6. pilot	11. trial	16. historic
2. vision	7. plant	12. change	17. cycle
3. sense	8. view	13. arrange	18. operate
4. polite	9. natural	14. likely	19. act
5. pleasure	10. locate	15. take	20. urban

2. Guess the meanings of the ten words listed below. Then check each guess against the dictionary. Use three columns, thus: *Word, My Guess, Dictionary Definition.*

1. bipartisan	6. mistranslate
2. impersonal	7. nonviolent
3. bimetallic	8. predigest
4. discredit	9. repeople
5. interlace	10. superstructure

GOING AHEAD

Here are ten common prefixes not listed above. Look them up in a good dictionary and make a list of them similar to the one for prefixes on page 163. If any prefix has more than one meaning, choose only one of the meanings.

1. ante–	3. con–	5. fore–	7. post–	9. semi–
2. circum–	4. contra–	6. mono–	8. pro–	10. tri–

Suffixes

A **suffix** is a syllable or syllables joined to the end of a word. Here are lists of the suffixes most useful in building vocabulary. They can be classified according to what they mean.

One group of suffixes means "one who." When any one of these suffixes is added to a verb or a noun, the resulting word means "one who performs or does" whatever is named. A few of these suffixes are listed below. Study the list and try to name one or two other examples for each suffix.

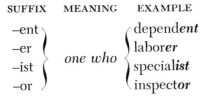

SUFFIX	MEANING	EXAMPLE
–ent		dependent
–er	one who	laborer
–ist		specialist
–or		inspector

Another group of suffixes means "state of being." One of them is *–ance.* Thus the word *annoyance* means "the state of being annoyed." Study the list below and give the meaning of each word:

SUFFIX	MEANING	EXAMPLE
–ance		importance
–ence		dependence
–hood	state of being	childhood
–ness		wordiness
–tion		temptation

Yet a third group of suffixes means "having the quality of." One of these suffixes is *–ish.* Added to the word *fool,* it results in *foolish,* which means "having the quality of a fool."

SUFFIX	MEANING	EXAMPLE
–ic		heroic
–ish	having the quality of	childish
–like		sphinxlike
–ly		friendly

There are three other suffixes which will help you build vocabulary. They are listed below:

SUFFIX	MEANING	EXAMPLE
–ful	*full of, full*	faithful
–less	*without*	faithless
–ward	*toward*	homeward

Exercise: Adding suffixes to words

Choose any ten of the suffixes listed above and write a word using each one. Use a dictionary to check meaning. Then use each word in a sentence.

EXAMPLE: *–ful*   playful
The seals are in a playful mood.

Roots

A **root** is a word, or part of a word, that is the base upon which other words may be built. An understanding of roots will help you build your vocabulary. One common root is *port.* As a verb, *port* came into English from Old French, which in turn got it from the Latin verb *portare,* "to carry."

In the following words, *port* is the root. Observe how the words are built from the root and the prefixes and suffixes.

export	portage	deport	reporter
import	portable	porter	transportation
transport	support	report	portfolio

Study these word parts, some from Greek, some from Latin:

ROOT	MEANING	EXAMPLE
ped	*foot*	*ped*estrian
voc	*call*	*voc*al
cide	*kill*	sui*cide*
geo	*earth*	*geo*graphy
logy	*science of*	bio*logy*
scribe, scrip	*write*	in*scribe*, in*scrip*tion
bio	*life*	*bio*logy

Exercises: Roots

1. Can you find one or two words which contain each of the roots listed above? After each word, write its meaning. Be sure you check with the dictionary. Compare your lists in class.

2. See how many words you can build by adding a prefix or suffix, or both, to these words: *print, appear.*

███ GOING AHEAD ███

See how many good English words you can build by putting two or three of these word parts together. You may need to add a prefix or suffix to some of your combinations.

auto—*self*	logy—*science, theory of*
bio—*life*	meter—*measure*
chrono—*time*	phono—*sound, voice*
geo—*earth,* or *the earth*	tele—*far, distant*
graph—*writing*	vis—*see, face*

Learning Words in Specialized Vocabularies

You will never use most of the approximately 600,000 words in the English language. So many of these words are found in the specialized vocabularies of sports, hobbies, occupations, professions, and other special fields of activity. However, the more varieties of experience and interest you have, the more interesting your vocabulary will be.

As you expand your interests, you will discover many new words to add to your vocabulary—words like *gantry, hypergols, telemeter,* in the field of rocketry, for example.

In addition to new words, you will learn new meanings for common words, like *positive,* which to a photographer may mean a print made from a film or a plate. Working in a garage; learning to cook, sew, dance, or play a musical instrument; and reading a book about sailing, jungle life, or space travel are only a few of the experiences from which you can draw words to enrich your vocabulary.

Here are lists of words taken from specialized fields. Look over the words in each list and be prepared to discuss them.

LIST 1	LIST 2	LIST 3	LIST 4	LIST 5
carburetor	measuring	placket	coda	cirrus
piston	cup	tuck	crescendo	front
crankshaft	sifter	piping	octave	horse lati-
differential	double	lining	percussion	tudes
radiator	boiler	bodice	stave	nimbus
axle	grater	gore	clef	precipita-
transmission	griddle	pinking	treble	tion
cylinder	casserole	shears	diminuendo	doldrums
battery	potholder	bias bind-	dissonance	troposphere
manifold	baster	ing	andante	isotherm
distributor	blender	pleat	pianissimo	cumulus

To discuss

1. What type of specialist do you think would use the words in each list above? If you cannot name the specialist, can you tell the activity or field in which these words would be used?

2. Which words gave you a clue?

3. Can you think of any words which can be added to each list above? You may use your dictionary if you need help.

Exercise: Specialized vocabularies

Write the four headings listed below on your paper. Under each heading, name the specialist who is likely to use the words listed under that heading. Then name an activity or field in which these words would be used. List the word or words that gave you the clue. If you do not know the answer, look up one or two words in the dictionary. Discuss your answers in class.

LIST 1	LIST 2	LIST 3	LIST 4
alpha particle	pistil	planetoid	scansion
commutator	mutant	planetesimal	couplet
conduction	photosynthesis	equinox	ode
decibel	node	solstice	iambic
diffusion	gene	nebula	meter
foot-pound	cytoplasm	corona	quatrain
grid	corolla	asteroid	alliteration
rectify	coccus	spiral nebulae	euphony

▬▬▬ **GOING AHEAD** ▬▬▬

Perhaps you have a special field of interest about which you know more than the average person. If so, think about the special vocabulary it requires and choose ten or twelve uncommon words from it. Remember, the words may seem easy to you because you are familiar with them, but they are probably not familiar to those who are not specialists.

Some fields about which you may have special knowledge are rocketry, sewing, sports, automobiles, model railroads, cooking, gardening, stamp collecting. Write your list of words on the board and see if the class knows to which specialty it refers.

Using Synonyms

How rich is your vocabulary? Do you use the same words over and over again until they lose their exact meaning? If you do, you should learn some synonyms—words that are similar in meaning. They will help you to express your ideas more clearly and more interestingly.

■ Words which have the same or nearly the same meaning are called **synonyms.**

Exercises: Synonyms

1. Below each of the sentences in this exercise are five words. One of the words is a synonym for the italicized word in the sentence. Choose the synonym and write it on your paper opposite the appropriate numeral.

1. The speaker's voice was *monotonous.*

   weak   harsh   unvarying   gruff   musical

2. The crew of the ship became *mutinous.*

   noisy   rebellious   silent   moody   wild

3. The captain of the ship was *imperious.*

   domineering   stubborn   serious   firm   fun-loving

4. The statue had a richly carved *pedestal.*

   head   body   base   case   surface

5. The *energetic* scout leaped across the rocky stream.

   unhappy   skillful   nervous   careless   vigorous

6. Was that child *pampered* by his parents?

   indulged   hampered   criticized   helped   punished

7. How *variable* the weather has been!

   rainy   warm   sunny   changeable   steady

8. Earl was a *novice* at the game.

   leader   beginner   expert   coward   authority

2. Beside each italicized word below are four other words, one of them a synonym for the italicized word. Choose the synonym and then use it in an original sentence.

1. *proceed*   march, proclaim, follow, continue
2. *dominate*   scold, rule, give, share
3. *pacify*   pack, soothe, annoy, convey
4. *surrender*   yield, encircle, delay, surprise
5. *prophesy*   predict, threaten, propose, predicate

ADJECTIVES

6. *impartial*   halfway, flimsy, neutral, prejudiced
7. *eternal*   heavenly, honorable, airy, everlasting
8. *abundant*   scarce, ample, happy, wealthy
9. *fragile*   pale, slender, frail, sweet
10. *able*   inept, active, exact, competent

NOUNS

11. *disciple*   assistant, founder, leader, follower
12. *statute*   law, image, proverb, monument
13. *petition*   division, request, banner, partnership
14. *prowess*   ship, huntress, valor, director
15. *fatigue*   weariness, brevity, sleep, relaxation

Avoiding overworked words

The word *nice* is one of the most overworked words in our language. We talk about a *nice* girl, a *nice* mess, a *nice* time, a *nice* book, a *nice* tree, a *nice* song, or a *nice* school. No one really knows just what we mean each time we use a word as often as this.

Another overworked word is the verb *strike*, which means "to hit or deal a blow." Here are some synonyms for *strike: smite, spank, cuff, thwack, thump, beat, buffet, thrash, pummel, lace, drub, trounce, flog, scourge, whip, cane, switch, pelt, stone.* There are also a few slang words, such as *biff, lambaste,* and *sock.* Here are four of these synonyms used in sentences:

1. The Black Knight *smites* his opponent with a mace.
2. The intruder *thwacked* the hero with a loose board.
3. The mother bear *cuffed* her cub amiably.
4. The little man was *buffeted* by the crowd.

To discuss

1. Do all the italicized words in the sentences above have identical meanings? Check your answer with the dictionary.

2. Can you think of other sentences in which the verbs *smite*, *thwack*, *cuff*, and *buffet* could be used appropriately?

3. How can an extensive knowledge of synonyms help improve a person's writing and speaking?

Avoid frequent use of overworked words. Choose words that have the exact shade of meaning you want to convey.

Exercise: Using vivid words

Read the sentences below. For each italicized word, see if you can name three substitutes that would be more exact or more colorful. Do not use fancy language where plain language would do.

1. The lecture was *great*.
2. The old gentleman wore *funny* clothes.
3. I have just read a *good* book.
4. The new girl wore a *pretty* dress.
5. The village at the foot of the hill looked *nice*.
6. Marjorie seems *happy* about her party.
7. Little Jimmy was a *marvelous* student.
8. Louise *said*, "Where can it be?"
9. Did Roy *make* that model plane?
10. On our return, we *went* through the Ozarks.

TO MEMORIZE

FROM *A Poison Tree*

I was angry with my friend:
I told my wrath, my wrath did end.
I was angry with my foe:
I told it not, my wrath did grow.

WILLIAM BLAKE

Poets interpret life in many ways. Sometimes, they describe a scene in nature or tell a story or ask questions about the meaning of life. At other times, they comment on the relationship between persons, as in the poem above. What do you think of William Blake's advice? You may want to find and read the entire poem.

Using Antonyms

Another way of keeping alert to words is to think of words which have opposite meanings. For example, the opposite of *white* is *black*; of *large* is *small*; of *man* is *woman*. What are the opposites of *happy*, *slow*, and *visible*?

■ Words which have opposite meanings are called **antonyms**.

Exercises: Antonyms

1. After each word in the left-hand column below are printed four other words. On your paper, write the word which is the antonym of the word in italics. When you have completed this exercise, check your answers in class.

| EXAMPLE: | 1. *child* | infant | adult | boy | girl |
| YOU WRITE: | *1. adult* | | | | |

1. *distant*	far	invisible	near	small
2. *lenient*	uneven	slanting	easy	severe
3. *slovenly*	modest	tidy	dull	joyous
4. *gallant*	petty	rude	brave	ridiculous
5. *idolize*	admire	hate	refuse	accept
6. *malice*	suitcase	thick mud	kindness	ill will
7. *offense*	absence	knowledge	barrier	defense
8. *perverse*	difficult	reasonable	opposite	insane

2. Name an antonym for each word below. It must be a single word of the same part of speech. Then use any five of the words below and their antonyms in sentences of your own. This means you have ten sentences to write. When you have completed this exercise, check your answers in the dictionary.

VERBS	NOUNS	ADJECTIVES
admire	boredom	ridiculous
construct	interior	defiant
retreat	anguish	antagonistic
notice	nonsense	usual
move	doubt	doleful
extend	force	varied
decline	kindness	irritable

Writing Homonyms

Words that sound alike but that differ in meaning and sometimes in spelling are called **homonyms.** When you are learning to spell homonyms, always learn them in meaningful phrases or sentences. When you test yourself on them, write them in meaningful phrases or sentences, or you will not know which homonym you are spelling.

Here are some homonyms which often cause trouble. Notice that they are written in sentences so that their meaning is clear.

all ready	We are *all ready.*
already	We have been paid *already.*
here	Come *here.*
hear	I *hear* the noises.
bear	The *bear* growled. I cannot *bear* the pain.
bare	Do not walk in your *bare* feet.
principle	Truth is my *principle.* (rule)
principal	The *principal* (main) building is on the corner.
	The *principal* of the school has left.
through	Look *through* the window.
threw	He *threw* the ball.
no	There is *no* reason to leave.
know	I *know* your neighborhood.
write	*Write* soon.
right	There is a *right* and wrong.
meet	I would like to *meet* your friend.
meat	The *meat* and potatoes are overcooked.
break	Did you *break* your arm?
brake	The emergency *brake* of the car needed adjustment.
great	He is a *great* leader.
grate	We need a fireplace *grate.*
stationery	*Stationery* is paper.
stationary	A *stationary* engine is an engine that cannot be moved.
whose	*Whose* book is it?
who's	*Who's* (who is) going?

Exercises: Writing homonyms correctly

1. On your paper, write the word which completes each sentence correctly.

1. The players must pass (threw, through) this entrance.
2. Try to (write, right) a polite answer.
3. His (principle, principal) purpose was to get out of work.
4. Before the accident, the car had been (stationery, stationary).
5. (Whose, Who's) friend are you?
6. The (principle, principal) of our school is Beth's father.
7. The (stationary, stationery) is in that desk drawer.
8. Can you (hear, here) the fireworks in the next town?

2. Write each word below in a sentence of your own:

all ready	no	meet	breaks	great
already	know	meat	brakes	grate

Using Words to Convey Feelings

If you call a girl *skinny,* she will probably not like it. If you call her *thin,* she may have no reaction at all. On the other hand, if you call her *slender,* she will probably react favorably.

As another example, take the synonyms *cold, frigid, chilly, cool, icy, wintry, raw, bitter, nipping, fresh.* Clearly they are not identical, although they all have similar meanings.

Read this sentence and then discuss the questions which follow.

The knight rode out into the __?__ morning air.

To discuss

1. If you wanted to suggest that a knight found the cold air pleasant, which of the synonyms above might you use?

2. If you wanted to make sure the reader knew that the air felt unpleasant, which words would· you use?

3. Which of the synonyms above conveys a neutral feeling?

You can see that many words suggest particular feelings. Because the feeling of a word is part of its meaning, you must choose words carefully. Remember, the more words you know, the more appropriately and exactly you can express yourself and your feelings.

Exercise: Words and feelings

Some of the following words are neutral, while others give a favorable or an unfavorable impression. Make three columns on your paper and label them *Favorable, Neutral,* and *Unfavorable.* Then write each word of the group, starting with numeral 1, under one of the headings. In some of the groups, you may have more than one word in one column and none in another.

EXAMPLE: cur, dog, puppy, mongrel

YOU WRITE: *Favorable   Neutral   Unfavorable*

        puppy   dog   cur
                           mongrel

1. clever, cunning, sly
2. shack, house, cottage
3. agent, spy, observer
4. waste, garbage, refuse
5. crew, gang, mob
6. plump, fat, stout, chubby
7. scold, reprimand, chide
8. breeze, wind, gale
9. stubborn, persistent, steady
10. car, heap, buggy
11. graveyard, cemetery, memorial park
12. make, create, fashion

━━━━ GOING AHEAD ━━━━

Sometimes people do not like to see or hear words that say directly and plainly something that is unpleasant. Instead, they substitute a pleasanter expression to say the same thing. For example, instead of saying, "She died," they will say, "She passed away," or instead of saying "fat people," they will say "stylish stouts." These less direct and milder expressions are called *euphemisms.* Advertising is full of them.

During the next few days listen, watch, and read carefully to see how many euphemisms you can find. List them, and beside each one, write its direct translation.

EXAMPLE: EUPHEMISM   DIRECT EXPRESSION

        motion discomfort   air sickness

Choosing Words with Specific Meanings

Some writers use too many words which have a *general* meaning, rather than a *specific* one. For example, a general word is *food*. Some words which name specific foods are: *beef, eggs, milk, bread*. A word more specific than *food* but rather general is *meat*. Under *meat* one can include the specific words *pork, beef, veal, hamburger, hot dogs*. Under *veal* one can be even more specific with words like *veal roast, veal chops, veal cutlets*.

Your writing and speaking will usually be more interesting if you express yourself in quite specific terms, rather than in general ones. It is better to say, "We ate bacon, eggs, and coffee cake for breakfast," than to say, "We had food for the meal." Your reader would rather know that "Mrs. Crenshaw's Packard crept down Willow Avenue" than "A lady's car went slowly down the street." Remember that specific words make your writing come alive.

To discuss

Discuss the following pairs of sentences. Which sentence in each pair do you find the more interesting? Why?

1. The animal went into his home.
2. The bear lumbered into his cave.

3. Under the piece of furniture he saw a cooking utensil.
4. Under the rocker Mike noticed a spatula.

The person with a large vocabulary will find it easier to choose words with specific meanings and thus to write and speak better.

Exercise: Using specific words

Rewrite the following sentences, making the general words more specific:

1. Into the building walked a man.
2. They ate food and played games.
3. The trees looked beautiful.
4. Those boats are moving across the water.
5. The boy made a pleasant remark to the old person.
6. The animals in the zoo made a variety of noises.
7. In the recent past the girl has read several good books.
8. Those dogs are always bothering members of our family.

A Book to Read

Otto of the Silver Hand
by Howard Pyle
Illustrated by the author
Charles Scribner's Sons

This is the story of a poor, motherless waif who was placed in a monastery as an infant and raised in that pleasant, peaceful, and safe atmosphere for twelve years. Young Otto was certainly ill prepared for the cruelty and brutality of the outside world when his father, Baron Conrad, came to the monastery door to claim him. These were the days of the dark Middle Ages, the days of the robber barons who ruled from ancient castles and terrorized the people with their lawlessness and savage ways. Otto, caught in a feud between his father and the cruel, vengeful Baron Henry, was kidnaped and imprisoned. How he got his silver hand and how, because of his great courage, this hand became a family crest make a moving and exciting story.

About the author

In school Howard Pyle was a very poor student, neglecting his studies so that he could draw or read. Later, he was on the point of starvation when he sold a picture to a magazine for $75. That was the turning point of his career and led to his great success as illustrator and author.

Test I

Copy the italicized words in the following sentences and write the meaning for each one. Figure out the meaning from the context of the sentence if you do not already know the word.

1. The long-winded speaker *expounded* for a dreary hour on sparrows' eating habits.
2. Suddenly a noise *emerged* from one of the broken windows of the deserted building.
3. The *invincible* baseball team finished their fourth winning season.
4. Samuel Clemens was the real name of the author who used the *pseudonym* Mark Twain.
5. Since a guinea pig isn't *carnivorous*, it couldn't have eaten the meat.

Test II

1. On your paper, write only the prefix from each of the following words. Beside each prefix, write its meaning.

1. mistreat	6. cooperate
2. superhighway	7. extend
3. subtopic	8. transfer
4. prehistoric	9. unfolded
5. interact	10. recount

2. Write two words that end in suffixes meaning *one who.*
3. Write two words that end in suffixes meaning *state of being.*
4. Write the root in each of these words and give its meaning:

1. importer   2. vocalist   3. subscription   4. pedestal

Test III

1. Beside each italicized word are four other words, one of which is a synonym for it. Write the italicized word and its synonym.

1. *procrastination*   misery, acme, delay, complaint
2. *malice*   consideration, quarry, spitefulness, thoughtfulness
3. *precarious*   searching, risky, secure, insane
4. *anguish*   agony, diversion, audition, happiness
5. *comprehend*   subside, ignore, emphasize, understand

2. Beside each italicized word are four other words, one of which is an antonym for it. Write the italicized word and its antonym.

1. *mad*   wild, stuttering, engulfing, sane
2. *joyous*   horrendous, considerate, unhappy, intellectual
3. *meagerness*   relaxation, richness, playfulness, minuteness
4. *monotony*   anxiousness, stability, variety, assurance
5. *discreditable*   scalable, implorable, honorable, caustic

Test IV

For each word below, write its homonym, using it in a sentence of your own.

1. here	6. right
2. bear	7. meet
3. principal	8. brakes
4. threw	9. grate
5. no	10. whose

Test V

Write two headings on your paper: *Favorable* and *Unfavorable*. Decide which feeling is carried by each word in the pairs listed below, and write it in the appropriate column.

1. alibi—apology	6. eager—grabby
2. odor—stench	7. clique—group
3. intellectual—highbrow	8. fence—barrier
4. gang—club	9. teacher—schoolmarm
5. inquisitive—prying	10. delicate—weak

Test VI

The following sentences are of two kinds. Some choose specific words quite carefully; some are too general. After the appropriate numeral on your paper, write *specific* or *general*.

1. Brilliant sunshine lit the silver fish as they leaped in the air.
2. A tree with bark and branches was growing along the side of the road.
3. The animal ate his food at night.
4. The gray damp walls of the jail rose behind the spikes.
5. The player failed to reach the football.

Review and Practice

Exercise I

1. Review "Learning Words from Context" on pages 161–62.

2. Write meanings for the italicized words in the following sentences. If you don't already know the word, you are expected to figure out the meaning from context.

1. His stern father *coerced* the boy into staying home from the game and washing all the windows.
2. The *inundated* streets were like rivers of flowing water.
3. *Enervated* after his exhausting climb, the mountaineer collapsed as he was staggering to the peak.
4. The meeting ended *congruently,* with all the members voting "yes" to the new proposal.

Exercise II

1. Review "How Words Are Built" on pages 163–66.

2. Following is a list of prefixes. For each prefix, write one word in which it is used. Then write the meaning of the word. The meaning of the word should include the meaning of the prefix.

    1. bi–   2. auto–   3. re–   4. non–   5. pre–

3. In your dictionary, find ten words that begin with different prefixes. Write each prefix after the word and write the meaning of the prefix.

4. Write the suffix alone in each of the following words and give its meaning:

1. brotherhood	6. exhaustion
2. devilish	7. negligence
3. cheerful	8. skyward
4. actor	9. housekeeper
5. neatness	10. typist

5. Think of words which include the following common word parts. Write at least two words for each one.

duct (to lead)	audit (to hear)	gress (step)
ped (foot)	voc (call)	cide (kill)
geo (earth)	capit (head)	logy (science of)
scribe (write)	bio (life)	port (carry)

Exercise III

1. Review "Using Synonyms" and "Using Antonyms" on pages 169–70 and 172.

2. The following pairs of words are synonyms. Use each in a sentence that shows the slight difference in meaning. You may use your dictionary.

1. bench–pew	3. door–entrance
2. house–home	4. animal–pet

3. For each of the following words, write an antonym. It should be the same part of speech that is given in parentheses below. You may use your dictionary.

1. decline (verb)	3. offensive (adjective)
2. conquer (verb)	4. abundant (adjective)

Exercise IV

1. Review "Writing Homonyms" on page 173.

2. Copy the pairs of homonyms on page 173. Use each word in a sentence of your own to illustrate its meaning.

Exercise V

1. Review "Using Words to Convey Feelings" on page 174.

2. The following words are more or less neutral in tone. Find words which give a favorable impression for each one. Then find words which give an unfavorable impression. You may use your dictionary.

1. argument   2. (war) veteran   3. talk   4. smell

Exercise VI

1. Review "Choosing Specific Words" on page 176.

2. Which sentence in each of the following pairs is more specific and therefore more interesting? Explain your answer.

1. The things hung on the line.
   The white sheets spanked the wind.

2. The coat was a mess.
   The smudgy raincoat had lost its buttons.

3. The dog came up to me.
   The puppy bounced into my lap.

CHAPTER 7

Pronouns and Their Correct Use

Here are two versions of the first paragraph of a short story called "Ebenezer and Aunt Elspeth." Version 1 was written by a seventh-grade author; Version 2 was changed to show you something about pronouns. Read the two paragraphs and then answer the questions that follow them.

Ebenezer and Aunt Elspeth
(Version 1)

Little Ebenezer stood by his tricycle and kicked it. He was angry at his father because he had ordered Ebenezer to come in to say hello to Aunt Elspeth. "I hate her! I hate her!" Ebenezer whispered. Two seconds later he felt strong hands grab his shoulders and squeeze them hard. He knew that a decision had been made for him. It was not a decision he liked.

Ebenezer and Aunt Elspeth
(Version 2)

Little Ebenezer stood by Ebenezer's tricycle and kicked the tricycle. Ebenezer was angry at Ebenezer's father because Ebenezer's father had ordered Ebenezer to come in to say hello to Aunt Elspeth. "Ebenezer hates Aunt Elspeth! Ebenezer hates Aunt Elspeth!" Ebenezer whispered. Two seconds later Ebenezer felt strong hands grab Ebenezer's shoulders and squeeze the shoulders hard. Ebenezer knew that a decision had been made for Ebenezer. The decision was not a decision Ebenezer liked.

Which paragraph reads better? Explain.

What is the difference between the two paragraphs?

Do you remember enough about pronouns to tell how many there are in Version 1? If you can, name them.

What function does each pronoun perform in the paragraph?

Which paragraph is longer? What does this show about pronouns?

Personal Pronouns

Your discussion of the paragraphs on page 182 should have demonstrated to you that a pronoun is a word that is used in place of a noun. It enables a writer to avoid tiresome repetition and to save space and time.

Pronouns, like nouns, can show *number* and *possession*.

Singular and plural pronouns

The typical noun shows *plural number* by adding *s* (cat, cats). Pronouns, however, show number by changing their form, never by adding *s*. Here is a list of the singular and plural forms of some common pronouns, called **personal pronouns:**

FIRST PERSON (person speaking)
Singular: I, me, my, mine, myself
Plural: we, us, our, ours, ourselves

SECOND PERSON (person spoken to)
Singular: you, your, yours, yourself
Plural: you, your, yours, yourselves

THIRD PERSON (person spoken of)
Singular: he, him, his, himself, she, her, hers, herself, it, its, itself
Plural: they, them, their, theirs, themselves

■ A **pronoun** is a word that is used in place of a noun.

Exercise: Singular and plural pronouns

Write the headings *Singular* and *Plural* on your paper. Find the pronouns in the following sentences and list each one under the correct heading. In one case, the pronoun should be written under both headings.

1. You mustn't hit her or me.
2. Theirs is larger than mine.
3. Of themselves they said, "Our family was poor."
4. She always sat on her front steps and watched our games.
5. Ours are not as fancy as hers.
6. He patted himself on the back, saying, "I am the best!"
7. "Fix it yourself," they said.
8. He and I easily beat her at Ping-pong.

Rewrite the sentences in the previous exercise. Make all singular pronouns plural and all plural pronouns singular. Often there will be more than one correct possibility. If the form of the verb or another word needs changing to agree with the pronoun, change it.

EXAMPLE: 1. We like to cook dinner ourselves.

YOU WRITE: *1. I like to cook dinner myself.*

Possessive pronouns

Personal pronouns show possession quite differently from nouns.

PRONOUNS	POSSESSIVE PRONOUNS	
I own a box.	It is *my* box.	The box is *mine.*
You own a pen.	It is *your* pen.	The pen is *yours.*
He owns a car.	It is *his* car.	The car is *his.*
She owns a boat.	It is *her* boat.	The boat is *hers.*
It has short legs.	*Its* legs are short.	
We own a mop.	It is *our* mop.	The mop is *ours.*
They own a pig.	It is *their* pig.	The pig is *theirs.*

Notice that you never use an apostrophe with a possessive pronoun. You would say, "The boat is Anne's," using an apostrophe to form the possessive of the noun *Anne.* But with a pronoun you would say, "The boat is hers," with no apostrophe.

Its–it's. The pair of homonyms (words that sound the same) *its–it's* causes more trouble than almost any other pair of words in the English language. Just remember that the possessive form of a pronoun has no apostrophe: "*Its* paw was sore." *It's* is a contraction of *it is,* as, "*It's* a nice day." (*Remember*: *it's* always means *it is.*)

Their–they're–there. Another set of homonyms that causes trouble is *their, they're,* and *there.* Keep alert and remember that:

Their is a possessive pronoun   (*Their* faces were red.)
They're is a contraction of *they are*   (*They're* my best friends.)
There is (1) An adverb telling *where*   (I put it *there.*)
(2) A word that often starts sentences in which the subject follows the verb   (*There* are forty students here.)

Remember: Possessive personal pronouns never have apostrophes.

184

Exercises: Possessive pronouns

1. Pick out all the possessive pronouns in the following sentences:

1. My house is full of your possessions.
2. That car is yours, not his.
3. We like her apple pie, but we are not hungry.
4. Theirs is a lovely house, but its back porch is too close to our front door.
5. Your house and my house are on the border of his land.

2. On your paper, write a possessive pronoun for each blank below. Try not to use any pronoun more than twice.

1. John, that desk is __?__; this one is __?__.
2. Sally said it was __?__ mother who came to pick up __?__ friends.
3. Those people lost __?__ heads in the mob. I'm glad you didn't lose __?__.
4. As for the monster, it raised __?__ immense claw and bashed in the hero's car as well as __?__ terrace furniture.
5. Gladys has __?__ boat, I have __?__ boat, and you have __?__ boat, but when I look at the Smiths, I wonder who has __?__ boat.

3. On your paper, write *its* or *it's* for each blank below:

1. __?__ a great day for a ride!
2. We sell popcorn at __?__ best.
3. "I think __?__ lost," said Harry.
4. When he thinks of his club, he thinks of __?__ motto: "__?__ never too late to learn."
5. During the storm, our house lost __?__ roof, __?__ south wall, and half of __?__ attic.

4. On your paper, write *there, their,* or *they're* for each blank in the sentences below:

1. __?__ is no reason to cry.
2. I left __?__ money right __?__ on the sofa.
3. __?__ lucky not to have lost __?__ car if they parked it over __?__.
4. __?__ over __?__, not here!
5. __?__ radio is much better than __?__ TV set.

Pronouns and Their Antecedents

A pronoun usually refers to a noun which has come earlier in a sentence or paragraph. This noun which *goes before* the pronoun is called the **antecedent of the pronoun.** (In Latin *ante*– means "before" and *cedere* means "go.")

Now study these three brief passages containing pronouns. From each pronoun an arrow is drawn back to its antecedent.

1. The early morning sun spread its light across the sky.

2. The flight commander gave his instructions to the crew.

3. The engineer tested the rockets. He announced them A–OK.

4. As the rocket left its launching pad, the pupils held their breath.

Do you see how each pronoun is preceded by a noun, its antecedent?

■ The noun to which a pronoun refers is called the **antecedent of the pronoun.**

Exercises: Finding antecedents of personal pronouns

1. Read the following report. Then list all of the pronouns on your paper. Next to each pronoun, write its antecedent in parentheses.

Cat and Dog Trouble

In Maud's block there are many small children. They all ride tricycles fast and recklessly. Yesterday Maud's dog Bowser was trotting down the walk when two small pedaling demons bore down on him. They tried to dodge Bowser, but he dodged left at the same moment they dodged right. The result was that his tail was run over. It wasn't hurt badly, but Bowser was so surprised he snapped at the neighbor's cat and bit *her* tail. So Maud tells the story, calling it "The Tale of Two Tails."

2. List all of the pronouns in Version 1 of "Ebenezer and Aunt Elspeth" on page 182. Then write the antecedent of each pronoun in parentheses.

3. Write five sentences of your own with a personal pronoun and its antecedent in each one. Then underline the pronoun and draw an arrow to its antecedent.

Sentence Patterns

So far you have learned to build sentences following combinations of these symbols:

$$\textbf{N} = \text{Noun}$$
$$\textbf{V} = \text{Action verb}$$
$$\textbf{V}^{\textbf{be}} = \text{Verb of being used as linking verb}$$
$$\textbf{V}^{\textbf{h}} = \text{Helping verb}$$

Because a pronoun is a word used in place of a noun, we will keep the symbol **N** for a noun with the addition of a small **p**.

$$\textbf{N}^{\textbf{p}} = \text{Pronoun}$$

In the examples below, notice that pronouns are used in sentences wherever nouns are used:

PATTERN 1:   N V

N *always* **V**   Monkeys always chatter.
Np *always* **V**   They always chatter.

PATTERN 2:   N V N

A **N V**h *already* **V** *the* **N**   A boy has already eaten the apples.
Np **V**h *already* **V N**p   He has already eaten them.

PATTERN 3:   N Vbe N

The **N V**be *not a* **N**   The heroine was not a student.
The **N V**be *not* **N**p   The heroine was not she.

In addition to the noun signals, words that often come between the parts of a verb are included in the examples above.

● Now build sensible sentences, according to the following combinations of symbols. Vary your sentence ideas.

1. **N**p **V**
2. **N**p **V**h **V**
3. **N**p **V N**
4. A **N V**h **V**h **V N**p
5. **N**p **V**h *always* **V** *the* **N**
6. **N V**h *never* **V N**p
7. *The* **N V**h *not* **V N**p

8. **N**p **V**h **V**be **N**
9. *The* **N V**h **V**be **N**p
10. *The* **N V**h *soon* **V N**p
11. **V**h **N**p **V** *a* **N**?
12. **N V**h *not* **V**h **V N**p
13. **N**p **V**h **V**h **V N**p
14. **N**p **V**h **V**h **V**be *the* **N**

Subject and Object Pronouns

Pronouns change form when they move from the subject position to the object position in a sentence. For example:

SUBJECT POSITION: *I* praised Mary Smith.
OBJECT POSITION: Mary Smith praised *me*.

SUBJECT POSITION: Did *he* hit the neighbor's boy?
OBJECT POSITION: Did the neighbor's boy hit *him*?

You see that *I* and *he* are used as subjects; they are **subject pronouns.** The pronouns *me* and *him* are direct objects. They receive the action of the verbs *praised* and *did hit*; they are **object pronouns.**

Here are some personal pronouns listed in their subject and object forms and used in a sentence:

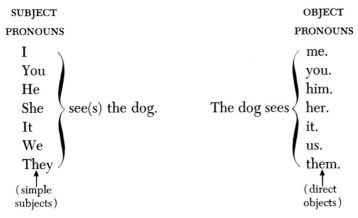

Which pronouns have the same form for the subject and object?

Exercise: Subject and object pronouns

Choose the correct pronoun from each pair in parentheses below. Then tell whether it is used as a subject or direct object.

1. My big brother ate (they, them) before I could get one.
2. (We, Us) are happy to come to the party.
3. (He, Him) battered his opponent.
4. That policeman arrested (I, me) yesterday.
5. Under the sofa (he, him) crawled.
6. After dinner (I, me) like a short nap.
7. (She, Her) has already suffered very much.
8. The new team defeated (we, us).

Pronouns in compound subjects and objects

You come now to what many people find a more difficult point of grammar.

Look at the sentences below. Can you see what the difference is between them and the sentences in the exercise on page 189?

1. John and I went to school.

2. Did Mary or she eat the hamburger?

3. Our pet skunks bit Oscar and me.

4. Did the crash injure Sue and him?

Sometimes the subject of a sentence is made up of two nouns or pronouns, or one of each, joined by the word *and* or *or*. These subjects are called **compound subjects.** What is the compound subject in sentence 1 above? in sentence 2? Are the pronouns subject or object pronouns?

Direct objects, too, can be compounded in the same way as subjects. They are called **compound objects.** What is the compound object in sentence 3 above? in sentence 4? Are the pronouns subject or object pronouns?

If you have trouble knowing whether to say "John and her went to town" or "John and she went to town," try this device: Quickly say the sentence to yourself, omitting the *John and* so that only the doubtful pronoun remains. Then your ear will tell you to say, "*She* went to town." (You would never say "*Her* went to town.")

Try the same device for these sentences. Which sentence in each pair is correct?

(Lorna and) he spoke to the storekeeper.
(Lorna and) him spoke to the storekeeper.

The falling rocks hit (Mabel and) I.
The falling rocks hit (Mabel and) me.

Can you *hear* why the pronouns *he* and *me* are correct?

Use a **subject pronoun** in the subject position in a sentence.
Use an **object pronoun** in the object position in a sentence.

Exercise: Compound subjects and objects

Read the following sentences aloud, choosing the correct form from the two given in parentheses. Explain your choices.

1. The little kitten and (she, her) played on the kitchen floor.
2. A kettle of boiling water scalded Archie and (I, me).
3. Mr. Ellis and (I, me) bandaged Larry and (he, him).
4. Laura and (she, her) are climbing an apple tree.
5. Our parents encouraged you and (they, them) with loud cheers.
6. (He, Him) and (I, me) swam across the lake.
7. We will meet Sarah and (they, them) at the entrance.
8. Were the dog and (he, him) still walking at midnight?
9. The ball almost hit the umpire and (he, him).
10. Cressida and (we, us) volunteered for the assignment.

Subject Pronouns After Linking Verbs

You may remember from Chapter 3, page 92, that nouns are used as subject complements when they follow a verb of being and refer to the subject, as in the sentence "My uncle was the *president*." The same thing is true with pronouns, as you can see in the following sentences:

	SUBJECT	LINKING VERB	SUBJECT COMPLEMENT
1.	The visitor	was	she.
2.	The men at the window	were	they.
3.	It	is	I.

Notice that each pronoun follows a verb of being that is used as a linking verb. Each pronoun means the same person or thing as the subject of the sentence.

Another common name for a pronoun that is used as a subject complement is **predicate pronoun.**

Look at the sentences again. What form of pronoun is needed in the subject complement position—a subject or object pronoun?

Concerning example 3 above, in informal speech "It is me" is widely accepted. Informal speech is not always grammatically logical. "It is me" is not acceptable in formal speech or writing.

Compound subject complement

Look at the examples that follow. Notice that there are two subject complements in each sentence.

SUBJECT COMPLEMENTS

1. The women at the door were *Kitty* and *she.*
2. The losers were   *he* and *I*

It may help you in using a subject pronoun in the subject complement position to think of the linking verb as making a sort of equation of a sentence. In the equation the subject and the subject complement are equal:

$$\text{The worst boys in the class were Jake and } \textit{he!}$$

$$\text{Jake and he were the worst } \textit{boys} \text{ in the class.}$$

A pronoun used as a subject complement must be a subject pronoun.

Exercises: Subject and object pronouns

1. On your paper beside the appropriate numeral, write the correct pronoun from each pair in parentheses below. The sentences all require a subject complement. Read each sentence aloud two or three times to establish the correct version in your mind.

1. The small boy at the left is (he, him).
2. The old woman on the mountain is (she, her).
3. One person without ambition is (I, me).
4. The guilty ones are (they, them).
5. My favorite singers are Martin and (he, him).

2. Of the ten sentences below, five contain *verbs of action* and therefore require *object pronouns.* The other five contain *verbs of being* used as linking verbs and require *subject pronouns.* Choose the correct pronoun from each pair in parentheses.

1. That dog always nips Jerry and (I, me).
2. We boys are fighting the Zoots and (they, them) with all our strength.
3. Before the debate my favorite speaker was (she, her).

4. After the debate the winners were Jean and (they, them).
5. Across the large room I saw the boys and (they, them).
6. The prettiest child in the second grade is (she, her).
7. The driver of that overturned truck was not (he, him) but his father.
8. The movie frightened my sister and (I, me).
9. Those exhaust fumes covered (she, her) and (I, me) with soot.
10. After three weeks of competition, the champs were Peter and (they, them).

TO MEMORIZE

FROM *A Dedicatory Ode*

From quiet homes and first beginning,
  Out to the undiscovered ends,
There's nothing worth the wear of winning
  But laughter and the love of friends.

HILAIRE BELLOC

This verse sings the praises of laughter and friendship. According to Belloc, only these are the important things in life worth our energy and effort. The lines have an easy flowing rhythm that matches the thought they express.

Object Pronouns After Prepositions

Study the pairs of sentences below, noticing especially the italicized parts. Do you know what the italicized words are called?

1. Give it *to Dad*. Give it *to him*.
2. John went *with Jim and Mike*. John went *with them*.
3. He painted a picture *of Oscar*. He painted a picture *of me*.

The groups of italicized words above are called **prepositional phrases.** Each one begins with a preposition and ends with a noun or pronoun. In the pair of sentences marked 1, the preposition is *to*. What are the prepositions in the other pairs of sentences?

The noun or pronoun that follows the preposition and comes at the end of the phrase is called the **object of the preposition.** In the first pair above, the objects of the prepositions are *Dad* and *him*. What are the objects of the prepositions in 2 and 3?

Compound objects of a preposition

You will probably have little trouble using the correct form of the pronoun when there is a single object of the preposition. However, when there is a *compound object*, there is more chance of error. Now read each of these samples aloud several times to fix the correct form in your mind:

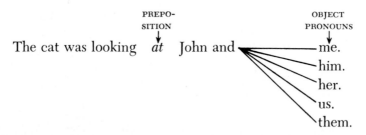

PREPO-SITION

OBJECT PRONOUNS

The cat was looking *at* John and — me.
him.
her.
us.
them.

If you have difficulty with a compound object of a preposition, try omitting the "John and" part in your mind. When you do that, your ear will tell you what the correct form of the preposition is:

The cat was looking at (John and) me.
The car crashed into (the Smiths and) us.

You would never say "at I" or "into we." Your ear makes it clear to you that you say "looking at *me*" and "crashed into *us*." In that case, you also say "at John and *me*" and "into the Smiths and *us*."

> A pronoun used as the object of a preposition must be an object pronoun.

Exercises: Pronouns as objects of prepositions

1. Read aloud the following pairs of sentences five times to fix in your mind the correct form:

1. Give the book to *me*. Give the book to John and *me*.
2. Throw the ball to *him*. Throw the ball to Mary and *him*.
3. Come with *us*. Come with *them* and *us*.
4. Look at *her*. Look at Mike and *her*.

2. Read the following sentences aloud and decide which pronouns should be used. Be prepared to explain to the class the reason for each choice.

EXAMPLE: 1. Andrew and (she, her) annoyed the baby and (I, me).

YOU SAY: 1. Andrew and *she* annoyed the baby and *me*.
She is used as a subject.
Me is used as a direct object.

1. Please, Miss Smith, don't scold Matthew and (he, him).
2. The principal called Jim and (I, me) to his office.
3. There he spoke to the teacher and (we, us).
4. Joan and (she, her) went to Florida for their vacation.
5. In Florida they saw Betty and (he, him).
6. Who is walking with your mother and (she, her)?
7. A drunken driver and (he, him) were arrested.
8. My best friends are Molly and (she, her).
9. "The champions are Zeke and (he, him)!" shouted Mr. Jay.
10. Lucas and (she, her) annoyed Mrs. Smith and (we, us).
11. That handsome fellow with Mary and (they, them) was (I, me).
12. Nothing will please Josh and (they, them) more.
13. Will Ike and (I, me) be invited to the party?
14. With the policemen and (they, them) were two detectives.
15. Jessie won't share the popcorn with Ned and (I, me).
16. The rest of the work will be divided between Patrick and (he, him).

Some Special Problems of Pronoun Usage

You must be careful to use pronouns correctly and in a way to make your meaning clear. Some of them have characteristics which need special attention.

Pronouns that are always singular

The pronouns *each, either, neither,* and *one* are always singular. When they are used as subjects, they must take the singular form of the verb.

1. *Each* of us is glad to go. (Think: "Each one is . . .")
2. *Either* of the girls was willing to try. (Think: "Either one was . . .")
3. *Neither* was uncooperative. (Think: "Neither one was . . .")
4. *One* of those houses has collapsed.

Now examine these same pronouns in the following sentences:

1. *Each* of them looks *his* best.
2. *Either* of the boys is able to make *his* own bed.
3. *Neither* of us wants *his* picture taken.
4. *One* of those books has lost *its* cover.

What is the antecedent of the pronoun *his* in sentence 1? in sentence 2? in sentence 3? What is the antecedent of *its* in sentence 4? The arrows above show the relationship between the pronoun and its antecedent. The pronoun must agree in number with its antecedent.

Pronouns that are always plural

There are some pronouns that are always plural. As subjects, they must take the plural form of the verb. Their antecedents must also be plural. The pronouns *both, several,* and *many* are examples.

1. *Both* of the partners are here.
2. *Several* of the performers forgot *their* lines.
3. *Many* in the room are unhappy with *their* assignments.

Exercise: Using pronouns correctly

Rewrite the following sentences, using the correct pronouns and the correct forms of the verbs in parentheses:

1. Each of those cats (loves, love) (his, their) mistress.
2. Neither dog (wants, want) to give up (his, their) bone.
3. Several of the students (has, have) (his, their) hands up.
4. Each of them (wants, want) to express (his, their) opinion.
5. Both of those games (is, are) fun to play.
6. Neither (has, have) enough money for (his, their) ticket.
7. Each (is, are) ready to play (his, their) part in the festival.
8. Neither of the boys (wants, want) to cause trouble for (his, their) friends.
9. One of us (is, are) going to speak to the teacher.
10. When the teacher returns, many of those boys (is, are) going to enjoy the praise (he, they) (deserves, deserve).

We boys, us boys

Sometimes you may wonder whether to say or write, "*Us* boys had a fine camping trip," or "*We* boys had a fine camping trip."

The question is easily answered. Just mentally omit the word *boys*, and it will be clear that you should say:

> *We* (boys) had a fine camping trip. (*We* is the subject of the sentence.)

Here are other examples of the correct use of *we* and *us*. Read each one twice, once omitting the words in parentheses and once leaving them in.

> We (boys) were the first ones on the scene.
> The mayor agreed with us (students).
> The football players defeated us (soccer players).

In each case, can you explain why the *we* or *us* is used?

Use the expression **we boys** if it is the subject of a sentence or the subject complement.

Use **us boys** when it is a direct object or the object of a preposition.

Exercise: Using pronouns correctly

Choose the correct pronoun from the two given in parentheses.

1. (We, Us) boys are sorry to have broken the window.
2. The noisy people in the yard last night were (we, us) girls.
3. Down the long hallway marched (we, us) four soldiers.
4. The closing of the factory was very hard on (we, us) workers.
5. The audience saw (we, us) actors peeking out from behind the curtains.

Superfluous pronouns

Something is *superfluous* when it is unneeded, when it is too much. In the sentences below, can you pick out the superfluous pronouns?

1. My father he gets home too late to eat dinner with us.
2. That pig over there it is always eating.
3. John and I we hope you will stay for a while.

The pronouns *he, it,* and *we* are not needed because each sentence already has a subject. The meaning of each sentence is perfectly clear without them. Therefore, do not say "My father he . . ."; simply say "My father . . ."   Read sentences 1, 2, and 3 as they should have been written.

Exercise: Correcting the double subject

In each of the following sentences, pick out the superfluous pronoun and read the sentence aloud twice without it:

1. That department store it charges too much for sports equipment.
2. All of my teachers they are quite kind to me.
3. Down in the cellar my brother he has some very fine tools.
4. Napoleon he was really a dictator.
5. My mother and I we always like to go to an afternoon movie.

Making the meaning clear: pronouns and antecedents

Read the following sentences and see if you can explain why the meaning in each one is not clear:

1. George and Bob ran into his house.
2. Mary gave a doll to little Suzie, but she broke it.

If you are to rewrite the sentences above—or sentences like them which you have written—it will help to know *why* they are not clear. Look at the pronoun *his* in sentence 1. What is its antecedent—the noun it stands for? It could be *George* or it could be *Bob*. The reader does not know whose house the boys entered.

In sentence 2, to whom does the pronoun *she* refer? You do not know if it is Mary or Suzie who broke the doll.

The first step in solving a problem of unclear meaning is to explain why the meaning is unclear. The next and more important step is to remedy the problem. Consider now how you might rewrite sentence 1 above. Depending on what you want to say, you could write:

George and Bob ran into Bob's house.

or

George and Bob ran into George's house.

In these rewritings, the pronoun has been replaced with a noun.

Another way to proceed would be to recast the sentence completely:

George ran into his house, accompanied by Bob.

or

George ran into his house. Right behind him ran Bob.

How would you rewrite sentence 2?

Remember: When the antecedent of a pronoun is not clear, it is better to repeat the noun than to use the pronoun.

Exercise: Writing clear antecedents

Rewrite each of the following sentences so that its meaning is absolutely clear:

1. Marge and Kay were talking about her vacation.
2. Remove the violin from the table before you wipe it off.
3. Gretchen walked out into the garden to pick a rose. It was beautiful.
4. Jerry entered the movie house with a package under his arm and left it at nine-thirty.
5. Leonard made the appointment with the dentist for later in the week because of his busy schedule.

Test I

Write the headings *Singular* and *Plural* on your paper. Find the personal pronouns in the following passage and list each one under the proper heading. Next to each pronoun, write its antecedent in parentheses.

Little Joey likes birthdays best of all. They cannot come too often for him. He doesn't understand why his mother does not want them all the time, too. Each year she has to give a party and invite all the children in the neighborhood. When it is all over, they leave her in absolute exhaustion, with two days' cleaning to do by herself.

Test II

1. Copy the following sentences, using *there, their,* or *they're* in place of each blank:

1. __?__ ideas shock my mother.
2. Please go in __?__ and get __?__ cat.
3. __?__ is so little time and so much to do.
4. They brought __?__ bottle-cap collection with them.
5. __?__ giving a party at __?__ house.

2. Copy the following sentences, replacing each of the italicized word groups with *its* or *it's*:

1. *It is* time to get up.
2. *It is* too dark to be morning.
3. *The belt's* buckle is broken and *it is* too late to fix it before school.
4. Give the cat *the cat's* milk before you leave.
5. *The whooping crane's* feeding habits are being studied.

Test III

On your paper next to the appropriate numeral, write the correct pronoun from each pair in parentheses.

1. Sally and (I, me) are going to cut each other's hair.
2. The victim of the snowball was (he, him).
3. Rain was the last straw for Cal and (I, me).
4. The teacher praised Betsy and (I, me).
5. My mother and (she, her) enjoy shopping.

Test IV

Copy the following sentences, choosing the correct word from each pair in parentheses:

1. Either of the jobs (is, are) difficult.
2. Several (has, have) asked to bring (her, their) parents.
3. One of the animals (is, are) always getting lost.
4. Each of the telephone calls (has, have) been mysterious.
5. Neither of the boys (likes, like) (his, their) picture.

Test V

There are two kinds of mistakes in some of the following sentences. There are superfluous pronouns and mistakes in the use of expressions such as "we boys" and "us girls." If the sentence has no error, write "correct" next to the appropriate numeral. If it contains an error, rewrite the sentence correctly on your paper.

1. The coach is always getting angry at we boys.
2. The boy and his dog they are really moving fast.
3. You and your sister are late.
4. The voices you heard were us choir members.
5. Us students want to rest.
6. Their second team played us girls.
7. That teacher he will make you work.
8. Us seventh-graders we go in first.
9. My uncle he has a million dollars.
10. The winners were we boys.

Test VI

Number your paper from 1 to 5. Next to the appropriate numeral, write the pronoun in each of the following sentences that does not have a clear antecedent:

1. Get some new marbles for these games before you lose them.
2. Laura took her book to the window and closed it.
3. Sally, Joanne, and Candy were feeding her dog his supper.
4. Jay looked up the month and the day of his sister's birthday on the calendar and circled it.
5. Miss Dewslip found her glasses near her books and put them in her briefcase.

Review and Practice

Exercise I

1. Review the lessons on pronouns on pages 182–83 and 187.

2. Write the headings *Singular Pronouns* and *Plural Pronouns* on your paper. Find the personal pronouns in the following passages and write each one under the proper heading. Next to each, write its antecedent in parentheses.

> 1. Greg loves figure skating, but he is finding it very difficult. His instructor told him that it takes a great deal of skill and practice. Now every afternoon Greg practices by himself at the Cold Springs Creek.
> 2. "Mother, I am certainly not going to enjoy myself this weekend. Mrs. Bell gave the class too much homework," Bill complained. "She said that it will be easier to do than we think. Did you and Dad get so much homework when you were in school?"

3. Copy the following paragraphs, replacing all the italicized nouns and noun signals with personal pronouns. Note that you may have to change some verbs to match the pronouns you use.

> Catherine said, "*Catherine* is hungry. That hot dog looks delicious to *Catherine*."
>
> "*Catherine* may eat *the hot dog*," *Catherine's* mother said.
>
> "Catherine, *Catherine* is going to gain weight," Father said. "*Catherine* should stop *Catherine* from eating so much."

Exercise II

1. Review the lesson on possessive pronouns on page 184.

2. Choose the correct word from each pair in parentheses.

> 1. (Its, It's) not my umbrella.
> 2. (There, Their, They're) are two reasons why you should not go.
> 3. (There, Their, They're) planning to have folk singing.
> 4. The ostrich stretched (its, it's) head over the fence.
> 5. (There, Their, They're) contribution to the charity is very generous.

3. Write ten sentences in which you use *its, it's, their, they're,* and *there* twice each.

Exercise III

1. Review the lessons on subject and object pronouns on pages 189–92 and 194–95.

2. Choose the correct pronoun from each pair in parentheses.

1. She encouraged Ned and (I, me) to read about satellites.
2. The present was from Alan and (she, her).
3. Will you call Susan and (I, me) when you are ready?
4. Our grandparents and (we, us) will spend the holidays with (they, them).
5. The leaders are Joey and (she, her).

Exercise IV

1. Review the lesson on page 196.

2. Copy the following sentences, choosing the correct word from each pair in parentheses:

1. Many of them (brings, bring) (his, their) skates.
2. Either of the recipes (is, are) good.
3. One of the books (has, have) been torn.
4. Each of the buildings (has, have) a doorman.
5. Neither of the buildings (has, have) lost (its, their) roof.

Exercise V

1. Review pages 197–98.

2. Copy the following sentences, correcting the mistake in each one:

1. Us members want to call a special meeting.
2. The usher he told me that this was my seat.
3. The bouquet was tossed to we girls.
4. Those sounds they were disturbing all the neighbors.
5. That man he sells vacuum cleaners.

3. Write five sentences showing the correct use of each of these phrases: *us baseball fans, we students, we girls, us boys, we boys.*

Exercise VI

1. Review pages 198–99.

2. Turn to Test VI on page 201. Rewrite each of the sentences so that the pronouns have clear antecedents.

CHAPTER 8

Writing Letters

In the name of the Empress of India, make way,
    O Lords of the jungle, wherever you roam,
The woods are awake at the end of the day,
    We exiles are waiting for letters from home.
Let the robber retreat—and the tiger tail—
    In the name of the Empress, the Overland Mail.

        from *Departmental Ditties and Ballads,*
            by Rudyard Kipling

Luckily, we do not have to worry about robbers and tigers in getting our mail today. But receiving letters is just as important to us as it was to a British soldier in India, thousands of miles away from England, in Kipling's time.

Writing Friendly Letters

You know how pleased you are to receive a letter from a friend, and how eagerly you open and read it. Reading friendly letters is always an enjoyable experience. Actually, it is a way of visiting those friends and family members we cannot see and talk to every day.

When you write a letter, think about the person to whom you are writing. What will *he* want to know? Try to put yourself in his place.

In answering a letter, first respond to the questions your friend may have asked. Comment on what he has told you. Also write about the things you would tell your friend if he were sitting beside you—about an exciting game, a party, or a camping trip you have enjoyed. Tell whom you met, what they said, and in general how things are going. You may ask questions in your letter. A person likes to know you are interested in what he may say in reply.

On the next page, read and plan to discuss a letter written by George to his older brother Dick.

61 Maple Street
Trenton, New Jersey 08608
February 13, 19—

Dear Dick,

What a pal! With all you have to do at college, you still wrote to me.

Your new job as a waiter sounds like a lot of work, and fun, too. Your story of how you knocked the peas and catsup over the hamburgers and how your customers insisted on eating them that way made us laugh. Betty and I combined these ingredients for lunch. We called them "Green Hamburgers à la Dick". Tell us more about what you do at college. It really brightens our days.

Your issues of <u>Science Magazine</u> are still being delivered here. I read them first before sending them on to you, hoping that it will help my marks in science.

Terry had her puppies — eight of them. I am enclosing a snapshot. Did you know that she still sleeps in your room?

You are probably taking your exams right now. Good luck! Let us know the results.

Best regards,
George

To discuss

Discuss the following questions about George's letter:

1. How does George begin his letter? Does he show how much he appreciated Dick's letter?
2. How does George show that he has read Dick's letter?
3. How does George show that he is interested in Dick?
4. Which paragraphs contain information that Dick will be glad to have?
5. Which paragraphs sound like conversation?
6. Does George include any touches of humor?
7. What do you think of the appearance of the letter?

Guides for writing friendly letters

1. Write naturally, as if you were talking.
2. Write with pen or typewrite, whichever is easier for you.
3. Write about what the other person will want to know.
4. If you are replying to a letter written to you, begin by reacting to the other person's letter. Answer any questions he has asked or make comments about what he has written. Be appreciative.
5. Remember, courtesy demands that your letter be neat and legible. Follow the standard form for writing friendly letters, as shown in the model letter on the opposite page.

Exercises: Topics for letterwriting

1. Write the following two headings on a sheet of paper: *General Interests* and *Special Interests*. Under the first heading, list some of the things you have been talking about this week with your family and friends. For example, list local and school events and amusing personal experiences. Under the second heading, list the items which would be of special interest to one particular person you know. Include his interests as well as your own.

2. Take turns reading some of the lists aloud. Discuss why some of the items are good and why others are not.

3. Write a letter to the person you had in mind for the *Special Interests* list in the first exercise above. Use some suggestions from both of the lists you made.

4. Read a few of the letters aloud in class and discuss them.

The body of a friendly letter

Here are some things to avoid when you write a letter:

1. Don't start by stating that you hate to write letters.
2. Don't apologize for a poorly written letter. Write it over.
3. Don't make excuses for closing your letter. Just close it.
4. Don't write in anger. If you have something unpleasant to discuss, wait until you are calm. Then write about it only if you are sure you must. Remember, you will not be there when your letter is received to explain or to hear explanations.
5. Don't use a letter for gossip, for complaining, or for telling unnecessary things that will merely make the reader unhappy. If you can think only of unfriendly things to say, it is better not to write.

Study the following seven excerpts from letters. In each case you are told who is writing to whom. Be prepared to discuss whether or not you think each excerpt is acceptable.

1. *Girl to younger sister*
   Honestly! As soon as I go away from home for a visit, you have to start borrowing my things. Look, just stay out of my closet until I get back, see?
2. *Daughter to parents*
   Well, the end of the sheet is approaching, and I have to get back to my books, so I'll stop. Excuse the messy letter.
3. *Girl to friend who has moved away*
   Your friend Molly may still be writing to you in a friendly way, but you should hear the things she says about you to the other girls. I bet she would not dare say them to your face.
4. *Girl to older sister*
   Grandmother has not been very well this week, and I think Dad is worrying a lot about her. It still may not be serious, but I thought I ought to keep you posted. If you have time, write her a letter. She needs cheering up, and nothing makes her happier than one of your newsy notes.
5. *To your father away on a business trip*
   Mom gave us our allowances and we are upset. You promised us a raise this month, but Mom wants to wait until you return. Please write and settle the argument because I need the money.

6. *Girl to a pen pal overseas*

   I have blue eyes, brown hair, and weigh eighty-six pounds. I am in the seventh grade of the Coleman Junior High School, and my teacher's name is Mrs. Cripps. She told me to write to a pen pal, and so here is my letter. Write to me soon.

7. *Pupil to a former teacher*

   Our new school is a lot bigger and more modern than Platt Memorial, but the teaching cannot equal what we had at Platt. Every day that I sit in English class I long for those interesting stories you used to tell us and even for the hard work you gave us. Maybe I did not always seem to appreciate you at the time, but now I think you were the toughest teacher we ever had and the best. I will never forget what you taught us.

To discuss

Using the list of "things to avoid" on page 208 as a basis for discussion, answer the following questions about each excerpt above. Do not be concerned if all members of the class do not agree. After all, people are individuals and write differently.

1. Is the excerpt acceptable?
2. Which sentences are good, thoughtful sentences?
3. Which passages should have been omitted? Why?
4. How would you rewrite some of the sentences to make them acceptable?

Exercise: Writing friendly letters

Choose three of the excerpts above which can be improved, and rewrite them.

Matters of Form

What you say in your letters is the most important part of letter writing. However, there are certain matters of form which you should know, too. Your letter represents *you* to the person who receives it. If it is sloppy and incorrectly written, it will not represent you favorably.

Generally, you should write friendly letters on plain white paper, not on highly colored paper. The envelope should match the letter paper. When you write, be sure to leave a good margin on the left-hand side of the paper. Leave some margin, also, at the top, bottom, and right-hand side.

Parts of a letter

A friendly letter has five parts. Take a few minutes now to discuss the contents of each part. Learn its name and placement.

1. Heading	*231 Ash Avenue* *Lima, Ohio 45805* *April 3, 19—*
2. Salutation (*or* Greeting)	*Dear Annie,*
3. Body	*Your ticket is enclosed. Meet us at the reception desk.*
4. Closing	*Sincerely,*
5. Signature	*Margot*

A Zip Code identifies "a delivery unit and associates that unit with a major post office through which mail is routed for delivery." What is the Zip Code above? Is there a punctuation mark between the state and the Zip Code?

It is generally considered better not to use abbreviations in the heading and within the body of a letter. For example, the words *street* and *avenue* and the names of cities and states should not be abbreviated. However, abbreviations for titles before names, such as *Mr.*, *Mrs.*, and *Dr.*, are exceptions.

Indented or block form

There are two forms for arranging a friendly letter: the **indented form** and the **block form.** The block form is most commonly used in typewritten material.

Look at the following outlines. Notice that the two forms differ only in the arrangement of the heading and signature. Use the form that is recommended by your teacher.

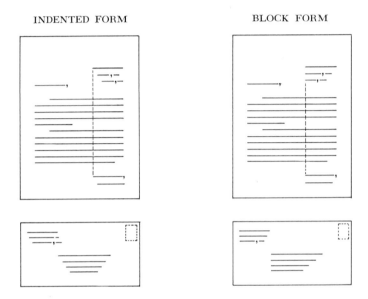

INDENTED FORM   BLOCK FORM

Capital letters and punctuation

In earlier grades you have studied the rules for capitalizing and punctuating all parts of a letter. If you are not certain about these rules, review them briefly here.

Heading:
1. Capitalize all proper names.
2. Place a comma between the name of the city and state.
3. Put the Zip Code after the state. Do not put a punctuation mark between them.
4. Place a comma between the day and year.
5. Never put a comma at the end of any line in the heading.

> 21 Park Lane
> Newark, New Jersey 07102
> February 9, 19—

Salutation:

1. Capitalize all proper names.
2. Capitalize the first word of the salutation.
3. Put a comma at the end of the salutation of a friendly letter.

Dear Aunt Matilda,   My dear Harold,   Dear Mrs. Bell,

Closing:

1. Capitalize only the first word of the closing. The other words should begin with small letters.
2. Place a comma at the end of the closing.

Sincerely yours,   Very sincerely yours,   Love,

Signature:

Never put a punctuation mark after your name.

Exercises: Capitalization and punctuation

1. Write the following headings correctly, using the arrangement recommended by your teacher:

1. 115 kirby avenue—falls church virginia—july 23 19—
2. 11 forest hill terrace—billings montana 59107—january 4 19—
3. parker road—sundance wyoming—august 3 19—
4. 315 prescott circle—camden new jersey 08101—may 6 19—
5. 6035 sunset boulevard—pittsburgh pennsylvania 15219— december 8 19—

2. Write the following salutations correctly:

1. dear uncle oscar
2. dear cousin philip
3. dear mother
4. dear mr bernstein
5. dear mike
6. my dear friend

3. Write the following closings correctly:

1. love—albert
2. lovingly yours—peggy
3. sincerely—william
4. very sincerely yours—edward

Preparation for Mailing

Make it a practice to reread and check your letter before you mail it. Poor writing, a blot or two, misspelled words, incorrect use of capital letters and punctuation marks—all these score against you. Check your spelling of words like *dear, truly, sincerely, received, avenue, appreciate*, which recur in letters.

Personal letters are most commonly written on a small sheet of paper, sometimes a double sheet folded at the left. The paper should be folded just once and placed into the envelope with the crease at the bottom. Thus, when the receiver takes it from the envelope, it will be right side up and ready for him to read. The sketches below show the correct method:

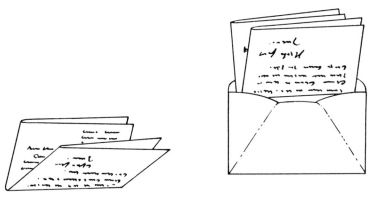

If you write your letter on regular 8″ by 11″ typewriter paper, fold it as shown below.

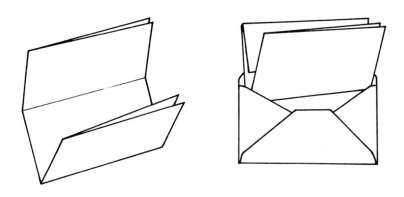

Addressing the envelope

The envelope of the letter should be plainly and fully addressed, not only with the address of the person to whom the letter is sent, but also with your address. Use the same form for the address— indented or block—that you used in the heading of your letter.

The Post Office Department asks that you do not use abbreviations for the names of cities and states, because they are easily misread in the sorting of the mail by post-office workers.

It is more convenient for the post office to have the return address written on the front of the envelope in the upper left-hand corner than on the back of the envelope. Can you explain why?

Here is the envelope for George's letter on page 206:

George McVay
61 Maple Street
Trenton, New Jersey 08608

                    Mr. Richard McVay
                    332 Holworthy Hall
                    New Brunswick
                    New Jersey 08901

Exercise: Writing a friendly letter

Write a friendly letter to someone who would like to hear from you. A friendly letter written as an exercise in English class need not sound artificial. Do your best to make it sound like yourself. Address an envelope for your letter.

If you prefer not to write a letter to a real person, then follow one of the suggestions below, making up whatever facts you need:

1. Write a letter to a friend who has been out of town for a month visiting relatives.
2. Write a letter to your father, who is on a business trip.
3. Write a letter to a friend who lives in a distant city.
4. Write a letter to a former teacher.
5. Write a letter to an older brother or sister who is away.
6. Write a letter to a brother or sister who is in the hospital.

FROM *The World Is Too Much with Us*

The world is too much with us; late and soon,
Getting and spending, we lay waste our powers:
Little we see in Nature that is ours;
We have given our hearts away, a sordid boon!

WILLIAM WORDSWORTH

Wordsworth is one of England's greatest and most popular poets. He is often called the poet of Nature and of the common man, for he chose the simple common experiences of life to write about.

In the four lines above, he says that most men spend so much time worrying about material comfort that they forget to look around them at Nature, which feeds the heart and the spirit. Do these lines apply to our life today? You may want to find and read the entire poem.

215

Social Notes

Courtesy, which includes being thoughtful toward other people, helps to make and keep friends. Writing notes of thanks, apology, invitation, regret, or acceptance is an important part of courteous behavior. Always be sincere and thoughtful in what you say, even though occasionally you may, for example, need to thank a person for a gift that you do not really like. In such cases, you want to tell the truth, and yet you would be rude to state the whole truth. You can solve the problem by expressing your appreciation for the thoughtfulness of the donor. That is the important thing.

On the pages that follow are models of several kinds of social notes. Study them. However, when the time comes for you to write your own social notes, do not copy the models. You should express your own ideas.

Thank-you Note

> 221 Hunter Lane
> Ames, Iowa 50010
> February 12, 19—
>
> Dear Grandmother,
> This morning I woke from a sound sleep with the strange feeling that my face was being washed. I opened my eyes and there on my bed was the silkiest, wiggliest little puppy I ever saw. The card on his collar told me he was a gift from you.
> How did you know what I wanted most? Thanks a million!
> Please visit us soon. You will never believe how adorable Binkie is until you see him.
> Love,
> Kathy

Letter of Invitation

321 Valley Road
Provo, Utah 84601
December 9, 19-

Dear Todd,
The day after Christmas we leave for Uncle Burt's ranch in Arizona. We hope to visit some Indian reservations.
Aunt Lil wants you to come too. I hope you can. We could have such fun together.
Your cousin,
Chuck

Note of Regret

2201 Post Street
Ogden, Utah 84404
December 12, 19-

Dear Chuck,
Why do all the best things have to happen at once? You and I have been crazy about Indians ever since we were kids. Do you remember how Mrs. Busby's old turkey gobbler treed us when we tried to pluck out his feathers for headdresses?
Now you give me my big chance to see some real Arizona Indians, and I have to turn you down. That same day we leave for a week's visit to California.
It was nice of you and your Aunt Lil to ask me. How I wish I could be in both places at once!
Yours as ever,
Todd

Note of Acceptance

2201 Post Street
Ogden, Utah 84404
December 12, 19—

Dear Chuck,

I sure am glad you and your Aunt Lil included me in the visit. Many thanks to you both. To see Arizona Indian life will be a dream come true for Indian buffs like you and me.

What time are you starting? Dad will get me there early.

All the best,
Todd

Note of Apology

December 13, 19—

Dear Mr. Treadway,

For the first time in ages I really had a good excuse for being late, but this did not give me the right to speak to you the way I did yesterday. Most of my excuses for tardiness to class have been flimsy, and you did right in talking to me about it. Please accept my apology for being discourteous.

Sincerely yours,
Polly Pemberton

2201 Post Street
Ogden, Utah 84404
January 4, 19—

Dear Mrs. Porter,

How can I ever thank you enough for the wonderful time I had during my visit! It was good of you to put up with me. I do appreciate your kindness.

Please tell Mr. Porter how much I enjoyed the visits to the Indian reservations. I have never had anything interest me so much before. I plan to use the notes I took and the Indian pictures for a report. The set of pictures I have enclosed are for you and the family.

Mother is going to write to you. She hopes you will come up to see us the next time you visit Chuck's folks—and so do I.

Sincerely,
Todd Kimball

Guides for writing invitations and replies

1. Always specify the date, place, time, type of activity, and where the reply should be sent.
2. If a written invitation is received, send a written reply, unless a telephone number is given on the invitation.
3. Reply promptly. Never wait until the last minute, for this makes it difficult for the host or hostess to make plans.
4. Never issue or reply to invitations when others are around. It causes embarrassment to those who may not be invited.

Exercise: Writing social notes

Write two notes, using any two of the following ideas:

1. An invitation to a picnic at your house
2. A note of regret to a friend for not being able to accept an invitation to attend a Big League baseball game for which he has tickets
3. A note congratulating a cousin for winning a college scholarship
4. A note of apology for having accidentally broken down a neighbor's hedge
5. A note of thanks for the gift of a book you have already read and did not like   (This will be a test of your tact.)
6. A bread-and-butter letter to the mother of a classmate at whose house you have stayed
7. A note of acceptance to a friend who has invited you to spend a week end at her house
8. Any other social note that you may need to write

✓ Check Test 9: Adjectives and adverbs

Take this test to find out how much you remember about using adjectives and adverbs.

Write the sentences listed below, choosing the correct word from each pair in parentheses:

1. I can't sing (good, well) in front of an audience.
2. My father was ill, but he is now (good, well).
3. Before Paul finished the book, he solved the mystery (easy, easily).
4. Lucille always plays chess (good, well).
5. I can climb that pole (easy, easily).
6. My bicycle rides (good, well) uphill.
7. These cookies are quite (good, well).
8. I can tell the twins apart (easy, easily).
9. We will (sure, surely) know the results by Monday.
10. That fisherman is (sure, surely) trying to get our attention.

If you made any mistakes in Check Test 9 above, turn to pages 435 and 445 in the Review Handbook. Study the lesson or lessons you need and then do the practice exercises.

The Business Letter

You have been discussing friendly letters and social notes written to family, friends, and acquaintances. In these letters your writing is conversational and personal; it reflects your personality, your likes, and your dislikes. We come now to another type of communication—the business letter—which is written for specific purposes and requires a different kind of writing. Letters for ordering magazines or goods, requesting information, or requesting adjustments are business letters.

A good business letter should be as brief as possible, clear, and to the point. It should also reflect courtesy. Its form should be correct and its appearance neat.

If you type well, it is preferable to type business letters. If you do not type, be sure that your writing is especially neat and clear. The paragraphs in the body of a typewritten business letter may be indented or not, as you wish. If the letter is handwritten, the paragraphs should be indented.

Letter of request

Here is a typical business letter—a *letter of request:*

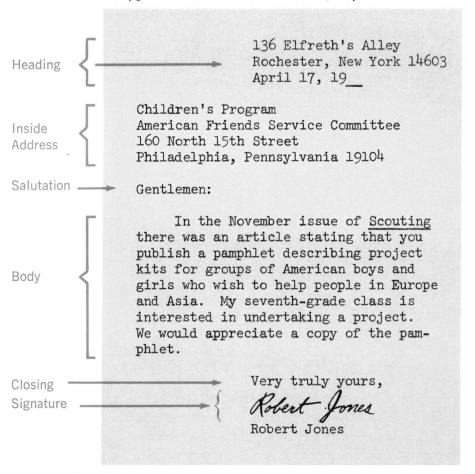

Heading

136 Elfreth's Alley
Rochester, New York 14603
April 17, 19__

Inside
Address

Children's Program
American Friends Service Committee
160 North 15th Street
Philadelphia, Pennsylvania 19104

Salutation

Gentlemen:

Body

    In the November issue of <u>Scouting</u>
there was an article stating that you
publish a pamphlet describing project
kits for groups of American boys and
girls who wish to help people in Europe
and Asia. My seventh-grade class is
interested in undertaking a project.
We would appreciate a copy of the pamphlet.

Closing

Very truly yours,

Signature

Robert Jones
Robert Jones

To discuss

Discuss the following questions about Robert's letter above:

1. Is Robert's letter brief and to the point?
2. How many parts does a business letter have?
3. Which letter part is not included in a friendly letter? What information does this part give?
4. Does a business letter have block or indented form?
5. How do the salutation and closing above differ from the ones in a friendly letter? What mark of punctuation is used after the salutation of a business letter?
6. Why is the signature both typed and handwritten?

An order letter

Another common type of business letter is the order letter. In the following example, notice how carefully Ronald has given all the information the company needs to fill the order:

```
                          3620 Passayunk Avenue
                          Baltimore, Maryland 21233
                          May 13, 19__

Holiday Hobby and Supply Co.
37 Crenshaw Boulevard
Chicago, Illinois 60607

Dear Sirs:

Please ship to me in the best way the following
items advertised in your spring catalog:

     No. 432  1 Gang-way bicycle horn
                (blue)                       $2.89
     No. 437  2 Lookee handlebar
                streamers (2 for 39¢)          .39
     No. 303  1 spoke wrench                    .45
     No. 214  1 kick stand (14")              1.32
                                             $5.05

I enclose a money order for $5.05.  I'd appre-
ciate prompt delivery.

                     Very truly yours,

                     Ronald Yungblut
                     Ronald Yungblut
```

Notice the exact information that is given in the order letter above: (1) catalog number of each item; (2) number and description of articles desired; (3) advertised prices; (4) total cost; (5) method of payment; (6) amount of money enclosed. An order that is as exact as this one will be easy to fill without mistakes.

Letter of adjustment

Sometimes you have to write a letter to call attention to an error in a bill or in filling an order. Study the following model letter:

```
                              187 Alden Place
                              Buffalo, New York 14219
                              November 30, 19__


Audio-Visual Helps, Inc.
38 Main Street
Portland, Maine 04101

Dear Sirs:

     On November 20 I ordered a Slide-Set of
"Birds of America" and an accompanying record,
priced at $3.50, as advertised in North Amer-
ican Birds magazine. I received your ship-
ment yesterday, but I find that the slides are
badly scratched. I am returning the entire
shipment today by parcel post.

     I should appreciate your sending me
another one.

                              Yours truly,

                              Vera O'Connor

                              Vera O'Connor
```

Here are excerpts from some poorly written business letters. Read them and be prepared to discuss what is wrong with each one.

1. *Letter of adjustment*
   You sent me a broken camera lens. Now I can't use my camera next week during my camping trip.
2. *An order letter*
   My dog has fleas. Please rush me two cans of D-Flea-Dog. My dad will pay when he gets his next pay envelope.

3. *Letter of request*

Please send me one of those booklets you mentioned on the radio or TV a few days ago.

4. *Letter of request*

Dear Government Printing Office,

5. *Letter of adjustment*

Dear Sirs:

It came broken and I am returning it. Please refund my money.

Hoping to hear from you,

Joe

6. *An order letter*

Will you please send me some grass seed for our new lawn? It is about a half acre, I think. Please send your best quality seed, provided it is not too expensive.

Yours Truly,

To discuss

1. In the first excerpt, what kind of effect do you think the complaining tone will have on the reader? In requesting adjustments, why is it better to assume that the company will be reasonable? What else is wrong with the letter?

2. Can you explain what is wrong with each of the remaining excerpts above?

Guides for writing business letters

1. Write your letter neatly, politely, and clearly.
2. Include your address, city and state, Zip Code, and the date in the heading.
3. Include the inside address. Make sure that it is identical with the address on the envelope.
4. Use block form.
5. Use a colon after the salutation.
6. Give all the needed information, as, for example, prices, sizes, dates, and quantities, in an order letter.
7. Avoid giving any unnecessary information.
8. Close in the standard way:

Yours truly,   Very truly yours,   Sincerely yours,

Exercises: Writing business letters

1. Choose one of the items below and write the letter described. Make up any names and facts needed to have a complete letter, but sign your own name. Then exchange letters with a classmate and write an answer to his letter.

1. Order two of the items described in the following advertisement from a local newspaper. State your choice of type and your first and second color choice.

ON SALE * $1.99 * $1.99 * $1.99

Men's Short-Sleeve Sport Shirts
* Comparable values are $2.95, $3.95, $4.95

Here are the types available:
a. Yorbel triacetate and cotton, regular collar, small plaid in blue, tan, gray, or gold.
b. Cotton hopsacking, regular collar, solids of white, blue, tan, or green.
c. Wash-and-wear cotton, regular collar, stripes in blue, tan, gray, or green.
d. Cotton chambray, regular collar, solids of blue, tan, or gray, with contrast trims on pocket and collar.

Sizes: small • medium • large

HoLLAdAy's 1303 Front Street
Merchantville, New Jersey 08109

In the answer to the letter, say that the type ordered is out of stock and that the money is being returned.

2. Write a letter of adjustment concerning a shipment of one dozen plates, two of which arrived broken. Write to the China Shop, 7 Main Street, Springfield, Massachusetts 01101.

3. You are interested in going away to summer camp for two weeks. Write to Camp Central Information Service, 3654 57th Street, Chicago, Illinois 60607, requesting information about locations, cost, and other practical details.

4. You think you left a school bag on a public bus. Write to the Safeline Bus Company, Paterson, New Jersey 07509. Describe the bag, tell when it was lost, and inquire as to what you should do.

5. A neighboring school runs summer sessions for junior high school pupils. You wish to do some advanced work in the subject you are most interested in, or to get some special help in the subject which gives you the most difficulty. Write to Mr. Charles O'Brien, Director, Summer Session, Brownlow Junior High School, Manchester, New Hampshire 03105, explaining your needs and requesting information.

2. Address envelopes for your letters.

3. Discuss some of the letters you have written in class.

Post cards

When few details are needed and no money is required, it is acceptable to write a request on a post card. Follow this model:

```
                            October 10, 19__

    Please send me the booklet "How to
Overcome Dinginess" which was offered on
the Joey Walsh show last evening.

                       Charles Smith
                       17 South Street
                       Flint, Michigan 48502
```

```
Charles Smith
17 South Street
Flint, Michigan 48502




            Glorious Color Company
            Bankers Trust Building
            Syracuse, New York 13201
```

Exercise: Writing post cards

Write a post card, requesting a pamphlet, brochure, or some information.

A Book to Read

Night of the Wall
by Priscilla Goldthwait
Illustrated by Denny McMains
G. P. Putnam's Sons

One night in August, 1961, the East German government suddenly built a high, rough, ugly wall through the middle of Berlin, Germany. They topped it with barbed wire and thus sealed off the Communist from the non-Communist part of the city. The wall also sealed off from each other members of the same families.

Hans Starrholm's mother failed to come home on "the night of the wall." She had taken fresh vegetables to Cousin Hannah in East Berlin. Hans succeeded in crossing the wall and making his way to Hannah's home. During the course of a dreadful, dangerous night and following morning, he learned how his father had died and the secret reason for his mother's visits. During these suspense-filled hours, Hans experiences things that force him to outgrow his boyhood.

About the author

Priscilla Goldthwait, now the mother of four children, was sent to Germany shortly after World War II to set up a displaced persons' camp for Russian refugees. It was operated by the United Nations. When she returned to the United States, she spoke wherever possible about refugee and immigration problems. She later returned to Europe and met the "real Hannah" who inspired her to write *Night of the Wall*. In August, 1963, Mrs. Goldthwait visited the infamous Berlin Wall.

Test I

Read the following parts of letters. Choose the better one in each pair. On your paper, write *A* or *B* next to the appropriate numeral.

1. A. Dear Grandma,

    I don't have anything to say, but Mother says I have to write, so here goes.

    B. Dear Grandma,

    Things haven't been very exciting here lately, but Mother says you would like to hear about the book I've been reading.

2. A. 611 Randolph St.   B. 611 Randolph Street
   Philadelphia, Pa.   Philadelphia, Pennsylvania

3. A. Well, it's getting late and I'm out of ink, so I better stop.

   B. Please write again soon. I really like hearing from you.

Test II

Number your paper from 1 to 5. Write the names of the five parts of a friendly letter, numbered in the diagram below. Give an *example* for parts 1, 2, 4, and 5. Use your own name and address.

Test III

1. Number your paper from 1 to 4. Correcting the capitalization and punctuation, rewrite these parts of friendly letters:

    1. 97 north lincoln avenue   2. my dear uncle joe
       los angeles cal.   3. dear doctor ames
       july 18 19—   4. very sincerely yours

2. Rewrite and arrange this envelope address correctly:

mrs. e. w. kendall—99 lexington ave.—ny, ny

Read the following pairs of excerpts from social notes and decide which one is the better example in each pair. On your paper, write the letter *A* or *B* next to the appropriate numeral.

1. A. Thanks very much for sending me a book for my birthday. It would be nice if I liked to read. My mother tells me I should read more, so I'll use your book.
   B. Thanks very much for remembering my birthday. It makes me feel good to realize you think that much of me. The book you sent will be ideal for my next book report.
2. A. I'm having a party Saturday night. I hope you can come. Don't worry about what to wear. It's going to be an informal barbecue in the yard.
   B. Please come to an informal barbecue in our yard next Saturday, April 11, at 5 P.M.
3. A. I'm really sorry I can't come to your barbecue next Saturday night. My grandparents will be visiting us, and my parents say I've got to stay home.
   B. I'm sorry I can't come to your barbecue tomorrow night. I hope you can get someone to take my place.
4. A. I apologize for being rude during the game yesterday, but you had no right to call that foul on me.
   B. I apologize for being rude during the game yesterday. I know it's your job and not mine to decide who has committed a foul.

Test V

1. Number your paper from 1 to 4. Answer the following questions about business letters:

   1. What information does the inside address give?
   2. Which form is correct—block or indented form?
   3. What mark of punctuation is used after the salutation?
   4. What are the names of two types of business letters?

2. Write an imaginary letter, ordering for yourself *The Students' Dictionary*, 4th edition, at $3.95, from the North American Book Company, 95 Washington Boulevard, Fair Meadows, Connecticut. Parcel post will cost $.35. Include all the parts of a business letter.

Exercise I

1. Turn to pages 205–10 and review the lessons on writing friendly letters.

2. Rewrite the following excerpts from letters and correct any mistakes in the form or content:

1. Dear Mom,
   I hate writing letters, but I'm sorry you're in the hospital.
2. 42 N. Pierce St.
   Franklin, Tenn.
3. Well, I'm running out of ideas so I'll close this letter now.
4. I know you'd rather hear about the baseball team, but I'll write to you about science class.
5. Glad you made a good record in baseball this year, but you should see me in action. They made me the pitcher.

Exercise II

1. Review the parts of a friendly letter in the lesson "Matters of Form" on pages 210–11.

2. Write the names of the parts of a friendly letter. Using your own name and address, write examples of each part. Arrange them in good letter form on your paper.

Exercise III

1. Review pages 211–12.

2. Write the following letter parts, capitalizing and punctuating each one correctly:

1. 2002 liberty crescent—nashville tennessee—april 19 19—
2. 41 east new avenue—martindale michigan—october 12 19—
3. 9 golden gate st.—san fran. california—january 7 19—
4. dear mrs albertson
5. my dear uncle john
6. dear mom
7. dear friend
8. very sincerely yours
9. yours truly
10. with love

Exercise IV

1. Review "Social Notes" on pages 216–19.

2. The contents of the following social notes need changes and corrections.   Study them and rewrite them on your paper.

1. Dear Chuck,

   Since Bob is moving to California next week, I thought it would be nice to have a surprise party for him next week-end.   Please bring a small humorous present and be on time so that we'll all be here before he is.   I hope you can come.

2. Dear Aunt Agatha,

   Thanks very much for sending me such a nice sweater for Christmas.   You can tell how much I like it by the fact that I already bought one just like it.   You really know how to choose nice clothes.

3. Dear Mr. Wilson,

   I had a field trip in science yesterday, and that's why I didn't come in for the help you offered to give me in math.   I hope you'll give me another appointment some other time.

Exercise V

1. Review "The Business Letter" on pages 221–25.

2. There are mistakes in the following business letter.   Copy the letter on your paper, correcting the mistakes.   You may have to change whole sentences.   If needed information is missing, make up something that makes sense.

New York City
March 19—

McHenry Watson Co.
9782 West 111th St.
New York, New York 10011

Please send me blue jeans, catalog number LX923, size 10.   (Don't send size 6 the way you did last year.   I haven't been size 6 since 4th grade.)   Enclosed is my father's check for $2.75 to pay for the jeans. I didn't know how much postage so I didn't send any.

Love,
Hank Burns

CHAPTER 9

Adjectives and Adverbs: How They Modify

By using only subject nouns and verbs, you can write sentences, but they will be rather bare sentences like these:

1. Children are playing.   2. Actors are rehearsing.

By adding words that enlarge the picture of each noun and verb, you can create much more interesting and useful sentences. Notice that the sentences listed below have the same foundation—skeleton—as the sentences above.

1. { Several naughty little children are still playing upstairs.
{ Those considerate children are not playing loudly today.

2. { The two leading actors are rehearsing inside.
{ The other actors are not rehearsing today.

Do you see how the words *several, naughty,* and *little* have added meaning to the subject noun *children?* These words are called **modifiers.** To *modify something* means "to change it." This can be shown in a simple chart, in which you put *children* in the center, with its modifiers clustering around it:

For the verb *are playing,* a similar chart can be made:

upstairs ⟶ (are playing) ⟵ still

Draw similar charts for the remaining three sentences above.

Exercise: Using modifiers

As a basis for class discussion, have three or four class members write some skeleton sentences on the board. The sentences should be made up only of subject nouns and verbs, for example: *Boys play. Apples fell.* Then see how many interesting and vivid ways you can think of to modify the nouns and verbs. As you experiment, notice how modifiers like *not* and *never* completely reverse the meaning of the sentence, and those like *good* and *bad* or *one, five,* and *no* may almost change it completely.

Adjectives: Modifiers of Nouns and Pronouns

Look at the pictures and words below and observe how the meaning of the noun *boy* can be changed by the addition of modifiers. The words that have been used to modify *boy* are **adjectives** of various kinds. Read them over aloud to remind yourself of the kinds of words that can be adjectives.

Adjectives, in addition to modifying nouns, modify pronouns, as in this sentence:

He is humorous and intelligent.
  (adj.)   (adj.)

What pronoun do the two adjectives above modify?

■ An **adjective** is a word used to modify a noun or a pronoun.

Tall, slender,   Strong, active,
studious **boy**   muscular **boy**

Subject complements

Adjectives usually appear before the words they modify, as,

The *black* mask was found in the *dark, ghostly* attic.

Sometimes, however, they follow the noun or pronoun they modify, as,

The mask was *black*.   It was *dark* and *ghostly*.

An adjective that follows a linking verb and modifies the subject is called a *subject complement*. You have already studied subject complement nouns and pronouns. Another name for an adjective used as a subject complement is **predicate adjective.**

Exercises: Recognizing and writing adjectives

1. Pick out the adjectives in the following sentences and write them on your paper with the nouns or pronouns they modify. Then underline each adjective and draw an arrow to the noun or pronoun it modifies.

EXAMPLES: 1. The large snake was hungry and cranky.

YOU WRITE: *1. the snake; large snake;*

hungry snake; cranky snake

1. The new grass was smooth and green.
2. I will trade this large old desk for that small modern one.
3. Long, serious books are difficult for poor readers.
4. They were kind and considerate to me.
5. That noisy starling cackled constantly.

2. Copy the sentences below and provide adjectives for the blanks. (Words like *the, a, an, some, that,* and *this* are adjectives.)

1. __?__ __?__ girl was always trying to help __?__ __?__ dog.
2. __?__ birds can be found in __?__ bird cages.
3. __?__ man is quite __?__ and __?__.
4. __?__ __?__ tools are more __?__ than the __?__ ones we have at home.
5. "Please put away __?__ __?__ books," said our __?__ chairman, "and listen with __?__ attention to the __?__ records I shall now play."

Sentence Patterns

Review the three basic sentence patterns you have used thus far:

PATTERN 1:   N V   Children play.
PATTERN 2:   N V N   Children play games.
PATTERN 3:   N Vbe N   Children are people.

Now, with your knowledge of adjectives, add the symbol **Adj.** to form a fourth sentence pattern:

PATTERN 4:   N Vbe Adj.   Children are playful.

In Pattern 4, an adjective follows a linking verb (verb of being) and describes the subject.

Study the following examples of Pattern 4 sentences with their symbols on the left. Keep in mind that the symbol **Adj.** will also represent the noun signals *a*, *an*, and *the* from this point on.

PATTERN 4:   N Vbe Adj.   (Subject—Verb—Subject Complement)

Adj. N Vbe Adj.   The animals are fierce.
Adj. Adj. N Vbe Adj.   A fierce animal is dangerous.
NP Vh Vbe Adj.   He has been kind.

● Write Pattern 4 sentences according to the following combinations of symbols:

1. **N Vbe Adj.**   4. **NP Vbe Adj.**
2. **Adj. N Vbe Adj.**   5. **NP Vh Vbe Adj.**
3. **Adj. Adj. N Vh Vbe Adj.**   6. **Adj. Adj. N Vbe Adj.**

● Write sentences according to the following combinations of symbols. After each sentence, indicate in parentheses whether it follows *Pattern 1, 2, 3,* or *4*.

1. **N Vbe Adj.**   8. **Adj. Adj. N Vbe NP**
2. **N V**   9. **Adj. N V Adj. N**
3. **N Vbe N**   10. **NP Vh Vbe Adj. N**
4. **N V N**   11. **Adj. Adj. Adj. N Vh V**
5. **NP Vbe Adj.**   12. **NP Vh Vbe Adj.**
6. **NP V**   13. **Adj. Adj. N Vh Vbe Adj.**
7. **N V NP**   14. **Adj. Adj. N Vh Vh V**

Two classes of adjectives

It is useful to group adjectives into two classes. One class *describes,* as do the italicized adjectives below. They answer the question *what kind?*

small window	*enormous brown* bear
empty room	*strong, quick,* and *ferocious*
warm fire	animal

These adjectives are called *descriptive adjectives.*

Other adjectives do not describe; they *limit* by telling *how many* or *which one.* Such adjectives are italicized below:

that boy	*this* place
three girls	*most* people
a cow	*some* students
the child	*these* houses

These are called *limiting adjectives.* The noun signals *a, an,* and *the* are the most common limiting adjectives. They are called **articles.**

(You may want to study and practice diagraming sentences which contain adjectives. If so, turn to pages 394–95.)

Exercises: Descriptive and limiting adjectives

1. Here are ten descriptive adjectives and ten limiting adjectives. Copy them on your paper. Next to each adjective, write a noun that it can modify.

DESCRIPTIVE ADJECTIVES		LIMITING ADJECTIVES	
lively	friendly	the	several
slippery	ugly	a	this
rapid	clean	an	many
long	awkward	that	few
delicate	large	those	seven

2. Use the following nouns in sentences of your own, modifying each noun with one or two adjectives:

streets	man	book	clouds	trucks
ocean	child	river	wind	comedian
parks	city	hills	tree	politician

This kind—these kinds

The word *kind* is singular. Therefore, the singular form, *this* or *that*, must modify it:

this kind   *that* kind

The plural of *kind* is *kinds*. With the plural form you use *these* or *those:*

these kinds   *those* kinds

Exercises: Using this kind *and* these kinds

1. Here are four correct sentences. Read each aloud four times to establish in your mind the correct use of *these* and *those* with *kinds*, and *this* and *that* with *kind*.

1. *This kind* of person annoys me.
2. *These kinds* of canned goods are all satisfactory.
3. *That kind* of language sounds bad.
4. *Those kinds* of people always succeed where I fail.

2. Read these sentences aloud, choosing the correct limiting adjective from each pair in parentheses:

1. I am fond of (this, these) kind of cooky.
2. (This, These) kind of morning makes me feel happy.
3. I want (that, those) kinds of fish kept out of the lake.
4. (This, These) kinds of candies give you quick energy.
5. The ones on the shelf are (that, those) kind.

Modifiers That Show Possession

One way to modify, or change, a noun or a pronoun is to show who owns what; that is, to show possession. Words used to show possession are a type of limiting adjective. We call them **possessive modifiers.** As you can see, they are simply nouns or pronouns used as adjectives.

the *pupils'* library   *our* party
David's toys   *your* posture
James's room   *his* chances
my book   *its* tail

A possessive noun or pronoun may follow a verb and modify the subject noun.

This money is *ours*.   The fault is *Bob's*.

(You may want to study and practice the diagraming of sentences which contain possessives. If so, turn to pages 392–93 in Chapter 15, "Making Sentence Diagrams.")

Exercise: Finding possessive modifiers

List the possessive nouns and pronouns in the following sentences. After each, write the noun it modifies.

1. My story is about Jerry's pets.
2. His copy of the book came from our library.
3. Their hunting days together were enjoyable.
4. Lonny's first lesson was about the school's safety program.
5. I hope you and your friends will visit Happy's camp.
6. Jane and her mother were invited to spend their vacation at Mr. Gates's farm.
7. Her coat is in my closet, but your hat is on that chair.
8. Ellen's books are in Joan's locker.
9. The child's toys were piled high upon his bed.
10. The dog brought its master the stick.

TO MEMORIZE

FROM *Byron*

In men whom men condemn as ill
I find so much of goodness still,
In men whom men pronounce divine
I find so much of sin and blot,
I do not dare to draw a line
Between the two, where God has not.

JOAQUIN MILLER

This poet lived in the Old West during the hectic and heroic days of the westward movement. Working in a mining camp, living with an Indian tribe, working as an editor and in the pony express, studying law, and becoming a judge were only a few of the experiences which acquainted him with people in all segments of American life. What is he saying about judging people in the lines above? Do you agree with the idea he expresses?

239

Adverbs: Modifiers of Verbs

In language, not only do you need to modify nouns and pronouns to express your ideas; you need also to modify verbs. Look at the verb *pulled* in the following sentence:

This old mule *pulled* the wagon.

You may want to give further information and answer for your reader the questions:

How did he pull the wagon?
When did he pull the wagon?
Where did he pull the wagon?

Words that answer such questions are called **adverbs.** Here are examples of adverbs used in the same sentence:

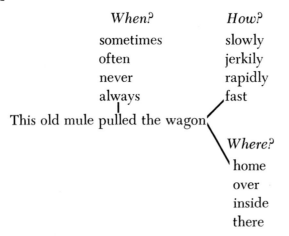

When?	*How?*
sometimes	slowly
often	jerkily
never	rapidly
always	fast

This old mule pulled the wagon

Where?
home
over
inside
there

In addition to the types of adverbs explained above, perhaps the most common adverb is *not*, which modifies a verb and changes the meaning of the entire sentence:

This old mule did *not* pull the wagon.

Another interesting fact about adverbs is that so many of them can be made by adding *–ly* to adjectives. For example:

ADJECTIVE	ADVERB	SENTENCE
quick	quickly	I *quickly* hid.
intelligent	intelligently	He studied *intelligently*.
smooth	smoothly	The motor ran *smoothly*.

Here are some adverbs that do not end in *–ly*:

soon	not	seldom
always	never	often

Exercises: Recognizing and writing adverbs

1. Pick out the adverbs from the following sentences and write them on your paper. In parentheses after each, write the verb it modifies. Then tell which question it answers: *how? when?* or *where?* (except for *not*).

EXAMPLE: 1. Yesterday he quietly left the house.

YOU WRITE: *1. Yesterday (left) when?*
quietly (left) how?

1. The dog barked softly.
2. He usually barks loudly.
3. Today my cousin devoured his meat hungrily.
4. Bob suddenly threw his wallet down.
5. He will surely not return soon.
6. I always answer letters quickly.

2. On your paper after the appropriate numeral, write one or more adverbs to go in each blank below. Then read the sentences aloud. Do not use any adverb more than once.

1. The tree swayed __?__.
2. Bob __?__ likes to sail.
3. Mathematics is __?__ the easiest subject in school.
4. My little friend fell __?__ to the ground.
5. The leader's hand began to rise __?__ and __?__.
6. The teacher __?__ sat down and began __?__ and __?__ to prepare her lesson.

Adverbs That Modify Adjectives and Other Adverbs

In each of the following four sentences there is one adverb or adjective shown in italics:

1. A *beautiful* girl walked across the street. (adjective)
2. That monkey climbed the tree *quickly*. (adverb)
3. My opinions on the question are *strong*. (adjective)
4. The gale blew *noisily* through the streets. (adverb)

Each of these adjectives or adverbs can be modified by the word *very*:

A *very beautiful* girl walked across the street.

Read sentences 2, 3, and 4 with *very* inserted before the adjective or adverb.

Very is a special kind of adverb. It modifies an adjective or another adverb.

There are other adverbs that act in the same manner. One of them is *rather*.

A *rather beautiful* girl walked across the street.

These adverbs that can modify adjectives or other adverbs answer the question *how much?* or *to what extent?* Some of the most common ones are:

slightly	hardly	rather	too
extremely	almost	really	very
more	quite	so	somewhat

(You may want to study and practice diagraming sentences which contain adverbs. If so, turn to pages 395–96.)

■ An **adverb** is a word used to modify a verb, an adjective, or another adverb.

Exercises: Special adverbs

1. Taking turns in class, read aloud the two sentences below, using adverbs to fill in the blanks:

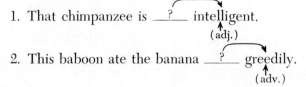

1. That chimpanzee is ___?___ intelligent.
   (adj.)

2. This baboon ate the banana ___?___ greedily.
   (adv.)

2. In each sentence, name the adverb or adverbs. Tell whether each modifies a verb, an adjective, or another adverb.

1. Strange knockings were heard rather often in the old castle.
2. Evidently a house spirit had settled there.
3. Hinzelmann, the spirit, soon became truly courageous.
4. Quite agreeably he would chat with the castle occupants.
5. He was almost always friendly to everyone.
6. The women of the castle liked him especially well.
7. Hinzelmann usually proved an extremely obliging spirit.
8. He worked very diligently at all the household tasks.
9. In the stables he labored equally hard.
10. In fact, he really never stopped his work.
11. But did Hinzelmann work too industriously?
12. For what reason did he live so contentedly in the castle?

3. Use any six of the adverbs listed in the lesson above in six sentences of your own. In three of the sentences, use adverbs that modify adverbs. In the other three sentences, use adverbs that modify adjectives.

Using Adjectives and Adverbs to Compare

Often modifiers are used to compare things. For instance, you might say: "This wrestler is *strong*; that wrestler is *stronger*; but the third wrestler is *strongest*." Here you are using the adjective *strong* to compare wrestlers.

Also, you might say: "This jet flew *fast*; that jet flew *faster*; but the third jet flew *fastest*," using the adverb *fast* to compare.

Both adjectives and adverbs have three forms of comparison, which are called **degrees of comparison.** Here they are:

POSITIVE DEGREE	COMPARATIVE DEGREE	SUPERLATIVE DEGREE
fine	finer	finest
sweet	sweeter	sweetest
intelligent	more intelligent	most intelligent
helpful	less helpful	least helpful
fast	faster	fastest
slowly	more slowly	most slowly
interestingly	more interestingly	most interestingly

Some very common irregular adjectives and adverbs form their comparisons by changing form entirely:

POSITIVE	COMPARATIVE	SUPERLATIVE
good } well	better	best
many } much	more	most
bad	worse	worst
little	less	least

Here is a check list of rules for forming comparisons:

1. Most one-syllable adjectives and adverbs show comparison by adding *–er* and *–est*:

> big, bigg*er*, bigg*est*
> late, lat*er*, lat*est*

2. Some two-syllable words show comparison with *more* and *most* (or *less* and *least*) and some use *–er* and *–est.*

> spiteful, more spiteful, most spiteful
> lovely, lovel*ier*, lovel*iest*

3. Words of three or more syllables show comparison with *more* and *most* (or *less* and *least*):

> conspicuous, more conspicuous, most conspicuous
> alertly, more alertly, most alertly

Making comparisons correctly

When comparing *two* things, use the **comparative** degree. When comparing *three or more* things, use the **superlative** degree.

> Of the two tomatoes, that one is *redder.*
> Of the three tomatoes, that one is *reddest.*

> She dances *more gracefully* than I.
> Of all the girls in the class, she dances *most gracefully.*

In making comparisons, be sure to use only the one method that is needed, *–er–est* or ***more–most.*** Never use both the ending and the word *more* or *most* together.

244

Spelling notes

1. When adding *–er* or *–est* to a word ending in *y* following a consonant (*friendly, pretty*), change the *y* to *i* and then add the suffix (*friendlier, friendliest; prettier, prettiest*).

2. When adding *–er* or *–est* to an adjective ending in a consonant following one vowel, double the final consonant (*big, bigger; hot, hottest*).

Exercises: Comparison of adjectives and adverbs

1. Write the positive, comparative, and superlative degrees of the following adjectives and adverbs:

1. nice	6. ambitious
2. deep	7. well
3. generous	8. slowly
4. good	9. enthusiastically
5. lucky	10. properly

2. On your paper beside the appropriate numeral, write the correct form for the word in parentheses.

(busy) 1. Of all my friends, John is the __?__ one.

(clumsy) 2. Of the two apes, that one is __?__.

(fast) 3. The __?__ boy on the team is Jerry.

(energetic) 4. Jean is the __?__ of the two candidates for office.

(fearfully) 5. Today we proceeded __?__ than yesterday.

(well) 6. I feel __?__ today than I did yesterday.

(good) 7. The __?__ play of the season was *The Prince and the Pauper*.

(many) 8. I want to see even __?__ people in the stands than last week.

(far, friendly) 9. Between Boston and Philadelphia, I think the city __?__ south is the __?__.

(soon) 10. Between the two workers, Jerry can finish the job __?__.

3. Use each of the words that follow in two sentences, one comparing two persons, places, or things, and one comparing three or more persons, places, or things.

1. little	3. happy
2. bad	4. beautiful

5. slowly

Sentence Patterns

Learn this new symbol:

Adv. = Adverb

Study the sentences below. Notice that only the skeleton words (underlined below) in each sentence represent its basic pattern. Without these words, the sentence could not be complete grammatically.

PATTERN 1: N V

Adj.   N   V   Adv.
The <u>performers</u> <u>arrived</u> today.

PATTERN 2: N V N

Adj. Adj.   N   Adv.   V   Adj.   N
Those funny <u>clowns</u> always <u>do</u> dangerous <u>tricks</u>.

PATTERN 3: N Vᵇᵉ N

Adj. Adj.   N Vᵇᵉ Adv. Adj.   N
The trained <u>seals</u> <u>are</u> always the <u>favorites</u>.

PATTERN 4: N Vᵇᵉ Adj.

Adj.   N   Vᵇᵉ Adv. Adv.   Adj.
The <u>tickets</u> <u>are</u> not very <u>expensive</u>.

Adjectives and adverbs add color and meaning to sentences, but, with one exception, they do not change the basic patterns. The exception is the adjective which follows the linking verb (verb of being) and modifies the subject in a Pattern 4 sentence.

246

Here are the skeleton words, the words that form the basic pattern of each sample sentence on page 246.

PATTERN 1: N V — Performers arrived.
PATTERN 2: N V N — Clowns do tricks.
PATTERN 3: N Vbe N — Seals are favorites.
PATTERN 4: N Vbe Adj. — Tickets are expensive.

Can you see now why the skeleton words which form the sentence patterns are the framework to which all other words are added? The symbols above each word in the sample sentences include the symbols for the basic pattern plus the ones for adjectives and adverbs.

● Each of the following groups of symbols can be matched with two of the sentences listed below. Next to the appropriate numeral, write the letters of the two sentences that fit.

1. **Adj. Adj. N Vh Vbe Adj. N**
2. **Adj. Adj. N Vh Adv. V NP**
3. **Adj. Adj. N Vh Adv. Vbe Adj.**
4. **Adj. Adj. N Vh Vh V Adv.**

a. The scurrying mice will surely frighten her.
b. The hungry cow has been mooing loudly.
c. Our nervous neighbors have often been angry.
d. A considerate visitor would have spoken softly.
e. That lucky person will surely be famous.
f. The black horse will be a winner.
g. This friendly policeman will gladly help us.
h. The little acorn will become a tree.

● On your paper, list the letters *a* to *h*. Tell which pattern each sentence above follows by writing down *Pattern 1, 2, 3,* or *4.*

● Write sentences of your own, following the groups of symbols below. Try to vary your sentence ideas. You may find this exercise easier if you first list all the symbols you have studied so far and their meanings next to them.

1. **NP Vbe Adv. Adj.**
2. **Adj. Adj. Adj. N V Adj. N**
3. **Adj. Adj. Adj. N Vh Vh V**
4. **Adj. N Vh V Adj. Adv. Adj. N**
5. **Vh N V Adv. Adv.?**

Choosing Between Adjectives and Adverbs

Sometimes choosing between an adjective and an adverb can cause difficulty. In the following sentences, for example, an adverb should be used—not an adjective. The adverbs tell *how* something is done. Each one modifies a verb.

> 1. Pauline spoke (polite, politely).
> 2. He blew the trumpet (noisy, noisily).
> 3. We can solve that problem (easy, easily).

Read aloud each sentence above a few times, using the adverbs *politely, noisily, easily.*

The words *polite, noisy,* and *easy* are adjectives and must modify nouns or pronouns, as,

> 1. Pauline is *polite.*
> 2. The sounds of the trumpet are *noisy.*
> 3. That is an *easy* problem.

Use an adverb—not an adjective—to modify a verb.

Exercises: Adjective or adverb?

1. Choose the correct modifier from each pair in parentheses.

> 1. I can answer the question (easy, easily).
> 2. She always behaves (polite, politely).
> 3. Uncle Bill speaks (interesting, interestingly) about his travels.
> 4. The children are playing (noisy, noisily) outside.
> 5. Her room is always (neat, neatly) cleaned.
> 6. Usually Bert was (happy, happily), but he is not speaking (happy, happily) today.
> 7. My desk isn't (neat, neatly) now, but I cleaned it (neat, neatly) this morning.
> 8. That's an (easy, easily) job. I can do it (easy, easily).

2. Use each of these words in a sentence of your own:

1. polite	3. noisy	5. easy	7. neat
2. politely	4. noisily	6. easily	8. neatly

Good and well

A common problem is to know when to use *good* and when to use *well.* *Good* is always an adjective; it cannot modify a verb—only a noun or pronoun.

1. A *good* job gives satisfaction.
(adj.)

2. Mother's pies are always *good.*
(adj.)

Well is sometimes an adjective meaning "healthy."

1. He is now a *well* boy.
(adj.)

2. John looks *well* after his operation.
(adj.)

In sentence 2, *well* describes the noun *John*; it is an adjective. It does not modify the verb *looks.* The verb *looks* acts in the same way as a verb of being; it links the adjective to the subject of the sentence.

However, *well* is mainly used as an adverb, meaning "in a satisfactory manner."

Aunt Inez sings *well.*
(adv.)

He came through the test *well.*
(adv.)

> Use the adverb **well**—not **good**—to tell how something is done.

Bad and badly

Another problem is *bad* and *badly.* *Bad* is an adjective.

He is a *bad* boy.   He was *bad.*

Badly is an adverb:

He played *badly.*   The child reads *badly.*

Many people make the mistake of saying, "He feels *badly*." They do not say what they mean. They do not mean that he lacks a good sense of touch or feeling. What they mean is that the way he feels is *bad*; *bad* modifies *he*. Therefore, it is correct to say:

He feels *bad*.   He looks *bad*.

The opposite of "He feels *bad*," as you have seen, is "He feels *well*." In this case, *well* is used as an adjective, just as *bad* is.

Exercises: Using good–well and bad–badly

1. Choose *good* or *well* for each of the blanks below. Be prepared in each case to explain your choice.

1. My father is now __?__ after his rest in the hospital.
2. The film is very __?__ and I advise you to see it.
3. The sheep dog did his job very __?__.
4. His training was __?__.
5. The shepherd felt __?__ about it.
6. That car rides __?__ and steers __?__.
7. It does not do very __?__ on steep hills.
8. The engine is not __?__.
9. The students always behave __?__ when the faculty is here.
10. Their success shows that they planned __?__.

2. Choose *bad* or *badly* to complete the blanks.

1. The accident was very __?__.
2. The driver steered his car __?__.
3. He felt __?__ about causing so much suffering.
4. She always looks __?__ when she leaves the roller coaster.
5. A __?__ sport acts __?__ in a __?__ situation.

Most and almost

Do not make the mistake of leaving off the first syllable of the adverb *almost*. You must say, "She was *almost* ready"; "Henry has *almost* finished his supper."

Almost is always an adverb and must be used as an adverb. *Most* is usually an adjective (*Most* birds sing. *Most* boats float.) or a noun (*Most* of the people were happy. *Most* thought well of him.). *Most* is rarely an adverb.

Note these examples. Read each one aloud twice.

The fog had almost lifted.
Most of the fog had lifted.
She was almost drowned by the time they pulled her out.

Exercise: Using *most* and *almost*

Read the following sentences aloud, choosing the correct word in parentheses:

1. The trip had (most, almost) discouraged us.
2. We were (most, almost) ready to give up and return home.
3. The weather was (most, almost) all bad.
4. It rained (most, almost) every day.
5. The cold was (almost, most) more than we could endure.
6. (Most, Almost) of us were really upset.
7. There was one storm that (almost, most) drowned us.
8. Terrific winds (most, almost) always blew.

Double Negatives

What is the difference between the four sentences on the left and the four on the right?

I do love you.	I do *not* love you.
You may have some candy.	You may have *no* candy.
Some of us will go.	*None* of us will go.
Somebody is whispering.	*Nobody* is whispering.

The sentences on the left make *affirmative* statements; those on the right make *negative* statements. Affirmative means *yes*; negative means *no*. Read aloud the italicized words in the sentences on the right. These words are *negatives*.

Some people make the mistake of using two negatives in a sentence. When they do this, they spoil the meaning of the sentence and are using substandard English. *Do not use two negatives in a sentence.* (The introductory word *No*, as in "No, I didn't see him," is an exception.)

WRONG: I *never* asked *no one*.
RIGHT: I *never* asked *anyone*.

WRONG: He *never* went *nowhere*.
RIGHT: He *never* went *anywhere*.

WRONG: He *doesn't* have *no* money.
RIGHT: He *doesn't* have *any* money.

Exercise: Avoiding the double negative

Read aloud the sentences below, choosing the correct word from each pair in parentheses:

1. Isn't (nobody, anybody) going to help?
2. There isn't (any, no) money in my purse.
3. You cannot have (any, no) cake today.
4. We couldn't see (any, no) mountains in the distance.
5. None of us (is, isn't) going to that party.
6. Henry didn't do (nothing, anything).
7. He didn't find (any, no) friends (nowhere, anywhere).
8. Never say (nothing, anything) like that to me.
9. Our house (has, hasn't) never been painted.
10. Don't sit (nowhere, anywhere) near that boy with mumps.

Test I

There are twenty adjectives in the sentences below. Copy each one on your paper. Then, in parentheses, write the noun or pronoun it modifies. Do not include *a, an,* or *the.*

EXAMPLE: 1. That question was rude.

YOU WRITE: *1 That (question)*

rude (question)

1. Many queer birds nest on these two remote islands.
2. This kind of brilliant windy day will become warmer by the afternoon.
3. An angry brown bear terrified four families in the park.
4. Those unusual kinds of snowflakes fall on high mountains.
5. They were angry and unhappy.
6. The last meeting of the year was shorter and quieter.

Test II

Number your paper from 1 to 5. Choose the correct word from the pair in parentheses and write it on your paper next to the appropriate numeral.

1. (This, These) kinds of mushrooms are poisonous.
2. (This, These) beautiful kinds of orchids are very common.
3. I would like three of (this, these) crisp kind of cooky.
4. (That, Those) kind of evening proved relaxing.
5. (That, Those) kind of grape makes good raisins.

Test III

There are ten adverbs in the following sentences. Copy each one on your paper. Then, in parentheses, write the word it modifies.

1. His offer was very suspicious.
2. The team seldom has played there successfully.
3. The coach had not thought optimistically about the game.
4. Yesterday Jerry eagerly offered help.
5. He cleaned the garage quite slowly.

Test IV

1. Make three columns on your paper headed *Positive, Comparative, Superlative.* Place each of the adjectives and adverbs listed below in its correct column. In the remaining two columns, write its other two forms.

EXAMPLE: 1. biggest

YOU WRITE: *Positive Comparative Superlative*
1. *big bigger biggest*

1. kindest
2. sadder
3. dark
4. casually
5. friendlier

6. better
7. more quickly
8. many
9. quickest
10. sleepy

2. On your paper beside the appropriate numeral, write the form of the adjective or adverb in parentheses which will fit correctly in the blank.

(hard)   1. Bobby works __?__ of all the class members.

(dark)   2. Your picture is __?__ than mine.

(bad)   3. As far as I'm concerned, pistachio is the __?__ kind of ice cream.

(sluggishly)   4. The third hippopotamus walked __?__ of all.

(good)   5. Between the two speeches, Carolyn's was __?__.

Test V

Choose the correct words from the pairs in parentheses. Write each word on your paper next to the sentence numeral.

1. Isn't (anybody, nobody) interested in that movie?
2. Calvin had the flu, but he is (good, well) now.
3. That boy can fix the bike (easy, easily).
4. Neither of my sisters wants (any, no) dessert.
5. Joe swims (good, well) in races.
6. I am doing (bad, badly) in science.
7. The teacher spoke (stern, sternly) to us.
8. The rain has (most, almost) stopped.
9. No one said (nothing, anything).
10. Marilyn told the teacher she didn't feel (good, well) and went to the doctor.

Review and Practice

Exercise I

1. Review the lessons on adjectives on pages 233–35 and 237.

2. Here are some short sentences. Rewrite them, adding adjectives that modify the italicized nouns in each one.

1. *Students* complained about the *rules*.
2. The *baby* smiled at the *visitor*.
3. *Boys* are playing in the *yard*.
4. *Parents* make *decisions*.
5. The *car* stalled in the *street*.

Exercise II

1. Review the use of *this kind* and *these kinds* on page 238.

2. Using *this, these, that,* and *those* each at least once, put the following phrases in sentences of your own:

kind of apple

kinds of disturbances

kinds of classes

kinds of diseases

kind of game

kind of explosion

Exercise III

1. Review "Adverbs" on pages 240–42.

2. Pick out the adverbs from the following sentences. Then tell which question each one answers: *how? when? where?* or *to what extent?*

1. Janice quickly purchased a new raincoat.
2. Sometimes he growls quite angrily.
3. The falls splashed the rocks below noisily.
4. He always counts money too rapidly.

3. Copy the following sentences on your paper, adding adverbs that will modify the italicized adjectives and adverbs. Try to use as many different adverbs as you can.

1. The *old* man walked *slowly*.
2. He was *tired* and *uneasy*.
3. A *small* child *quietly* offered to carry the man's parcel.
4. The *old* fellow was *deaf* and didn't hear the boy.
5. The boy looked *hurt* when the feeble man went *wearily* on without answering.

Exercise IV

1. Review "Using Adjectives and Adverbs to Compare" on pages 243–45.

2. Below, you are given several adjectives and adverbs in the positive degree. Use each one in a sentence showing the comparative degree and a sentence showing the superlative degree.

EXAMPLE: 1. intelligently

YOU WRITE: *1. He handled the problem more intelligently than I.*
             ✔ *Of all the scouts, he acted most intelligently.*

1. good	3. late	5. carefully
2. often	4. recently	6. skillful

Exercise V

1. Review "Choosing Between Adjectives and Adverbs" and "Double Negatives" on pages 248–51 and 252.

2. Study the italicized words in the following sentences. Tell whether each is an adjective or an adverb. Then give the word that is modified.

EXAMPLE: 1. Clarence had finished the game *easily*.

YOU WRITE: *1. easily -- adverb which modifies had finished*

1. The floor was polished *well*.
2. The *better* team was defeated *badly* because of injuries.
3. Pilots land planes *really carefully* in fog.
4. Sailors *almost always* resist seasickness.

3. Choose the correct word from each pair in parentheses.

1. The evacuation order affected (almost, most) every soldier on the base.
2. I play chess (bad, badly).
3. I had pneumonia, but I feel (good, well) now.
4. He (most, almost) lost his gear.
5. I didn't eat (no, any) green apples, but I feel (bad, badly).
6. Our homework is seldom done (easy, easily).
7. He doesn't play (happy, happily) with strangers.
8. We never travel (nowhere, anywhere).

CHAPTER 10

Giving Explanations and Reports

One very practical use of language is to explain to others how to do something, get somewhere, or solve some problem. Knowing how to explain things clearly and logically is a valuable skill. You know how satisfied you can be when a person says "Let me explain," and then proceeds to do so, especially if he knows his subject and how to organize his ideas.

Another skill which requires clear thinking and organization is the writing of reports. Many times between now and your graduation from school you will be required to report on an experience you have had, some special subject you know about, or some special reading or research you may have done. And after school, whether in college or on a job, you may be called upon to report to others.

Giving Explanations

Think for a moment about the explanations you have read or heard recently. Were they confusing? Were they too simple for you or too difficult? Certainly, some explanations interested you, and others bored you. Why? What makes a good explanation?

Here is an explanation. Read it carefully and be prepared to tell whether you think it is well organized.

Things to Remember in Setting Up an HO Train

If you set up an HO electric train carefully, it can be a lot of fun. If set up incorrectly, it will be a constant source of trouble.

Remember that an HO electric train operates on two kinds of electric current: direct current (D.C.) and alternating current (A.C.). The locomotive is on D.C., and this makes it possible to reverse the engine by pushing a lever on the power pack, the small box which plugs into your house current. The accessories—lights, switches, and

other equipment—are on A.C. They can be operated even when the locomotive is not running. Be sure to wire the track to the D.C. terminals of the power pack and the accessories to the A.C. terminals. Otherwise, your train will not operate properly and may be damaged.

As you put your tracks together, do not leave gaps between the sections of track. Make sure the track lies on a really smooth surface.

Be careful about dirt. Some railroaders lay their sets on the floor and allow dust and dirt to get on the track. From the track it is drawn up into the delicate machinery of the locomotive and soon causes wear and rough running. It is best to set up the train tracks on a raised platform above the dirt of the floor and the feet of smaller children.

When you first get your set, and after each eight hours of operation, you should lubricate all moving parts with a very small amount of light machine oil. Dip a toothpick about an eighth of an inch into the oil and then touch it lightly on each part, especially the wheel bearings and the engine parts. Be careful not to overoil. If you do, the rolling stock collects dust, and the oil runs out on the track, making it slippery. It also prevents the engine from picking up electricity from the rails efficiently. Too little oil and too much are equally bad.

So remember, to have a smoothly operating HO train, (1) keep the A.C. and D.C. straight, (2) set up the track with great care, (3) keep it clean, and (4) lubricate the rolling stock regularly with a very small amount of oil.

258

To discuss

Look again at the explanation on pages 257–58. Discuss in class the following questions about it:

1. Can the explanation be outlined easily? Take a few minutes now in class to outline it. One of you can work at the board as suggestions for the outline are given.
2. Does the explanation keep on the subject?
3. Does it present its ideas in logical order? Look at the first sentence. Does it introduce the topic well? Does the last paragraph summarize all the main points in the explanation?

Guides for giving an explanation

1. Organize your material in logical steps.
2. Present the steps in the order in which they should be followed.
3. Give accurate and complete information.
4. Stay on the subject.
5. Use specific words.
6. Explain any difficult or unfamiliar terms.
7. Keep your information simple and clear.
8. Use models, diagrams, pictures, maps, or charts if they help make your meaning clear.

Exercise: Giving an explanation

Write or tell orally how to make or do something that you know how to make or do quite well. If you do not have an idea, perhaps these suggestions will help:

1. How to collect, label, and exhibit rock specimens
2. How to bake a coffee cake
3. How to care for a cat or a dog
4. How to build a wooden fence
5. How to build a bookcase with bricks and boards
6. How to take care of African violets
7. How to build a fire for outdoor cooking
8. How to set up a tent
9. How to perform a magic trick
10. How to water-ski

Writing Personal Notes of Explanation

At home or in school, the need to make brief explanations in writing often arises. In the following example, Muriel informs her friend Florence of a change in rehearsal plans. Unable to see her until rehearsal time, Muriel left the following note on Florence's desk:

Dear Flo,

We tried to get the auditorium for three-thirty this afternoon as planned, but the orchestra members had first claim on it. Instead of postponing the rehearsal, Jack suggested we meet at his house at four o'clock. Don't forget to bring the extra copy of the play. We'll need it for the prompter.

Love,
Muriel

To discuss

1. What important facts did Florence need to know in order to be present at the rehearsal? Did Muriel supply the information in her note? Did she tell where the rehearsal will be and the time it will start?

2. Did Muriel tell why the plans were changed?

3. What might have happened if Muriel's note had not given all the information?

In writing any note, a person must keep in mind what the reader will need or want to know.

Exercise: Writing a note of explanation

Here are four situations in which a note of explanation is required. Choose one of them and write the note.

1. You have offered to lend your camera to your cousin who does not know how to use it. Write a note explaining how to load and use the camera. Also, give him any photography hints that may be helpful. (If you prefer, choose an object other than a camera.)

2. Your uncle has said he will come in his car to pick you up after a basketball game at another school. He does not know which school or how to get there. He will come to the office at your school to find out. Write a note explaining all that he will need to know.

3. You and your family are to be away over the weekend, and your neighbor has agreed to come to your house to feed and care for your pet. Write the neighbor a note which will be put in his mailbox. Tell him where he will find the food and how to prepare it.

4. Your friend was not able to attend the final Science Club meeting of the year. He and his family were already at their summer cottage at the lake. At this final meeting, each club member chose a project to work on for the summer. The projects will be discussed and screened by the club members at the first meeting in the fall. The best ones will be submitted to the Junior Science Exhibit Committee for exhibition at the state fair in October. Write to your friend, explaining what happened at the meeting, what project he was assigned, and why he was chosen for it. Tell him to write to the club president if he doesn't like the assignment and has another project he'd rather do. Be sure to give him all the important facts.

Making Announcements

In writing a public notice to be posted or read aloud, you must be sure to make everything clear. A notice that is to be posted should be attractive in order to catch people's attention. The important information should be plainly stated.

A notice that is to be read aloud must read smoothly. Any information about time, dates, and places should be repeated, since most people do not remember such details on the first hearing.

Examine the example of a good typical bulletin-board notice on the next page and be prepared to discuss it.

FOR THE BIRDS?

MR. CADBURY WILL CONDUCT

ANOTHER ONE OF HIS FAMOUS

BIRD WALKS

NEXT WEEKEND

DATE: SATURDAY, APRIL 13 (IN CASE OF RAIN, WILL BE POSTPONED)

TIME: 7:00 to 10:00 A.M.

STARTING PLACE: END OF POSSUM HOLLOW BUS LINE

EQUIPMENT: OLD CLOTHES. BRING FIELD GLASSES IF YOU HAVE THEM.

FOR WHOM? GRADES SEVEN AND EIGHT

STEVENS NATURE CLUB

SEE BOB HIBBS
RM. 223 IF YOU
HAVE QUESTIONS.

To discuss

1. Is the bulletin-board notice on the opposite page attractive?

2. Is all the important information plainly stated?

3. What device is used to catch people's attention?

4. Is the nature of the event or activity given?

5. Who may participate? Where does the event take place? When?

6. Is there an admission charge? Are tickets needed? Is any equipment needed?

7. If the reader had any questions about the "bird walk," what would he do?

8. Is it likely that there would be any questions after reading this notice?

In general, when writing notices, try to use your imagination. Put yourself in the place of the reader or hearer. Figure out what he will need to know. Usually it is safe to assume that he will not know very much and that his interest will have to be attracted.

Exercises: Making announcements

1. Prepare a notice for a school bulletin board, announcing some event or activity of interest to the students in your grade. If possible, announce something that will actually take place in your school. If there is nothing that is appropriate to announce, make something up. If you cannot think of anything, perhaps the following suggestions will help:

    1. Rehearsals for a class play
    2. Organizing a hobby club
    3. Student elections
    4. A sale
    5. A cultural event which students are encouraged to attend
    6. A school game

2. Prepare an announcement that will be read aloud to a home room rather than posted on a bulletin board.

3. When you have written your announcement, try to arrange to have someone else read it to the class. Then question the class about the principal items of information in the notice in order to see if they were understood by the majority. If they were not, revise your notice so that it will be more effective.

Gathering Information for Reports

A report may be on any one of many topics: books you have read, some aspect of history, the life of a famous man, a scientific subject, a trip, a movie you have seen, or any other topic that interests you or is required by the subject you are studying.

Once you have decided on your topic, your job is to gather information about it. *It is important to think about where you are likely to find your information before you start the search.*

Using written sources

For some subjects you may find it helpful if you first make a list of the main categories under which you might expect to find information. For example, if you are to do a report on easy-to-grow vegetables, you might find material under "Vegetables," "Gardening," and possibly under the names of certain vegetables, such as "Carrots," "Beets," "Tomatoes." This list of categories would give you a good start on gathering information for your report. It would be much more useful than trying to find something under the heading "Easy-to-grow Vegetables." Then, as you read in various books, encyclopedias, and magazines, other categories or topics will suggest themselves.

If, on the other hand, you are doing a report on a famous person, you will not need a list of categories. You can go directly to possible sources, looking up your information under the name of the famous person you have chosen.

If your subject is a historical one, like the Louisiana Purchase or William the Conqueror, you will probably find most of your information in history books and encyclopedias. If it is a contemporary subject, like highway safety or modern dance steps, for example, much of your information may come from magazines, newspapers, or perhaps recent books.

Reference books which are generally useful are biographical dictionaries, the *Readers' Guide to Periodical Literature*, almanacs, atlases, and, of course, encyclopedias.

You have probably had some experience in finding information about report topics. If not, you will want to refer to Chapter 12, "How to Study More Efficiently," which gives you instructions on using the library, reference books, dictionaries, and periodicals. It also gives you information about note-taking.

Using your memory and experiences

Someone once said that the brain is the least-used muscle in the human body. Well, of course, the brain isn't a muscle, and many of us do make good use of it. It is true, however, that you often could save yourself much time and trouble in writing a report if you just sat down, pencil in hand, and *thought* about the personal experiences you have had. You may recall information you have read and heard that might be useful to include in your report. Of course, before you use the facts or figures that you think you remember, you should *check them for accuracy.*

To discuss

Suppose you are assigned a report on the subject of highway safety. Discuss in class the following questions, using only information the class already possesses:

1. What have you read or heard that might be useful in your report? List your sources.
2. Have you ever been in an automobile accident? What did you learn from it? Have you ever seen accidents? How might they have been avoided?
3. Do you know people who have had accidents? How does their experience dramatize the need for highway safeguards?

Exercises: Listing ideas and facts

1. Here are eight suggested report topics about which you probably already have some information. Choose any two of these topics and, using only your own memory and experience, jot down some of the ideas you might put into a report on them.

1. Family Life in the United States
2. Caring for __?__ (name a pet)
3. Ways for Young Teen-agers to Earn Money
4. Safety Hazards in the Home
5. Why __?__ Is My Hobby
6. Do Rules at School and at Home Work?
7. What Makes a Good TV (or Radio) Program?
8. The Place of Sports in Education

2. For each of your report topics above, list two facts found in a reference book, magazine, or newspaper. Name your sources.

Interviewing

Another source of material for your reports is people who have special knowledge or interesting opinions about the subject of your report. After you have thought out your topic thoroughly, have done as much reading as possible, and have your subject pretty well organized, you might want to get some additional facts and opinions from certain people in your community. To do this, you would arrange an interview. It is important not to waste the time of busy people by coming to interview them badly prepared. As soon after an interview as possible, write it up carefully.

Before you interview anyone, study the following sample write-up of an interview:

Interview with Mr. George Hessel, Principal of Lincoln Junior High School; February 10, 19—   Subject: School Rules

Mr. Hessel believes that the fewer rules a school has, the better. He thinks it is better for students to control themselves than to be controlled by rules. He told about a school he used to teach in where there were many complicated rules and where the student behavior was poor.

When asked "Why do we not abolish rules completely, then?" he replied that certain rules have proved to be necessary. He gave as examples our rules at Lincoln about running in the halls, about promptness to class, about leaving school during the school day, and about throwing snowballs. "Actually," he said, "students should make up their own rules and then discuss them with the teachers." He thinks it would be a good project for the student council to review the present rules at Lincoln and to suggest any changes.

Mr. Hessel believes that if rules are reasonable and well understood by students, they will be obeyed almost all the time. When we asked him what should be done when students disobeyed the rules, he said, "I believe in being very strict. Either we mean business or we don't." He thinks, though, that before a student is punished for disobeying a school rule, his home-room teacher or guidance counselor should discuss the matter with him and try to understand why the student did not obey.

Mr. Hessel thinks that the students themselves should help enforce the rules and told of several examples where students had done a better job of this than the teachers could have done. He thinks highly of the system of monitoring in the halls that the council has worked out this year.

To discuss

1. Is the report above well organized? Do you think that the student who interviewed Mr. Hessel came to the interview well prepared? Give reasons for your answer.

2. Read the first paragraph of the report again. What question do you think Mr. Hessel was asked before he gave his opinion about school rules?

3. What other questions do you think Mr. Hessel was asked? You can probably guess what the questions were from Mr. Hessel's answers. Two of the questions are stated in the report.

4. Did the interviewer use direct quotations to help make his report lively and interesting?

5. Can you think of any questions that you would have asked which the interviewer apparently omitted?

Guides for interviewing

1. Make a definite appointment. Be sure the person you interview knows who you are and why you want to interview him.
2. Think carefully in advance about the questions you want to ask. Write them down. Do not ask questions you could easily answer by reference to the library.
3. Arrive for your appointment a few minutes ahead of time.
4. Give your name and purpose.
5. Ask your questions, one at a time, but do not force the person you are interviewing to follow *your* order of questions. If he wishes simply to talk about the subject, listen attentively and save your questions until the end. You may then find that you do not need to ask them.
6. Take notes, especially on names and figures. Do not trust your memory. Be sure you note the exact name of the person you are interviewing, his position, and the date of the interview. While taking notes, listen carefully and politely.
7. At the end of the interview, thank the person with whom you have talked. It is also polite to write a note of thanks soon afterwards.
8. Go over your notes as soon after the interview as possible, or they may grow cold. Then expand and clarify your notes if you need to.

Exercise: Interviewing

Divide the class into several committees and have each committee decide on a person it would like to interview and a subject for an interview. Plan your questions carefully before the interview. It may be a good idea to ask your teacher to check the questions you plan to ask before you have the interview. After the interview, have each member of the committee write it up carefully either as a part of a report you may be doing or as a separate paper.

Organizing Your Report

The best way to organize your facts and ideas into a report is to make an outline. *Remember*: An outline is not something to make for its own sake. It is a *tool* to help you to present your ideas more clearly and logically.

Making a rough outline

Some of you may find it more helpful to organize a rough temporary outline of what you think may go into your report even before you begin gathering information. For example, if you are doing a report on highway safety, you might, just out of your head, sketch out the subject something like this:

Highway Safety

Statistics of accidents
Killed and injured
Cost of accidents
Causes of accidents
Mechanical difficulties
Poor driving
Bad road conditions
Methods for improving safety
Individual drivers
Safety laws
Highway engineering
Personal experience to illustrate my points
Our family accident last summer
Accidents on our street
Interview with Mr. Stilz, policeman
Conclusion

If you are doing a report on the life of a person, you might jot down some main points as follows:

Life of Thomas Jefferson
The importance of Thomas Jefferson
  How he became famous
  How he helped mankind
Family background
Childhood experiences
Education
Important influences on his life
His traits of character
His accomplishments
What you and I can learn from his life

Such an organization of a report on a person's life is more interesting than the typical report which grinds out the facts of a man's life from birth until death.

Revising your outline

The examples above are not finished outlines. They merely give a framework within which you may work as you organize your information. You will probably find that you need to rearrange your outline *as you go*, adding some topics, dropping others, and changing the order. For example, in the outline above, you may find that the information you have for the topic "His accomplishments" can be combined with the facts you have for the topic "How he helped mankind." You may then want to drop one of these headings. By the time you have gathered all of your information and are ready to put it together, most of your job of organization has already been done. All you will have to do, then, is to write a more finished outline, with only minor revisions, before you actually start writing. Detailed instructions for making an outline are on pages 330–31.

Exercise: Making a rough outline

Here are ten topics on which you would probably need to look up information before you could make a report. Choose one and make a rough pencil outline of how you think you would organize a report on the subject. Leave plenty of space between parts of the outline so that additions can be made.

1. The First Twenty-five Years of __?__ (name of your community)
2. The American Indian in My State
3. Paper-making
4. Lewis and Clark and the Westward Expansion
5. The Causes and Cures of Seasickness
6. Plastics and the Toy Industry
7. Food from the Sea
8. Hunting: Sport or Menace?
9. Washington Irving's Home (or the home of any other famous American)
10. The Training of an Astronaut

TO MEMORIZE

If thou hast, of all the world's goods, but two loaves of bread remaining, sell one of them and buy hyacinths to feed thy soul.

CONFUCIUS

Does the author actually mean "loaves of bread" and "hyacinths," or are these words used as symbols to represent a larger, more important meaning? In your own words, tell what you think the author means. Do you see a similarity in theme with Wordsworth's "The World Is Too Much with Us" on page 215?

You may enjoy reading these lines from a poem which is an adaptation of the theme in Confucius's statement above. Notice that the symbols of the loaves and the hyacinths are used again in the poem.

FROM *Not by Bread Alone*

If thou of fortune be bereft
And in thy store there be but left
Two loaves, sell one and with the dole
Buy hyacinths to feed thy soul.

JAMES TERRY WHITE

Writing Your Report

You are now ready to choose a topic and write a report. When you have completed your first draft, you will want to read it over, pencil in hand, correcting errors and clarifying anything that is not clear. Think back to the discussion of the explanation "Things to Remember in Setting Up an HO Train," page 259. Check your organization, your spelling, your punctuation, and your sentences. Before doing these things, you may find it helpful to read the section on proofreading on page 378. Your teacher may want you to submit your first draft before you write the final one.

To make your report more attractive, you can design a cover for it and print an attractive title page. Be sure to arrange any maps and illustrations carefully and to label them neatly.

Use the following guides to help you in writing your report:

Guides for writing reports

1. Choose an interesting, manageable topic.
2. Make a rough outline, covering the main points in your topic.
3. Gather your information.
4. Make a careful outline before you start to work. (See pages 330–31.)
5. Start your report with an introductory paragraph that arouses interest and tells the purpose of the report.
6. Write your report in well-constructed paragraphs, following your outline. Center each paragraph around one idea. (See pages 108–12.)
7. Increase interest by including pictures, graphs, charts, and maps, if appropriate.
8. List your sources of information at the end of the report.

Exercise: Writing a report

Choose a topic from the lists in the exercises on pages 265 and 271, or one of your own. Gather and organize information about it, and then write the first draft of a report 250 to 350 words in length. If you wish, and your teacher approves, you may do a report in connection with another subject you are studying, such as social studies or science. Follow the guides above as you work.

Write the final draft of your report, proofread it, and hand it in.

A Book to Read

John F. Kennedy and PT–109
by Richard Tregaskis
Illustrated with photographs
Random House

During World War II, one of the most difficult jobs was that done by the men and commanders of the U.S. Navy PT boats, relatively light, fast torpedo boats used to seek out and sink Japanese warships. By far the most famous of these was PT–109, because it was commanded by John F. Kennedy, later to become the thirty-fifth President of the United States. *John F. Kennedy* is a fast-moving story of Kennedy's young years. It recounts in exciting detail how his ship was sliced in two by a Japanese destroyer and how Kennedy and most of his men surprised everyone by coming out alive—thanks, largely, to the bravery, coolness, and physical endurance of one man. The book contains many excellent photographs.

About the author

Richard Tregaskis was born in 1916 in Elizabeth, New Jersey. He graduated from Harvard and has spent much of his life as a war correspondent. During World War II he flew 23 combat missions over Europe and received the Purple Heart. He also wrote the famous *Guadalcanal Diary* and several other war books.

Test I

The following explanation has some faults. Number your paper from 1 to 3. Read the explanation and answer the questions below.

Keeping in Condition

A. Avoid a heavy diet of sweet things and soft drinks, for example. They are not very nourishing and take away your appetite for foods that are. Good food is essential for a good physical condition. Regular exercise is particularly important.

B. Since sleep is also important, don't stay up too late. Everyone needs a certain amount of sleep regularly. Although some people can get along on eight hours, others need ten.

C. Sleep will also help your looks. People with bags under their eyes are not very attractive.

D. Students spend so much time sitting at desks that they need to exercise to keep their muscles from getting flabby. Regular vigorous exercise and fresh air are most essential if you want to keep in good physical condition.

1. Write the letter (*a*, *b*, or *c*) of the item below that completes this statement correctly: The first sentence in paragraph A should

(a) Stay as it is.

(b) Be replaced by a topic sentence.

(c) Follow a good topic sentence like "One of the ways to stay in condition is to be careful about what you eat."

2. There is one sentence which does not belong in paragraph A at all because it does not keep to the topic of the paragraph. Copy this sentence on your paper.

3. Which paragraph is completely off the subject of the explanation and should be removed? Write the letter of the paragraph.

Test II

Arrange a clear, legible bulletin-board announcement relating the following information. Use a whole sheet of paper.

Your English class is presenting a comedy called *I Was a Ten-year-old Genius*, written and directed by two class members. Tell the date, time, and place the event will occur. Tell who is invited and whether there is an admission charge.

Test III

Suppose that you are going to have an interview with a fireman in preparation for a written report about what people can do at home to prevent fires. Study the following questions. Copy the numerals of those questions that are appropriate for this interview.

1. Can you, sir, remember fires in our area which could have been prevented by the people involved?
2. How many fires in our town were caused by carelessness?
3. What steps should people take to save water during drought?
4. Are fires in factories usually caused by carelessness?
5. What kinds of fire extinguishers are effective and safe to have in the house?
6. Where are the best places in the house to have fire extinguishers?
7. What steps should a person take when he discovers a fire in his house?

Test IV

Here are some random notes and an outline about the life of Madame Curie and her discovery of radium. Copy the outline on your paper, leaving space between items. Read the notes and write the numeral of each note under the appropriate outline heading.

1. Father, a professor of physics in a Polish high school
2. 1893–1894, received her Master's degrees in physics and math
3. Intellectual atmosphere in her childhood home
4. College education in Paris
5. Existence of radium doubted by scientists
6. Had very little money; no grants and fellowships available
7. Born in Poland
8. 1902, after 45 months of work, she and her husband isolated pure radium
9. 1898, she and her husband discovered radium
10. No laboratory, needed a large one

Outline:

    I. Early life and influences
   II. Education
  III. Difficulties she had to overcome in isolating radium

Exercise I

1. Review "Giving Explanations" on pages 257–59.

2. The explanation which follows is not clear and needs to be re-written. Rewrite it by following these instructions: (a) write a topic sentence, (b) arrange the steps in clear order, (c) eliminate the parts that are off the subject, and (d) rewrite the sentences that do not say what they mean.

How to Make Cocoa

You are very foolish if you add the dry cocoa to the milk while you're heating it. The box usually says quite clearly that you should mix the cocoa with sugar and a little water first. Then you don't get lumps. Lumpy cocoa is just disgusting to drink. With a smooth syrup of cocoa, water, and sugar, you slowly add a little hot milk. Then you'll have nice, smoothly mixed hot cocoa to drink, after you've added all the milk.

Exercise II

1. Review "Making Announcements" on pages 261–63.

2. Which announcement below is better? Explain your answer.

A. The contest begins tomorrow and lasts until next Friday. Each poster has to be 24 by 48 inches on heavy paper. It has to announce some event at school. You can get more information from the art teacher after school tomorrow. First prize is two super banana splits. Second prize is two hot fudge sundaes. Third prize is two ice-cream cones.

B. *You* can win two banana splits, two hot fudge sundaes, or two ice-cream cones at DeHaven's Drugstore if you enter the school events poster contest. The contest begins tomorrow, October 5th, and ends October 12th. Anyone in the junior high is eligible to submit one poster, 24″ x 48″, announcing an event to be held at school. Those interested should come to the art room tomorrow, October 5th, after school. The art teacher will give details. That's tomorrow after school for all those entering the poster contest.

3. Write your own announcement to be read aloud. Announce a school event. Be sure to include all the necessary information.

Exercise III

1. Review "Interviewing" on pages 266–67.
2. Prepare a list of questions for one of the interviews below:

   1. An interview with the school guidance counselor, in preparation for writing a school newspaper article entitled "Ways to Earn Money"
   2. An interview with a policeman in preparation for a written report about the safe play areas in your town

Exercise IV

1. Review "Organizing Your Report" on pages 269–70.
2. Copy the rough paragraph outline below, leaving space between each heading. Expand the outline by adding detailed notes under each heading.

Copy the title and fill in the blank spaces with places that you know. A museum, or a picnic ground, or a theater are examples you may use.

Instructions for Going from __?__ to __?__

   I. Means of travel
   II. Amount of time required
   III. Streets and other landmarks indicating where to turn
   IV. How to recognize destination

CHAPTER 11

Prepositions and Conjunctions: Connecting Words

The words in two parts of speech are used especially for the purpose of joining two or more words or word groups. These words are often called *connecting words*.

Prepositions and Prepositional Phrases

Suppose we wish to show the relationship between the two nouns *fox* and *coop*. We can use the preposition *in* to connect *fox* with *coop*. If we use the noun signal *the* before the second noun, we have *fox in the coop*. It is not a sentence, but the preposition *in* does show the relationship between the two nouns.

Words such as *behind, beside, in,* and *on* are **prepositions**. The relationship between *fox* and *coop* is illustrated in the pictures above.

Thirty of the most common prepositions are listed here. Read the list aloud to familiarize yourself with them.

about	before	for	over
above	behind	from	through
across	below	in	to
after	beside	inside	under
along	between	into	up
among	by	near	with
around	down	of	
at	during	on	

Groups of words that begin with a preposition and end with a noun or pronoun are called **prepositional phrases.** The noun or pronoun which follows the preposition is the **object of the preposition.** The object of the preposition in the phrase *in the coop* is the noun *coop.*

Here are some more examples of prepositional phrases:

into the swamp	from the old barn
at him	through a broken window
between them	with her

What is the preposition and the object of the preposition in each phrase above? Which objects are nouns and which are pronouns?

■ A **prepositional phrase** is a group of words that begins with a preposition and ends with a noun or pronoun as the **object of the preposition.**

Exercises: Prepositional phrases

1. In each of the following blanks, a preposition is needed to complete the idea. Think of at least two prepositions that can be used in place of each blank. Write them after the appropriate numeral on your paper. You may use the list on page 279 to help you.

1. That cat __?__ the sofa is not ours.
2. He bought the house __?__ Prospect Park.
3. The four cars __?__ the garage are total wrecks.
4. Several robbers __?__ the forest were plotting the theft.
5. A good football game __?__ dinner makes life worth while.
6. All the lawns __?__ our house and yours are covered with snow.
7. I am fond of those pictures __?__ Harry.
8. The rush of water __?__ the streets alarmed us all.

2. Use each of the following prepositional phrases in a sentence of your own:

1. near the wall
2. to us
3. inside it
4. around our apartment
5. between that big tree and her
6. from their products

Adjective phrases

All of the prepositional phrases you completed in the first exercise above modify nouns. For example, in sentence 1, the phrase *on the sofa* modifies the noun *cat*. This phrase is called an **adjective phrase,** because it modifies a noun just as an adjective does. Look at the phrases in sentences 2 to 8 above and name the noun each phrase modifies.

Here are five examples of adjective phrases in sentences, with an arrow pointing to the noun or pronoun that each phrase modifies:

1. The back *of the room* was dark.
2. This book *of poetry* pleases me.
3. There are many dogs *without leashes!*
4. See the snow *on the mountaintop!*
5. Several *on the desk* are his.

■ An **adjective phrase** modifies a noun or pronoun.

280

Adverb phrases

Prepositions also show the relationship between a *verb* and a *noun* or *pronoun*. Consider the verb *are running*. The picture above shows some of the ways that prepositions can relate the verb to the noun *school*. Some of the prepositional phrases illustrated in the picture are:

PREPOSITIONAL PHRASES

The students *are running* to the school.
by the school.
into the school.

(prepo-   (object of
sition)   preposition)

Each prepositional phrase modifies the verb *are running* and is therefore called an **adverb phrase.**

(You may want to study and practice diagraming sentences which contain prepositional phrases. If so, turn to page 397.)

■ Most **adverb phrases** modify verbs.

Exercises: Prepositional phrases used as adjectives and adverbs

1. Supply a preposition for each blank below. Then tell what verb each phrase modifies. Refer to the list of prepositions on page 279 if you need to.

1. Little Suzie eats __?__ her fingers.
2. The truck roared __?__ the highway.
3. __?__ the barn flew two swallows.
4. My mother always relaxes __?__ the evening meal.
5. Enormous mushrooms were growing __?__ the old tree.
6. Bob threw the book __?__ the room.

2. Find the prepositional phrases in the sentences below. Tell whether each phrase is an *adjective phrase* or an *adverb phrase*. (One sentence contains more than one phrase.)

1. A large new pet shop opened on Clarke Street.
2. Joel and I were browsing around the shop Saturday.
3. The owner of the store became friendly and talkative.
4. Joel pointed to the aquariums.
5. The water-filled tanks along the wall contained many beautiful species of tropical fish.
6. The owner gave us much information about them.
7. Usually, goldfish and tropical fish cannot live in the same tank.
8. The water temperature in a goldfish tank should be cool.
9. Tropical fish require a constant warm temperature of 70 degrees Fahrenheit.
10. Aquatic plants and aerating pumps supply the fish with oxygen.

3. Use each of the following prepositional phrases in two sentences, first as an adjective phrase and then as an adverb phrase. See how interesting you can make your sentences. Be prepared to tell what noun, pronoun, or verb each phrase modifies.

1. up the hill
2. under that chair
3. on the paper
4. with him
5. near their back door

Preposition or adverb?

Many words can be used both as prepositions and as adverbs. When they are used as prepositions, they introduce a prepositional phrase and are always followed by a noun or pronoun object. Study these examples of words used as adverbs and prepositions:

1. Mary walked *in*.   (adverb)
   Mary walked *in the garden*.   (preposition)

2. The child fell *down*.   (adverb)
   The child fell *down the stairs*.   (preposition)

3. That old car chugged *along*.   (adverb)
   That old car chugged *along the lane*.   (preposition)

Exercise: Preposition or adverb?

Use each of these words in two sentences. Use the word as an adverb in the first sentence and as a preposition in the second.

up   in   down   along   above   below

Some Usage Problems

There are a number of errors that people commonly make in using prepositions. Study the meaning and use of each preposition below.

At—to

Use *at* when you want to say that "someone or something is already in a certain place."

> George is *at* school.
> My father was *at* the office.
> He remains *at* the office until five o'clock.

Use *to* when you want to show "movement toward something, someone, or some place."

> George went *to* school.
> My father drives *to* the office.

> WRONG: Mary is ⤬ school today, not ⤬ the Smiths'.
> RIGHT: Mary is at school today, not at the Smiths'.

284

In—into

Use *in* when you mean "already inside."

> They were *in* the barn.
> She slept *in* the house.
> We stood *in* the vestibule.

Use *into* when you mean "movement from outside to inside."

> They ran *into* the house.
> Water poured *into* the pool.
> After the wedding we threw rice *into* the car.

Among—between

Among refers to three or more people or things.

> I was *among* friends.
> *Among* the trees were bears.

Between refers to two only.

> I was *between* Mike and Zeke.
> *Between* the two trees hung a hammock.

Beside—besides

Beside means "at the side of."

> Will you sit *beside* us?
> The ladder is *beside* the house.

Besides means "in addition to."

> Two others *besides* me were chosen.
> Who else wants to go *besides* us?

Unnecessary prepositions

Where means "in what place?" Therefore, if you want to ask in what place something is or to what place someone is going, you say:

> *Where* did he put it?   or   *Where* did he go?

Do not say:

> WRONG: Where did he put it ~~at~~?
> WRONG: Where did he go ~~to~~?

Exercises: Using the correct preposition

1. Choose *at* or *to* in place of each blank. Explain each choice.

1. Yesterday I stayed __?__ home.
2. He travels __?__ Chicago tomorrow.
3. John was __?__ my house when she called.
4. Mabel was __?__ the post office all day.
5. Jim ran __?__ his mother for help.

2. Choose *in* or *into* in place of each blank. Explain each choice.

1. We all ate dinner __?__ the cabin.
2. When the supper bell rang, Ted ran __?__ the cabin.
3. __?__ the water jumped Sylvia.
4. Please do not poke that stick __?__ the lawn.
5. She got out of one difficult situation and __?__ another.

3. Choose *among* or *between* in place of each blank. Explain each choice.

1. __?__ us all there is a fighting spirit.
2. There is an empty seat __?__ Mary and Zelda.
3. I will sit __?__ Frank and Howie.
4. It is friendly to circulate __?__ the guests.
5. One poor mouse had to live __?__ all those rats.

4. Choose *beside* or *besides* in place of each blank. Explain each choice.

1. __?__ squirrels, there were chipmunks all over the place.
2. __?__ the life belts, we need a first-aid kit.
3. Please sit __?__ me.
4. __?__ the wall stood many spectators.
5. Who __?__ us asked for help?

5. If you have the habit of using the preposition *to* or *at* at the end of a sentence that starts with *where*, read each of the sentences below aloud five times. Repeat the process for several days.

1. Where did he find it?
2. He didn't know where he was going.
3. He couldn't find where she hid it.
4. Where was John going?
5. Where did Dora put it?

6. Choose the correct preposition from each pair in parentheses.

1. They all went (at, to) the baseball game.
2. He was (at, to) the dentist's office on Tuesday.
3. The fish (in, into) the lake were dying.
4. We put those fish (in, into) the lake.
5. (Among, Between) seven campers there was not a single match.
6. Please divide it (among, between) Josh, Jed, and Jarvis.
7. (Beside, Besides) the speaker sat two students.
8. Who (beside, besides) me wants to go?
9. I was (at, to) Mary's house doing my homework.
10. There is no need for tact (among, between) you and me.
11. He had been (in, into) the house for an hour before he decided to go (in, into) the cellar.
12. (Beside, Besides) my friend, my sister sat (beside, besides) me.

Reviewing object pronouns after prepositions

Remember: When you use a pronoun as the object of a preposition, you must use the object form.

Throw it to *him*.   Divide it between Paula and *me*.
Take it from John and *her*.   It was news to *him* and *us*.

Think: from (John and) *her*; between (Paula and) *me*; to (him and) *us*.

If you need more explanation and drill on this point, review pages 194–95 in the chapter on pronouns.

Exercise: Choosing the correct pronoun

Choose the correct pronoun from each pair in parentheses. Then read each sentence aloud twice. In each case, explain your choice.

1. Put it between John and (I, me).
2. Please go with (they, them) and (we, us).
3. All he could see were the rapidly disappearing heads of Will and (she, her).
4. If you want to eat with (he, him) and (I, me), please be early.
5. Mother placed a light blanket over the baby and (she, her).

Sentence Patterns

These are the symbols you have studied this year. Notice the addition of one new symbol, which stands for *preposition*.

N	= Noun	**V**h	= Helping verb
Np	= Pronoun	**Adj.**	= Adjective
V	= Action verb	**Adv.**	= Adverb
Vbe	= Linking verb	**P**	= Preposition

With the new symbol **P**, you can now add prepositional phrases to the sentences you are building. Prepositional phrases begin with prepositions and end with nouns or pronouns, for example:

P N	after school
P Adj. N	in the soup
P Adj. Adj. N	under the blue skies
P Np	with me

Prepositional phrases are modifiers. They are used in sentences in somewhat the same way that adjectives and adverbs are used.

Now study these example sentences that contain prepositional phrases. The third example has a conjunction which is written out. Conjunctions are words such as *and*, *but*, and *or*.

1. **Adj. N P Adj. N V Adj. N**

   The man on the bridge repaired the cable.

2. **Adj. N V**h **V P Adj. Adj. N**

   The prisoner had run into the large crowd!

3. **Adj. N** *and* **Adj. N V P N**

   Young Leroy and the troupe traveled to Europe!

● On your paper, write the symbols for the four basic sentence patterns you have studied this year. Label each pattern as *Pattern 1, 2, 3,* or *4*. Then write out the names of the basic sentence elements which each pattern contains.

● Close your textbooks and see how many symbols you can remember. Write down the symbols and their descriptions.

● Write sentences following these groups of symbols. In some of the groups, conjunctions have been written out for you.

1. **Adj. Adj. N V P Adj. N**
2. **Adj. N P Adj. N V^be Adj.**
3. **N^P V Adj. N P Adj. N**
4. **N V Adj. N P Adj. Adj. N**
5. **Adj. N P Adj. Adj. N V Adv.**
6. **V^h Adj. Adj. N V P Adj. N?**
7. **Adj. Adj. N P Adj. N V^h Adv. V Adj. N P Adj. N**
8. **N** *and* **Adj. N V P N**
9. **Adj. N P Adj. N V** *and* **V**
10. *Either* **N V^h V Adv.** *or* **N^P V^h V P N^P**

Subject and Verb Agreement

You know that the subject and verb in a sentence must agree in number. Adding a prepositional phrase modifying the subject does not change the number of the subject.

SINGULAR: The leaf of oaks is handsome.

PLURAL: The leaves on the tree are falling.

SINGULAR: One of those melons has spoiled.

PLURAL: Several kinds of melons are delicious.

Exercise: Subject and verb agreement

Choose the correct verb from each pair in parentheses. Check your answers in class. Then read each sentence aloud three times.

1. The bottom of the stairs (is, are) wet.
2. The courses of the school (is, are) thorough.
3. The ends of his shoelace (was, were) frayed.
4. Catsup on hamburgers (improves, improve) the flavor.
5. Four different types of aircraft (flies, fly) this route.
6. The cries of the baby (is, are) ear-splitting.
7. The breeze from those lakes (feels, feel) fine.
8. One of the members (was, were) absent today.
9. The noise of the buses (keeps, keep) me awake.
10. Not a single one of the buildings (looks, look) shabby.

Compounding with Conjunctions

Read the following sentences. There is a joining word in each one that connects the italicized words or word groups which are named in parentheses.

1. *Tom* and *Nancy* ate lunch. (two subject nouns)
2. Nancy ate *lunch* or *dinner* with Tom every day. (two object nouns)
3. *Sadly* but *eagerly* they ate together. (two adverbs)
4. They were *strong* and *brave*. (two adjectives)
5. That crocodile never *thrashed* his tail or *clashed* his teeth. (two verbs)
6. *Outside the house* but *inside the yard* was a large pile of furniture. (two prepositional phrases)
7. The *officer, she,* and *I* made a list of safety rules. (three subjects—a noun and two pronouns)

The joining words *and, but,* and *or* are called **conjunctions.** These conjunctions are like links which connect two or more words or word groups of equal rank. They are shown above joining nouns, pronouns, verbs, adjectives, adverbs, and prepositional phrases.

In the following sentences there are two-word conjunctions which act in the same way that *and, but,* and *or* do:

1. *Both* Irma *and* Wilma like fattening foods.
2. *Neither* you *nor* he can stop me.
3. I will *either* call you tonight *or* wait until morning.

Which words do the conjunctions join in sentence 1? in sentence 2? in sentence 3?

Exercises: Conjunctions

1. On your paper, write the conjunction or conjunctions in each sentence below. On both sides of the conjunction, write the words or word groups joined by it.

EXAMPLE: 1. I gave the saddles to Bill and Theresa.
YOU WRITE: *1. Bill and Theresa*

1. You must obey the riding master or his assistant.
2. Should we gallop or trot?

3. The instructor asked both Arnold and me to sit up straight.
4. This horse is old and lazy.
5. Both the wind and the rain spoiled our plans last week.
6. We rode over the hill and into the woods.
7. Janet rides swiftly but carefully.
8. Arnold, the instructor, and I rushed ahead of the group.
9. We explored the trail and then returned.
10. The advanced class is practicing jumps over those logs and across the narrow stream.

2. Beside each answer you have written for the exercise above, tell what elements are joined by the conjunction—*nouns, pronouns, adjectives, adverbs, verbs,* or *prepositional phrases.*

3. Use each of the conjunctions below in a sentence. Follow the directions in parentheses.

1. and   (Join subject nouns.)
2. and   (Join verbs.)
3. or   (Join prepositional phrases.)
4. neither . . . nor   (Join pronouns.)
5. both . . . and   (Join adjectives.)
6. either . . . or   (Join verbs.)
7. and   (Join object nouns.)
8. but   (Join adverbs.)

Compound Subjects

You know what a simple subject is.

That black bat is flying near the girls.

(simple
subject)

You know that the simple subject can be plural and that it then takes the plural form of the verb.

Those black bats are flying near the girls.

(simple
subject)

Another form of the subject is the **compound subject.** In the sentences listed below, the compound subjects are underlined once and the verbs in the predicate are underlined twice.

COMPOUND SUBJECTS	PREDICATES
1. That skunk *and* this cat	are my pets.
2. *Both* boys *and* girls	like Halloween parties.
3. These nails in the box *and* that hammer	were found in the garage.
4. A beautiful view *and* a cooling breeze	add to the pleasures of a summer vacation.
5. John *or* Mary	has the schedule.
6. *Either* a pencil *or* a pen	is acceptable.
7. *Neither* a stick *nor* a stone	is a very heroic weapon.
8. *Either* roses *or* camellias	make beautiful corsages.

(Turn to pages 398–99 if you want to study and practice diagraming sentences which have compound subjects.)

■ A **compound subject** contains two or more subjects that are connected by a conjunction.

Subject and verb agreement

The verbs in sentences must agree in number with compound subjects. With the conjunctions *and* and *both . . . and,* the verb must be plural. Which sentences above illustrate this point? Read them aloud.

With the conjunctions *or*, *either . . . or*, and *neither . . . nor*, the verb must be singular if the two parts of the compound subject are singular. Which sentences on page 292 illustrate this point? Why does sentence 8 have a plural form of the verb?

Exercises: Subject and verb agreement

1. Choose the correct verb from each pair in parentheses.

    1. Our dog and your cat (is, are) great friends.
    2. Both that wig and this cloak (was, were) used in the play.
    3. Either apples or oranges (is, are) good ingredients for this salad.
    4. Neither the fox nor the wolf (like, likes) to hear the sound of shooting.
    5. He and she (play, plays) tennis on Tuesdays.
    6. Neither Cindy nor her mother (admire, admires) the sort of language he uses.
    7. The trees and the grass (is, are) green.
    8. Mary or Josephine (go, goes) to the market tomorrow.

2. Below are six predicates without subjects. Provide compound subjects. Use the conjunction (or conjunctions) given for each one. Be sure the verb and the compound subject agree.

    1. __?__ and __?__ were riding down the long, shady lane.
    2. __?__ or __?__ makes me angry.
    3. Both __?__ and __?__ have frequently seen that shark swim by the beach.
    4. Neither __?__ nor __?__ are going to help us much now.
    5. Neither __?__ nor __?__ was placed on the table.
    6. Either __?__ or __?__ is joining us at the ice-cream parlor.

3. Below are six compound subjects. Some need predicates with the singular form of the verb, some with the plural form. Copy each compound subject and provide a predicate.

    1. The highways and the skyways of America . . .
    2. Neither my teachers nor my parents . . .
    3. Below us both he and she . . .
    4. Either a horse or a cow . . .
    5. Much noise and utter confusion . . .
    6. She and I . . .

Compound Predicates

Conjunctions are used to join predicates also, as in these sentences. The subjects are underlined once, and the verbs in the predicate are underlined twice.

1. The policeman walked up Fifth Avenue *and* turned east on 86th Street.
2. Our sandlot baseball team played four games *but* won only two.
3. The hippopotamus looked around, opened his mouth, *and* yawned.

Notice that the conjunctions *and* and *but* connect two or three verbs in each sentence above. The predicate of each sentence is called a **compound predicate.**

(Turn to pages 398–99 if you want to study and practice diagraming compound predicates.)

■ A **compound predicate** contains two or more verbs that are connected by a conjunction.

Exercise: Compound predicates

Name the compound predicate in each sentence below. Then name the two (or more) verbs in each predicate that each conjunction connects.

1. Read quietly or leave the room.
2. The villain startled and terrified his victims.
3. I dug my shovel into the ground and uncovered a broken vase.
4. The apples fell to the ground and rotted away.
5. A frightened rabbit raised his ears, shivered a moment, and then hopped away.
6. The fleet of ships sailed slowly out of the harbor but disappeared suddenly from sight.
7. I slid behind the wheel, turned the ignition on, and released the brake.
8. The judge lifted the gavel, pounded on the desk, and asked for order.

Compound Sentences

Study these sentences, which have one subject and one predicate each:

1. The batter hit the ball.
2. I ran to second base.
3. The batter hit the ball and ran to first base.

Such sentences are called **simple sentences.** A simple sentence has one subject and one predicate and these parts may or may not be compound. Notice in sentence 3 that there is a compound predicate—two verbs are joined by a conjunction.

If two separate sentences, however, are joined with a conjunction, we have a different kind of sentence.

4. The batter hit the ball, and I ran to second base.

Such a sentence is called a **compound sentence.** Here are three more examples:

1. The detective ran around the corner, but the thief had scurried out of sight.
2. Our football team played four games, and Mike scored all the touchdowns.
3. The truck parked in the middle of the block, and we were delayed for half an hour.

The word groups on both sides of each conjunction above are called **independent clauses.** Notice that each has a subject and a predicate and can stand alone as a simple sentence. Read each clause aloud.

What punctuation mark did you notice in each example of a compound sentence above?

(If you want to study and practice the diagraming of compound sentences, turn to Chapter 15, "Making Sentence Diagrams," and do the lesson on pages 399–400.)

■ **A compound sentence** consists of two or more independent clauses joined by *and, or,* or *but.*

Punctuation of compound sentences

Make sure that you know the difference between a *compound predicate* and a *compound sentence*. Study these examples:

SIMPLE SENTENCE WITH COMPOUND PREDICATE

The wind ripped the shutters off and blew them out to sea.

COMPOUND SENTENCE

The wind ripped the shutters off, and the rain soaked the rug.

Notice the comma just before the conjunction in the compound sentence above. There is no comma between the parts of a compound predicate.

Remember: Do not use a comma before the conjunction in a simple sentence with a compound predicate.

If a compound sentence is very short, the comma may be omitted:

Tracey stood and Maxine sat.

The wind whistled and the lightning snapped.

> Place a comma before the conjunction in a compound sentence, unless the sentence is very short.

Exercises: Compound sentences

1. Find the conjunction in each of the compound sentences below. Then write the simple subject and verb in each clause and the conjunction that connects them.

1. Aunt Polly hadn't heard of Pain Killer, but she ordered it.
2. She tasted it, and her heart was filled with gratitude.
3. She had expected something fairly strong, but this stuff was fire in liquid form.
4. Tom's unconcern about everything made him a better boy, but his indifference must be broken up at any cost.
5. Tom swallowed some of the liquid, and his aunt watched him anxiously.
6. It was only a mouthful, but the results were spectacular.
7. Tom's interest was wild and hearty, and at last his indifference was broken up.
8. Her troubles were at rest, and her soul was at peace.

2. Some of the following sentences are compound sentences, and others are simple sentences with compound predicates. Copy the compound sentences only and punctuate them correctly.

1. The emperor was excessively fond of new clothes and spent all his money on them.
2. He neglected his soldiers and scorned the theater.
3. Either the emperor was trying on new clothes all day or he was forever gazing at himself in the mirror.
4. Hosts of strangers visited the town and among them one day were two swindlers.
5. They could weave the most beautiful materials imaginable but the materials would be invisible to most people.
6. Anybody not fit for his job could not see the materials and would therefore give himself away.

3. Write two sentences for each conjunction below, making one a simple sentence with a compound predicate and the other a compound sentence. Pay special attention to the punctuation before the conjunction in a compound sentence.

1. and   2. but   3. either . . . or   4. or

The Coin

Into my heart's treasury
   I slipped a coin
That time cannot take
   Nor a thief purloin—
Oh, better than the minting
   Of a gold-crowned king
Is the safe-kept memory
   Of a lovely thing.

SARA TEASDALE

In this poem Sara Teasdale expresses her feelings about the appreciation of beauty. She does not strive for extra meaning as Robert Frost does in "The Road Not Taken" on page 28. Using an easy, relaxing rhythm, she makes a comparison between the storing of money and of lovely memories. "The Coin" is one contribution to beauty that can be appreciated and remembered.

Discuss the meaning of the words *purloin* and *minting*.

Improving Your Writing

In good writing, the conjunctions *and, but,* and *or* join items that are grammatically equal. This means that you should not join nouns and adjectives, or phrases and adverbs, or adjectives and verbs. For example:

NOT ACCEPTABLE: The stranger acted *strangely* and *with suspicion.*

ACCEPTABLE: The stranger acted *strangely* and *suspiciously.*

NOT ACCEPTABLE: The girl was *rude, troublesome,* and *made a lot of noise.*

ACCEPTABLE: The girl was *rude, troublesome,* and *noisy.*

NOT ACCEPTABLE: The boy was *strong, brave,* and *a hero.*

ACCEPTABLE: The boy was *strong, brave,* and *heroic.*

Use compound sentences only when you want to join two or more ideas that are closely related. Sentences should not be joined together without reason.

Study these examples:

POOR: We planned an overnight stop at the Browns' shack on the beach, and the waves were beautiful.

GOOD: We planned an overnight stop at the Browns' shack on the beach, but the hurricane had destroyed it.

With the conjunctions **and, but,** and **or,** join items that are grammatically equal.
In compound sentences, join two or more closely related ideas.

● In the following sentences, grammatically unequal elements have been combined. Revise each sentence so that each conjunction joins equal elements.

1. The stranger was tall and a mystery.
2. Her parties are always enjoyable and a success.
3. She spoke loudly, impressively, and at a slow speed.
4. After the dance, they all became merry and talked a lot.
5. The wolves attacked quickly and with much ferociousness.

● Four of the compound sentences below have two or more closely related ideas joined together. Four are poor examples of compound sentences. Next to the appropriate numeral, write "Poor" or "Good."

1. The traffic policeman put his hand up, but the car did not stop.
2. The two of us volunteered, and I always like to help.
3. Ponce de Leon was looking for the Fountain of Youth, and many people want to stay young.
4. Martin can walk to the stadium now, or he can ride there in our car later.
5. The crops need water, but there has been no rain.
6. We went on a tour of the cattle ranch, and everyone in our house likes steak.
7. The old lady sits on her porch every afternoon, and Bobbie helped her across the street yesterday.
8. There are two parties Saturday night, and Bess received an invitation to both of them.

Punctuating Items in a Series

When you use a conjunction to join more than two items, the result is called a *series*. Perhaps the most common series is made up of nouns: "Pigs, horses, ducks, *and* chickens are common on a farm." But many other kinds of words or word groups may make up a series. Notice, in the following examples, how words in a series are punctuated:

1. The clown threw *pots, pans, rolling pins,* and *dishmops* all over the arena.
2. The campers *ate, swam,* and *slept* for four days.
3. The new bridge was *wide, strong,* and *graceful.*
4. He read the book *quickly, happily,* and *thoughtlessly.*
5. *Across the yard, onto the porch,* and *into the house* marched the column of ants.
6. *The ship swayed, the waves glistened,* and *the iceberg towered in the moonlight.*

Use **commas** to separate items in a series.

Exercise: Using commas

Copy the following sentences, inserting commas where they are needed:

1. Apples pears and peaches are delicious fruits.
2. The wire ran under the table through the door and up the wall.
3. The storm approached passed over and disappeared without a drop of rain falling.
4. Those students use the dictionary shrewdly energetically and constantly.
5. Mrs. Smith Dr. Jones and Mrs. Perlmutter held a meeting in our kitchen.
6. The guard scolded threatened and frightened the mischief-makers.
7. Men shouted women applauded and children waved their arms in the air.
8. The water at the bottom of the well was shallow ghostlike and shimmering.

Subordinating with Conjunctions

The conjunctions you have been studying so far—*and, but, or, both . . . and, neither . . . nor, either . . . or*—have joined equal elements. They have joined nouns to nouns, adjectives to adjectives, verbs to verbs, phrases to phrases, and clauses to clauses.

There are other conjunctions that perform differently. They join clauses (word groups that contain a subject and a verb) and *make them unequal*. They make one clause depend upon the other so that the one clause is *subordinate* and cannot stand alone. Here are examples, with the conjunction italicized:

MAIN (INDEPENDENT) CLAUSES	SUBORDINATE CLAUSES
My sister ate in her room	*because* she had been naughty.
I cannot watch TV	*unless* my homework is done.
That chair will upset	*if* you lean back too far.
Mother praises me	*when* I clean up my room.

Read aloud the subordinate clauses in the right-hand column above. Notice that they do not sound complete by themselves.

They *depend* upon the main clause to complete their meaning. They are fragments of sentences, which cannot stand alone. Each one needs a sentence to go with it, thus:

My sister ate in her room *because she had been naughty.*
Because she had been naughty, my sister ate in her room.

The conjunctions *because, unless, if,* and *when* are called **subordinating conjunctions.** Here is a list of twelve very common ones:

after	as	before	since	until	where
although	because	if	unless	when	while

You will notice that changing the subordinating conjunction may change the meaning of a sentence considerably. Read aloud the following two sentences, using different subordinating conjunctions in the blank, and you will see how the meaning changes:

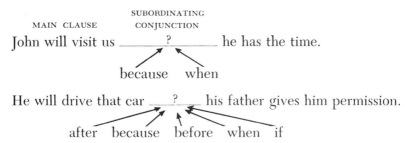

Exercises: Subordinating conjunctions

1. Copy the subordinate word group in each of the following sentences and underline the subordinating conjunction:

EXAMPLE: 1. He put his coat where it would keep dry.
YOU WRITE: *1. where it would keep dry*

1. A mongoose does not frighten easily because he is eaten up from nose to tail with curiosity.
2. Rikki-Tikki roamed about the house until he knew it well.
3. When the boy went to bed that night, Rikki-Tikki went, too.
4. He didn't stay, since he had to investigate night noises.
5. If a snake had come around, he would have attacked.
6. In the morning, after he had eaten, he went to the garden.
7. While he snuffled around there, he heard sorrowful voices.
8. Darzee, the tailorbird, and his wife were crying as they sat on the brim of their nest.

301

2. For the blank in each of the following sentences, choose a subordinating conjunction from the list above the sentences. Write the conjunction on your paper after the appropriate numeral. Do not use any conjunction more than twice.

although	as	since	when
because	if	unless	while

1. __?__ a baby had fallen from the nest, Nag had eaten him.
2. __?__ Rikki-Tikki was a stranger, he didn't know Nag.
3. He probably wouldn't recognize Nag __?__ he met him.
4. __?__ he stood there, a hiss came from the thick grass.
5. He jumped __?__ the hiss had such a horrid sound.
6. __?__ Rikki-Tikki watched, inch by inch out of the grass rose the head and spread hood of Nag, the cobra.
7. Rikki-Tikki perceived a deadly enemy __?__ he had never seen a cobra before.
8. A mongoose meant death to Nag __?__ Nag killed first.

3. Combine each pair of sentences into a single sentence, using a subordinating conjunction. In some cases you may subordinate either the first or the second sentence. Underline the conjunction.

EXAMPLE: 1. He turned on the heat. He was uncomfortable.

YOU WRITE: *1. He turned on the heat because he was uncomfortable.*

(or)

After he turned on the heat, he was uncomfortable.

1. The forest fire raged. The fire fighters put it out.
2. The teacher likes Jane. She always pays attention.
3. The TV set works better. The repairman has made his visit.
4. I don't want to go. You come with me.
5. The mason's wife brewed coffee. He left to go to work.
6. I will be very happy. Mother is coming with us.
7. The little girl put her head under the pillow. There was a thunderstorm.
8. You must not eat your dinner. You wash your hands.
9. Pamela is staying indoors. She is afraid of this dog.
10. The ship stayed in port. The passengers returned on board.

Test I

Copy the prepositional phrases that you find in the following sentences. Decide and write down whether each is an adjective or an adverb phrase. Then write the word that is modified by the phrase.

EXAMPLE: 1. The giant walked over the mountains.
YOU WRITE: *1. over the mountains*
adverb phrase walked

1. The explosion in the street frightened the baby.
2. The movie about the dinosaurs is wonderful.
3. We practice basketball during the afternoon.
4. The lawyer for the defense stood before the witness.

Test II

Number your paper from 1 to 10. Choose the correct words from the pairs in parentheses and write them on your paper.

1. My uncle stays (at, to) his garage all day.
2. That basketball coach doesn't show favoritism (between, among) his players.
3. Have you heard about Janice and (she, her)?
4. Please walk (in, into) the theater with me.
5. They couldn't decide (between, among) Howie and (I, me).
6. Where are you (going, going to)?
7. The guard must stay (at, to) his post for hours.
8. Put the cash (beside, besides) the bills.
9. They had no food (beside, besides) one candy bar.
10. Are those presents for (she, her) and (I, me)?

Test III

Number your paper from 1 to 5. Copy the compound elements in the sentences below, underlining the conjunctions:

1. Smoke from the fire ruined the rugs and curtains.
2. I will never ski beautifully or rapidly.
3. The good skier relaxes and concentrates at the same time.
4. Neither Bertram nor Bunter went swimming today.
5. The rabbit went under the fence and into the garden.

Test IV

1. Eight of the sentences below require one or more commas; two of the sentences are correct as they stand. On your paper, copy only those sentences which need commas and punctuate them correctly.

1. My little brother Ricky is upset today and will not go to the playground.
2. He has a bump on his forehead a black eye and a bruise on his nose.
3. Yesterday he was in the playground and someone pushed him off the slide.
4. Mother feels sorry for him but I think he bullied somebody.
5. He often startles shoves and irritates little girls.
6. They either ignore him or fight him back.
7. Perhaps one girl quietly carefully and determinedly pushed him off the slide.
8. He would be infuriated hurt and too proud to cry.
9. Everyone probably jeered and he ran home.
10. The experience may have taught him a lesson but I doubt it.

2. Four of the sentences above are compound sentences. Write their numerals on your paper.

Test V

Number your paper from 1 to 5. Choose the correct verb from each pair in parentheses and write it on your paper.

1. The snow on the mountains (is, are) visible.
2. Polish on shoes (prevent, prevents) scuffing.
3. Both cinnamon and ginger (is, are) good in spice cakes.
4. Sally or he (was, were) responsible for the noise.
5. One of those students (need, needs) help.

Test VI

Copy the subordinate clause in each of these sentences and underline the subordinating conjunction:

1. I'll learn if you will teach me.
2. Unless he calls, I am leaving without him.
3. I received poor grades because I did not work hard enough.
4. Mr. Carter won't visit us until we invite him.
5. As I turned the corner, the little dog disappeared.

Review and Practice

Exercise I

1. Review "Prepositions and Prepositional Phrases" on pages 278–81 and 284.

2. Copy the following sentences on your paper. Circle each prepositional phrase and draw an arrow to the word it modifies. In parentheses, write whether the phrase is an adjective or adverb phrase.

1. The view through the west window is dull.
2. The bobsled whizzed around the curve.
3. Peter completed his posters for the school dance.
4. My money fell under the chair.
5. The jury of twelve men stared at the witness.

3. Tell whether each italicized word below is used as a preposition or an adverb in the sentence:

1. A bullet had passed *through* the window.
2. Are the painters *through* now?
3. The meteor shot *across* the Milky Way.
4. The log *across* the river is too narrow.
5. We can jump *across* easily.

4. Write six sentences, using these prepositions in prepositional phrases: *across, over, behind, through, around, inside.*

Exercise II

1. Review "Some Usage Problems" on pages 284–85 and 287.

2. Copy the following sentences on your paper, choosing the correct words from the pairs in parentheses:

1. My mother is now (at, to) home.
2. Where is that rocket (going, going to)?
3. There is a problem (among, between) my sister and (I, me).
4. The cows were (in, into) the barn asleep.
5. Put the garbage (in, into) the ash can.
6. We couldn't choose (among, between) the four puppies.
7. (Beside, Besides) one dollar, there is no money in our bank.
8. Do not put crayons (beside, besides) the baby or (he, him).
9. They live near the Bucks and (we, us).
10. May I sit (beside, besides) him at dinner?

Exercise III

1. Review "Compounding with Conjunctions," "Compound Subjects," and "Compound Predicates" on pages 290, 292, and 294.

2. The following word groups have missing parts which are described in parentheses. Make each a complete sentence, adding the compound element indicated.

1. . . . broke their legs skiing. (compound subject)
2. The cocker spaniel fought . . . (compound object nouns)
3. She cried . . . whenever she was left alone. (compound adverbs)
4. The announcer's voice was . . . (compound adjectives)
5. A colony of ants . . . (compound predicate)
6. Our visiting cousins played with . . . (compound object of preposition)
7. The ball rolled . . . (compound prepositional phrase)
8. . . . met us at the station. (compound subject)

Exercise IV

1. Review "Compound Sentences" and "Punctuating Items in a Series" on pages 295–96 and 299.

2. Make a compound sentence of each independent clause below by adding the conjunction *and*, *but*, or *or* and another independent clause. The ideas in the two clauses should be closely related. Punctuate your sentences correctly.

1. Sports may be important to you . . .
2. I invited Janet to join us . . .
3. Pet animals take a lot of time . . .
4. I voted for Jerry . . .
5. You should apologize to Jean . . .

3. Copy the following sentences on your paper, punctuating each one correctly:

1. Peaches plums and grapes were loaded onto the trucks.
2. Ted studied all night but he did not finish his homework.
3. The reptile zoo contained alligators snakes and lizards.
4. They stopped the car on a hill put it in neutral turned off the ignition and pulled up the hand brake.
5. The disabled tractor slowly made its way from the fields through the orchard and into the barn.

Exercise V

1. Review "Subject and Verb Agreement" on pages 289 and 292–93.

2. Below are word groups that can be used as subjects. Make each one a complete sentence by adding words of your own. Use one of these verbs in each sentence: *is, are, was, were, am.*

1. Neither my father nor I . . .
2. The sun on the clouds . . .
3. One of my partners . . .
4. Either a bus or a truck . . .
5. Both the President and the Vice-president . . .
6. Posters and signs . . .
7. A beetle or a spider . . .
8. Either footballs or basketballs . . .
9. The box of pins . . .
10. The boys in the class . . .

Exercise VI

1. Review "Subordinating with Conjunctions" on pages 300–01.

2. Using the subordinating conjunction in parentheses, add a subordinate clause to each sentence below. Write the complete sentences on your paper.

1. The rain didn't fall . . . (until)
2. Accidents occur . . . (when)
3. Mimi is wearing a costume . . . (because)
4. We ought to hide the birthday cake . . . (before)
5. Let's go to the stadium . . . (where)

PART II

Language Study and Appreciation

CHAPTER 12

How to Study More Efficiently

Your assignments are getting longer and more complicated each year, yet you are expected to do them with less and less guidance from your teacher. Actually, you are developing study habits now that will influence all your future school work and whatever work or profession you choose later.

It is impossible for anyone to carry all the information he needs or wants in his memory. Neither teacher nor employer will expect you to know everything. You are expected, however, to know *where* and *how* to find the information you need when you need it. Do you know how to find information? Are you at home in a library? Once you find your information, do you know how to organize it? Concentrate this year on developing efficient study habits. Then you will be ready to explore by yourself the vast and fascinating world of knowledge. The lessons in this chapter will help you to achieve this goal.

The Library

If you know your way around the library, you have at your disposal a treasure of information and pleasure. Obviously, since libraries contain thousands of books, pamphlets, and magazines, there must be a method for organizing them so that readers like yourself can easily find what they want. This lesson tells you how libraries are organized and how to use them. In most situations, you should be able to find things yourself. If you have difficulty, you should not hesitate to ask the librarian, who will be glad to help you. However, you will enjoy the library more and work more efficiently if you learn to be independent.

The card catalog

Every book in a well-organized library is listed on a card. These cards are filed alphabetically in a card catalog. For many books, there are three cards. On the *author card* the author's name is printed at the top, last name first. If you want a book by a particular author, you would look for the author card.

Author Card

```
j960      Davidson, Basil, 1914-

D281g        A guide to African history.  Rev. and
          edited by Haskel Frankel.  Illustrated by
          Robin Jacques.  Doubleday  [ᶜ1965]

             118 p.     (Zenith books)
```

On the *title card* the book title is first. The title cards are arranged alphabetically by the first word (not counting *a, an,* or *the*). If you know the book title but not the author, look for the title card.

Title Card

```
             A guide to African history.
j960      Davidson, Basil, 1914-

D281g        A guide to African history.  Rev. and
          edited by Haskel Frankel.  Illustrated by
          Robin Jacques.  Doubleday  [ᶜ1965]

             118 p.     (Zenith books)
```

On the *subject card* the general subject appears first. You use this card when you have no particular author or title in mind but want to find what books are available on a given subject.

Subject Card

```
                        ●
             AFRICA -- HISTORY
j960
          Davidson, Basil, 1914-
D281g
             A guide to African history.  Rev. and
          edited by Haskel Frankel.  Illustrated by
          Robin Jacques.  Doubleday  [ᶜ1965]

             118 p.     (Zenith books)
```

The *call number* of the book appears on all three cards. Each book in the library has a different call number. This number also appears on the book itself. With only the call number, you can find any book.

The letter *j* in the call number of the cards on the opposite page means that the book is in the juvenile collection and that it is a book for young people. The letter *D* is the first letter of the author's last name. The letter *g* is the first letter in *guide*.

To discuss

Examine the author card shown on page 312 and answer the following questions about the book:

1. What is the title?
2. What is the author's name?
3. How long is the book? Is it illustrated?
4. Who published the book?
5. When was it published?
6. What is the call number?

The Dewey Decimal System

The Dewey Decimal System, developed by the New York librarian Melvil Dewey, is an ingenious system for classifying and arranging books of nonfiction in a library.

Nonfiction. Nonfiction includes all books except short stories and novels. There are ten categories, as follows:

000–099 General works (encyclopedias, periodicals, newspapers)
100–199 Philosophy (conduct, ethics, psychology)
200–299 Religion (Bible stories, myths, churches)
300–399 Social sciences (customs, commerce, education, government, law, economics)
400–499 Language (dictionaries and languages)
500–599 Pure science (mathematics, astronomy, plants, animals, chemistry, physics)
600–699 Applied science (engineering, radio, aeronautics)
700–799 Arts and recreation (architecture, music, sports)
800–899 Literature (poems, plays, essays)
900–999 History (travel, geography, biography)

Each of the categories is subdivided into narrower subject fields. An expert librarian could tell in some detail just what the subject of a book is merely by reading the call number. However, there is no point in your memorizing the Dewey Decimal System unless it interests you. You should be familiar with it and know how to refer to it. In most libraries there is a Dewey Decimal System chart to which you can refer. Often the chart will indicate where in the library the different categories of books are located.

Fiction. Novels and other books of fiction are not classified under 800–899, Literature, as you might expect them to be. They are placed in a special section of the library, arranged on the shelves alphabetically by authors' last names.

To discuss

Referring to the Dewey Decimal System chart on page 313, classify the following books in their proper hundred:

1. *The Wonderful World of Mathematics,* by Lancelot Hogben
2. *In Bible Days,* by Gertrude Hartman
3. *Engineers' Dreams,* by Willy Ley
4. *Benjamin Franklin,* by Carl Van Doren
5. *Making of a Democracy,* by Gertrude Hartman
6. *Parents Keep Out; Elderly Poems for Youngerly Readers,* by Ogden Nash
7. *Exploring Art,* by Luise C. Kainz and Olive L. Riley
8. *Television Story,* by John Joseph Floherty
9. *Pioneer Art in America,* by Carolyn Sherwin Bailey
10. *Wider than the Sky: Aviation as a Career,* by Charles M. Daugherty

Exercises: Investigating the library

Divide the class into three groups. Each group should do one of the three exercises below. Then each group should report to the class the results of its investigations.

1. Here is a list of six topics for investigation. Share the topics in your group so that each group member works with one topic. Find in the card catalog the authors, titles, and call numbers of three books dealing with the topic. On a piece of paper, write the topic and list the books by call number, author, and title.

1. swimming	4. transcontinental railroad
2. Cape Horn	5. Abraham Lincoln
3. weeds	6. baby care

2. Here are the titles of ten books. Dividing the titles among the group members, see whether these books are available in your library. Write the title of each book on your paper and, after it, write either the call number or "not available."

1. *Kon-Tiki*, by Thor Heyerdahl
2. *Horses of Destiny*, by Fairfax Downey
3. *Teaching Your Dog Obedience*, by Elliott Blackiston
4. *Basketball Techniques Illustrated*, by Forrest Anderson and Tyler Micoleau
5. *The Story of Medicine*, by Joseph Garland
6. *The Earth for Sam*, by William Maxwell Reed
7. *The Story Behind Great Inventions*, by Elizabeth R. Montgomery
8. *Tropical Fish as a Hobby*, by Herbert R. Axelrod
9. *Sewing Made Easy*, by Mary Lynch
10. *Fun for Young Collectors*, by Joseph Leeming

3. Assign each group member at least one of the following authors. Using the card catalog, see whether your library contains titles by these authors. Write down the titles of all the books in the library by a given author.

1. Louisa M. Alcott	6. Laura Benét
2. Thomas Bailey Aldrich	7. MacKinlay Kantor
3. Joseph A. Altsheler	8. Jeannette C. Nolan
4. Elliott Arnold	9. Jeanette Eaton
5. Walter D. Edmonds	10. Cornelia Spencer

The Reference Books in the Library

How often do you find that the knowledge of certain facts and figures can clarify a discussion or an argument? How often do questions arise for which you want to find answers? The reference books in the library can give you answers on most factual questions and can give you information on almost any subject in which you are interested. Reference books are especially important when you have a school assignment which requires information that is not included in your textbooks. Refer to these special books often. They are designed to inform you.

Encyclopedias

Encyclopedias are wonderful books. They contain information about almost any subject you can think of. Most libraries have some encyclopedias written especially for young people. The four sets that you will find very helpful are *Compton's Pictured Encyclopedia*, *The Book of Knowledge*, *The World Book Encyclopedia*, and *Britannica Junior*.

Most sets of encyclopedias have many volumes, arranged from A to Z to show you the initial letters of the topics in each volume. Within each volume, arranged alphabetically, are interesting articles about famous people, places, and things. These articles may be historical, biographical, geographical, scientific, and so on.

Encyclopedias have indexes to help you locate an article. The index may be at the back of each volume or may be a separate volume, depending on the set of encyclopedias you are using.

Guide words at the top of each page of the encyclopedia can also help you to locate an article. They name the first topic and sometimes the last topic on the page. Be sure to use these guide words to help you find your topic.

When you use an encyclopedia, remember to pay attention to cross references. These pages will refer you to another article relating to the topic you are reading.

Almanacs and atlases

When you are looking for brief information, such as an important date, the name of a Nobel prize winner, or the population of your state, turn to an almanac or an atlas. These books are two of the handiest reference books in your library. The *World Almanac*, which is published every year, gives statistics of all kinds and up-to-date information about government and world geography. You will also find countless facts about the entertainment, sports, political, and business worlds.

The sizes of countries and cities and their populations are usually found in both an almanac and an atlas. An atlas, however, is mainly a collection of maps, with tables of geographical information.

Readers' Guide

Another valuable set of reference books is called the *Readers' Guide to Periodical Literature.* It lists by subject and by author all of the articles in over a hundred of the best-known magazines. There is a separate volume for each year, and a larger volume which combines three years. To find recent articles on a subject or by an author that interests you, refer to recent volumes of the *Readers' Guide.* Before you do so, you should ask the librarian for a list of the magazines subscribed to by your library. Find out whether back issues of these magazines are available.

Exercises: Reference books

1. Appoint two small committees, one to go to the library and list the titles and dates of publication of all the encyclopedias found there; the other to list the titles of all other important reference books which might be of interest to your class. Both of these committees should report to the class.

2. Let each member of the class write a question at the top of a sheet of paper. Each question should ask for a single fact which might be found in a reference book. Exchange papers. Then arrange for the class to go to the library so that each student can look up the answer to his question. Let him write the answer to the question, the title of the reference book in which he found the answer, the volume, and the page.

> EXAMPLE: ONE STUDENT WRITES:
> Who invented the first submarine and when?
> ANOTHER STUDENT ANSWERS:
> The first underwater craft is said to have been invented by Cornelius van Drebbel in 1620. From *Compton's Pictured Encyclopedia,* Vol. 13 (S), pages 494–95.

The Dictionary

There is no book more useful than a good dictionary. We turn to a dictionary most frequently to find (1) the meaning of a word, (2) its spelling, or (3) its pronunciation. But a dictionary gives you much more information than that. Turn now to the table of contents in your dictionary to discover how many different kinds of information it has to offer.

A dictionary is of little use unless you can find the words you are looking for in it. To use your dictionary easily and efficiently, you need to master alphabetical order.

There are many people who do not know the order of the letters unless they start with the letter *a* and go through the whole alphabet. They cannot tell immediately that *r* follows *q*, that *i* appears before *j*. Take the time now to memorize the alphabet so well that you will recognize the order of individual letters.

Exercises: Alphabetical order

1. On your paper, copy the following names, arranging them in alphabetical order. If two or more names begin with the same letter, you will need to look at the second letter in each name. If the second letter is the same for both names, look at the third letter.

Vivian	Richard	Anne	Pamela	Sophie
Jack	Barbara	Susan	Lynne	Oscar
Margaret	Elizabeth	George	Matthew	Bromley
Florence	Leigh	Phyllis	Lucy	Erma
Dorothy	Vera	Xerxes	Maud	Charlotte

2. On a separate sheet of paper, arrange the following words in alphabetical order. In these words you will need to consider the fourth letter or beyond.

fortunate	forever	forehead	fortress
force	fortify	foreign	forecast
forgive	forage	former	forfeit
fork	formal	forgery	forward
forest	forbid	formula	fortune

Guide words

Many students forget to use the helpful *guide words* at the top of each page of most dictionaries. Look at the sample dictionary page from the *Thorndike-Barnhart Advanced Junior Dictionary* on page 324 and notice the guide words. The guide words are **buck** and **buffalo grass**. This means that all the words on that page of the dictionary come alphabetically between these two entries: that *buck* is the first entry on the page and *buffalo grass* is the last.

The meanings of words

When you do locate a word that you need, remember that it may have more than one meaning. It is important to read all of the meanings listed in the dictionary to be sure you find the one you want for a sentence you are reading or writing.

Exercises: Finding words and their meanings

1. If the guide words on the page of a dictionary are **minimize** and **minute**, which words in the list below will be found on that page? Write them down.

minister	mining	mirror	minstrel
minor	mirage	minuet	mink
mint	minutely	minimal	mingle
minus	minority	miniature	minnow

2. Which words in the list below would be found on the page of a dictionary for which the guide words are **grate** and **gray**?

gravel	grateful	graze	grapple
grating	grate	gratis	grave
grassy	gravity	gratification	grapefruit
grasp	graybeard	grant	gratitude

3. Look up each italicized word below in the dictionary. Copy the definition that best describes the meaning of the word as it is used in the sentence.

1. John will *catch* a small fish.
2. The fifth problem is a *catch* question.
3. His *sentence* was three years at hard labor.
4. That is a grammatical *sentence*.
5. Judges *sentence* criminals.
6. He *pounds* the door, demanding entry.
7. We need four *pounds* of cabbage to make cole slaw.
8. The dogs in the *pounds* were restless.

The Dictionary Shows Pronunciation

In English, unfortunately, it is not always possible to know how to pronounce a word, even if you see it spelled correctly. In every dictionary there is a *pronunciation key* which explains the symbols and special spellings used to show how to pronounce words. It is a good idea to look at the full pronunciation key, which is usually printed inside the front and back covers. Many dictionaries also list the key, in abbreviated form, at the bottom of every other page.

Diacritical marks

The marks used to indicate the pronunciation of words are called **diacritical marks.** Since there are so many of them and they differ from dictionary to dictionary, you need not memorize them.

Long vowels. There is one mark you should know, and that is the **macron** (¯). It marks a *long vowel.* If you say the vowels *a, e, i, o, u* aloud, you will hear the sound of the long vowels. Each long vowel sound is identical to the sound of its name.

EXAMPLES OF LONG VOWELS

plate	plāt
she	shē
sigh	sī
boat	bōt
use	ūz

Exercise: Marking the long vowels

Copy the following words. Show each long vowel—each vowel that says its own name—by putting a macron over it. Use the dictionary where you need to.

1. date	6. tight	11. finite
2. poke	7. wholesale	12. lion
3. even	8. obedience	13. purity
4. oppose	9. music	14. equalize
5. emancipate	10. holy	15. intermediary

Short vowels. Short vowels are pronounced with a shorter sound than long vowels. The most common way for a short vowel to be marked is with a **breve** (˘). For example, here are long and short vowels for you to compare. The long vowels are marked with a macron; and the short vowels, with a breve.

LONG VOWELS	SHORT VOWELS
fāte	făt
Pēte	pĕt
sīte	sĭt
hōpe	hŏp
hūge	hŭg

The schwa. Another common way to mark vowels is to use the **schwa**, which looks like an upside down *e*: ə. The schwa is used to show an unaccented vowel sound, whether the vowel be *a, e, i, o,* or *u.* (In some dictionaries it is also used to indicate the short *u,* accented or not.)

EXAMPLES OF THE USE OF THE SCHWA

b*a*n*a*n*a*	bənanə
sl*i*pp*e*r	slipər
cl*a*r*i*fy	klarəfi
c*o*llect	kəlekt
foc*u*s	focəs

Exercise: Using diacritical marks

Copy this list of ten words containing short vowels. Find the short vowels and mark each one with a breve (˘). Then check your answers in a dictionary to be sure you have picked out the short vowels.

1. scrapbook
2. dictionary
3. picture
4. obligation
5. representative
6. passion
7. construct
8. contemptible
9. heartily
10. cultural

Accent marks. All dictionaries show you through the use of an **accent mark** which syllable is accented. In most dictionaries the accent is shown by a ' *after* the accented syllable:

ex ter nal (eks tėr'nəl)

In some dictionaries, the accent is indicated by a ' *before* the accented syllable:

ex·ter·nal (eks-'tərn-l)

Many words have two accents—a heavy one and a light one. The word *insulation* is an example. The syllable *in* is the light or **secondary accent**; the syllable *la* is the heavy or **primary accent**. These two types of accents are indicated thus:

in′sə lā′shən

Another way of marking accents is to have the primary and secondary accents before the syllables, with the primary one at the top and the secondary one at the bottom:

′dand-l-,ī-ən

Syllabification

A syllable is a word or part of a word which can be pronounced with a single sounding of the voice. *Child* is a one-syllable word; *chil·dren* is a two-syllable word.

The dictionary tells you how to syllabize a word. You need to know this in order to divide a word correctly at the end of a line. It also helps you learn to spell a word. Dictionaries indicate syllabification in several ways, as shown in the following examples:

hon·est·ly   hon est ly   hon-est-ly

Exercises: Using accent marks

1. Use your dictionary for this exercise. Copy the following words on your paper, using dots to divide them into syllables. Then place the accent mark before or after the accented syllable, whichever method your dictionary uses.

EXAMPLE: 1. repair
YOU WRITE: *1. re·pair′ (or) re·′pair*

1. occur
2. oblong
3. absolute
4. typical
5. powerful
6. tragedy
7. comedy
8. comedian

2. Follow the directions for the first exercise above. With these words, indicate the primary and secondary accents.

1. caterpillar
2. nevertheless
3. numerator
4. firewater
5. estimation
6. pessimistic

The Dictionary Shows Spelling and Capitalization

Most of the words in our language have only one spelling. When a word has more than one spelling, however, the dictionary lists all of them. Do not consider any one spelling better than the other; they are all correct. Sometimes, the first spelling listed is the one judged by the makers of the dictionary to be the spelling most commonly used. Here is a sample entry:

jin rik i sha or **jin rick sha** (jin rik′shə), a small, two-wheeled, hooded carriage pulled by one or more men, used in Japan, China, etc. *n.* Also, **rickshaw, ricksha.**

Jinrikisha

There are several things you need to know about the use of a dictionary to find the correct spelling of a word.

1. **The dictionary shows the spellings for the plurals of nouns which form their plural in an irregular way.** For example, you will find the plurals of words like *ox* and *woman—oxen, women.*

   However, the dictionary does not list the plurals of nouns which form their plural in the regular way; that is, by adding *s* or *es*. For example, you will find the entries for the words *apple, wish,* and *box,* but you will not find the plurals *apples, wishes,* and *boxes.*

2. **The dictionary shows the past tense and the past participle forms of irregular verbs.** If you look up the verbs *choose, buy,* and *try,* you will also find the past tenses *chose* (and *chosen*), *bought, tried.*

3. **The dictionary lists the –ing form of irregular verbs.** If the spelling changes in any way, the verb is listed. For example, you will find *put—putting* in the dictionary because the *t* is doubled when *–ing* is added.

4. **The dictionary tells you whether a word should be hyphenated or written as a solid word or as two words.**

Examine the sample dictionary page which follows. Then discuss the questions on page 325.

buck[1] (buk), 1. a male deer, goat, hare, rabbit, antelope, or sheep. 2. dandy. 3. *Informal.* man. *n.*

buck[2] (buk), 1. *U.S. Informal.* fight against; resist stubbornly. 2. *U.S. Informal.* push or hit with the head; butt. 3. *U.S. Informal.* rush at; charge against. 4. in football, charge into (the opposing line) with the ball. 5. jump into the air with back curved and come down with the front legs stiff: *His horse began to buck, but he managed to stay on.* 6. a throw or attempt to throw by bucking. 1–5 *v.*, 6 *n.* —**buck'er**, *n.*

Bucking bronco

buck[3] (buk), *Informal.* **Pass the buck** means to shift the responsibility, blame, work, etc., to someone else. *n.*

buck[4] (buk), *U.S. Slang.* dollar. *n.*

buck a roo (buk'ə rü), *U.S.* cowboy. *n., pl.* **buck a roos.**

buck board (buk'bôrd'), an open, four-wheeled carriage having the seat fastened to a platform of long, springy boards instead of a body and springs. *n.*

Buckboard

buck et (buk'it), 1. pail made of wood or metal. Buckets are used for carrying water, milk, coal, etc. 2. amount that a bucket can hold. 3. scoop of a dredging machine. *n.*

buck et ful (buk'it fúl), amount that a bucket can hold. *n., pl.* **buck et fuls.**

bucket seat, a seat in an airplane, sports car, etc., set close to the floor, with a rounded back.

buck eye (buk'ī'), tree or shrub closely related to the horse chestnut, with showy clusters of small flowers, large divided leaves, and large brown seeds. *n.*

Buck ing ham Palace (buk'ing əm or buk'ing-ham), official London residence of all British sovereigns since 1837.

buck le (buk'əl), 1. catch or clasp used to fasten together the ends of a belt, strap, etc. 2. a metal ornament for a shoe. 3. fasten together with a buckle. 4. bend; bulge; kink; wrinkle: *The plaster has buckled because of the settling of the house.* 1,2,4 *n.*, 3,4 *v.*, **buck led, buck ling.**

buck ler (buk'lər), 1. a small, round shield. 2. protection; defense. *n.*

buck private, *Slang.* a common soldier below the rank of private first class.

Soldiers with bucklers

buck ram (buk'rəm), a coarse cloth made stiff with glue or something like glue. *n.*

buck saw (buk'sô'), saw set in a light frame and held with both hands. *n.*

buck shot (buk'shot'), a large lead shot used for shooting deer, foxes, etc. *n.*

buck skin (buk'skin'), a strong, soft leather, yellowish or grayish in color, made from the skins of deer or sheep. *n.*

buck skins (buk'skinz'), breeches made of buckskin. *n.pl.*

buck thorn (buk'thôrn'), *U.S.* 1. a small, sometimes thorny tree or shrub with clusters of black berries, each containing several nutlets. 2. a low, thorny tree with black, cherrylike fruit that grows in the southern United States. *n.*

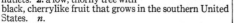

Man using a bucksaw

buck wheat (buk'hwēt'), 1. plant with brown, triangular seeds and fragrant white flowers. 2. the seeds, used as food for animals or ground into flour. 3. meal, flour, or batter made from buckwheat. *n.*

buckwheat cake, pancake made of buckwheat flour.

bu col ic (bü kol'ik), 1. of shepherds; pastoral. Bucolic poetry is seldom written by shepherds themselves. 2. rustic; rural. 3. poem about shepherds. 1,2 *adj.*, 3 *n.*

bud (bud), 1. a small swelling on a plant that will develop into a flower, leaf, or branch. 2. put forth buds: *The rosebush has budded.* 3. graft (a bud) from one kind of plant into the stem of a different kind. See **graft** for picture. 4. time or state of budding: *The pear tree is in bud.* 5. a partly opened flower. 6. anything not yet developed; beginning stage. 7. child; young girl. 8. begin to grow or develop. 9. a minute, bud-shaped part or organ: *a taste bud.* 1,4–7,9 *n.*, 2,3,8 *v.*, **bud ded, bud ding.**

nip in the bud, stop at the very beginning.

Bu da pest (bü'də pest), capital of Hungary, on the Danube River. 1,058,000. *n.*

Bud dha (bud'ə or bü'də), 563?-483? B.C., great religious teacher of Asia, founder of Buddhism. *n.* Also, **Gautama.**

Bud dhism (bud'iz əm or bü'diz əm), religion that originated in the sixth century B.C. in N India and spread widely over central, SE, and E Asia. It teaches that right living will enable people to attain Nirvana, the condition of a soul that does not have to live in a body and is free from all desire and pain. *n.*

Bud dhist (bud'ist or bü'dist), 1. having to do with Buddha or Buddhism. 2. believer in Buddhism. 1 *adj.*, 2 *n.*

bud dy (bud'i), *Informal.* 1. *U.S.* brother; comrade; pal. 2. a little boy. *n., pl.* **bud dies.**

budge (buj), move or cause to move (usually with negative): *He wouldn't budge from his chair.* *v.*, **budged, budg ing.**

budg et (buj'it), 1. estimate of the amount of money that can be spent, and the amounts to be spent for various purposes, in a given time. Governments, schools, companies, and persons often make budgets. 2. make a plan for spending: *budget your time.* 3. stock or collection: *a budget of news.* 1,3 *n.*, 2 *v.*, **budg et ed, budg et ing.**

budg et ar y (buj'ə ter'i), of a budget. *adj.*

Bue na Vis ta (bwā'nə vis'tə), village in NE Mexico. The Americans defeated the Mexicans there in 1847.

Bue nos Ai res (bwā'nəs ī'riz or bō'nəs är'ēz), capital of Argentina, on the Plata River. 3,368,000.

buff (buf), 1. a strong, soft, dull-yellow leather, made from buffalo skin or oxhide. 2. a soldier's coat made of this. 3. made of buff leather. 4. dull yellow. 5. a polishing wheel or stick covered with leather. 6. polish with such a wheel or stick. 7. *Informal.* bare skin. 1,2,4,5,7 *n.*, 3,4 *adj.*, 6 *v.*

buf fa lo (buf'ə lō), 1. the bison of America, the male of which has a big, shaggy head and strong front legs. Herds of buffalo used to graze on the plains of middlewestern United States. See **bison** for picture. 2. any of several kinds of oxen. The tame **water buffalo** of India and the wild **Cape buffalo** of Africa are two different kinds. 3. *U.S. Slang.* intimidate or overawe. 4. *U.S. Slang.* puzzle; mystify. 1,2 *n.*, **buf fa loes, buf fa los,** or (*esp. collectively*) **buf fa lo;** 3,4 *v.*, **buf fa loed, buf fa lo ing.**

Water buffalo (body 6 ft. long)

Buf fa lo (buf'ə lō), port in W New York State, on Lake Erie. 577,000. *n.*

Buffalo Bill, 1846-1917, William F. Cody, American frontier scout and showman.

buffalo grass, a short grass of central and western North America, often used for pasture.

To discuss

Look at the sample dictionary page opposite and answer the following questions based on it. Take turns writing some of your answers on the board.

1. What is the plural of these nouns: *buckaroo, bucket, bucketful, buddy, buffalo?*
2. What is the past tense and the *–ing* form of these verbs: *buckle, budge, bud?*
3. Find the following entries. Are they written as one word or as two words? Write each of them correctly on the board.

   buckboard   buckprivate   buckwheat
   bucketseat   buckeye   buckskin

4. How long is a water buffalo?
5. How many verb meanings of the word *bud* are given? How many noun meanings?
6. Can you find three words in which the schwa is used—one to show an unaccented *o,* one to show an unaccented *a,* and one for *e?*
7. A dictionary gives usage labels, such as "informal" or "slang." Can you find two expressions or forms that are labeled "informal" and two that are labeled "slang"?
8. Can you name three kinds of buffaloes and the country in which each kind is found?

Exercises: Using the dictionary

1. Look up the following nouns in the dictionary. Write the plural of each one on your paper.

1. cargo	5. half
2. soprano	6. roof
3. hippopotamus	7. brother-in-law
4. cupful	8. Negro

2. Add *–ing* to the following words. Look each word up in the dictionary unless you are certain of the spelling.

1. singe	3. diagram
2. benefit	4. occur

5. occupy

3. All of the words below are written as one word. Some of them should be written as solid words, some hyphenated, and some as two words. Consult your dictionary before deciding how to write each word. If the dictionary gives a choice, write down both forms.

1. airmail	5. teenager
2. airplane	6. selfreliant
3. icecream	7. expresident
4. fountainpen	8. undergraduate

4. Look up a few of the words above in more than one dictionary. Did you find that dictionaries disagree on some words? What does this show about the English language?

5. Write the past tense and past participle of each of these verbs. Use your dictionary to make sure. If there is a choice, write all of the acceptable forms.

    1. stride   2. chide   3. bid   4. wring   5. wear

Capitalization

The dictionary tells you when a word is ordinarily capitalized. Often a word is listed twice—once capitalized and once not. In such cases you must look carefully to see which meaning you want.

Exercise: Capitalization

Check your dictionary to see if each of the following words is capitalized. On your paper, copy only those words which need capitals. Be sure you capitalize them.

1. egret	4. indonesia	7. geranium
2. dresden china	5. hesperus	8. beetle
3. elixir	6. island	

GOING AHEAD

Use each word below in a brief sentence, capitalized or not, as required by the information you find in the dictionary. If there is a choice—that is, if the word is listed once capitalized and once not —use the word in two sentences and illustrate both uses.

1. cork	4. civil war	7. jimson weed
2. caucasian	5. cocker spaniel	8. arctic
3. chipmunk	6. herculean	

Note-taking

If you had a perfect memory, perhaps you would not need to take notes. Most of us, however, need reminders of what we have read or heard, especially if we are to use this information later in a written or oral report. Notes can be written on a pad or in a notebook. However, there is some advantage in putting notes on 3″ x 5″ cards so that you can later rearrange the ideas and facts you have collected.

Keep in mind your purpose for taking notes. Write down only the facts and ideas which serve your purpose. For example, if you are doing a report on penguins and find some information about them in an article on Antarctica, do not make notes on such topics as the area of the region, the history of explorations there, or other animal life found there. Note only those things which tell about penguins and how they live.

In general, you should not copy whole sentences and paragraphs into your notes. Read the material and then note down the main ideas as you yourself would say them. Sometimes you will want to record the idea of an author in his exact words. Be sure you put the words within quotation marks both in your notes and on your paper. Copying another writer's words without quotation marks and using them as your own is dishonest. The word which describes this deliberate use of someone else's writing as your own is called *plagiarism*.

Name the sources of your information: authors, titles, dates of publication, and page numbers of the books you use.

Suppose you want to write a report on penguins and you come across these paragraphs from the book *Through the Frozen Frontier* by Rear Admiral George J. Dufek. Read the paragraphs and then examine the notes which follow them.

The best-known of Antarctic natives are the penguins. There are millions of penguins south of the equator. Most of them build their nests and hatch their eggs on the frozen shores of Antarctica. Penguins like to live in a very cold climate. However, there are penguins on the Galapagos Islands near the equator, where it is ordinarily very warm, but a cold water current flows in the ocean nearby. This water current, called the Humboldt Current, cools off the islands. Although it is cold in the north-polar regions, no penguins

live there, perhaps because—while in Antarctica there are no land animals to kill the penguins—in the north-polar regions there are many land animals that eat practically anything to stay alive.

There are seventeen different kinds of penguins. You can tell them apart by their size, shape, and coloring. . . .

The Adélie penguin is the most amusing of all. He is known as Mr. Curiosity. Mr. Curiosity is two to two and one half feet tall and weighs six to fourteen pounds. He looks as if he were wearing a formal dress suit. The top of his head and his back are covered with bluish-black feathers, the front with dazzling white feathers. The sailors like to put black bow ties around the necks of these penguins. Then Mr. Curiosity struts around and looks funnier than ever.

Notes on "Penguins"
from
Through the Frozen Frontier
by Rear Admiral George J. Dufek,
1959, pp. 22-24
Like cold climate
Live on frozen shores of Antarctica
Some live on Galapagos Islands
  near equator where the Humboldt
Current cools off the islands
No penguins live in Arctic
Too many land animals would
  kill penguins for food
17 different kinds of penguins
Adélie penguin is one kind
"Known as Mr. Curiosity"
Sailors enjoy his amusing antics
2-2½ tall; 6-14 lbs.
Black, bluish feathers on top of
  head and back; white feathers
  in front — coloring similar to
  formal dress

Guides for note-taking

1. State the general topic.
2. Do not note everything. Select only the facts you need.
3. Write the notes in your own words. Use words and phrases, not sentences.
4. If you quote directly, use quotation marks.
5. Label your notes with a complete reference to your source of information.

Exercises: Taking notes

1. What facts must you include in your notes to identify each source of information?

2. Explain the meaning of the word *plagiarism*.

3. Have someone read a passage of four or five paragraphs. Take notes on the main points. Compare your notes in class.

Outlining

An outline is a tool; it is of no use for its own sake. Making an outline should help you to organize your ideas in proper order. It should also help you to sort these ideas into main topics and subtopics. If you can learn to organize your ideas in an outline, your reports and oral talks will improve.

Of course, your outline cannot do your thinking for you. You must decide on the order of your ideas and on their relative importance to each other. If your thinking is not clear and logical, your outline will not be clear and logical. However, the outline can *help* you to clarify your thoughts.

Outlines have a definite form which you should follow. To observe that form, examine the outline on the next page and answer the following questions about it. The outline is based on the notes about penguins on page 329.

To discuss

1. Which topics are labeled with Roman numerals? Are these the main topics?

2. Which topics are labeled with capital letters? What are these topics called?

3. How are the most subordinate ideas labeled?

4. How many topics are listed under each main topic?

5. What mark of punctuation is used after each numeral and letter?

6. How does the first word of each topic begin?

Whenever you are dividing a topic, remember that you can never have a I without a II, an A without a B, or a 1 without a 2. Place a period after each letter and numeral. Begin the first word of each main topic and subtopic with a capital letter.

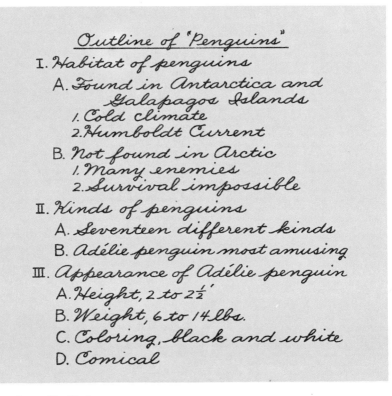

Outline of "Penguins"

I. Habitat of penguins
   A. Found in Antarctica and Galapagos Islands
     1. Cold climate
     2. Humboldt Current
   B. Not found in Arctic
     1. Many enemies
     2. Survival impossible
II. Kinds of penguins
   A. Seventeen different kinds
   B. Adélie penguin most amusing
III. Appearance of Adélie penguin
   A. Height, 2 to 2½'
   B. Weight, 6 to 14 lbs.
   C. Coloring, black and white
   D. Comical

Exercises: Outlining

1. Copy the twenty-one numerals and letters which follow and then see if you can arrange them in proper outline form. There are several ways of doing this. Remember to indent the items properly as in the model.

C, 2, B, I, III, 1, 2, B, C, 1, 3, A, 2, 2, IV, II, A, 1, A, B, 1

2. The next time you have a talk or report to make on any subject, make an outline of it first. Then show it to your teacher for suggestions.

Learning How to Spell

No one can be a perfect speller; everyone has to look up a word in the dictionary now and then. However, you should not have to look up the common, easy, everyday words. You should know these words by heart.

Keeping a list of the words you have looked up and studied will help you to be a good speller. Write the words in a small *alphabetized notebook* that you can carry around with you for ready reference. Refer to it whenever you have forgotten a word.

Here are six steps to help you learn the spelling of a word:

Step 1. Find the word in the dictionary. If necessary, have a good speller help you. Copy it carefully into your notebook. Then look at the word and pronounce it correctly several times.

Step 2. Divide the word into syllables by underlining each syllable in this way:

unfortunately

Step 3. Take another good look at the word you wrote in your notebook. Then cover it with your finger. Now uncover the word, syllable by syllable, pronouncing each syllable as it becomes visible. Then say the whole word. Repeat this process several times.

Step 4. When you are quite sure that you know the word, close your notebook and write it.

Step 5. Compare what you wrote with the model in your notebook. If you misspelled it, cross out the incorrect version (do not patch it up) and start again.

Step 6. If you spelled the word correctly, write it a few more times to be sure of it. Write it from memory; do not copy it. Check with the model each time. Eventually, the correct spelling will begin to "look right" to you.

With this system, you can learn a word in about a minute. You will also be likely to remember its correct spelling in the future.

If you can possibly avoid it, never write a word unless you are sure of its spelling. Every time you misspell a word, you have made a bit more permanent the error-habit that causes you to misspell it.

Remember: First say and see the word correctly.

Next, get an image of the word in your head.

Finally, write the word correctly on paper.

Exercises: Starting your spelling notebook

1. Buy a small notebook and cut out an alphabetized thumb-index so that the notebook is easy to use. (See the illustration on page 160.)

2. As an experiment, see if you can learn to spell these eight rather hard but commonly used words in our language. Start by copying them carefully into your spelling notebook. Check the words to make sure that you have not miscopied them.

1. exaggerate
2. picnicking
3. conscientious
4. hippopotamus
5. occasionally
6. schedule
7. embarrassment
8. disappearance

Perhaps your teacher will give you a test on the words above after you have studied them.

(Apply the spelling method you have just studied to the words that sound alike, listed on page 173. In the Review Handbook on pages 432–33, there is a list of one hundred spelling demons. You should learn them, since they are often used and often misspelled.)

━━━ **GOING AHEAD** ━━━━━━━━━━━━━━━━━━━━━━━━━

1. The words in the following list are frequently used in your other subjects in school. Working in pairs, have your partner dictate the words to you. Then, using the system suggested above for learning to spell a word, study any of the ones you misspelled.

seismograph	evaporation	hypotenuse	circumference
astronaut	perpendicular	protoplasm	perimeter
photosynthesis	diameter	revolution	carbohydrates
metamorphosis	radius	civilization	chlorophyll

2. Just for fun, and if there is time, see if you can learn to spell the following two words. (The second is one of the longest words in the English language.) If you are successful, it will prove to you that the system suggested here really works. Look up the meanings of these words in an unabridged dictionary.

antidisestablishmentarianism
pneumonoultramicroscopicsilicovolcanoconiosis

333

Memorization

There are many different ways of memorizing something. No one can be certain which way will be best for you. You will need to experiment and see for yourself. For some people, memorization is very easy; for others, nearly impossible. However, if you are blessed with a good memory, nothing can give you more satisfaction than a stock of memorized poems and quotations which you like and enjoy repeating.

Here are some suggestions which may help you to memorize more efficiently:

1. Read over the passage to be memorized and be sure you understand the meaning.
2. Read over the passage three or four times *aloud*, with full expression in your voice.
3. Put the text aside and see how much of the passage you can now say from memory.
4. Take a few lines at a time and memorize them. Read the lines and then close your eyes and say them.
5. When you have finished step 4, try saying over the entire passage again, but have the book in front of you to glance at.
6. Work with a partner, who can prompt you as you try saying the passage.
7. If a certain few lines are giving you trouble, concentrate on them and master them.
8. Do your memory work in short spurts, perhaps five to ten minutes each, rather than all at once.
9. Repeat the passage two or three times before you go to sleep.
10. After you have memorized the passage, say it over every other day or so to fix it in your mind.

In memorizing lines for a play, be sure to memorize your cues (the words of another actor that tell you when to speak) as well as your own lines.

Exercises: Memorizing poetry

1. Choose a poem or brief passage you enjoy and memorize it.
2. Using the method you have just studied, memorize the poem printed on the opposite page.

A Nation's Strength

Not gold, but only man can make
   A people great and strong;
Men who, for truth and honor's sake,
   Stand fast and suffer long.

Brave men who work while others sleep,
   Who dare while others fly—
They build a nation's pillars deep
   And lift them to the sky.

RALPH WALDO EMERSON

The American essayist and poet, Ralph Waldo Emerson, spoke for the importance of the common man and the self-sufficiency of the individual. To him, each man's work had an important place in the scheme of American life. He pointed to the early settlers in America as a shining example of the great contribution that can be made by those who practice the doctrine of self-reliance. Could the same thing be said of the workers of today? Do they make a contribution to American life? Is the poem a patriotic poem?

335

Homework

Perhaps the most important study skill is that of doing homework. Homework really should be called "independent work," because it should be done independently, by you alone, not jointly with a classmate or your parents. Occasionally, you may be told specifically that you may get help or do your work with someone else, but otherwise, you should do it yourself.

If you do your homework with another person, these bad results are likely:

1. You become dependent upon someone else.
2. You may hide from yourself the fact that you do not know something; and you may hide it for a month or two from your teacher, who then will not be able to give you help as soon as you should have it.
3. You tend not to ask questions in class because you always feel you can get help at home or elsewhere. You should ask questions in class.
4. When you are *alone in a test*, you will be poorly prepared to work well independently.

There are a few ways in which others may help you from time to time if your teacher does not object. They may help you . . .

    . . . to get ideas for things to write about.
    . . . to find materials for projects.
    . . . to test you on routine tasks like spelling or memorization.
    . . . to plan a regular schedule for homework.
    . . . to listen to a speech you have prepared.

Suggestions for doing your homework

1. As soon as an assignment is given, write it down in your home-work notebook completely and accurately. If the assignment is not clear to you, ask the teacher then and there to explain it.
2. Have a definite time for home study. Establish a schedule and let the schedule provide the will power for you, if you do not have enough of your own.
3. Have a quiet place that has good lighting for study, if you can possibly manage it. Have your materials available: paper, pen, pencil, ruler, books, dictionary. Eliminate any distraction such as radio or TV.
4. Know the *purpose* of the assignment before you start. Do not just do the work blindly. Be sure you are clear about how it fits in with what you are studying and what you are supposed to get from it.
5. Note any questions that arise while you are doing the work and be ready to ask them next day in class, if there is an opportunity to do so.
6. If you have no assigned homework, spend your scheduled homework time reading for pleasure. There is no better way to improve your English.

Exercises: Improving your study conditions

1. Survey the physical conditions in which you do your home-work. Are they ideal? If not, why not? If you live in a crowded, busy house, there may be little you can do except to learn to concentrate amid the turmoil. On the other hand, many students could improve their study conditions if they gave some thought and care to the problem. Are you one of these?

Write two or three paragraphs on the subject: "My Homework Problems."

2. Give some thought to your daily schedule and then write down the schedule for a typical day. Include such things as sleep, meals, relaxation, TV, sports, homework, and time spent in class.

After you have completed your schedule for a typical day, write a paragraph or two on the topic: "What Changes in My Schedule Would Improve My School Work?"

Test I

On which of the three kinds of library cards would you look to find each of the following? Write your answers next to the appropriate numerals on your paper.

1. A book by Louisa May Alcott
2. A description of an astronaut
3. A book called *Television Story*
4. Books about television
5. The book *Kon-Tiki*

Test II

1. Listed below on the left are three kinds of reference works. Assume you are trying to find the things listed on the right. Number your paper from 1 to 5. Write the kind of reference work in which you would be most likely to find the information quickly.

Encyclopedias   1. Short biography of Franklin D. Roosevelt
Almanacs   2. Description of a bathyscaph
Atlases   3. Map of Madagascar
                 4. Winner of the Nobel Prize for Literature in 1954
                 5. Alaskan seals

2. Next to the appropriate numeral on your paper, write the letter *a*, *b*, or *c* of the item which completes the sentence correctly.

1. The Dewey Decimal System classifies books of nonfiction into (a) four categories, (b) ten categories, (c) three categories.
2. Nonfiction includes all books except (a) short stories and novels; (b) poems, plays, and essays; (c) dictionaries and languages.
3. The *Readers' Guide to Periodical Literature* lists by subject and author (a) magazine articles; (b) short stories; (c) encyclopedia articles.

Test III

1. Copy the words in the following list that will be found on a dictionary page with the guide words **idolize** and **immature**:

ignition	idyll	illustrate	ideal
immediate	immaterial	idleness	illuminate
imagine	immature	identity	ignorance

2. Number your paper from 1 to 5. The word *catch* is used in five sentences below. Beneath the sentences are five different definitions. Next to the appropriate numeral, write the letter *a, b, c,* etc., of the one definition that best describes the meaning of the word as it is used in each sentence.

1. His *catch* was a dozen lobsters.
2. The *catch* on the door is broken.
3. He made his *catch* in far right field.
4. Let's play *catch.*
5. Don't *catch* your sweater on this nail.

    a. become caught
    b. act of catching
    c. thing caught
    d. game of throwing and catching ball
    e. thing that catches

Test IV

1. Write three of the guides for note-taking.

2. Explain in one or two sentences the meaning of the word *plagiarism.*

3. On your paper, arrange the following items into correct outline form, putting the main topics and subtopics in logical order. Capitalize and punctuate the outline correctly.

ways to improve my homework

II	place of study
B	knowing purpose
A	proper lighting
I	assignments
C	asking questions
B	materials at hand
1	radio
3	dictionary
A	writing in homework notebook
III	time of study
2	television
C	no distractions
1	paper, pen, pencil, and ruler
2	books

Review and Practice

Exercise I

1. Review "The Library" on pages 311–14.

2. Draw three boxes, three inches by five inches, on your paper. Study the following information about a book. Then print carefully inside the boxes: an Author Card, a Title Card, and a Subject Card for the book. It is in the Juvenile Collection. Make up a call number for it after you check the numbers in the Dewey Decimal System categories.

> The book is *Canada: Mounted Police* written by Richard Lewis Neuberger and published in 1953 by Random House in New York. It is an illustrated 182-page book.

Check your cards with the models on page 312.

3. On which of the three kinds of cards would you look to find each of the following?

1. A book by Lancelot Hogben
2. A book about Abraham Lincoln
3. Information about Washington, D.C.
4. The book *How to Hit*
5. A book by MacKinlay Kantor

Exercise II

1. Review "The Reference Books in the Library" on pages 316–17.

2. Number your paper from 1 to 10. Write the kind of reference work in which you are most likely to find quickly the numbered items listed below. Choose from these reference works: *encyclopedias, almanacs, atlases.*

1. Names of cities in New York State
2. The population of Detroit, Michigan
3. Location of the Alps
4. Information about the habits of bees
5. The names of the senators in Congress in 1964
6. Map of the United States
7. Oscar award winner for the best leading actor in 1963
8. A biography of Shakespeare
9. Information about cattle raising
10. The names of the pitchers for the New York Yankees

Exercise III

1. Review the lessons on the dictionary on pages 318–26.

2. In each of the columns below, one word is out of alphabetical order. Which one is it?

boar	dampen	shipmate
boat	damper	sinkage
bag	dampest	sinking
bog	dampness	sinkhole
boss	dampish	sunk
bout	damsel	sunken

3. List ten words that might be found on an (imaginary) dictionary page between the guide words **educate** and **extract**.

4. Each of the following words has two or more meanings listed in the dictionary. Look up each word and use it in two sentences that illustrate two of the meanings you find in the dictionary.

   1. pen   2. chair   3. coat   4. step   5. table

Exercise IV

1. Review "Note-taking," "Outlining," and "Homework" on pages 327–31 and 336–37.

2. Explain in your own words the guides for taking notes.

3. On your paper, arrange the following items into correct outline form, putting the main topics and subtopics in logical order. Capitalize and punctuate the outline correctly.

the armadillo

I	appearance	1	insects
II	habits	3	exposes only bony,
B	vulnerable abdomen		scalelike plates to
A	feeding		enemy
1	moves quickly	2	worms
C	short legs	2	rolls up into ball to
A	armorlike covering		protect abdomen
B	night creature	C	protection from danger

4. Write a paragraph about the topic "Improving Your Homework."

CHAPTER 13

Listening: Receiving Ideas

Teachers have always said, as they still say, "Listen carefully" or "Pay attention." However, recently teachers have become more interested in listening as a part of a student's education. Tests have shown that some people listen much better than others, and that there are times when one listens well and times when one does not. Certainly, you will want to do what you can to improve your listening habits. The lessons in this chapter will help you to evaluate these habits and suggest ways to improve them.

The Importance of Listening

Listening is an important skill, a skill which you can develop if you really want to. A good listener takes in many more ideas than does a poor one. He probably does better in school or in his job or profession. He also gets more pleasure from the sounds around him. A good listener gives pleasure, too, for we all like to talk to an attentive listener.

To discuss

Discuss the importance of learning to listen well. Write on the board as many situations as you can where it was important to listen carefully.

As a start, you might list the following listening situations:

Directions given by a policeman on how to reach a certain street address

Your mother explaining what you are to do about supper on a night when she is to be away

The school fire marshal explaining what you should do during a fire drill

Exercise: Judging your listening skills

Write a short set of instructions telling someone how to do something, giving directions for getting somewhere, or assigning homework in one of your subjects. Take turns reading some of them to the class. Listen carefully and take notes as each paper is read aloud. Write down the important facts. When the paper is read again, check your notes to see how carefully you have listened.

Your Purpose in Listening

Your listening will improve if you *listen with a purpose.* Sometimes when you hear something read or spoken, you have no idea why you are supposed to be listening to it. If you have a definite purpose in mind when you listen to a speech or conversation or a radio or TV program, you are likely to get more out of it than if you merely listen. If you are assigned some listening to do for homework, be sure that you know the purpose for listening.

Exercise: Listening

Listen to the paragraph which will be read by your teacher or someone in the class. At the end, you will be asked a single question which can be answered by giving a single figure. Now close your textbooks and listen.

A bus is traveling through a city. It has seven passengers on it. It stops at State Street, and five passengers get off and two get on. Next, it stops at Forest Avenue, and three passengers get off and four get on. At the next stop, seven passengers enter the bus and only one gets off. Four blocks later another stop is made and eight passengers are discharged and none get on. The next stop is Third Avenue, where one passenger gets off and thirteen get on. At this time the bus begins a long express run into the suburbs.

Question: How many stops did the bus make?

Were you able to answer the question correctly? Why not? What were you listening for? You probably were able to tell how many passengers were on the bus as it began its express run to the suburbs: 15. Now, if you listen again to the paragraph, knowing in advance what the question will be, it will be easy to answer the question. Try it.

Hearing and Listening

As a first step toward understanding what listening is, examine carefully for a moment the things you can *hear*. You may be surprised at the number of things that come to your ears. For example, on a summer's day, you may hear sounds like these:

A thrush singing
Automobiles on a nearby highway (both heavy trucks and cars)
A person walking heavily in the kitchen
A crow cawing
A dog barking
Your own breathing
The creaking of a chair
A fly buzzing
Automobile horns
Papers rustling in the breeze
Some boys shouting in a game they are playing

To discuss

Stop what you are doing, either in class or at home, and list everything that you can hear during a three-minute period. Share some of these lists by asking a few class members to read their lists to the entire class. Can you explain why we *hear* much more than we *listen* to?

Someone who lived in an extremely crowded neighborhood in New York next to the railroad track once commented, "The only time there is quiet around here is when the train goes by." Of course, he meant that the only time he could think was when the very loud noise of the train drowned out all the distracting neighborhood noises. The noise of the train created a kind of quiet during which he could concentrate.

The difference between *hearing* and *listening* is that you hear all the sounds that reach you, but you listen only to those sounds which catch your attention or to which you make yourself pay attention. The human nervous system has ways of turning off other sounds, and it is a good thing. If you listened to everything you hear, you would soon get very confused. You must select what you will listen to and shut off most other sounds so as to permit concentration on what you need to listen to.

Exercise: Hearing and listening

Take a survey of the kinds of listening and hearing you did between the time you left school yesterday and the time you went to bed. You will include hearing and listening to such things as directions, radio, TV, telephone, conversations in other rooms, noises in other parts of the house or the outdoors. Tell how much time you spent on each listening situation and how beneficial you think it was to you. Explain why you think it was beneficial or harmful. Use the following rating scale:

> 1. very beneficial
> 2. beneficial
> 3. no particular effect

> 4. a bit harmful
> 5. very harmful

EXAMPLE: On my way home from school, my friend Larry and I were talking for about a half-hour. This listening was *beneficial* because he was explaining how I can make my own display cases for my rock collection.

EXAMPLE: I heard my brother playing the bongo drums in the next room for an hour. This was *very harmful* because I was trying to study for a test.

To discuss

Discuss in class the results of your survey above.

1. Do you think you make good use of your listening time? Was the day surveyed typical?
2. Are there things you should listen to more? less?
3. Did the survey illustrate anything to you about the difference between hearing and listening? If so, what?

Critical Listening: Radio and TV

You have just read that your mind, often unconsciously, *selects* from the things you hear the things you actually listen to. But you should do some conscious, planned selecting, too. A good place to start would be with the radio and TV programs you spend time on. Both radio and TV influence your life probably more than you realize. If you select your programs wisely, your experiences with radio and TV can be cultural and educational, as well as entertaining. If you do not, listening to radio and TV can be a waste of time.

To discuss

1. Take a survey of your radio and TV listening habits by answering the following questions:

1. How much time do I spend each day listening to the radio and watching TV?
2. Do I really listen, or do I merely listen with "half an ear" while I do something else? Should I always listen carefully, or are there programs and occasions when half an ear is sufficient?
3. What programs do I listen to daily? Have I developed a wide range of interests?
4. Which of these programs add to my cultural or educational experience? Which provide entertainment? Which are a waste of time?
5. Am I truly critical of the programs that I listen to?
6. Which is my favorite program? Why do I like it best?

2. As a result of the individual surveys, plan to have a group discussion of the following questions. Each person should have an opportunity to express his opinion.

1. Should you limit the amount of time you spend on radio and TV? How?
2. Should leisure time be budgeted so that an equal amount of time is devoted to reading, hobbies, exercise, visiting with friends, radio, and TV?
3. Should the radio be turned on while you are reading or studying?

3. As a class, attempt to set up some standards by which radio and TV programs may be judged. In your discussion, consider these points:

PURPOSE: Is the program really worth while? If it is, what makes it so?

UNITY: Does the program hang together or are there some parts that seem needless?

ACTORS: Do the actors do a good job? If they are comedians, are they really funny? Do the actors speak their lines clearly and vividly? Do they seem real to you? Are there several different styles of acting that appeal to you? Explain your answer by giving examples.

It may help you in making decisions on these three points to choose a program that many or all of you consider the best of its kind. Then compare other programs of the same kind with it.

Exercise: Choosing radio and TV programs

Make a list of recommended radio and TV programs in each of the three categories: cultural (such as music, book reviews), educational, amusement. Try to make your decisions on the basis of the standards the class agreed upon. Compare your lists in class.

TO MEMORIZE

FROM *The Vision of Sir Launfal*

And what is so rare as a day in June?
    Then, if ever, come perfect days;
Then Heaven tries earth if it be in tune,
    And over it softly her warm ear lays;
Whether we look or whether we listen,
We hear life murmur or see it glisten.

JAMES RUSSELL LOWELL

You have memorized poems written by Robert Frost, Emily Dickinson, and Ralph Waldo Emerson. Here is another famous New England poet, James Russell Lowell. The lines above are taken from a long, romantic narrative poem about a young knight's search for the Holy Grail. He finally found the Grail—it turned out to be the cup he shared with a beggar. These lines from the poem are favorites.

Improving Your Listening in Class

If you have done the exercises in the earlier part of this chapter carefully and thoughtfully, you probably now understand why some people are poor listeners and why some things are difficult to listen to. Consider the following suggestions for developing good listening habits in one important situation in which all students find themselves: the classroom.

Guides for listening in the classroom

1. Come to class *ready to listen.* Sit where you can see and hear.
2. *Be comfortable* but alert; do not slouch or fidget. *Look at the speaker.*
3. *Clear your mind* of distracting thoughts. Make a conscious effort to forget the hobby you cannot wait to get back to or the friend you hope to see between periods.
4. *Listen actively.* This means to have a pencil in hand and your notebook open so that you can note down anything especially important. Take notes.
5. *Listen for special signals* that something is important. For example, never be caught napping when the teacher says, "Make a note of this"; or "There may be a test on this"; or "Here are three (or any number) points"; or "Look this up."
6. *Ask questions* if you are puzzled (but be sure not to interrupt unless the teacher has made clear that interruptions are acceptable).
7. *Try to remember what you have heard.* Right after class, or during a pause, restate briefly in your mind what was said. Look at your notes. If you can, *use* the material you have heard or tell somebody about it. All of these suggestions will help to implant the material in your mind.

Exercise: Judging yourself

Think back over the past five classes you have attended and rate yourself on the seven suggestions just given. Use the following system: 5: perfect; 4: very good; 3: good; 2: fair; 1: poor. A total score of 22 to 28 on the seven suggestions would be very good. Keep your rating, and rate yourself again a week from now, after you have thought about the suggestions and tried to apply them.

Listening Courtesy

Courteous listening brings out the best in those to whom you are listening. This is true whether you are involved in individual or group conversations or as part of a large audience.

Listening in conversations

Everyone knows that some people are much more fun to talk with than others. Haven't you found that there are some teachers, friends, and parents of friends to whom you just feel like talking, while there are others who make you feel that you are dull and uninteresting or that you have nothing to say? Can you explain why this is so?

Don't you enjoy talking to the person who is *truly interested* in what you have to say and *shows* it? To make yourself a good conversationalist, one of the easiest things to do is to be a *creative listener*. This means you must show that you are interested in what is being said. You cannot just sit back and be quiet. On the other hand, a creative listener does not constantly interrupt or wait breathlessly for a pause so that he can say what is on *his* mind.

Guides for listening in conversation

1. Look at the speaker with an interested expression.
2. Do not fiddle with keys, a pencil, a book, or other objects.
3. Indicate interest by nodding, frowning, or smiling at the right time so that the speaker knows that you are listening.
4. Make brief comments or ask brief questions from time to time. *Examples*: "Really?" "Amazing!" "I've often thought so myself." "Go ahead." "Then what happened?"

Of course, all of this can be quite artificial if it does not spring from a true interest in what the person is saying.

To discuss

Think about the four or five people you like most to talk with. Try to notice carefully the next time you see them what makes conversation with them such a pleasure. Make notes on your observations. Have a class discussion during which you compare notes on the good listeners you have observed.

Listening in an audience

The reaction of an audience is important to a performer or speaker. This is one reason why radio or TV studios often arrange for a studio audience. There are many times in school assemblies, at public meetings, or at the theater when you can contribute greatly to the success of the occasion (and thus, indirectly, to your own enjoyment) by your behavior as a member of the audience. Speakers who go around to various schools can tell the difference between a good audience and a dull and unresponsive one. A good audience can actually stimulate and help a speaker give his best.

To discuss

Think over the following questions about audience behavior. Then write down your answers and discuss them in class. As you answer these questions, keep in mind the underlying question: "How can I help the performer or speaker accomplish the purpose of the assembly or meeting successfully?"

1. Where should you look during a speech or performance?
2. What kind of expression should be on your face?
3. What should be the posture of your body?
4. What should you do with your hands and feet?
5. When should you laugh? when not?
6. When is it right to applaud? when not?
7. What should you do when the performance or speech is over?

Listening on the Telephone

A special situation where skillful and considerate listening is necessary occurs when you are using the telephone. Today most children learn to use the telephone at a very early age. Probably you have been quite expert at it for some time. To make sure that you are well informed, however, go over the directions given below:

Guides for using the telephone

1. To be thoughtful and courteous when receiving a call:
   a. Answer promptly.
   b. Identify yourself:
      "Hello, this is Becky Smith speaking"; or "Hello, this is Victor 8–3238."
   c. If the call is for someone else, call the person promptly, but do not shout into the receiver.
   d. If the person is not in, offer to take a message. Write down the message.
2. To be thoughtful and courteous when placing a call:
   a. Identify yourself as soon as the person answers, as: "This is George Beck speaking."
   b. Courteously request the person to whom you wish to speak: "May I please speak to John?"
   c. If the person is not in, politely give your message to the person answering, as: "Would you mind asking John to call when he comes in?" or "May I leave a message for Jack, please?"
3. Never talk at great length. Others may need the phone or wish to call you or the party you are calling.
4. Business calls should be brief and courteous and cover all details accurately. Example:

   OFFICE SECRETARY: Dr. Adler's office.

   MAUD: This is Maud Muller. Could you give me an appointment with Dr. Adler, please?

   OFFICE SECRETARY: Can you come on Thursday at four?

   MAUD: That would be fine. I'll note it down. Thursday, January 15th, at four. Thank you very much. Good-by.

   OFFICE SECRETARY: Doctor will expect you then.

You have to listen with special care on the telephone. You have only the speaker's voice to give you his meaning. There is no facial expression; there are no gestures. You must also remember that the speaker has no way of knowing you are listening unless you give an occasional clue, such as "Yes," "Really?" or "How interesting!"

If you are speaking, it is well not to speak very long without a pause to be sure that your listener is with you. You can check now and then by some question like "Do you understand?" or "Do you see what I mean?" or "Am I making myself clear?"

Exercises: Using the telephone

1. Using your telephone directory, prepare a brief report to the class and give information on the four points listed below. If you can do so without inconveniencing your family, bring in a telephone directory to show where the information is found.

1. How to dial (or call) a number
2. How to place an emergency call (fire, police, etc.)
3. How to call long-distance
4. How to report telephone trouble

2. Prepare with a partner a brief social call and demonstrate it to the class. Ask for suggestions and criticisms afterwards. Here are some ideas for calls:

1. Invite a friend to a game or motion picture
2. Explain to your scout leader why you will be absent
3. Congratulate a friend who won an honor in school
4. Call a classmate's home to inquire how he is recovering from a recent illness
5. Call your mother to explain why you will be late for dinner

3. With a partner, prepare and demonstrate a brief business call. Make a call to:

A bus station to inquire the time and the price of a trip to a nearby town or city, naming the day and the time preferred, morning or afternoon

A dentist or doctor for an appointment

The public library to reserve a book

The newspaper to report nondelivery of your paper

The police station to report some kind of emergency

Listening to Poetry

Most poetry is made to be heard. It is very difficult to enjoy a poem fully unless you hear it read aloud or read it aloud yourself. Good poetry is usually vigorous, alive, and fresh. The thoughts expressed in a poem are often so concentrated that it cannot be read idly. Good poetry also requires a special kind of listening—a word-for-word listening that commands all of your attention. Do not expect to understand a poem completely the first time you hear it. In fact, one of the tests of a good poem is whether you like it better after several readings than after the first. One of the great pleasures in literature is to hear good poetry read aloud by a good reader.

Rhyme

With most poetry, the sounds at the ends of some of the lines of the poem are alike; that is, they **rhyme.** In poems that rhyme, there is usually a rhyme scheme or pattern which the poet has created. We have a special way of labeling the rhyme or rhyme scheme of a poem. The sound at the end of the first line of the poem is labeled *a*. The next line that rhymes with the first (if there is one that rhymes with it) is also labeled *a*. If the next line does not rhyme, it is labeled *b*.

A great humorous rhymster is Ogden Nash. It is a delight to hear how the lines of his poems rhyme so neatly. Read aloud the following verse:

The Centipede

I objurgate * the centipede,	a
A bug we do not really need.	a
At sleepy-time he beats a path	b
Straight to the bedroom or the bath.	b
You always wallop where he's not,	c
Or, if he is, he makes a spot.	c

Notice that the first end-of-line sound that does not rhyme with the first line is labeled *b*, and so forth through the poem.

Notice, also, the way in which Nash has used rhyme to emphasize the humor in his poem.

* objurgate: rebuke, scold.

In serious verse, rhyme increases the power and beauty of the words. Read aloud this poem:

The Eagle

He clasps the crag with crooked hands;
Close to the sun in lonely lands,
Ringed with the azure world, he stands.

The wrinkled sea beneath him crawls;
He watches from his mountain walls,
And like a thunderbolt he falls.

ALFRED, LORD TENNYSON

Exercises: Listening to rhyme and writing poetry

1. Listen carefully as someone in the class reads aloud Tennyson's "The Eagle." Do not look at the poem. As you listen, label the rhyme scheme for the poem.

2. Try to write two lines of poetry, making the first line rhyme with the second. Read some of these lines aloud in class.

Rhythm

Most poems, in addition to rhyme, have **rhythm.** This means that the syllables in the lines are arranged in a regular pattern, creating a beat somewhat like the beat in music. Here is a verse by Gelett Burgess, printed with some words and syllables underlined to show the rhythm. Read it aloud.

Felicia Ropps

Funny, how Felicia Ropps
Always handles things in shops!
Always pinching, always poking,
Always feeling, always stroking
Things she has no right to touch!
Goops like that annoy me much!

How many strong beats do you hear in each line? The pattern of beats in a line of poetry is called the **meter** of a poem.

Now, read the verse again, this time naturally, not emphasizing the meter. Notice that you hear the meter even when no special effort is made to bring it out. Meter, like rhyme, should not be specially emphasized in reading a poem. The rhythm in a poem should be allowed to come out naturally as you read for meaning.

Exercises: Listening to rhythm

1. Read again "The Centipede" and "The Eagle." Do you hear their rhythm?

2. Listen to the verses below as they are read aloud, noticing especially how the poet has used rhythm to get his effects. What natural motion is the author imitating with the sound of his words?

The Highwayman

The wind was a torrent of darkness among the gusty trees.
The moon was a ghostly galleon tossed upon cloudy seas.
The road was a ribbon of moonlight over the purple moor,
And the highwayman came riding—
  Riding—riding—
The highwayman came riding, up to the old inn door.

He'd a French cocked hat on his forehead, a bunch of lace at his chin,
A coat of the claret velvet, and breeches of brown doeskin;
They fitted with never a wrinkle; his boots were up to the thigh!
And he rode with a jeweled twinkle,
  His pistol butts a-twinkle,
His rapier hilt a-twinkle, under the jeweled sky.

ALFRED NOYES

(*Note:* These are only two verses of a long poem. You will enjoy looking up the poem and reading it all.)

Repetition

Poetry uses repetition. Rhyme is repetition of sound; rhythm is repetition of stress, a regular pattern of beats. You have already heard this in the poems you have listened to in this chapter.

Poets also make delightful use of repetition of sound at the beginning of words. This is called **alliteration.** One fine, ridiculous example of alliteration is this famous tongue-twister, which has been giving pleasure to listeners for generations:

Peter Piper

Peter Piper picked a peck of pickled peppers;
A peck of pickled peppers Peter Piper picked;
If Peter Piper picked a peck of pickled peppers,
Where's the peck of pickled peppers Peter Piper picked?

A more serious use of alliteration is found in William Rose Benét's "The Skater of Ghost Lake." Here are the first two verses. You will enjoy reading the complete poem.

The Skater of Ghost Lake

Ghost Lake's a dark lake, a deep lake and cold:
Ice black as ebony, frostily scrolled;
Far in its shadows a faint sound whirrs;
Steep stand the sentineled deep, dark firs.

A brisk sound, a swift sound, a ring-tinkle-ring;
Flit-flit—a shadow, with a stoop and a swing,
Flies from a shadow through the crackling cold.
Ghost Lake's a deep lake, a dark lake and old!

Exercises: Listening to poetry

1. Number your paper from 1 to 10. Have someone read aloud each item listed below. Listen carefully to each of the items. Then decide whether you think it is poetry. If you think it is, write *poetry* beside the appropriate numeral on your paper; if it is not, write *prose*. (Anything that is not poetry is prose.) If you are not sure, write a question mark. Be prepared to explain your opinion in each case. Keep in mind rhyme, rhythm, and alliteration.

1. Fee, faw, fum! bubble and squawk!
2. Alone, alone, all, all alone.
3. Please sit up straight and take out your notebooks.
4. But look, the morn in russet mantle clad
   Walks o'er the dew of yon high eastward hill.
5. See how the rising sun is making the dew sparkle on the hill to the east of us.
6. Listen to me, people of Rome, who are my friends and countrymen.
7. Friends, Romans, countrymen, lend me your ears.
8. Never have I been so embarrassed!
9. Roll on, thou deep and dark blue ocean. Roll!
10. "Celery, raw,
    Develops the jaw,
    But celery, stewed,
    Is more easily chewed."

Red Horse Hill

by Stephen W. Meader
Illustrated by Lee Townsend
Harcourt, Brace & World, Inc.

This is a story of Bud Martin, an orphan from the city, who goes to live on a farm in New Hampshire. On an old abandoned farm near his new home, Bud and his friend Cal find the will of Bud's grandfather in the ruins of the old house. They also find a half-starved boy who is watching over the horses stolen by his thieving master. Suddenly Bud finds himself, through his grandfather's will, the owner of the old farm. From then on, things really begin to happen. There is action on every page of the book. Who will win the thrilling show races? Bud's lightning-swift colt Cedar is stolen. Will they find him? Is the horse thief caught? In addition to all these fast-moving events, this book describes everyday life on a busy New England farm. Both boys and girls will enjoy this book.

About the author

As a boy, Stephen Meader himself swam, fished, hunted, skated, and went to school in New Hampshire. He knows all about life on the kind of farm he writes about. After college, he went into social work, a profession that serves the needs of people. Then he discovered he liked to write. Now writing is his hobby. He also likes to draw and to make canoe trips through the wilds of our country.

Test I

On your paper, write the letters that label the rhyme scheme in the following verses. The first verse is from "Daniel Boone" by Arthur Guiterman, and the second verse is from "The Deacon's Masterpiece" by Oliver Wendell Holmes.

1. Daniel Boone at twenty-one
   Came with his tomahawk, knife, and gun
   Home from the French and Indian War
   To North Carolina and the Yadkin shore.
   He married his maid with a golden band,
   Builded his house and cleared his land;
   But the deep woods claimed their son again
   And he turned his face from the homes of men.

2. Have you heard of the wonderful one-hoss shay,
   That was built in such a logical way
   It ran a hundred years to a day,
   And then, of a sudden, it—ah, but stay,
   I'll tell you what happened without delay,
   Scaring the parson into fits,
   Frightening people out of their wits—
   Have you ever heard of that, I say?

Test II

Copy the verses in Test I above and underline the syllables which are stressed. Remember, in the rhythm of a line the stressed syllables are those which have a heavy beat.

Test III

Following are lines quoted from various poems. Select and write down next to the appropriate numeral the words which are examples of alliteration.

1. "But ever he dreamed of new domains
   With vaster woods and wider plains."
2. "And his horse in the silence champed the grasses
   Of the forest's ferny floor."
3. "A line of black that bends and floats
   On the rising tide, like a bridge of boats."

Exercise I

1. Review pages 354–55.

2. On your paper, write the letters that label the rhyme scheme in these verses from "Casey at the Bat" by Ernest Lawrence Thayer.

> It looked extremely rocky for the Mudville nine that day;
> The score stood two to four, with but one inning left to play.
> So, when Cooney died at second, and Burrows did the same,
> A pallor wreathed the features of the patrons of the game.
>
> A straggling few got up to go, leaving there the rest
> With that hope which springs eternal within the human breast.
> For they thought: "If only Casey could get a whack at that,"
> They'd put even money now, with Casey at the bat.

Exercise II

1. Review page 355.

2. Copy the verses in Exercise I on your paper. Underline the stressed syllables—those syllables which have a heavy beat.

Exercise III

1. Review pages 354–58.

2. How does the following verse from "Casey at the Bat" use poetic forms of rhyme, rhythm, and repetition?

> Oh, somewhere in this favored land the sun is shining bright,
> The band is playing somewhere, and somewhere hearts are light;
> And somewhere men are laughing, and somewhere children shout,
> But there is no joy in Mudville—mighty Casey has struck out.

3. Only three of the following groups of words are poetry. Copy them on your paper. Then discuss your answers in class.

1. Wailing, wailing, wailing, the wind over land and sea.
2. Outside the wind sounds very loud.
3. I hated him with the hate of hell.
4. She disliked the handsome man intensely.
5. The water in the lake was almost black.
6. The reddening rippling water blushed like blood along their tracks.

CHAPTER 14

Reading

Do you waste hours of time reading the wrong way? Plan now to improve your reading. Once you learn to read efficiently, you will be prepared for all the reading you will do in the future. You will read more quickly, with more understanding, and with more pleasure whether you are reading for school work or for yourself.

Reading for Pleasure and Appreciation

Persons who enjoy reading may read with no special purpose in mind except enjoyment and relaxation. Read the following passage. It illustrates this type of reading, which can usually be done rapidly, with no strain or conscious effort involved.

Passage 1

I remember that every Saturday night Mama would sit down by the scrubbed kitchen table and with much wrinkling of usually placid brows count out the money Papa had brought home in the little envelope.

There would be various stacks.

"For the landlord," Mama would say, piling up the big silver pieces.

"For the grocer." Another group of coins.

"For Katrin's shoes to be half-soled." And Mama would count out the little silver.

"Teacher says this week I'll need a notebook." That would be Christine or Nels or I.

Mama would solemnly detach a nickel or a dime and set it aside.

We would watch the diminishing pile with breathless interest.

At last, Papa would ask, "Is all?"

And when Mama nodded, we could relax a little and reach for schoolbooks and homework. For Mama would look up then and smile. "Is good," she'd murmur. "We do not have to go to the bank."

from *Mama's Bank Account*, by Kathryn Forbes

Reading for pleasure has value over and above pure enjoyment. You pick up vocabulary, information, and ideas. You live through experiences as though they were actually happening to you, whereas they are really happening to someone else. Your life is enriched and your understanding of people deepened.

In reading for pleasure alone, you will read as you feel like reading: rapidly or slowly, carelessly or carefully. However, you can increase your appreciation and therefore your enjoyment of a book by observing a number of things about it.

It is interesting to notice how different writers select words and put them together. Some authors have a smooth, flowing style; others, a quick, snappy style. Some styles make you feel calm and relaxed; others give you a feeling of excitement, eagerness, and suspense.

Reread Passage 1 on page 363 and then read the following three passages from well-known authors. Read them to note especially each author's style. To get the full flavor of the style, you may find that reading the passage aloud helps. Be prepared to discuss the author's style later by comparing each passage with the brief descriptions of style on the next page.

Passage 2

Slasher, or any experienced wolf or fox, would have smelled the man coming and slunk out ahead of him without being seen. An inexperienced beast might have waited until Jake was very near, then broken, run, and offered Jake a good shot. But Sean had stayed right where he was, never moving at all. None knew better than he that men had great and mysterious powers at their command; what besides man could reach out and injure a thing that he could not personally touch? But when it came to woodcraft, the keenest man could not compare to the dullest wild creature.

from *Outlaw Red*, by Jim Kjelgaard

Passage 3

At daybreak Billy Buck emerged from the bunkhouse and stood for a moment on the porch looking up at the sky. He was a broad, bandy-legged little man with a walrus mustache, with square hands, puffed and muscled on the palms. His eyes were a contemplative, watery gray and the hair which protruded from under his Stetson hat was spiky and weathered. Billy was still stuffing his shirt into his blue jeans as he stood on the porch. He unbuckled his belt and tightened it again. The belt showed, by the worn, shiny places opposite each hole, the gradual increase of Billy's middle over a period of years. When he had seen to the weather, Billy cleared each nostril by holding its mate closed with his forefinger and blowing fiercely. Then he walked down to the barn, rubbing his hands together.

from The Red Pony, by John Steinbeck

Passage 4

The boys still listened and watched. Presently a revealing thought flashed through Tom's mind, and he exclaimed:

"Boys, I know who's drowned—it's us!"

They felt like heroes in an instant. Here was a gorgeous triumph; they were missed; they were mourned; hearts were breaking on their account; tears were being shed; accusing memories of unkindnesses to those poor lost lads were rising up, and unavailing regrets and remorse were being indulged; and best of all, the departed were the talk of the whole town, and the envy of all the boys, as far as this dazzling notoriety was concerned. This was fine. It was worth while to be a pirate, after all.

from The Adventures of Tom Sawyer, by Mark Twain

To discuss

Compare the descriptions of style below with the passages you have just read. Tell which passage each one describes. Point out the reasons for your choice.

1. The author uses much detailed description of small things and small actions. The words chosen tell a great deal about the character described. The sentences are rather long and complicated.

2. The author uses exaggeration and uncommon words to be humorous. One sentence is a long series of half-humorous emotional statements, and it is followed by two short, plain sentences such as boys might use. The style has great variety.

3. The style is easy, lively, and smooth. The author talks directly to the reader, using short sentences and dialogue natural to the characters.

4. The author uses long sentences which have a rolling rhythm. The writing gives the reader a feeling of the excitement and mystery of nature.

The plot

When we read a good story, we are usually carried along by the events and give little thought to how the story is put together. And yet in most novels those events are used by the author to create a definite plan or plot. It is interesting to observe how the author works out the story. The plot often has to do with the facing and solving of some kind of problem, for example:

1. Trying to solve a mystery
2. Trying to meet a physical challenge like a storm or a mountain
3. Trying to escape from danger
4. Trying to defeat an enemy
5. Achieving an ambition
6. Trying to win the love of another person

Usually the plot will involve a number of smaller problems within a larger one.

To discuss

Discuss some well-known books and stories in class. As a group, decide whether the main plot of a story can be described by one of the problems stated above. Give specific reasons for your choice.

Exercise: Telling plots

In a paragraph or two, write the plot of a book you have read and enjoyed. Tell only the bare bones of the story.

While the plots of the various stories are being read (or told) in class, write down the authors and titles of any that you think you might be interested in reading.

The characters

It will add to your enjoyment of a book to observe how the author describes the characters, especially the principal ones whom you get to know very well. If they are true to life, they will have both strengths and weaknesses, which you will understand as you see the characters meeting the various situations in the story. For instance, Jim Hawkins, the hero of *Treasure Island*, a book you will certainly want to read if you have not already done so, is honest, as you observe when he refuses to break his word and flee to safety from his enemy, Long John Silver. He is respectful, as you observe

in the loving way he cares for his mother and the quick way he obeys Dr. Livesey. But he is rash and thoughtless, as shown when he goes ashore with the pirates without telling anyone or cuts loose the ship from its moorings. He becomes easily overconfident, as shown when he manages to kill Israel Hands and then walks right into the hands of the pirates.

How a character *acts* and how he *changes* as the story develops are much more interesting than a mere description of his appearance. By noticing the characters and trying to identify yourself with them, you will experience much pleasure.

To discuss

Choose one character from a well-known book which most class members have read. Discuss these questions about each character:

1. What are two or three of his principal traits?
2. How are these traits brought out by the events in the story?
3. Does the character change during the story? If he does, how does he change?
4. Does the character seem true to life?
5. Is he a likable character? Did you care about what happened to him as you read the book?

GOING AHEAD

Survey the reading tastes of your English class and make a list of recommended books for your classmates. Post the list on the bulletin board. It would be useful to write beside the author and title of each book the name of the pupil who recommends it. Then your classmates may ask for more information about a book they think they might want to read.

How to Read Poetry

Good poetry is carefully created. Each word is chosen by the poet to give just the feeling, meaning, sound, and rhythm that he wants. In order to be appreciated, or even sometimes to have its simplest meaning understood, good poetry must be read with great care. Every word must be appreciated by the mind and by the ear. That is why poems should be read aloud.

Read the poem "Steam Shovel" aloud to yourself:

Steam Shovel

The dinosaurs are not all dead.
I saw one raise its iron head
To watch me walking down the road
Beyond our house today.
Its jaws were dripping with a load
Of earth and grass that it had cropped.
It must have heard me where I stopped,
Snorted white steam my way,
And stretched its long neck out to see,
And chewed, and grinned quite amiably.

CHARLES MALAM

How well did you read the poem above? Did you read it for meaning? Or did you read it in singsong fashion?

In many poems, there is a rather even beat, or meter, in each line. It is easy to place too much emphasis on these heavier beats and to emphasize the words that rhyme. Do not allow an even beat to distort the sense of the words or your reading will become singsong like this:

Its *jaws* were *dripping with* a *load* (pause)
Of *earth* and *grass* that *it* had *cropped.*

When you read, also keep in mind that poetry is written in sentences. The end of a line of poetry is not the end of a sentence unless there is an end punctuation mark—a period, a question mark, or an exclamation point. When you come to the end of a line that has no end punctuation, keep your voice up. Do not pause, or the listeners will think a sentence has ended. Lines 5 and 6 of "Steam Shovel," for example, must be read in a way that will show that they are one sentence. The phrase "load of earth and grass" should be read as one phrase, even though there is a break in the line.

To discuss

Examine the poem "Steam Shovel" and answer these questions about it:

1. How many sentences are there in the poem?
2. How many lines are there with no punctuation at the end, so that the sense of the poem requires carrying the meaning over from one line to the next?
3. How many lines are there in the second sentence? Try reading those lines as one sentence, as if they were written in prose and not poetry.

Guides to reading poetry

1. Read a poem for the meaning; then the rhythm and rhyme will take care of themselves.
2. Pay attention to the punctuation of a poem.

Exercises: Reading poetry

1. Reread "Steam Shovel" aloud. Put variety and expression into your voice.

2. Look for poems in books of poetry. Find a poem that you would enjoy reading to the class. First, practice reading it aloud.

Similes and metaphors

The language of poetry is full of vivid comparisons. Instead of saying "very black ice," one poet, for example, said "Ice black as ebony." The poet William Rose Benét was comparing the blackness of the ice to the blackness of ebony wood.

Read the four familiar expressions below. They show one way in which comparisons are commonly made.

1. He is as quick as lightning.
2. He is as sly as a fox.
3. She is as big as a house.
4. His mind is like an open book.

Notice that the words *as* and *like* are used in the comparisons above. A comparison which contains the word *as* or *like* is called a **simile.**

In each simile above, what is being compared to what? Can you think of other familiar similes?

Now read these sentences:

1. The waves trampled the rocks.
2. My room is a prison.
3. Cars travel in packs along the highway.

These three sentences show another way in which comparisons are made. They are called **metaphors.** Compare them with the similes on page 369. What major difference do you notice between a simile and a metaphor?

A metaphor is a comparison of one thing to another without the use of the word *as* or *like*.

Read the following poem aloud. Notice that the poem does not have a regular rhyme and meter. Such poems are called **free verse.**

Fog

The fog comes
on little cat feet.

It sits looking
over harbor and city
on silent haunches
and then moves on.

CARL SANDBURG

To discuss

1. Study the comparison you find in "Fog" on page 370. Discuss why the comparison is a good one. Is it a simile or a metaphor?

2. Look again at the poem "Steam Shovel" on page 368 and discuss these questions:

1. The entire poem is a comparison. What does the poet see when he looks at a steam shovel? Is the comparison a simile or a metaphor?

2. In some words and phrases, the poet makes a comparison by describing the *appearance* of the steam shovel. Can you find some examples?

3. At other times, the poet makes a comparison by describing the *actions* of the steam shovel. Which parts show this? Read them aloud.

3. In class, discuss the comparison expressed in each of the following bits from poems. The title of the poem from which the lines are taken may help you. In each comparison, what is compared to what? Is the comparison a simile or a metaphor?

1. "In the morning the city
   Spreads its wings . . ."
   from "City," by Langston Hughes

2. "Moan like an autumn wind . . . "
   from "Jazz Fantasia," by Carl Sandburg

3. "His hands are gentle with beast or child
   And strong as hardwood timber."
   from "Father," by Frances Frost

4. "Like an army defeated
   The snow hath retreated . . ."
   from "Written in March," by William Wordsworth

5. "He had a broad face and a little round belly
   That shook when he laughed like a bowlful of jelly."
   from "A Visit from Saint Nicholas,"
   by Clement Clarke Moore

■ **A simile** is a comparison of one thing to another and uses the word *as* or *like*.

■ **A metaphor** is a comparison without the use of *as* or *like*.

Read the following poem aloud once. Then study it to see how many metaphors you can find in it. After you have identified all the metaphors, read the poem aloud again and see how much more you enjoy it because you have studied it carefully.

Spring Cricket

He put away his tiny pipe
Last autumn, when the gale was chill;
And now in rusty coat and brown
He tries his strength upon the hill.

With fiddle tucked beneath a wing,
He staggers over a stubbled ground;
He climbs upon a sunny stone,
Shakes winter off, and looks around.

He polishes his dingy coat
And scrapes a valiant tune and high
To tell his tiny universe
That April's due to saunter by.

FRANCES RODMAN

TO MEMORIZE

Essential Delight

This life I've loved so dearly
  And grudgingly must leave—
Not for its pleasure merely
Do I grieve.
Not causes—joined, forsaken;
Nor loves—pledged or forsworn.
Only for roads untaken
Do I mourn.

GUSTAV DAVIDSON

What regrets does the speaker have in the poem above?

Notice that here again, as in Frost's poem on page 28, we find *roads* used as a symbol. Compare "The Road Not Taken" with this poem. How are they similar? In which poem has the speaker come toward the end of his travels? In which poem is the speaker still traveling the road of his choice? Which lines gave you the answers?

Choral Reading

Certain poems are enjoyable when read aloud by a group. Reading a poem with others is called **choral reading.**

Poems that have strong rhythm are especially good for choral reading. Those poems that tell a story or are humorous are also good. Whatever poems your group chooses to read to an audience, be prepared to read them with understanding and appreciation. Be sure that you pronounce all words correctly and that you articulate distinctly so that the audience can understand every word of the poem.

Mood and tone of voice

Different poems express quite different moods or feelings. Read the poem "The Wolf Cry" and be prepared to discuss the mood.

The Wolf Cry

The Arctic moon hangs overhead;
The wide white silence lies below.
A starveling pine stands lone and gaunt,
Black-penciled on the snow.

Weird as the moan of sobbing winds,
A lone long call floats up from the trail;
And the naked soul of the frozen North
Trembles in that wail.

LEW SARETT

To discuss

1. Is "The Wolf Cry" a gay, dancing, sprightly verse?
2. How would you describe the mood of the poem?
3. Do the words *cold, lonely,* and *sad* help to describe the mood?
4. Certain words in the poem have long vowel sounds which help bring out its mood. Which words are they? How can you use your voice to express the mood? Show the class by reading a few lines aloud.

Marking the poem

Your preparation for choral speaking should include *marking the poem.* Copy the poem and underline the words to be emphasized. Note in the margin the feelings that are to be expressed. Your group should decide how you will speak the lines. Lines to be spoken in unison (all together) should be marked *All.* Those to be spoken by boys should be marked *BC*, for boys' chorus; those for girls should be marked *GC*. If your poem seems to require three groups, mark the lines *Group 1, Group 2,* and *Group 3.* Some lines may be spoken as solo parts.

Exercises: Choral reading

1. Prepare the poem "The Wolf Cry" for choral reading. As you read it aloud, try to bring out its mood and feeling.

2. Prepare for choral reading and read aloud the poem below. In class, discuss the ideas in the poem before you present it to an audience.

What Do We Plant?

What do we plant when we plant the tree?
We plant the ship which will cross the sea.
We plant the mast to carry the sails;
We plant the planks to withstand the gales—
The keel, the keelson, the beam, the knee;
We plant the ship when we plant the tree.

What do we plant when we plant the tree?
We plant the houses for you and me.
We plant the rafters, the shingles, the floors,
We plant the studding, the lath, the doors,
The beams and siding, all parts that be;
We plant the house when we plant the tree.

What do we plant when we plant the tree?
A thousand things that we daily see;
We plant the spire that out-towers the crag,
We plant the staff for our country's flag,
We plant the shade, from the hot sun free;
We plant all these when we plant the tree.

HENRY ABBEY

Reading for Mastery

A type of reading quite different from that which we have been discussing is **reading for mastery**, which is reading for mastery of content. This is the sort of reading you do for the typical school assignment, say in science or English (except for literature).

Unfortunately, most students, when assigned a chapter to master, merely settle down and read it once or twice. This is a wasteful and inefficient way to study a chapter. Examine the following method. It can save you time and increase your learning.

Step 1: Know the purpose of the assignment before you start. What are you supposed to get out of it? How does it fit in with what you have already studied? If you do not know, ask questions.

Step 2: Examine the book in which the chapter is found. First, look at the *table of contents* (at the front) to see how the chapter fits into the book as a whole. It is important to know what comes before and what follows the chapter you are reading.

Step 3: Pre-read the chapter. This means that you should go over the chapter quickly to get a general idea of what it is about. Pre-reading involves:

a. Reading the title
b. Reading each heading as you come to it
c. Reading the first and last sentence of each paragraph
d. Glancing at the writing (called *captions*) under the pictures, charts, and graphs
e. Reading over any study questions at the end

Step 4: Read the chapter closely. Follow these suggestions:

a. Read it carefully.
b. At the end of each paragraph, stop to see if you can recall what you have just read. If you cannot, reread the paragraph.
c. Do the same at the end of each main section, if the chapter is organized into sections.
d. Notice carefully all *headings, italics, boldface words*, and *numbered items*. Also note pictures, charts, and their captions. They are probably put there by the author to emphasize or explain important ideas.
e. If there are words you do not know, look them up in a dictionary.

Step 5: When you have finished, think about the material you have just read. Try to *recall* all that you can. Reread any sections you are not sure of. See if you can answer any questions listed at the end of the chapter. If you cannot, look back and find the answers.

Step 6: On a sheet of paper, *write any questions* you have about the material. Ask these questions in class as soon as you are given an opportunity.

Step 7: When you discuss the chapter in class, have your pencil poised to *take notes* on any points the teacher explains or emphasizes.

Step 8: When reviewing a chapter later for a test, *do not read the chapter again.* Rather, read your class notes. Also read the headings and topic sentences to help you recall the chapter. Read again only the parts of the chapter which you do not remember.

To discuss

The next time you are assigned a chapter to master, study it *exactly* according to the plan just described. After the assignment, discuss in class whether you thought the method worked well.

Skimming

Still another type of reading is **skimming.** It is a great time-saver, if you do it for the right purposes. Skimming somewhat resembles pre-reading as described in Step 3 in "Reading for Mastery" on page 375. It is used mainly to grasp main topics quickly, to find a particular fact or piece of information, or to find the part or parts of a long article or chapter that are related to your topic of study. To skim, let your eyes run very quickly down the page. Glance at topic sentences and key words and phrases which give an idea of what the author is discussing.

Finding main topics

Very often the table of contents will tell you all you need to know about the main topics in a chapter. If it does not, turn to the pages you are interested in and glance quickly at the first and last sentences of each paragraph, plus any headings or captions. It may help to read carefully the first and last paragraph of the chapter.

Locating a fact

When you need to know a date, a name, or some other bit of information, you can skim quickly through several paragraphs to find the fact you want. For example, if you need to find out when and where Thomas Jefferson was born, you might first turn to the back of the book to the alphabetical list of all the topics in the book called the **index.** In the index, under the name *Jefferson, Thomas,* you might find a reference such as, *Early days, 37–38.* Turn to pages 37 and 38 and look rapidly through them to spot a date or place name. Do not read every word. Of course, you must read closely the sentence containing the information you are seeking.

Finding part of an article

Sometimes you need to skim through a long article or chapter to find the part of it that is related to your study. In this case you look for topic sentences and use them as guides. Suppose you wish to study the natural resources of California. In the encyclopedia you find an article on California. You skim through the article, passing over paragraphs that begin in this way:

"The climate of California is . . ."
"The scenery of California is unrivaled for beauty and . . ."

Then you come to a paragraph that begins:

"Under the soil of California there lie great riches."

This is what you are looking for. You read this paragraph closely, and perhaps the several that follow it. Skimming has served its purpose in helping you to locate information. Then you change to study-type reading—reading for mastery.

Exercises: Skimming

1. Skim "How Your Language Grew," the introduction of this book, until you find where it begins to discuss the "bow-wow" theory. On your paper, write the page and line number of the beginning of the discussion. Do the same for the chart called "Indo-European Languages."

2. Turn to the Review Handbook at the back. By skimming, find the punctuation rule which deals with the use of a comma to separate words in a series. Write the page and line number.

Proofreading

Proofreading is a special skill which you should learn. It means reading something to find and correct all mistakes. Publishers employ experts called proofreaders who have this special skill in detecting errors. Proofreaders try to find and correct any errors in a book in each stage of the publishing procedure.

Make a habit of proofreading your papers before you hand them in. Here are the types of errors you would look for in proofreading:

1. punctuation
2. capitalization
3. spelling
4. handwriting
5. sentence fragments
6. run-on sentences
7. usage

In proofreading, you will find that the Review Handbook at the back of this textbook can be a great help.

Guides for proofreading

1. If you can, let some time elapse after you have finished writing before you proofread.
2. Pretend you are a stranger who has never seen your paper and be tough on it!
3. Read your paper aloud at least once to bring out some errors that you may have overlooked in silent reading.
4. Have a dictionary at hand to check spelling and capitalization.
5. If you find many errors in your paper, you should copy it over. If you do, proofread the new copy.

Exercise: Proofreading

Proofread the following passage. There are fifteen changes that must be made. Indicate how you would correct the paper by writing the corrections on a separate piece of paper. Put each correction beside the numeral of the line. Some of the lines contain more than one error; others contain no errors.

EXAMPLE:
1. Johns father was not afraid of
2. dogs. Until he met Fido. That changed

YOU WRITE:
1. *John's* (One change was made.)
2. *dogs until* (Two changes were made.)

1   Whenever Johns mother goes threw his pockets, she finds
2   a surprising collection of things. Yesterday she says, "John
3   please be sure to empty out your pockets. Before I put your
4   pants in the laundry.
5   "All right, mother" said John.
6   Later, when his mother picked up the pants, they felt
7   very heavy she knew their was something in the pockets.
8   When she finished her search, she couldnt believe her eyes.
9   His pockets contained the following items: 1 rock, 2 paper
10   clips, 1 small book entitled *fury*, 4 hard candies, 1 empty
11   match box, 13 foreign coins and 1 lizard in a plastic box.

Word-for-Word Reading

When you have a mathematics problem to read or some complicated directions, you need to shift your reading into low gear and
move slowly. When each word is essential to a sentence packed
with meaning, you cannot afford to miss a single one. It is just as
foolish to tackle this kind of reading rapidly as it is to read a fast-
moving story word for word.

Directions must be read slowly, word for word. Do not jump to
conclusions, but always read through carefully to the end.

Exercise: Reading directions

Follow these directions, using a pencil and a piece of paper:

If *school* has five letters in it, draw a capital K about ¾″ high in
the center of your paper. If it has more than five letters, place
the K near the bottom left-hand corner of the paper. Just
above the K, place two capital O's, one above the other, unless
7 is 4 more than 4, in which case place the O's side by side to
the right of the K. If spinach is a vegetable, write a capital
I, the same height as the K, near the left-hand edge of the
paper, halfway between the top and bottom of the paper.
However, if automobiles are made entirely of rubber, use a
capital U instead of the I. Now, if ¼ is less than twice as large
as ⅛, write a capital H directly above the second O you wrote.
If it is not, and if pine trees are sometimes used at Christmas,
write an L instead. Lastly, if you are under twenty years of
age, say in a loud voice, "Young." Look on page 380 for the
answer.

The Parts of a Book

You will read books much more intelligently if you know what the various parts of a book are and how they can serve you.

The **table of contents** tells you how the book is organized, what the main divisions are, and what the chapter titles are.

At the back of most books, there is an **index.** The index is an alphabetical list of all the topics discussed in the book. If you want to know whether the book treats a comparatively small subject like *nouns of direct address,* the index will tell you. You might look up the subject under *nouns* or under *direct address*, or perhaps it would be listed under both entries. Look in the index of this book. How many pages are devoted to the subject?

To discuss

1. Find the table of contents of this book and use it to answer the following questions in class:

1. How many chapters are there in the book?
2. Is there a chapter devoted to the subject of speaking?
3. About what proportion of the book is devoted to the study of grammar? Explain your answer.
4. How many pages are devoted to the subject of speech?

2. Use the index of this book to answer these questions in class:

1. On what pages does the book treat these subjects: appositives, prefixes, the *ie—ei* spelling rule, *teach—learn*, exclamatory sentences, and pronouns?
2. Which of the following authors are represented in the book: Robert Louis Stevenson, Ralph Waldo Emerson, MacKinlay Kantor, Louisa May Alcott, Edgar Allan Poe, Robert Frost, Mark Twain, Charles Nordhoff, and Arthur Conan Doyle? Look under *Books.*

3. Which would be the better place to find the answers to the following questions—the table of contents or the index? Be prepared to explain your answers.

1. On which page is there a poem by Carl Sandburg?
2. Does the book contain a handbook?
3. Does the book tell about suffixes?
4. Does the book contain a chapter on letter writing?
5. Does the book give instructions on note-taking?
6. About how long are the chapters in the book?

There are other features of various books which may be useful. Look over a few of your textbooks to find some of the following parts of a book. You may not find all of the parts in one book.

1. *The title page*
   Gives title, names of authors, place of publication, publisher.
2. *The copyright page*
   Usually on the page following the title page; gives the year or years of publication, called the copyright date.
3. *The foreword*
   Here the author speaks directly to the reader about the book and acknowledges any help he may have received.
4. *List of illustrations*
5. *List of maps and tables*
6. *Bibliography*
   A list of books which give more information about the subject.
7. *Glossary*
   A list of technical or difficult words with their definitions which will help the reader understand the text. The words are arranged in alphabetical order.

To discuss

1. In a class discussion, show and compare the various parts of a book which you have found in your textbooks.

2. In a class discussion, answer these questions about this book:

1. When was the book first published?
2. What is the latest date of publication?
3. Where was the book published?
4. What are the names of the authors?

North Town
by Lorenz Graham
Thomas Y. Crowell

David Williams, a young Negro boy who had recently moved into New England from the South, had high hopes as he began school in North Town. But he was also worried about how he would be received and how he should behave, for this was the first school he had ever attended that enrolled both white and black students. There were some disappointments, true, but David managed to feel that he was adjusting little by little. And then two events changed his life. The first was an unexpected encounter with the law, and the second was a catastrophe in his family.

This honest, realistic, gripping story brings alive for the reader the struggles of an ambitious young boy faced with more than the usual odds against success.

About the author

Lorenz Graham, now the father of five children, was born in New Orleans, was educated in Washington state, and has traveled and taught in Africa. He has worked as an education officer in the Civilian Conservation Corps and as a probation officer in Los Angeles. His earlier book, *South Town,* which you also may want to read, received the Follett Award and the Child Study Award. In addition, Mr. Graham received a special citation from the Thomas Alva Edison Foundation for his adaptation of *The Ten Commandments.*

Test I

Here are four brief descriptions of authors' styles:

    A. Short sentences, natural dialogue
    B. Humorous exaggeration
    C. Detailed description of small things
    D. Long sentences, rolling rhythm

Match each quotation below with the letter of the style which fits it best. On your paper, write the letters next to the appropriate numerals.

    1. ". . . None knew better than he that men had great and mysterious powers at their command; what besides man could reach out and injure a thing that he could not personally touch? But when it came to woodcraft, the keenest man could not compare to the dullest wild creature."

    2. ". . . Here was a gorgeous triumph; they were missed; they were mourned; hearts were breaking on their account; tears were being shed. . . ."

    3. ". . . He unbuckled his belt and tightened it again. The belt showed, by the worn, shiny places opposite each hole, the gradual increase of Billy's middle over a period of years. . . ."

    4. ". . . 'For the landlord,' Mama would say, piling up the big silver pieces.

    " 'For the grocer.' Another group of coins.

    " 'For Katrin's shoes to be half-soled.' . . ."

Test II

    1. Write two headings on your paper: *Similes* and *Metaphors.* Copy each of the following items under the proper heading:

    1. Celia's face is as pale as new snow.
    2. Her words were drops of honey falling upon our ears.
    3. The kites are like floating bits of confetti in the sky.
    4. Tomorrow will be born at sunrise.
    5. The tree bowed gracefully to the wind.

    2. Write the things that are being compared in each statement above.

Test III

Copy the following paragraph on your paper, proofreading it and correcting any fragments and run-ons and mistakes in punctuation, capitalization, usage, and spelling.

Central Junior High staggered to a terrible defeat. At the hands of it's worst rivals on friday. The basketball team couldnt overcome the feirce Park St team. Even the principle admitted, "Your right today was not one of our best days.

Test IV

Below are various items that might be found in a book about snails. Next to the appropriate numeral on your paper, write the part of a book that would help you best to locate the item.

Index	Foreword
Glossary	Bibliography
Copyright page	List of maps, illustrations,
Table of contents	and tables
Title page	

1. Title of another book about snails
2. The author's comments to the reader about the book
3. The chapters about snails' habitat and their eating habits
4. The life span of a certain type of snail
5. A map showing where edible snails are found
6. A definition of the word "escargots" (French word for *snails*)
7. Whether the book has more than one author
8. A picture of the largest snail known to man
9. The year the book was published
10. The number of pages in the chapter "Cooking Snails"

Test V

Below are examples of things you might read. After each numeral on your paper, write the appropriate type of reading you should do for each one: *rapid, relaxed reading; skimming; reading to master facts; word-for-word reading;* or *proofreading.*

1. Newspaper, for time and location of play you want to see
2. Novel, for pleasure
3. Article you have just written for the school newspaper
4. Assignment in your science book
5. Math problem in your homework

Review and Practice

Exercise I

1. Review "Reading for Pleasure and Appreciation," pages 363–67.

2. Define *plot* in one or two sentences. Tell briefly the plot of a book or story you have read recently.

3. Imagine you are going to write a story which has as its main characters an old man and his teen-age grandson. List the qualities each one will have in the story. Be as specific as you can.

Exercise II

1. Review "How to Read Poetry" on pages 368–71.

2. Define the terms *simile* and *metaphor*. Find two examples of each in poems and copy them on your paper.

3. Write two *similes* and two *metaphors* of your own.

Exercise III

1. Reread the section "Proofreading" on page 378.

2. Copy the paragraph below, correcting any mistakes in fragments, run-ons, punctuation, capitalization, usage, and spelling.

> For a short time in the third quarter, it appearred that Central might gain the lead. Bobby Roberts had tossed in three baskets in a row he was put out of the game on foul's. The Central spectators was reprimanded. By the referee, who became quiet angry with the girls screeches and Bobbys behavior. All in all, it was a very bad day for central Junior High.

Exercise IV

1. Review "The Parts of a Book" on pages 380–81.

2. In your own words, tell the kind of information you will find in each of the following parts of a book: *Copyright page*; *title page*; *table of contents*; *index*; *glossary*.

Exercise V

1. Review pages 363–67 and 375–79.

2. List one or more types of reading matter for which you would use each of the following ways of reading:

1. Rapid, relaxed reading
2. Skimming
3. Mastering facts
4. Word-for-word reading
5. Proofreading

CHAPTER 15

Making Sentence Diagrams

(Optional)

This chapter teaches you how to make diagrams, or pictures, of English sentences. Because diagrams show the relationship of words and word groups in sentences, they can be an extra help in your understanding of grammar.

The Simple Subject and Verb   (See pages 21–22, 89, and 189)

A sentence diagram begins with a base line on which the simple subject and the verb are placed. Your first step, then, is to draw a base line and to pick out the verb from the sentence. Write the verb on the right-hand half of the line.

Rip Van Winkle slept for twenty years.

slept
_____

Next, find the simple subject by asking *who* or *what* did the action of the verb: "*Who* or *what* slept?" *Rip Van Winkle* slept, so you write the name on the left-hand side of the line. Separate the subject from the verb with a vertical line that crosses the base line:

Rip Van Winkle | slept

Sometimes, the verb may contain more than one word, as in the verb phrase *was sleeping*.

He was sleeping.

He | was sleeping

387

Exercise: Diagraming simple subjects and verbs

Find the simple subjects and the verbs in these sentences and show them on diagrams. Keep in mind that a verb may be one word or a verb phrase containing more than one word.

1. The little Dutch village lay in the Catskill Mountains.
2. Rip Van Winkle lived in the tiny village.
3. He disliked all kinds of profitable labor.
4. His own farm always suffered from neglect.
5. Rip would never refuse help to a neighbor.
6. The children of the village loved Rip.
7. Troops of children always followed him about.
8. One day Rip rambled into the mountains.
9. The steep climb had wearied Rip.
10. He rested in a shady spot.
11. The heat of the day finally lulled him into a deep sleep.
12. A band of queer-looking people appeared in his dreams.
13. They were playing a game of ninepins.
14. The noise of the rolling balls echoed like thunder.
15. Rip stared in wonder at the sight.
16. Then Rip awoke from his long sleep.
17. A long white beard had grown on his chin.
18. A badly rusted rifle lay at his feet.

Sentences in Inverted Order

Most sentences are in usual order: subject first, then predicate. However, sometimes it is desirable for purposes of variety or emphasis to put the predicate first and then the subject. This is called **inverted order.**

This change of order does not show on a diagram. The purpose of a diagram is to show grammatical relationship among words, not to show the word order. In a diagram, always put the subject first and the verb second.

Over the bridge marched John.

| John | marched |

Exercises: Diagraming simple subjects and verbs

1. The subjects and verbs in the following sentences are in inverted order. Decide on the simple subject and the verb in each sentence and place them on a diagram. Do not diagram any other words in the sentences, only the simple subject and verb.

1. Around the sun move nine planets.
2. Among these nine planets is our earth.
3. From the sun comes our light.
4. Nearest to the sun is Mercury.
5. Next outward from Mercury is Venus.
6. In the west at twilight shines bright Venus.
7. Farthest in distance from the sun is Pluto.
8. Among all the planets, the most beautiful is Venus.
9. Encircling Venus are rings of vapor.
10. From the planets is reflected the sunlight.
11. Around the earth revolves the moon.
12. Between the earth and the moon is a distance of about 240,000 miles.

2. The subject and verb in some of the following sentences are in inverted order, that is, the verb appears before the subject. The others are in usual order. Find the simple subject and verb in each sentence and place them on a diagram.

1. By a mountain stream camped the boys.
2. Above them towered a lofty mountain.
3. They were planning a week's stay.
4. Bill broke his hatchet handle on a rock.
5. Dan was building a fireplace for cooking.
6. The fish in the pool jumped noisily.
7. A frightened deer crashed through the brush.
8. Over the scene flickered the light from the fire.
9. In the distance sounded the hoot of an owl.
10. The boys' appetites were keen as a razor.
11. The odor of frying bacon filled the air.
12. Soon they were hungrily eating their supper.
13. Sleeping bags were soon unrolled.
14. The roaring stream lulled them to sleep.
15. They scarcely moved until daybreak.

The Four Types of Sentences (See pages 29–31)

The four types of sentences are listed below. The simple subject and verb in each one have been placed on a diagram.

DECLARATIVE: John went to town.

John	went

INTERROGATIVE: Did John go to town?

John	Did go

IMPERATIVE: Go to town.

(you)	Go

EXCLAMATORY: How rapidly John went to town!

John	went

In the interrogative sentence, the subject often comes between two parts of a verb.

In the imperative sentence, there is no subject expressed; it is *you* understood. See the example above.

Exercise: Diagraming simple subjects and verbs

Diagram the simple subject and verb in each of the following sentences. Refer to the models above if you need help.

1. Will the cat catch the mouse?
2. That bell is now ringing loudly.
3. Kindly remove the dog from the room.
4. What marvelous sights we saw!
5. How tremendous that elephant is!
6. Swat all those flies quickly.
7. Did that dictionary help much?
8. After the wind came the rain.

Direct Objects   (See pages 89 and 189)

So far, you have shown only the subject and the verb on the base line of your diagram. Now you are ready to add a third basic sentence element, the direct object.

SUBJ. VERB DIR. OBJ.
Birds eat seeds.

Birds	eat	seeds

You see that the vertical line which separates the subject from the verb crosses the base line. The line separating the verb from the direct object stops at the base line. Here is another example:

The dog ate John's steak.

dog	ate	steak

Exercise: Diagraming subjects, verbs, and direct objects

Find the simple subjects, the verbs, and the direct objects in the following sentences. Place them on a diagram.

1. Orioles build deep nests.
2. Eagles possess keen eyesight.
3. Ostriches lay eggs of huge size.
4. Parrots have long lives.
5. For its nest, the wood duck uses the hollow of a tree.
6. John James Audubon painted magnificent pictures of birds.
7. The mourning dove gives a sad call.
8. For its state bird, Indiana chose the lovely cardinal.
9. Do you know the name of your state bird?
10. Study the birds in your neighborhood.

Possessives and Articles (See pages 82, 84, and 184)

Possessive nouns and pronouns and articles are closely related to nouns, and this relationship is shown quite clearly on a diagram, thus:

Louise's cat ate its meal.

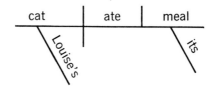

The cat's kittens have lost their mittens.

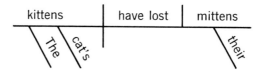

Using the following sentence, review the diagraming steps you have studied so far:

Does Mary's brother want an invitation?

Step 1: First pick out the verb and place it on the base line.

Does want

Step 2: Find and place the simple subject this way:

brother | Does want

Step 3: Find and place the direct object, if there is one in the sentence.

brother | Does want | invitation

Step 4: Find the articles and possessives, if any.

brother | Does want | invitation
Mary's · an

Exercise: Diagraming sentences

Diagram the subjects, verbs, articles, possessives, and any direct objects there may be in the following sentences. Be sure to look for the verb first. (Some of the sentences do not have direct objects.)

1. The boy stood on that burning deck.
2. Elsa's imagination worked all night.
3. My brother carried the large rock.
4. Do sailboats' skippers arise very early?
5. They chased the sparrows.
6. Their father had eaten his dinner.
7. The men's trip spoiled my holiday.
8. Do their canaries eat the pigeons' food?
9. I will read Esther's books.
10. A city's government should help its people.

Subject Complements   (See pages 92 and 192)

The subject complement is shown on the base line of a diagram.

Josiah was a pilot.

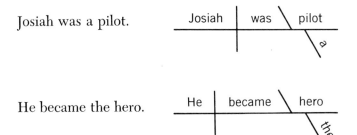

He became the hero.

The line between the verb and the subject complement slants toward the subject to show that the complement refers to the subject of the sentence.

Exercise: Diagraming sentences

Diagram all of the words in the following sentences:

1. They are men.
2. My books were dictionaries.
3. Their barn became the people's shelter.
4. Had the dog's father become a champion?
5. George's sunburn was a bother.

Adjectives   (See pages 234–35)

Adjectives modify nouns and pronouns, and this modification is simple to show on a diagram.

That large truck is stopping.

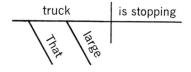

Her small chair collapsed.

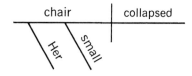

Exercise: Diagraming sentences

Diagram the following sentences:

1. The big black goat butted me.
2. George's tall friend admired my little sister.
3. This ugly worm will become a beautiful moth.
4. She had been a bothersome pest.
5. Tim's old aunt prepared this delicious supper.

So far, none of the adjectives you have diagramed are in the subject complement position. Now see how an adjective used as a subject complement is diagramed. The pattern is the same as for a subject complement noun or pronoun.

George is intelligent.

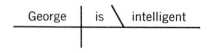

She became uneasy.

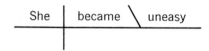

Exercise: Diagraming sentences with subject complements

Diagram all of the words in the following sentences:

1. Sue's brother is tall.
2. The postman was late.
3. Was Jerry absent?
4. Be careful.
5. Joe is ambitious.

6. The day was hot.
7. His actions were dangerous.
8. The light became dim.
9. The ladder looks unsafe.
10. That house appears vacant.

Adverbs   (See pages 240–41)

The principal function of adverbs is to modify verbs, and this relationship is shown thus:

Jean always eats fish.
(adv.)

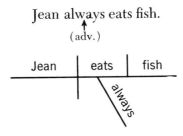

Yesterday my brother was almost elected.

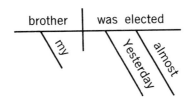

Notice that the adverb *Yesterday*, although it comes at the beginning of the sentence, is shown on the diagram directly under the verb it modifies. Remember, the order of words is not shown on a diagram. The first word of the sentence is always capitalized.

The adverb *not* or *n't* is shown just as any other adverb would be:

John wasn't happy.

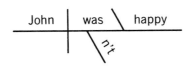

Diagram the following sentences:

1. James drove the car well.
2. John's sister didn't study her lessons thoroughly.
3. Tomorrow we shall certainly burn the trash.
4. Can't you see the airplane clearly?
5. The dog's leash was not long.

The special class of adverbs which answer the questions *how much?* or *to what extent?*, and which modify adjectives and other adverbs, are diagramed differently. Here is an example:

An *extremely* polite boy entered.

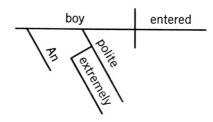

An adverb modifying an adjective that is used as a subject complement is diagramed thus:

The sea was *very* rough.

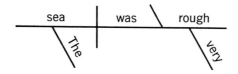

Exercise: Diagraming sentences

Diagram the following sentences, giving special attention to adverbs modifying adjectives or other adverbs. Be sure to include every word of each sentence on your diagram.

1. A really terrible flood washed our house away.
2. The boats were quite safe yesterday.
3. Gus is certainly handsome.
4. Our extremely tall tree completely destroyed the house.
5. The boy's lovely sister stood up rather quickly.

Prepositional Phrases (See pages 194 and 278–81)

A prepositional phrase is composed of a preposition and its object, plus any words that modify the object: *in barns; down the street; along the steep hillside.* Such phrases can modify either nouns or verbs and are called adjective phrases or adverb phrases. Here is how they and the words they modify are diagramed:

ADJ. PHRASE: piles *of coal*   ADV. PHRASE: walked *up the path*

Thus a sentence containing both an adjective phrase and an adverb phrase would be diagramed as follows:

The horsemen in the rear rode over the bridge.

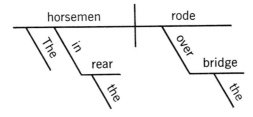

Exercise: Diagraming sentences

Diagram the following sentences. Although you should pay special attention to the prepositional phrases, these sentences will serve as a review of how to diagram the other elements you have studied.

1. They hunt for two weeks.
2. A school of ten whales is sighted.
3. The excitement of the men mounts.
4. The skipper's order for full speed goes to the first mate.
5. The boats tear through the water.
6. Head for that big whale!
7. The noise of the engines scatters the whales in all directions.
8. Will the whales dive to the bottom?
9. A cascade of foaming water spouts from a whale.
10. One of the whales swims toward an iceberg.

397

Conjunctions (See pages 290, 292–94, and 298)

The conjunctions *and, but,* and *or* join various elements in a sentence, and this relationship can be shown quite easily with diagrams.

Compound subjects and predicates

A compound subject is diagramed thus:

George and Mary were friends.

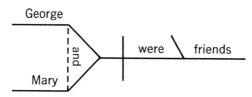

A compound predicate is diagramed thus:

George ate two sausages and drank milk.

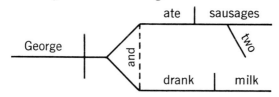

Compound objects and complements

Compound direct objects are diagramed thus:

Mother spanked Jane and me.

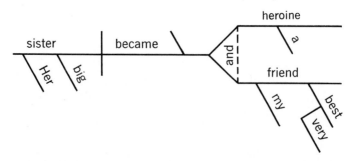

Compound subject complements are diagramed in nearly the same way:

Her big sister became a heroine and my very best friend.

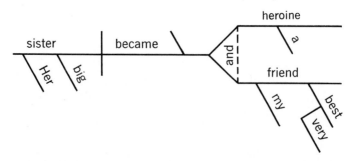

398

Compound adjectives, adverbs, and sentences

Compound adjectives and adverbs are shown thus:

His large and eager dog ate rapidly but carefully.

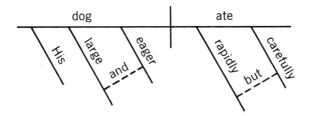

A compound sentence is shown thus:

The house on the hill burned, and the barn was barely saved.

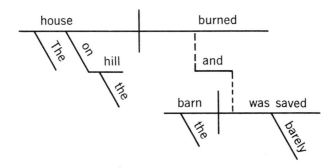

Exercises: Diagraming sentences

1. Diagram these sentences, each of which contains a compound subject or predicate:

   1. Coal and iron are mined here.
   2. The chicks scratched and pecked.
   3. Cactus and sagebrush grow on the high plains.
   4. The startled deer turned and fled.
   5. Fruits and vegetables are grown in abundance.
   6. Can you and Ellen go to the library?
   7. Here come Bob and his brother.
   8. The donkey started but moved quite slowly.
   9. Robins and thrushes belong to the same family.
  10. In the hall stood Andrew and his brother.
  11. Some elephants and their trainers marched in the parade.
  12. We ate our breakfast and later rested on the porch.

2. Diagram these sentences, each of which contains a compound direct object:

1. Bees store nectar and pollen.
2. This market sells fruits and vegetables.
3. Have you seen Tom and my brother?
4. I enjoy basketball and tennis.
5. Bring your notebook and a pencil.
6. We import coffee and tea.
7. The ship carried freight and passengers.
8. We passed tiny villages and some sizable towns.
9. Frank did not see the little boy and his dog.
10. This state produces iron and zinc.
11. Will you have fruit or sherbet for dessert?
12. My sister enjoys myths and legends.

3. Diagram the following compound sentences:

1. The dog barked, and the kitten vanished instantly.
2. The two robins toiled away, and soon the new nest was built.
3. I went to the door, and there stood Joe.
4. The wind blew furiously, and the old log house collapsed.
5. Tom came through the door, and every eye turned.
6. Are you going with us, or are you staying here?
7. They searched the cabin, but the jewels had disappeared.
8. Leigh washed the dishes, and I dried them.

█████ **GOING AHEAD** ███

See if you can write sentences that will fit the blank diagrams drawn below. For each diagram, hundreds of different sentences could be written, although all of the sentences for any one diagram would have the same grammatical pattern. Doing this exercise will give you practice in writing various patterns and also test your knowledge of diagraming.

For each item, draw the diagram on your paper and fill in the words, and also write the sentence out in normal English.

EXAMPLES:

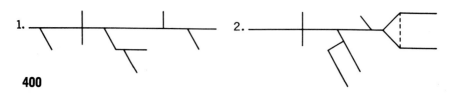

YOU WRITE:

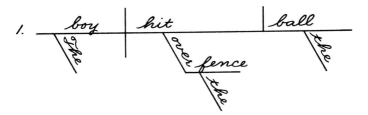

1. The boy hit the ball over the fence.

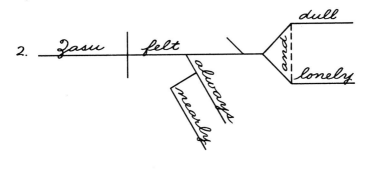

2. Zasu nearly always felt dull and lonely.

1.

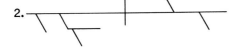

2.

3.

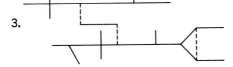

4.

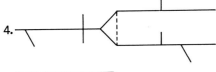

5.

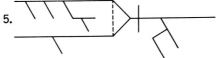

Mastery Tests

Test I

Diagram only the simple subject and the verb in each of the following sentences:

1. A short, yellow candle gently flickered on the table.
2. Mountains of snow blocked our entrance to the building.
3. Within the scientist's mind rested the formula.
4. Have you completed your report yet?
5. Measure the amount very accurately.

Test II

Diagram all of the words in the following sentences:

1. Our uncle had brought his camera.
2. The girl's father is the city's mayor.
3. This rusty old chest seems heavy.
4. Yesterday the time passed very slowly.
5. Alice did not design this floral arrangement.

Test III

Diagram all of the words in the following sentences:

1. Dad's new hat was rolling swiftly down the sidewalk.
2. A burst of applause greeted the performer on the stage.
3. The gentle breezes from the north flowed through the windows.
4. The gladiators of Rome had fought in this ancient arena.
5. A young man with a shiny trumpet stood in the soft blue spotlight.

Test IV

Diagram all of the words in the following sentences:

1. The councilman and his opponent argued publicly.
2. This water contains iodine and chlorine.
3. Hank and Jerry play guitars and sing ballads.
4. Janice speaks rapidly but distinctly.
5. Our days in the summer were long and lazy, but the nights were rather short.

Review and Practice

Exercise I

1. Review pages 387–90.

2. Diagram only the simple subject and the verb in each of the following sentences:

    1. Steak sizzled on the fiery-hot grill.
    2. Into the vast unknown soared the shiny rocket.
    3. Look at this flawless sculpture.
    4. Inside the police station was the lost boy.
    5. Can they fill your order in time?

Exercise II

1. Review pages 391–96.

2. Diagram all of the words in the following sentences:

    1. There the tropical storm raged quite violently.
    2. Eerie sounds were penetrating the hollow room.
    3. Their enthusiasm renewed the team's spirit.
    4. His sister is not my closest friend.
    5. Your hasty decision is unwise.

Exercise III

1. Review page 397.

2. Diagram all of the words in the following sentences:

    1. The soldiers marched around the field.
    2. The black bass in the tank was caught along this coast.
    3. Two of these boys carved small, wooden models of dogs.
    4. The cars in this lot will be loaded on a barge tomorrow.
    5. Piles of letters soon poured into the president's office.

Exercise IV

1. Review pages 398–99.

2. Diagram all of the words in the following sentences:

    1. Tuesday and Thursday are busy days.
    2. The old Ford started slowly but stopped suddenly.
    3. Have you ordered the paints and palettes?
    4. Two types of rodents are the mouse and the squirrel.
    5. Lenny likes geology, but his sister has little interest in rocks.

PART III

Review Handbook

CONTENTS

Composition

The Sentence
The Paragraph
The Letter

The Parts of Speech

The Noun
The Verb
The Pronoun
The Adjective
The Adverb
The Preposition
The Conjunction
The Interjection

Mechanics

Capitalization
Punctuation
Spelling

Usage

Composition

The Sentence

A **sentence** is a group of words that expresses a thought and makes sense by itself. In writing, the end of a sentence is marked by a period, a question mark, or an exclamation point. In speech, it is usually punctuated by a pause and a drop in voice pitch.

Types of sentences

There are four kinds of sentences, classified by the purpose they serve. Examine the end punctuation for each kind of sentence.

Declarative sentence—makes a statement:

My brother is a doctor.   Mountains can be dangerous.

Interrogative sentence—asks a question:

Is your brother a doctor?   Can mountains be dangerous?

Imperative sentence—makes a command or request:

Please put your books away now.   Go out quietly.

Exclamatory sentence—makes an exclamation:

What big teeth you have!   How stupid those pigs are!

In an interrogative sentence, the subject often comes between two parts of the verb:

Did he drop the plate?   Can they stay all week?

In an imperative sentence, the subject *you* is understood:

(You) Give me that suitcase.   (You) Please sit down now.

Exercises

1. On your paper beside the appropriate numerals, write S for each sentence below and F for each fragment. (A fragment is a piece of a sentence punctuated as a sentence.) Revise each fragment so that it is a complete sentence.

1. My room is usually a terrible mess.
2. Because we did not have time.

3. That big ape in the zoo yesterday.
4. Did Howard fly both to Europe and Asia?
5. Be quiet.
6. As soon as we saw them.

2. The sentences below have no end punctuation. Tell which of the four types of sentences each is and indicate what the end punctuation should be.

1. Have you seen that grizzly bear in the first cage
2. What a lovely necklace Jean is wearing
3. The state of California is one of the fastest-growing areas in the country
4. Roger, please put all that chalk away now
5. I am very fond of apple pie with vanilla ice cream on it

3. Write one sentence of each type and label it.

Subject and predicate

Every sentence has a subject and a predicate. The **subject** names what the sentence is about.

The **predicate** tells something about the subject.

COMPLETE SUBJECTS	COMPLETE PREDICATES
My little dog	eats meat.
Those big nuclear submarines	are useful for defense.

The **simple subject** is the key word in the complete subject; it is usually a *noun* or a *pronoun*. The nouns *dog* and *submarines* are the simple subjects in the two sentences above.

The **simple predicate** is the key word (or words) in the complete predicate; it is always a *verb*. The verbs in the two sentences above are *eats* and *are*.

Inverted order

The **usual order** of a sentence is subject first and predicate second. Some sentences are in **inverted order.** Study these examples:

PREDICATES	SUBJECTS
Onto the truck jumped	a pack of dogs.
Between the two men stood	four grim soldiers.

Exercise

Copy the following sentences and draw a vertical line between the complete subject and the complete predicate in each. Underline the simple subject once and the verb twice.

1. That old mongrel gnawed angrily on his bone.
2. After the fight, up stood Albert.
3. Through that very door strode Elsa.
4. Corn grows well in this state.
5. Jonathan slipped on the ice.
6. Around the planet revolved the moons.

Direct object

Subjects and verbs sometimes need another word (or words) to complete the thought, as:

1. Jessie lifted the heavy *package*.
2. Beth saw *Mary* and *me*.

The nouns *package* and *Mary* and the pronoun *me* receive the action of the verbs in the sentences above. They are called **direct objects,** or *objects of the verb.*

A **direct object** is a word that receives the action of a verb.

Subject complement

In the following sentences, the subjects and the words which follow the verb refer to the same persons or things:

1. Carl is *president*. (predicate noun)
2. That one is *it*. (predicate pronoun)
3. Erma is *beautiful* and *kind*. (predicate adjectives)

The italicized words above follow verbs that do not express action. These words are called **subject complements.** The terms *predicate noun, predicate pronoun,* and *predicate adjective* classify the subject complements according to the part of speech to which each one belongs.

A **subject complement** is a word in the predicate of a sentence that names or describes the subject.

Exercise

Find and write down the direct objects or subject complements that follow the verbs in the sentences below. Then label each one.

1. We have a problem in our town.
2. The lake nearby is really a swamp.
3. Swamps are quite dangerous in hot weather.
4. Mosquitoes lay their eggs in water.
5. They annoy us during the entire summer.
6. Certain kinds carry malaria microbes.
7. Insecticides are sometimes helpful.
8. Unfortunately, they often kill harmless animals and plants.

Avoiding sentence fragments and run-on sentences

Fragments are pieces of sentences. The fragment below is connected to a sentence to make the idea complete:

WRONG: When she left home.

RIGHT: I saw my mother when she left home.

Break up a run-on by punctuating each part as a sentence:

WRONG: There goes Mary she looks lovely in her new coat.

WRONG: There goes Mary, she looks lovely in her new coat.

RIGHT: There goes Mary. She looks lovely in her new coat.

Exercises

1. On your paper, correct the fragments and run-ons below.

1. This book is too long for me, the author should have cut it.
2. Because the soldiers fought so bravely all during the war.
3. Please go now finish your homework before you return.

2. Rewrite the following paragraph correctly on your paper:

Armies of ants travel great distances. In search of new homes and feeding grounds. These ants maintain a formation as well as trained soldiers do on a march they march in a straight column. Which is about eight inches to a foot wide and may be several miles long. Ants move straight ahead they never turn aside. Fences, fallen logs, and trees do not deter them, they climb over anything that gets in their path.

409

The Paragraph

A **paragraph** is a series of sentences which develop one topic or idea. The first word in a paragraph is indented.

Many paragraphs begin with a **topic sentence,** which states the topic or subject of the paragraph. The rest of the sentences in the paragraph *develop* the topic.

To write a good paragraph, you must:

1. Indent the first word.
2. State the main idea in a topic sentence. This sentence often appears as the first sentence in a paragraph.
3. Develop the main idea (explanation or details) in your other sentences.
4. Give your paragraph unity by keeping to the topic.

Exercises

1. Read the paragraph below and then answer the questions that follow it:

Boys generally study less than girls. A recent survey showed that the average seventh-grade boy spends almost half the time on his homework that the average girl does. Perhaps the reason is that boys tend to have more outside interests than girls. I wish I were a boy, but I'm not. Despite the difference in study time, however, statistics show that boys usually do as well as girls in college or in comparable jobs. I spent an hour on homework last night.

    1. What is the topic sentence?
    2. What two sentences detract from the paragraph and should be dropped?

2. Write a paragraph on any subject. If you wish, you may choose one of the topic sentences listed below and develop the topic with at least three more sentences.

    1. It's better to hunt with a camera than with a gun.
    2. Three days on tea and toast are an ordeal.
    3. Nothing helps a child grow up more than being responsible for his own pet.
    4. The cracks in the ceiling of my room make strange patterns.
    5. I'd rather have a cat for a pet than a dog.

The Letter

Both friendly letters and business letters have these five parts: the *heading*, the *salutation* (or the *greeting*), the *body*, the *closing*, and the *signature*. In addition, the business letter requires an *inside address*. Read the business letter below:

> 1314 Horizon Street
> Salt Lake City, Utah 84101
> May 12, 19—

Flora's Bargain Basement
637 Wallingford Street
Pawtucket, Rhode Island 02860

Gentlemen:

Please send me by the best way the following items listed in your catalog:

3 No. 1685–M tank cars, @ $1.04	$3.12
16 No. 687–T straight track @ $0.14	2.24
8 No. 688–T curved track @ $0.15	1.20
Total	$6.56

I enclose a postal money order for $6.56.

> Very truly yours,
>
> *Joseph Spratt*
> Joseph Spratt

Social notes should generally be written in the form of a friendly letter. The main types of social notes are *thank-you notes, letters of invitation, notes of regret or acceptance, notes of apology,* and *bread-and-butter letters.* (See pages 216–19 for models.)

Exercises

1. Study carefully the six parts of the letter above. Then write a business letter of your own, with the book closed.

2. Write a friendly letter, an imaginary letter or one which you really plan to send to a friend. *Remember,* a friendly letter needs no inside address, and its greeting and closing contain less formal phrases, such as:

> Dear Sally,   Your friend,

The Parts of Speech

Words name things, describe things, tell what happens, and connect parts of sentences. They can be classified into **eight parts of speech: nouns, pronouns, verbs, adjectives, adverbs, prepositions, conjunctions,** and **interjections.** The part of speech that a word is often depends on its function in a sentence.

The Noun

A **noun** is a word used to name a person, place, or thing.

Concrete nouns name things you can see or touch: *sky, box.* *Abstract nouns* name things you cannot see or touch: *joy, horror.*

Nouns show **number.** A noun that names one is *singular.* A noun that names more than one is *plural.*

Nouns show **possession** or ownership:

The cat's   dish
↑   ↑
(pos-   (thing
sessive   pos-
noun)   sessed)

See pages 80–81 and page 82 for rules on forming plurals and possessives.

Exercises

1. Write four abstract nouns and four concrete nouns.
2. Write the plural of the following nouns:

1. church	4. pear	7. chief
2. ox	5. shelf	8. salmon
3. mouse	6. daughter-in-law	

The articles *a, an,* and *the* are **noun signals.** When one of these words appears in a sentence, a noun follows:

the baby   *a* big noise   *an* apple

There are two types of nouns:

A **proper noun** names a particular person, place, or thing: *Jack Snipe, Algeria.* Proper nouns are always capitalized. All other nouns are **common nouns.** (See pages 419–21 for the rules and exercises on the capitalization of proper nouns.)

Uses of nouns

A noun is used in sentences in the following ways:

AS SUBJECT

The *poem* is called "The Courtship of Miles Standish."

AS DIRECT OBJECT

Robert Louis Stevenson wrote this *poem*.

AS OBJECT OF A PREPOSITION

John Alden delivered a message for his good *friend*.

AS SUBJECT COMPLEMENT

The message was a marriage *proposal*.

AS APPOSITIVE NOUN

Priscilla, the fair *maiden* of Plymouth, listened carefully.

AS NOUN OF DIRECT ADDRESS

She then asked, "Why don't you speak for yourself, *John*?"

Exercise

Copy each italicized noun below. Then tell how it is used in the sentence.

1. *Miles Standish* was the *captain* of *Plymouth*.
2. He was a courageous *man* in *battle*.
3. The *author*, a famous *poet*, told a good *story*.
4. Would you like to read it, *Martha*?

The Verb

Every sentence contains a **verb**. Verbs express *action* or *being*.

Verbs of action tell what the subject does. They are verbs such as *kick, twist, run, disappear*, which express physical action; or *doubt, think*, and *want*, which express mental action.

The boy kicked the ball.

Her friend thought terrible things.

Verbs of being tell what or where the subject *is* or *what it is like*. The most common verb of being is *be*. Its forms are: *am, is, are, was, were*. Other verbs of being are *become, seem*, and *look*.

Our suitcases are very new.   George became a terrible pest.

413

Helping verbs

A verb may include more than one word:

Dolly | should have been elected.

Should have been elected is a verb phrase. *Elected* is the *main verb*; the words *should have been* are the **helping verbs.** Another term for *helping verb* is **auxiliary verb.**

Sometimes the helping verb is separated from the main verb by an adverb or by the subject, or both:

Oscar had seldom eaten so much.   Did Oscar often eat much?

Verbs and tense

Verbs express *time* (or *tense*) in two ways: by changing form and/or by adding helping verbs.

PRESENT TENSE:	I admire you.	I throw the ball.
PAST TENSE:	I admired you.	I threw the ball.
	I have admired you.	I have thrown the ball.
FUTURE TENSE:	I shall admire you.	I shall throw the ball.

All verbs have three forms through which they express tense. These are called **principal parts.** Regular verbs form the past and the past participle by adding *d* or *ed* to the present; for example:

PRESENT	PAST	PAST PARTICIPLE
report, reports	reported	(have, has, had) reported

For a listing of irregular verbs, see pages 446–47.

Exercises

1. Choose five verbs of action and use each in a sentence. Underline the verb twice and its subject once.

2. Use each of these verbs in a sentence: *am, is, are, was, were.*

3. Copy the verb phrases in the sentences below. Underline the helping verbs once and circle the main verb.

    1. The river will flood the town.
    2. Could John have helped you?
    3. Did you call yesterday?
    4. You have never really seen my new room.

4. Write the principal parts of these verbs: *hate, look, play.*

414

The Pronoun

A **pronoun** is a word that is used in place of a noun. This table will help you remember the different forms of important *personal pronouns*:

Subject Pronouns		Object Pronouns	
SINGULAR	PLURAL	SINGULAR	PLURAL
I	we	me	us
you	you	you	you
he, she, it	they	him, her, it	them

Possessive Pronouns	
SINGULAR	PLURAL
my, mine	our, ours
your, yours	your, yours
his, her, hers, its	their, theirs

The noun for which a pronoun stands is called the **antecedent.** A pronoun's antecedent should be clear.

ANTECEDENT CLEAR

George bought a dog and was kind to *it*.

ANTECEDENT UNCLEAR

George showed Bob where *his* wallet was hidden.

See the "Usage" section of this Review Handbook for study and practice on using pronouns correctly. The usage items are listed alphabetically.

Exercise

Write the thirteen pronouns in the following passage in the same order in which they appear. After each pronoun, write its antecedent in parentheses.

Joe wanted his breakfast, and he wanted it quickly. He called his mother and asked her to hurry.

"Why should I hurry?" she asked. "You didn't do your chores yesterday, and until you do them today, I am going to relax, too."

415

The Adjective

An **adjective** is a word used to modify a noun or pronoun. There are two categories: *descriptive* adjectives, which tell *what kind;* and *limiting* adjectives, which tell *how many* or *which one.* The noun signals *a, an,* and *the* are limiting adjectives, called **articles.**

DESCRIPTIVE ADJECTIVES: *Small* birds sing sweetly.

They were too *ugly.*

LIMITING ADJECTIVES: *That* horse trots fast.

I bought *some* doughnuts.

Exercise

Copy each sentence below. Underline each adjective and draw an arrow from it to the word it modifies. Above each adjective, write *D* if it is a descriptive adjective, and *L* if it is limiting. Ignore the articles.

1. That robin is so busy.
2. Those lovely hats cost only four dollars.
3. An old rusty spoon was lying in the messy yard.
4. An inexperienced person would not climb this dangerous peak.

The Adverb

Most **adverbs** modify verbs and answer the questions *how? when?* or *where?*

That man drives ← recklessly. (*how?*)
often. (*when?*)
away. (*where?*)
(adverbs)

An important special adverb which makes verbs negative is the word *not.*

A small group of adverbs modify adjectives and other adverbs and answer the questions *to what extent?* or *how much?*

My *rather* ugly face is at least friendly. (modifies adjective)

He spoke *very* softly. (modifies adverb)

Exercise

In the order in which they appear, list the eight adverbs in the following passage.   In parentheses after each adverb, write the word it modifies and what part of speech that word is: *verb, adjective,* or *adverb.*

Mary spoke softly into the microphone because she was very uneasy and quite uncomfortable.   Gradually she breathed more easily and spoke loudly to the audience in a rather firm tone.

The Preposition

A **preposition** is always followed by a noun or a pronoun called the **object of the preposition.**   Together with any modifiers of the object, these form a **prepositional phrase.**

Prepositional Phrases

PREPOSITION	MODIFIERS OF OBJECT	OBJECT OF PREPOSITION
into	the	cellar
behind		her
under	the black, stagnant	water

Prepositional phrases are modifiers.   When they modify nouns or pronouns, they are called **adjective phrases:**

The boy under the narrow bridge is Bob.   (adjective phrase)

When they modify verbs, they are called **adverb phrases:**

Joe ran into the cellar!   (adverb phrase)

Exercises

1. List the prepositional phrases in the sentences below.   Identify each phrase as an adjective phrase or an adverb phrase.

1. A codfish swam into my net.
2. My sister ran down the street.
3. A young man at the door wants some directions.
4. A bouquet of flowers was sent to my mother.

2. Use each of the following prepositions in two sentences, once in an adjective phrase and once in an adverb phrase: *through, over, at, between.*   Label each phrase.

The Conjunction

A **conjunction** is a word used to join words, phrases, or clauses. The most common conjunctions are *and, but, or, neither . . . nor, either . . . or,* and *both . . . and.* Here are examples of their use:

JOINING ADJECTIVES: That girl is <u>either</u> *unfriendly* <u>or</u> *shy.*

JOINING ADVERBS: The captain sailed *skillfully* <u>but</u> *recklessly.*

JOINING PREPOSITIONAL PHRASES: John Gilpin rode *through the town* <u>and</u> *across the fields.*

When conjunctions join subjects, objects, verbs, and clauses, they are called compound subjects, compound objects, compound predicates, and compound sentences:

COMPOUND SUBJECT: *George* <u>and</u> *Mary* ate dinner.

COMPOUND OBJECT: She was with *Frank, Mal,* <u>and</u> *them.*

COMPOUND PREDICATE: The horse *turned suddenly* <u>and</u> *threw off the rider.*

COMPOUND SENTENCE: *The horse turned suddenly,* <u>and</u> *the rider fell off.*

Exercise

Pick out the conjunctions in the following sentences. Tell what sentence parts are joined. Some of the conjunctions have two words, such as *either . . . or.*

1. Either the fox or the goose has left the area.
2. She hopped happily but slowly back to the barnyard and under the fence.
3. My lessons are very difficult for me and cause me much unhappiness.
4. Mary cried but Alice prayed.
5. Both the adults and the children saw the storm and ran for the house or barn.

The Interjection

An **interjection** is a brief expression, not a sentence, used to express strong feeling and is punctuated by an exclamation point:

Oh!   Ouch!   My goodness!   Wow!

Mechanics

Capitalization

Main Rule: Capitalize all proper nouns and proper adjectives.

A **common noun** is the name of any of a class of persons, places, or things:

boy   school   month

A **proper noun** is the name of a particular person, place, thing, or group:

John   Central *H*igh School   March

A **proper adjective** is an adjective formed from a proper noun:

PROPER NOUN	PROPER ADJECTIVE
Germany	German
Asia	Asian

Note: If a proper noun has more than one word, capitalize the first letter in the first word and in all the important words.

Main categories of proper nouns

1. Calendar items: months, days, holidays, and special days

   January   Tuesday   Labor Day   Easter   Yom Kippur

2. Organizations, institutions, businesses, government departments

   the American Red Cross   the Saxe Junior High School
   the Department of Commerce

3. Brands or trade names of products

   Spee-Dee carts   General Motors buses

4. Historical and special events, documents, and periods

   the French Revolution   the Louisiana Purchase
   the Gettysburg Address   the Middle Ages

5. Races, nationalities, and languages

   Negroes   Caucasians   French   Swahili

6. Geographical names

Ashby Street	Sacramento	the Amazon River
Skyline Drive	Sweden	Illinois

7. Names of persons, including initials and titles

Professor Eisley   Roger L. Schafer   Sergeant Smith

8. Names of relationships when used as a proper name

Hello, Mother, I'm back.   There is Uncle Frank.
Look at Father.

(These names are not capitalized when used merely to show relationship: *My mother criticizes me. I love my uncle.*)

9. Names of ships, planes, satellites

the *Independence*   the *Eastern Skyjet*   *Telstar*
Cosmos I

10. Names of buildings, monuments, and natural wonders

Lincoln Memorial   Grand Central Station
the Grand Canyon

11. Names of political parties and members

the Democratic Party   Republicans   a Tory

12. The Deity, sacred documents, and religions

Jehovah   the Bible   the Torah   Christianity

13. Abbreviations of proper names

Kans.   Mr. Long   Dr. Wm. Salter   Y.M.C.A.

Nouns that are not capitalized

1. Names of seasons

summer   winter

2. Names of breeds of animals and birds, unless they contain a proper adjective or noun

collie   French poodle   pheasant

3. Compass directions (north, east), unless referring to a region

He traveled south.   He traveled through the South.

4. Names of diseases, flowers, trees, games, foods, and musical instruments, unless they contain a proper adjective or noun

cheese   Swiss cheese   maple   Norway maple

5. Names of subjects in school, unless they contain a proper adjective or name a particular course

mathematics   Mathematics I   English history

Exercises

1. On your paper, write each sentence below correctly.   One sentence is correct as it stands.

1. He studies biology on thursday.
2. I am on the corner of maple street and longview drive.
3. This is the department of health and welfare.
4. They signed the declaration of independence.
5. It was a movie about the life of cowboys in the west.
6. They are over at mountain view junior high school.
7. Look at the top of the supreme court building.
8. Listen to the song of the wood thrush in the spring.
9. Was he killed in the french revolution?
10. The thompson products company sent us a sample.
11. On a cold february day our class in algebra II met.
12. The fourth of july fireworks were beautiful.
13. We used a peabody dog brush.
14. During the middle ages the knights wore armor.
15. That happened before the boston tea party.

2. On your paper, write the following sentences correctly:

1. My mother studied catholicism and buddhism at doorman institute of religions.
2. "Oh, mother, you are my favorite mother in all of montana!" said little oscar as they entered glacier national park.
3. A negro, a caucasian, and a mongolian were on the program to help celebrate the sixth annual brotherhood week.
4. Their italian maid speaks german, and their greek chauffeur speaks spanish and chinese but no greek.
5. She saw col. b. w. thorpe with mr. and mrs. jacobson.
6. The republican candidate and the democratic candidate were friends.

Other uses of capitals

1. Capitalize the first word:
   (a) In a sentence
   (b) In a quotation

   *T*hen Beatrice asked, "*M*ay we join you?"

   (c) In the greeting or closing of a letter

   *M*y dear Jack,   *Y*ours very sincerely,

   (d) In a line of poetry   (There are exceptions to this rule.)

   *T*he Lord in His wisdom made the fly
   *A*nd then forgot to tell us why.—OGDEN NASH

   (e) In a topic in an outline

   I. *U*ses of automobiles
      A. *C*ommercial
      B. *R*ecreational
   II. *T*hree types of automobiles

2. Capitalize the words *I* and *O*

   "*O* master, please!" *I* said.

3. Capitalize all words in a title except *a, an*, and *the*, short prepositions, and conjunctions, unless these appear as the first or last word in the title.

   May I borrow the book *Mutiny on the Bounty?*
   "*T*he *H*ighwayman" is my favorite poem.
   Washington Irving wrote "*T*he *L*egend of Sleepy *H*ollow."

Exercise

Copy and capitalize correctly the following items:

1. that man said, "leave now!"
2. dear Mr. Jones,   my dear Joseph,
3. yours sincerely,   gratefully yours,
4. I. proper lighting for studying
      A. placement of lights
      B. power of lamps
   II. equipment for studying
5. Did you read the book *the prince and the pauper?*

Punctuation

Apostrophe

1. **Use an apostrophe in a contraction to show where letters have been omitted.**

haven't   I'm   o'clock (of the clock)

2. **Use an apostrophe to show possession in nouns.**

(a) If the noun does not end in *s*, add an apostrophe and *s*:

Tom's hat   men's club

(b) If the noun ends in *s*, add only an apostrophe (unless it is a singular noun that ends in *s*).

ladies' shoes   boys' games   Chris's hat (singular noun)

3. **Use an apostrophe to form the plural of letters, figures, or words used out of context.**

There are three 5's and six *x*'s in that sentence.
He has too many *and*'s in his paragraph.

Exercises

1. Show the possessive form of each of the following nouns. After each one, write a noun to show what is possessed.

EXAMPLE: 1. teacher
YOU WRITE: *1. teacher's desk*

1. Mary   3. women   5. people   7. actors
2. man   4. ladies   6. captain   8. states

2. Revise the following phrases by using the possessive case instead of a prepositional phrase:

EXAMPLE: 1. the voice of the giant
YOU WRITE: *1. the giant's voice*

1. the wages for a week   3. wings of bats
2. a dormitory for boys   4. the menu for tomorrow

3. Copy the following sentences, using apostrophes correctly:

1. Dont you know where youre going?
2. Its my guess that weve heard the last of them.
3. Lets get there at four oclock.
4. You connect your thoughts with too many *ands*.

Colon

1. **Place a colon after the greeting in a business letter.**

   Dear Sir: Gentlemen: Dear Mr. Smith:

2. **Place a colon between the numeral that represents the hour and the numeral that represents the minutes.**

   7:35 A.M.   10:15 P.M.

Comma

1. **Place a comma between the parts of dates.**

   December 25, 1932   Tuesday, January 31, 1899

   If the date is within a sentence, use a comma after the year.

   On January 7, 1908, I first saw Oscar.

2. **Place a comma between the city and state within an address.**

   Minneapolis, Minnesota   Philadelphia, Pennsylvania

   If the address is in a sentence, separate the parts of the address in this way:

   His address is 734 East Brattle Lane, Concord, Massachusetts.

3. **Place a comma between the city and country.**

   Berlin, Germany   Calcutta, India

4. **Place a comma after the greeting in a friendly letter.**

   Dear Sue,   My dear Mr. Fox,

5. **Place a comma after the closing in a letter.**

   Sincerely yours,   Your friend,   Very truly yours,

6. **Use a comma between last and first names when listing last names first.**

   Frost, Robert   Sandburg, Carl

7. **Use commas to set off a noun in direct address.**

   Molly, please pass the sugar.
   Open it now, Jim, before I go.
   Listen carefully, class.

8. Use a comma to set off the introductory words *yes*, *no*, and *well* at the beginning of a sentence.

Yes, I shall come.   Well, don't you agree?

9. Use a comma to set off interrupting expressions, such as *however*, *therefore*, *for example*, and *in fact*.

However, we are pleased with it now.
The top, in fact, was still lost.

10. Use a comma to set off *too* when it means "also."

George, too, felt sad.   I want to go, too.

11. Use a comma to set off appositives.

I saw Mr. Kent, the president of the bank, this morning.
The Society of Friends, a religious sect, is usually known as the Quakers.

Note: Usually, an appositive of one word is not set off:

My brother Dick went away.

12. Use a comma to separate items in a series.

We bought apples, gum, and soda pop.
Down his sleeve, over his hand, and across the table ran the mouse.

13. In a direct quotation, use a comma to set off the quoted words from the rest of the sentence.

John said, "Please go away."
"Please stay for a while," said Bert.
"I think," moaned George, "that I have lost my wallet."

Note: The comma comes before the quotation marks.

14. Use a comma before a conjunction in a compound sentence, unless the sentence is very short.

Encyclopedias are quite expensive, but they are very useful.
Birds sing and dogs bark.   (very short)

15. Use a comma if you need one to make your meaning clear.

After cleaning, Mary took a nap.
Inside the door, mats were placed.

425

Exercises: Colon and comma (rules 1–5)

1. Copy the following parts of letters, adding commas and colons where they are needed:

1. *Friendly letter*

> Myrtlehill Avenue
> Pensacola Florida 32506
> Monday March 4 19–

Dear Sal

2. *Business letter*

Green Pastures Inn
Chester Pennsylvania 19014

Dear Mr. Jones
  Thank you for confirming our reservations. We will arrive at 2 30 P.M. on Saturday August 10.

> Yours truly
> Lawrence Falks

2. Copy and punctuate the following:

1. He was born on June 12 1944 in a log cabin.
2. He lives at 50 Brookside Drive Greenwich Connecticut.
3. My friend writes to a boy who lives in Dijon France.
4. We moved on Thursday December 31 1964 to 32 West Haines Street Lexington Massachusetts.

Exercises: Comma (rules 6–11)

1. Copy each of the following sentences and punctuate it:

1. Look here John don't wriggle about so.
2. That small house for example actually has five bedrooms.
3. Yes you are right about their behavior.
4. In fact I have always wanted to go on a camping trip too.
5. On the card his name was arranged this way: Smith Larry.

2. Copy each sentence on your paper and punctuate it correctly.

1. George the biggest bully in class was finally squelched.
2. My cousin Eileen saw the whole thing.
3. Old Mr. Cruthers told us a story a short and exciting one.
4. Miss Mithers our teacher is out of the room.

Exercise: Comma (rules 12–15)

Copy the following sentences, punctuating each one correctly. One of the sentences does not need a comma.

1. Howie saw helicopters jet liners and hydroplanes.
2. John speaks but Mabel acts.
3. "Please return the books" requested Mrs. Hall.
4. It was so hot dogs were panting.
5. The hound crept around the log over the mossy bank and into the black forest.
6. "I hope" said Fred "that he will help."
7. Skiing may be fun but it can also be quite dangerous.
8. On the mountain goats pranced merrily.

Exclamation point

1. **Place an exclamation point after an exclamatory sentence.**

   What a colorful sunset that is!   Run for your lives!

2. **Place an exclamation point after an exclamatory word or phrase and after a strong interjection at the beginning of a sentence.** *Note*: Do not overuse the exclamation point.

   How horrible!   "What a mess!" he said.
   Hooray!   Our team has won the championship.

Hyphen

1. **Use a hyphen to divide words between syllables at the end of a line.**

   His plans for the summer are indef-
      inite.

2. **Use a hyphen in writing certain number and compound words.**

   seventy-six   son-in-law

   Compound words beginning with *self-* and *ex-* followed by a noun usually need a hyphen.

   ex-president   ex-soldier   self-restraint

3. **Use a hyphen when two very closely related words are used as a modifier.**

   a two-thirds majority   a one-way street

427

Italics

See "Underlining."

Period

1. **Use a period to end declarative (statement) and imperative (request, command) sentences.**

   Denmark is a wealthy country.   Please eat quickly.

2. **Use a period after abbreviations or initials.**

   Mr. E. W. Lee   Sara Baird, R.N.   Y.M.C.A.   A.D. 1066

3. **Use a period after numerals and letters in an outline.**

   I. The benefits of air-conditioning
     A. The effect on health
       1. No swift changes in temperature
       2. No pollen in summer
     B. The ideal temperature
   II. The disadvantages of air-conditioning

Question mark

Place a question mark after an interrogative sentence.

Why are there so many cases of pneumonia?
"When did she arrive?" asked the boy.

Exercise: Exclamation points, hyphens, periods, and question marks

Copy and punctuate the following items correctly:

1. IV The advantages of sailing
     A Low cost
       1 No fuel needed
       2 Repairs simple and cheap
     B Excitement and relaxation
2. Was Dr E A Bridewell reading a book by C S Lewis
3. The man's son in law showed self restraint when the policeman said that Clark Street was changed to a one way street
4. "They were very old, weren't they" asked Harold
5. John joined the Y M C A the Young Men's Christian Association in the year A D 1960
6. My socks My socks They're burning up

Quotation marks

1. Use quotation marks to enclose words quoted.

"We are grateful to you," said my aunt.
Jessie says "Jeepers!" too often.

(a) If a sentence is divided into two parts by words such as
he said or *Max answered*, use two sets of quotation marks.

"Doing exercises," Mary said, "is a chore."

(b) If several sentences are quoted in a row, do not close the
quote until the speaker has finished.

"Look over there. I think I see a boat," said Bob.

(c) When you write conversation or dialogue, begin a new
paragraph whenever the speaker changes.

**2. Use quotation marks to indicate the title of a story, poem,
article, or chapter of a book, when these appear in a sentence.**

In this magazine there is a piece called "How to Keep Your
Children Out of Trouble."
Read the chapter, "How the West Was Won."

Exercise

Copy and punctuate the following. You will need to put in commas, quotation marks, and end punctuation.

1. Think before you leap warned John
2. Think warned John before you leap
3. Let's go It's raining exclaimed Jim I'm getting soaked
4. Sarah asked where are you going
5. Stop saying Gosh
6. My favorite poem is The Sea Gypsy

Underlining (italics)

Underlining is the way you indicate italics when you type or write
by hand.

**1. Underline the titles of books, plays, magazines, and the names
of newspapers.**

I saw the play The Merchant of Venice at the festival.

429

2. Underline the names of ships, planes, and trains when used in a sentence.

The <u>Super-Chief</u> arrived on schedule.

3. Underline a word, numeral, or letter used out of context.

When you use <u>sky</u> in the plural, spell it <u>skies</u>.

Exercise

Copy and punctuate the following items correctly, using underlining where necessary:

1. The ship Independence has a the before its name.
2. In the book Don't Get Perconel with a Chicken, the word personal is intentionally misspelled.
3. I'd rather read a magazine like Boy Adventure than a daily paper like the Trumpet.

Spelling

You need a good visual memory to be a good speller of English. Never risk misspelling a word. Look it up in a dictionary; learn it; then use it.

To improve your spelling, learn words by this system:

STEP 1: Pronounce the word.
STEP 2: Divide the word into syllables by underlining each syllable.
STEP 3: Finger the word, pronouncing each syllable as it becomes visible.
STEP 4: Write the word.
STEP 5: Compare; if wrong, start over.
STEP 6: Write the word three more times.

Master five spelling rules.

RULE 1: **One-syllable words and words accented on the last syllable, if they end in a single consonant after a single vowel, double the final consonant when you add a suffix beginning with a vowel.**

stop—stopped   begin—beginner

RULE 2: **When sound is *ee*,**
Put *i* before *e*
Except after *c*.   field, receive

When sound is not *ee*,
Put *e* before *i*.   height

As always, there are a few exceptions, but they are not hard to remember. There are five common words spelled *ei* and yet sounded as *ee*. They are all contained in this nonsense sentence:

He seized neither (either) weird leisure.

Memorize the sentence above.

Also, there are three common *ie* words that are not pronounced *ee*. They are: *friend, sieve,* and *mischief*. Remember them.

RULE 3: **Words that end in silent *e* drop the final *e* before a suffix beginning with a vowel, but keep the final *e* before a suffix beginning with a consonant.**

come—coming   use—useful   note—notable

Four common exceptions are *argument, judgment, ninth,* and *truly*.

RULE 4: **Words that end in *y* with a consonant before it change the *y* to *i* before any suffix except a suffix which begins with *i*.**

try—tries   study—studied   study—studying

RULE 5: **Prefixes are added to the root word without changing the spelling of the root word.**

mis + spell = misspell   dis + appear = disappear

One hundred spelling demons

There are a few words which cause more than their rightful share of trouble. *These few you should master!* They have been chosen by experienced teachers who have carefully studied thousands of student papers to see what the trouble-words are.

431

100 SPELLING DEMONS

(You will note that the syllables are underlined to help you learn these words according to the system explained on page 430.)

1. accept
   Please accept a gift.
2. across
3. affect
   Running will affect his heart.
4. all right
5. always
   Always write clearly.
6. among
7. angle
   a 90-degree angle
8. answer
9. argument
10. athletics
11. beginning
12. believe
13. business
14. busy
15. capital
    a capital letter
16. character
17. choose
    to choose sides
18. chose
    Last year I chose to go.
19. column
20. coming
21. committee
22. criticize
23. definitely
24. description
25. develop
26. different
27. disappear
28. disappointed
29. doesn't
30. effect
    to effect an improvement; a good effect
31. excellent
32. except
    All were invited except her.
33. familiar
34. February
35. finally
36. foreign
37. forty
38. government
39. grammar
40. height
41. immediately
42. independent
43. its
    down its throat
44. it's
    It's a rabbit. Means: *it is*
45. judgment
46. knew
    I knew that man.
47. know
    You know the question.
48. library
49. loose
    loose tooth
50. losing
    losing your money
51. meant
52. medicine

53. minute
54. necessary
55. niece
56. ninety
57. occurred
58. omit
59. peculiar
60. perhaps
61. pleasant
62. principal
   the principal of the school
   the principal thing;
   Means: *main*
63. principle
   My principle is perfect honesty. Means: *rule*
64. probably
65. proceed
   proceed rapidly
66. quiet
   the quiet night
67. realize
68. really
69. receipt
70. receive
71. recommend
72. repetition
73. schedule
74. separate
75. similar
76. sincerely
77. stationery
   Stationery is paper.
78. surprise
79. than
   wider than hers

80. their
   their dog
81. there
   Put it there.
   There is one.
82. therefore
83. they're
   They're nice. Means:
   they are
84. though
   tall though fat
85. threw
   I threw him out.
86. through
   through that tunnel
87. too
   too big; I went, too.
88. trouble
89. truly
90. Tuesday
91. two
   two monkeys
92. until
93. usually
94. weather
   beautiful weather
95. Wednesday
96. whether
   whether or not
97. who's
   Who's strong enough?
   Means: *who is*
98. whose
   Whose car crashed?
99. women
   two women
100. writing

Exercise: Spelling demons

This exercise will take you several days, or possibly two or three weeks. It should be done with another person, either a classmate, a member of your family, or anyone else who is willing to help you. The exercise is to learn the 100 spelling demons above. The following method is suggested:

1. Take a pretest on the first 25 words. That is, have the words dictated to you and write down only the words you are absolutely sure of. Leave the others blank. (Be sure to number each word with the same numeral used in the demons list.) If homonyms are involved, write the word in a meaningful phrase.

2. Have the pretest marked.

3. Learn the words you misspelled and the ones for which you left blank spaces. Use the system suggested on page 430.

4. Take a pretest on the next 25 words . . . and so on until you have learned all 100 demons.

5. Take a final test on all 100 demons.

6. If you missed any words on the final test, learn them. Have someone test you until you know all the demons perfectly.

Usage

A and an

Use *a* before a word that begins with a consonant.

Use *an* before a word that begins with a vowel, a vowel sound, or a silent consonant that precedes a vowel.

Exercise

Choose the correct word from each pair in parentheses.

1. (A, An) shark frightened (a, an) octopus.
2. Put (a, an) *m* before (a, an) *at* and you have (a, an) *mat*.
3. (A, An) honest man looked at (a, an) dishonest man.

Adjective or adverb?   (See also pages 248–51)

(See also "Comparison of adjectives and adverbs," page 442.)

Use an adjective to modify a noun or pronoun.   Use an adverb to modify a verb, adjective, or adverb.

It was an *easy* question.   He answered it *easily*.
　　　　(adj.)　　　　　　　　　　　(adv.)

He is *neat* in his work.   He did his work *neatly*.
　　(adj.)　　　　　　　　　　　　(adv.)

Exercise

Choose the correct word.

1. She dresses (neat, neatly).
2. She carried the pack (easy, easily).
3. Bob was working (careful, carefully).
4. The car can be repaired (easy, easily).
5. She stacked the books (neat, neatly).

Agreement   (See also pages 152, 196–97, 289, and 292–93)

A verb must agree with its subject in number and person.   A singular subject takes a singular form of the verb.   A plural subject takes a plural form of the verb:

Pauline bakes fresh bread each day.   (singular)

They bake fresh bread each day.   (plural)

The pronouns *I* and *you* are exceptions: I bake.   You bake.

435

A compound subject always takes a plural form of the verb except when singular words are joined by *or, either . . . or,* or *neither . . . nor.* (See also "Singular pronouns and verbs," page 453.)

> The owl *and* the pussycat go to sea.   (plural)
> The owls *or* the pussycats go to sea.   (plural)
> *Either* the owl *or* the pussycat goes to sea.   (singular)

Exercise

Choose the correct verb.

1. Those boys (go, goes) to that school.
2. That girl and her sister (likes, like) to study algebra.
3. The rain or the fog (have, has) spoiled the vacation.
4. Neither the wallpaper nor the paint (pleases, please) me.
5. Either a puzzle or a game (makes, make) a good gift.

Almost and most   (See also pages 250–51)

Almost is always an adverb and has two syllables.

> Bob *almost* broke it.   She is *almost* dead.

Most is an adjective or a noun.

> *Most* dogs bark.   (adj.)   *Most* of the boys left early.   (noun)

Exercise

Choose the correct word.

1. They (almost, most) never arrive late.
2. He (almost, most) destroyed all those old letters.
3. I like (almost, most) people, but I don't like Kim.
4. In the evening we (almost, most) always watch the sunset.

Among and between   (See also pages 285–86)

Use the preposition *among* for three or more people or things.

> *Among* my friends and me there is much laughter.

Use the preposition *between* for two people or things only.

> *Between* John and me was the teacher's desk.

Remember to use an object pronoun after a preposition.

> Put it between *him* and *me.*

Exercise

Choose the correct word.

1. (Among, Between) us all we have two dollars.
2. A book of poems stood (among, between) two novels.
3. Dave stands (among, between) Jim and (I, me).
4. Divide it (among, between) all those children.

Antecedents of pronouns   (See also pages 187, 196–97, and 198–99)

A pronoun must agree with its antecedent in gender (masculine—*he*, feminine—*she*, neuter—*it*) and number (singular or plural).

If the antecedent of a pronoun is singular, for example, *each*, *either*, *everyone*, *neither*, or *one*, the pronoun must be singular. If the antecedent is *both*, *several*, or *many*, the pronoun must be plural.

Each of the girls has *her* own idea.   (Think: Each *one* has . . .)
(anteced.)   (pron.)

Both of those houses lost *their* roofs.
(anteced.)   (pron.)

To make the meaning clear, avoid using a pronoun whose antecedent is unclear.

UNCLEAR: Take the *rack* off the *car* and then wash *it*.
(pron.)

CLEAR: Before you wash the *rack*, take *it* off the car.
(anteced.)   (pron.)

Exercises

1. Choose the correct pronoun.
   1. Each of you here will get (his, their) feet wet.
   2. Neither of the women ordered (her, their) groceries.
   3. One of those buildings should remove (its, their) billboards.
   4. Several requested (his, their) money back.

2. Revise the sentences below to make the meaning clear:
   1. That boy and a friend rode his bicycle.
   2. He tried to look over the wall and through the corn, but it was too high.
   3. The boys wanted to lend their towels to the visiting team, but they lost them.

437

Any and no

With words that have a negative meaning, such as *not, none, never,* or contractions ending in *n't,* use the word *any.*

> We haven't any paper.
> They *never* have *any* money.

Do not use two or more negative words in this way:

> WRONG: They never have no money.

Exercise

Choose the correct word.

1. They didn't have (any, no) friends.
2. Don't those men have (any, no) manners?
3. There is (any, no) time to lose.
4. In my sack I do not have (any, no) potatoes at all.
5. Doesn't Joe have (any, no) suggestions?

Are and our

Are and *our* are spelled differently and should be pronounced as they are spelled. Do not confuse them. *Are* is the verb; *our* is the possessive pronoun.

> Rocks *are* being thrown into *our* yard.

Exercise

Choose the correct word.

1. (Are, Our) opinions were ignored.
2. They (are, our) not sure of (are, our) good intentions.
3. (Are, Our) you borrowing (are, our) tools?

At and to   (See also pages 284 and 286)

Use *at* when you mean that "someone or something is in a certain place."

> WRONG: Mother is ✗ home.   He is ✗ the circus.
> RIGHT: Mother is *at* home.   He is *at* the circus.

Use *to* when you want to show "movement toward someone or something."

> He ran *to* his father.   Send the boy *to* me.

Do not use *at* or *to* needlessly with *where*. See how they are unnecessary in the sentences below:

WRONG: Where did he send it ̶a̶t̶? Where did he hide it ̶a̶t̶?
RIGHT: Where did he send it? Where did he hide it?

Exercise

Choose the correct word.

1. He was (at, to) the store all afternoon.
2. He walked quickly (at, to) the meeting.
3. Yesterday I spent two hours (at, to) George's house.
4. (At, To) the Joneses' store, they have baby rabbits.

Bad and badly   (See also pages 249–50)

Bad is always an adjective.

It was a *bad* day.   The weather is *bad*.

Badly is always an adverb.

He plays *badly*.

Always say: "He feels *bad*," and "Joan looks *bad*." *Bad* modifies *he* and *Joan,* and therefore is an adjective.

Exercise

Read aloud the sentences below several times.

1. He looks *well*.   He looks *bad* (unwell).
2. Elsa feels *well*.   Elsa feels *bad* (unwell).

Be   (See also pages 25–26)

Learn the various forms of the verb *be*, as they are used with pronoun subjects:

SINGULAR PRONOUNS	PRESENT	PAST	PLURAL PRONOUNS	PRESENT	PAST
I	am	was	we	are	were
you	are	were	you	are	were
he, she, it	is	was	they	are	were

Notice that the pronoun *you* must use the plural forms of the verb *be*: *are* and *were*.

439

Exercise

Choose the correct form of the verb *be* for each blank in the sentences below. Refer to the double underlined words in the list on page 439 if you need help.

1. You __?__ my best friend.
2. __?__ you with the others last night?
3. We __?__ happy yesterday, happier than they __?__.
4. It __?__ almost midnight before they __?__ finished.
5. Yesterday you __?__ hopeful, but today you __?__ sad.

Beat—beat—(have, has, had) beaten

Beat (past) should be used without a helping verb. *Beaten* needs a helper. (See pages 446–48 for practice on irregular verbs.)

Begin—began—(have, has, had) begun

Use *began* without a helping verb. Always use *begun* with a helping verb. (See pages 446–48 for practice on irregular verbs.)

Beside—besides

Beside means "at the side of."
Besides means "in addition to."

Will you sit *beside* me?
Who else *besides* her will help?

Exercise

Choose the correct word.

1. Stand (beside, besides) the usher.
2. Who saw the accident (beside, besides) me?
3. The chair was put (beside, besides) the furnace.

Between and among

See "*Among* and *between*," pages 436–37.

Blow—blew—(have, has, had) blown

Note the spelling of each principal part above. *Blew* should be used without a helping verb. *Blown* needs a helper. (See pages 446–48 for practice on irregular verbs.)

Break—broke—(have, has, had) broken

Broke (past) should be used without a helping verb. *Broken* (past participle) always needs a helping verb. (See pages 446–48 for practice on irregular verbs.)

When you want to say "to make come apart," always use *break, broke,* or *broken.* Do not use *bust* or *busted.*

WRONG: He *busted* the toy.   His toy was *busted.*
RIGHT: He *broke* the toy.   His toy was *broken.*

Bring and take   (See also pages 148–49)

Use *bring* when the action is *toward* the person who is speaking. Note that its principal parts are *bring, brought,* (have, has, had) *brought.*

Use *take* when the action is *away from* the person speaking. Its principal parts are *take, took,* (have, has, had) *taken.*

Don't *bring* that rat near me!   He *brought* me my spear.
Please *take* that rat away from me.   I *took* it to Molly.

Exercise

Choose the correct word.

1. He was always (bringing, taking) his sister's toys away.
2. (Bring, Take) some laughter into our house.
3. John (brought, took) a good book to his mother.
4. What do you think Dad will (bring, take) us from New York?

Burst—burst—(have, has, had) burst   (See also page 143)

All three principal parts have the same form. (See pages 446–48 for practice on irregular verbs.)

Choose—chose—(have, has, had) chosen

Note the spelling of the forms of this verb. Use *chose* (past) without a helping verb. Use *chosen* (past participle) with a helping verb. (See pages 446–48 for practice on irregular verbs.)

Come—came—(have, has, had) come

Use *came* without a helping verb. (See pages 446–48 for practice on irregular verbs.)

Comparison of adjectives and adverbs   (See also pages 243–45)

Adjectives and adverbs have three degrees of comparison. They are called the *positive degree,* the *comparative degree,* and the *superlative degree.*

Adjectives and adverbs may be compared as follows:

With one-syllable words, use the endings *–er* and *–est.*

POSITIVE	COMPARATIVE	SUPERLATIVE
sad	sadder	saddest
fast	faster	fastest

With words of three or more syllables, use *more* and *most.*

infrequently	more infrequently	most infrequently

Some two-syllable words use the endings *–er, –est;* some use the words *more, most, less, least;* and some use either. If in doubt, refer to a dictionary.

pretty	prettier	prettiest
sweetly	more sweetly	most sweetly

These common words are compared irregularly:

good ⎫ well ⎭	better	best
many ⎫ much ⎭	more	most
bad	worse	worst
little	less	least

Exercise

Write the three degrees of comparison of the following words:

1. much   3. delightful   5. ugly
2. bad   4. remarkably   6. shrilly

When comparing *two* things, use the comparative degree. When comparing *three or more,* use the superlative.

Of the two oceans, the Pacific is *deeper.*
The *highest* mountain of all is Mt. Everest.

Use only one method of comparison. Never use both the ending and the words *more* or *most.*

Exercise

Choose the correct word.

1. Which is (heavier, heaviest), your pack or mine?
2. Between the two boys, Lee sings (better, best).
3. John is the (more, most) intelligent boy in the class.
4. There are two stations in our town, of which the (more, most) modern one is (nearer, nearest) our house.
5. Louise is (friendlier, more friendlier) than Janet.

Could have

The word *of* is a preposition and may not be used as a helping verb. Use the helping verb *have* with the verb *could*. The same is true for the verbs *should*, *would*, and *must*.

Could Mary *have* gone without telling her mother?
They couldn't *have* done it without you.

Exercise

Read aloud the two sentences above, emphasizing *have* in each.

Do—did—(have, has, had) done

Use *did* without a helping verb. Use *done* with a helping verb. (See pages 446–48 for practice on irregular verbs.)

Doesn't and don't

When the subject is a singular noun or the pronouns *he*, *she*, or *it*, use the verb *doesn't*.
When the subject is plural, or *I* or *you*, use *don't*.

A boy *doesn't* like to wash.   Boys *don't* like to wash.
He *doesn't* eat bananas.   You *don't* eat bananas.

Exercise

Choose the correct word.

1. Marianne (doesn't, don't) know anything about it.
2. (Doesn't, Don't) the car and the trailer fit together?
3. Why (doesn't, don't) Jane call?
4. It (doesn't, don't) work.
5. He (doesn't, don't) like traveling long distances.

443

Double negative (See also page 252)

The contraction *n't* and the words *not, no one, hardly, no, never, none, nothing, nobody, nowhere* are **negatives.** Do not use two of them in one statement.

WRONG: He hasn*'t* got *no* reason.
RIGHT: He has *no* reason.   He hasn*'t* any reason.

Exercise

Use correctly each of the ten negatives above in a sentence.

Draw—drew—(have, has, had) drawn

Note the spelling of the past and past participle forms: *drew, drawn.* Use *drew* without a helping verb. Use *drawn* with a helping verb. (See pages 446–48 for practice on irregular verbs.)

Drink—drank—(have, has, had) drunk

Use *drank* without a helping verb. Always use *drunk* with a helping verb. (See pages 446–48 for practice on irregular verbs.)

Easy and easily (See also page 248)

See "Adjective or adverb?" page 435.

Eat—ate—(have, has, had) eaten

Use *ate* without a helping verb. (See pages 446–48 for practice on irregular verbs.)

Fly—flew—(have, has, had) flown

Use *flew* without a helping verb. Use *flown* with a helper. (See pages 446–48 for practice on irregular verbs.)

Freeze—froze—(have, has, had) frozen

Always use *froze* without a helping verb. Use *frozen* with a helping verb. (See pages 446–48 for practice on irregular verbs.)

Give—gave—(have, has, had) given

Use *gave* without a helping verb. Use *given* with a helping verb. (See pages 446–48 for practice on irregular verbs.)

Go—went—(have, has, had) gone

Use *went* without a helping verb. Use *gone* with a helping verb. (See pages 446–48 for practice on irregular verbs.)

Good and well (See also pages 249–50)

Good is an adjective.

This hash is *good.*   I like *good* food.

Well is mainly an adverb, but it can be used as an adjective when you want to say that someone is not ill.

The injured man is now *well.*   (adjective)
He played the game *well.*   (adverb)

Exercise

Choose the correct word.

1. The weather was (good, well).
2. Despite the weather, he played (good, well) tennis.
3. She sings (good, well).
4. He played tennis (good, well).
5. The patient feels (good, well) enough to leave the hospital.

Grow—grew—(have, has, had) grown

Note the spelling of the past and past participle forms: *grew, grown.* Use *grew* without a helping verb. Always use *grown* with a helping verb. (See pages 446–48 for practice on irregular verbs.)

Hear and here

The words *hear* and *here* differ in meaning and spelling.
Hear is a verb which means "to receive sounds."
Here is an adverb which means "this place."

Here I am.   Did you *hear* what I said?

Exercise

Choose the correct word.

1. You will find them (hear, here).
2. I can't (hear, here) you.
3. (Hear, Here) are the presents.

Himself and themselves

Pronounce these words and sentences carefully, with special emphasis on the *m:*   *himself*   *themselves*

1. The lion bit *himself.*
2. They admired *themselves.*

Exercise

Write two sentences using *himself* and two using *themselves.*

In and into   (See also pages 285–86)

In means "within or inside."

The mouse is *in* the box.
We are *in* a movie theater.

Into shows movement from outside to inside.

He jumped *into* the box.
Put the tools *into* the car.

Exercise

Choose the correct word.

1. The swimmer dived (in, into) the pool.
2. The ophthalmologist peered (in, into) my left eye.
3. The porpoises were very happy (in, into) the tank.
4. The icebreaker pushed slowly (in, into) the area of solid ice.
5. We rushed (in, into) the principal's office.

Irregular verbs   (See also pages 143–45)

Many common verbs do not form their past tense in the regular way, that is, by adding *d* or *ed* to the present tense.   They are called **irregular verbs.**

Here is a list of the principal parts of the irregular verbs you have studied this year and in earlier grades.

PRESENT	PAST	PAST PARTICIPLE
beat	beat	(have, has, had) beaten
begin	began	(have, has, had) begun
blow	blew	(have, has, had) blown
break	broke	(have, has, had) broken

PRESENT	PAST	PAST PARTICIPLE
bring	brought	(have, has, had) brought
burst	burst	(have, has, had) burst
choose	chose	(have, has, had) chosen
come	came	(have, has, had) come
do	did	(have, has, had) done
draw	drew	(have, has, had) drawn
drink	drank	(have, has, had) drunk
eat	ate	(have, has, had) eaten
fly	flew	(have, has, had) flown
freeze	froze	(have, has, had) frozen
give	gave	(have, has, had) given
go	went	(have, has, had) gone
grow	grew	(have, has, had) grown
know	knew	(have, has, had) known
lay	laid	(have, has, had) laid
leave	left	(have, has, had) left
let	let	(have, has, had) let
lie	lay	(have, has, had) lain
ride	rode	(have, has, had) ridden
ring	rang	(have, has, had) rung
run	ran	(have, has, had) run
say	said	(have, has, had) said
see	saw	(have, has, had) seen
set	set	(have, has, had) set
shake	shook	(have, has, had) shaken
shrink	shrank	(have, has, had) shrunk
sing	sang	(have, has, had) sung
sink	sank	(have, has, had) sunk
sit	sat	(have, has, had) sat
speak	spoke	(have, has, had) spoken
spring	sprang	(have, has, had) sprung
steal	stole	(have, has, had) stolen
swear	swore	(have, has, had) sworn
swim	swam	(have, has, had) swum
take	took	(have, has, had) taken
teach	taught	(have, has, had) taught
throw	threw	(have, has, had) thrown
write	wrote	(have, has, had) written

Exercises

1. Read over the entire list of principal parts of irregular verbs. Note those that cause you trouble, and learn them.

2. Tell the correct form of the verb.

(beat)   1. We have __?__ the Park team twice.
(begin)   2. The play has just __?__.
(blow)   3. The leaves __?__ away in the storm yesterday.
(break)   4. Has he __?__ his record?
(bring)   5. Yesterday he __?__ his sister here.
(burst)   6. The balloon has __?__.
(choose)   7. Last night I __?__ the TV programs.
(do)   8. Yesterday I __?__ my chores.
(draw)   9. I __?__ this picture in class last week.
(drink)   10. Larry __?__ all of his milk at breakfast this morning.
(eat)   11. Have the birds __?__ all the seeds?
(fly)   12. Uncle Bob has __?__ across the ocean.
(freeze)   13. The pond has __?__ over.
(give)   14. The prizes have been __?__ out.
(go)   15. They have __?__ already.
(grow)   16. My baby sister has __?__ two inches.
(know)   17. I __?__ the answers last night.
(ride)   18. Have you __?__ a horse before?
(ring)   19. At twelve o'clock yesterday, the bell __?__.
(run)   20. He has just __?__ out of the house.

3. Use each of the following verbs in a sentence, using the past tense form of the verb:

see	sink	swear
shake	speak	swim
shrink	spring	take
sing	steal	throw

4. Use the past participle form of each of the following verbs in a sentence. Be sure to include a helping verb.

write	lie
lay	say
leave	set
let	teach
come	sit

448

Its and it's   (See also pages 184–85)

Its is a possessive pronoun.

The dog lost *its* collar.

It's means "it is."

I think *it's* too late to change.

Exercise

Choose the correct word.

1. The bird saw (its, it's) young fall from the nest.
2. (Its, It's) a difficult question.
3. (Its, It's) a fine day today.
4. The weather was at (its, it's) best today.

Know—knew—(have, has, had) known

Note the spelling of the past and past participle.   Use *knew* (past) without a helping verb.   Use *known* (past participle) with a helping verb.   (See pages 446–48 for practice on irregular verbs.)

Lay and lie   (See also pages 146–47)

Lay means "to put or place something."

Today I *lay* it aside.   (present)
Yesterday I *laid* it aside.   (past)
I *have laid* it aside.   (past participle)
I *am laying* it aside.   (present participle)

Lie means "to rest or recline."

Now you *lie* down.   (present)
Yesterday you *lay* down after dinner.   (past)
He *has lain* down.   (past participle)
He *is lying* down.   (present participle)

Exercise

Choose the correct verb.

1. She (lies, lays) down after lunch for an hour.
2. That water has (lain, laid) in the gutter for a week.
3. She (lay, laid) her book on the desk.
4. A thick fog is (lying, laying) in the valley.

Learn and teach   (See also pages 149–50)

Learn means "to gain knowledge or skill."

I *learned* my lesson.

Teach means "to give instruction."

She *taught* the lesson to the class.

Exercise

Choose the correct verb.

1. Miss Jones (learns, teaches) us our lessons well.
2. The sergeant (learned, taught) me to shoot straight.
3. What did they (learn, teach) you at school today?
4. I have (learned, taught) to ski.

Leave and let

Leave means "to go away (from)."   *Let* means "to allow or permit."

I *let* him *leave* the house.   *Let's* go in.

Exercise

Choose the correct verb.

1. (Leave, Let) us see it closer.
2. I cannot (leave, let) you do that.
3. Please do not (leave, let) me by myself now.
4. I think I'll (leave, let) him fix the bicycle.

Most   (See also pages 250–51)

See "*Almost* and *most*," page 436.

Naming yourself last

When you speak of someone else and yourself, put the other person's name first:

Becky and I are glad to be here.
Give it to Carl and me.

Exercise

Write three sentences in which you talk about someone else and yourself.

Object pronouns

See "Subject and object pronouns," page 454.

Ought (See also page 148)

Ought has only one form in all tenses. Never use *ought* with a helping verb. *Ought* is almost always followed by *to* and another verb.

WRONG: He ~~had~~ ought to go.   RIGHT: He *ought* to go.
WRONG: He ~~hadn't~~ ought to go.   RIGHT: He *ought not* to go.

or

He *oughtn't* to go.

Exercise

Use *ought, ought not,* and *oughtn't* twice each in sentences of your own.

Our and are

See "*Are* and *our*," page 438.

Pronouns

See "Antecedents of pronouns," page 437, "Naming yourself last," page 450, "Singular pronouns and verbs," page 453, "Subject and object pronouns," page 454.

See "Adjective or adverb?" page 435.

Ride—rode—(have, has, had) ridden (See also pages 143–44)

Use *rode* without a helping verb. Use *ridden* with a helping verb. (See pages 446–48 for practice on irregular verbs.)

Ring—rang—(have, has, had) rung

Use *rang* without a helping verb. Use *rung* with a helping verb. (See pages 446–48 for practice on irregular verbs.)

Run—ran—(have, has, had) run

Use *ran* without a helping verb. (See pages 446–48 for practice on irregular verbs.)

Say and said

Do not use *say* or *says* when you are talking about something that has happened in the past. *Say* or *says* is present tense. Use *said* to show the past tense.

WRONG: I ~~says~~ to him.
RIGHT: I *say* (or I *said*) to him.

WRONG: Yesterday he ~~says~~ to me.
RIGHT: Yesterday he *said* to me.

Exercise

Use each of the following in a sentence: *say, says, said, have said.*

See—saw—(have, has, had) seen

Always use *seen* with a helping verb. Use *saw* without a helping verb. (See pages 446–48 for practice on irregular verbs.)

Set and sit

Set means "to place or put in order." Its forms are *set—set—set.*

Set your package on the table.

Sit means "to rest, as in a chair." Its forms are *sit—sat—sat.*

He *has sat* there for a while.

Exercise

Choose the correct verb.

1. I shall (set, sit) on the porch for a while.
2. The workman has (set, sat) the box on the piano.
3. Will you be (setting, sitting) on the balcony tonight?
4. Please (set, sit) the radio over there.

Shake—shook—(have, has, had) shaken   (See also page 143)

Shook is used without a helping verb. *Shaken* is used with a helping verb. (See pages 446–48 for practice on irregular verbs.)

Shrink—shrank—(have, has, had) shrunk   (See also page 143)

Always use *shrunk* with a helping verb. *Shrank* does not need a helper. (See pages 446–48 for practice on irregular verbs.)

Sing—sang—(have, has, had) <u>sung</u>

Always use *sung* with a helping verb. *Sang* does not need a helper. (See pages 446–48 for practice on irregular verbs.)

Singular pronouns and verbs   (See also pages 152 and 196–97)

Always use the singular form of a verb after a singular pronoun subject. The following are always singular pronouns:

SAMPLE SENTENCE

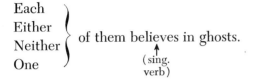

Each
Either
Neither
One
} of them believes in ghosts.
↑
(sing. verb)

Exercise

Choose the correct verb.

1. Neither of the boys (has, have) gone away yet.
2. Each of the ushers (takes, take) a turn at the ticket booth.
3. Either of the girls (plays, play) the game well.
4. One of us (wants, want) a chance to see the show.
5. Either of the boys (is, are) good for the leading character.

Sink—sank—(have, has, had) <u>sunk</u>   (See also page 143)

Always use *sunk* with a helping verb. *Sank* does not need a helper. (See pages 446–48 for practice on irregular verbs.)

Speak—spoke—(have, has, had) <u>spoken</u>   (See also pages 143–44)

Always use *spoke* without a helping verb. Use *spoken* with a helping verb. (See pages 446–48 for practice on irregular verbs.)

Spring—sprang—(have, has, had) <u>sprung</u>   (See also page 143)

Always use *sprung* with a helping verb. *Sprang* does not need a helper. (See pages 446–48 for practice on irregular verbs.)

Steal—stole—(have, had, had) <u>stolen</u>   (See also pages 143–44)

Stole (past) is used without a helping verb. *Stolen* (past participle) is used with a helping verb. (See pages 446–48 for practice on irregular verbs.)

453

Subject and object pronouns   (See also pages 189–91 and 194–95)

Most personal pronouns have a subject form and an object form:

SUBJECT PRONOUNS: I, we, he, she, they
OBJECT PRONOUNS: me, us, him, her, them

Use the subject pronoun as the subject of a sentence or as the subject complement after a verb of being:

Jill and *he* came home.   (subject)
Those women were Mother and *she*.   (subject complement)

Use the object pronoun as the direct object (object of a verb) or the object of a preposition:

Gordon lifted Jack and *her*.   (direct object)
Put it between Lisa and *me*.   (object of preposition)

Note: To make sure, use your ear. Omit the "Jack and" and say quickly in your mind, "Gordon lifted *her*." It will be obvious that you would never say, "Gordon lifted ~~she~~."

Exercise

Choose the correct pronouns.

1. The hose sprinkled the baby and (she, her).
2. Between Joe and (they, them) there was a friendly feeling.
3. Yesterday, Mrs. Schramm and (I, me) baked two cakes.
4. From under the chair peered Dick and (he, him).
5. The Queen of the May will surely be (she, her).

<u>Swear</u>—<u>swore</u>—(have, has, had) <u>sworn</u>   (See also pages 143–44)

Use *swore* without a helping verb. Use *sworn* with a helping verb. (See pages 446–48 for practice on irregular verbs.)

<u>Swim</u>—<u>swam</u>—(have, has, had) <u>swum</u>   (See also page 143)

Always use *swum* with a helping verb. *Swam* does not need a helper. (See pages 446–48 for practice on irregular verbs.)

<u>Take</u> and <u>bring</u>

See "*Bring* and *take*," page 441. See also the list of irregular verbs and practice on pages 446–48.

Teach and learn

See "*Learn* and *teach*," page 450. See also the list of irregular verbs and practice on pages 446–48.

Their, there, they're   (See also pages 184–85)

Their is a possessive pronoun.

> *Their* box is lost.

There is an adverb telling *where*.

> Our house is *there*.

There is a way of starting a sentence.

> *There* is fog in here.

They're is a contraction of "They are."

> *They're* lost in the woods.

Exercise

Choose the correct homonym to go in each blank: *their, there,* or *they're.*

1. I don't know why __?__ always squabbling.
2. __?__ is no reason for putting it __?__.
3. I think __?__ tire is flat.
4. __?__ hiding __?__ money in __?__.

Themselves and himself

See "*Himself* and *themselves*," page 446.

There with forms of is

There is never the subject of a sentence. It is often used as a way to get a sentence started. In such a sentence, the subject follows the verb:

> There are John and Pauline in the shop.
>
> There is a ghost in the attic.

The verb must agree with the subject: John and Pauline are; ghost is. With a singular subject you may say *there's*: "There's a mouse here."

Exercise

Choose the correct verb.

1. There (was, were) many reasons for leaving.
2. There (is, are) loose boards down in the playroom.
3. (There's, There are) a song I'd like to sing to you.
4. There (is, are) Mel and his brother on the truck.

This, that, these, and those   (See also page 238)

Do not use the words *here* and *there* between the limiting adjectives *this, that, these,* and *those,* and the nouns they modify.

RIGHT: This mouse is dead.   That puddle is muddy.
WRONG: This h~~ere~~ dog is mine.   That th~~ere~~ kitten is noisy.

Use *this* and *that* with *kind;* use *these* and *those* with *kinds.*

RIGHT: *Those kinds* of raincoats tear easily.
WRONG: Those k~~ind~~ of raincoats tear easily.

Exercise

Choose the correct word in each sentence below:

1. (This, This here) story will make you cry.
2. These (kind, kinds) of days are perfect.
3. (That, That there) poster is torn.
4. Those (kind, kinds) of lamb chops are expensive.

Those and them

Them is an object pronoun. It is *never* an adjective.

WRONG: Th~~em~~ books are quite old.
RIGHT: *Those* books are quite old.

Exercise

Read the following sentences aloud several times, emphasizing the word *those:*

1. *Those* flowers are wilting.
2. Please don't eat *those* cookies.

Throw—threw—(have, has, had) thrown

Threw is used without a helping verb. *Thrown* is used with a helping verb. (See pages 446–48 for practice on irregular verbs.)

To, too, and two

To often means "in the direction of."

He walked *to* school.

Too means "also" or "excessively."

I want to go, *too.* (also)
The stone is *too* heavy. (excessively)

Two means 2.

I saw *two* ducks swimming there.

Exercise

Choose the correct word: *to, too,* or *two.*

1. They are kind __?__ me.
2. The __?__ of them ran __?__ the beach, __?__.
3. Those __?__ boys went __?__ bed __?__ late.

Unnecessary pronouns (See also page 198)

Do not use an unnecessary pronoun after a noun subject.

RIGHT: My father likes lobsters.
WRONG: My father ~~he~~ likes lobsters.

Exercise

Choose the correct subject.

1. (Mabel, Mabel she) stayed home all last week.
2. (Boys, Boys they) are usually louder than girls.
3. After the fire, (that dog, that dog it) howled all night.

We or us with nouns (See also pages 197–98)

Use expressions like "we boys" and "we girls" when they are subjects or when they are subject complements after a verb of being.

RIGHT: *We* boys like to fish.
WRONG: ~~Us~~ boys like to fish.

Use "us boys" and "us girls" when they are direct objects (objects of a verb) or objects of a preposition.

RIGHT: Mary included us girls.
WRONG: Mary included ~~we~~ girls.

457

Exercise

Choose the correct word.

1. The teacher and (we, us) boys went on a trip.
2. Later the president introduced (we, us) girls.
3. They spoke to Mr. Smith and (we, us) boys.
4. The guilty ones are (we, us) boys.

Well

See "*Good* and *well*," page 445.

Write—wrote—(have, has, had) written

Use *wrote* without a helping verb. Use *written* with a helping verb. (See pages 446–48 for practice on irregular verbs.)

Your and you're

Your is a possessive pronoun. *You're* is a contraction of "you are."

Your pig has won a prize.
You're lucky.

Exercise

Choose the correct word.

1. He walked all over (your, you're) clean floor.
2. (Your, You're) remarks were very witty.
3. If (your, you're) going to stop, stop now.
4. (Your, You're) my favorite actor.

INDEX

Numerals in heavy black type indicate the teaching pages.

Book to Read, A (*cont.*)
  Night of the Wall by Priscilla Goldthwait, 228
  North Town by Lorenz Graham, 382
  Otto of the Silver Hand by Howard Pyle, 177
  Red Horse Hill by Stephen W. Meader, 359
  These Happy Golden Years by Laura Ingalls Wilder, 73
Books:
  arrangement of, in library, **312–15,** 338, 340
  excerpts from:
    The Adventures of Tom Sawyer, by Mark Twain, 365
    The Bible (in Old, Middle, and Modern English), 1–2
    The Book of the Camp Fire Girls (1959 Edition), 108
    The Call of the Wild, by Jack London, 109
    A Christmas Carol, by Charles Dickens, 105
    "A Day's Wait," from *Winner Take Nothing,* by Ernest Hemingway, 114
    The Great Houdini, by Beryl Williams and Samuel Epstein, 109
    "The Mahogany Fox," by Samuel Scoville, Jr., 114
    Mama's Bank Account, by Kathryn Forbes, 363
    Outlaw Red, by Jim Kjelgaard, 364
    "The Ransom of Red Chief," from *Whirligigs,* by O. Henry, 118
    The Red Pony, by John Steinbeck, 364–65
    Shane, by Jack Schaefer, 105
    "Snapshot of a Dog," from *The New Yorker,* by James Thurber, 105
    "Stolen Day," from *This Week,* by Sherwood Anderson, 114, 115–16, 117
    Through the Frozen Frontier, by Rear Admiral George J. Dufek, 327–28
    Treasure Island, by Robert Louis Stevenson, 102

  The White Company, by Sir Arthur Conan Doyle, 102
  parts of, **375, 377, 380–81, 384, 385**
  reference, **316–17,** 338, 340
  See also Book to Read, A
Breve, **320–21**

Capital letters:
  for abbreviations, **420**
  to begin sentences, 36, 113, **422**
  in business letters, **222–24,** 225, 232, **422**
  for first word in a line of poetry, **422**
  in friendly letters, **211–12,** 229, 231, **422**
  for *I* and *O,* **422**
  for "Mother," "Father," etc., **88,** 97, **420**
  in outlines, 95, **330–31, 422**
  for proper adjectives, 113, **419, 421**
  for proper nouns, 36, **86–87, 88,** 97, 99, 113, 385, **419, 420, 421**
  in quotations, **119, 422**
  rules for, **419–22**
  in titles, **422**
Card catalog, **312–**13, 315, 338, 340
Chairman of meeting, **66–68, 70, 72**
Check Test:
  on adjectives and adverbs, 220
  on capital letters, 36, 95, 113
  on friendly letter, 95
  on irregular verbs, 140
  on punctuation marks, 19, 95
  on *sit–set* and *leave–let,* 150
  on using words correctly, 120
  on verbs and pronouns, 52
Choose, 140, **441, 447, 448**
Choral reading, **373–74**
Clauses:
  independent, **295, 300,** 301
  subordinate, **300–01,** 302, 304, 307
Clubs:
  conducting meetings of, **66–72**
  constitutions of, **67**
  minutes of, **69**
Colon, **222,** 225, 230, 232, **424, 426**
Comma:
  with appositives, **93,** 97, 99, 304, **413, 425, 426**

in compound sentences, 295, **296–97**, 304, 306, **425, 427**
with introductory words, 19, **425, 426**
in letters, 19, 95, **211–12, 222–24,** 229, 231, 232, **411, 424**
with nouns of direct address, 19, **413, 424, 426**
in quotations, 19, **119–20,** 129, 131, **425,** 427
rules for, **424–25**
in series, 19, **290, 299, 300,** 306, **425,** 427
Commands. *See* Imperative sentences
Common nouns, 36, **86–87, 88,** 97, 99, 113, **412, 419, 420–21**
Comparison of adjective and adverb, **243–45,** 254, 256, **442–43**
Complete predicates, **22–23, 407,** 408
Complete subjects, **21, 407,** 408
Composition. *See* Writing; Creative writing
Compound objects, **194,** 195, **290,** 291, **398, 400,** 402, 403, **418**
Compound predicates, **294, 296,** 303, **398, 418**
Compound sentences, **290, 295–96,** 297, 304, 306, **399, 400,** 402, 403, **418, 425**
Compound subjects, **290–91, 292–93,** 303, 306, **398,** 403, 418
Compound verbs. *See* Compound predicates
Conjunctions:
compounding with, **290–91, 292–93, 294, 295, 298–99,** 303, 306, **398–99, 400,** 402, 403, **418**
defined, **290–91, 418**
subordinating with, **300–01,** 302, 304, 307
Contents, table of, **375, 380,** 381, 384, 385
Contractions, 19, **137,** 155, **423, 449, 455, 458**
Conversation:
art of, **55–56,** 59
courtesy in, **55, 56, 350**
guides for, **56**
listening and, **55, 56, 350**
using stories or anecdotes in, **60–61,** 62

writing, **115–16, 118–20,** 129, 131
Courtesy:
in business letters, **221**
in club meetings, **72**
in conversations, **55, 56, 350**
in friendly letters, **207, 216,** 229, 231
in listening, **350–51**
in social notes, **216, 219,** 232
Creative writing:
checking and revising in, **125–26**
and choosing a topic, **121–24**
of descriptions, **101–02, 103, 104–05, 106,** 107, 128, 130
of dialogue, **118–20,** 129, 131
of friendly letters, **205–09, 214,** 229, 231, **411**
of a paper, **121–22, 125–26**
of paragraphs, **108–13,** 130–31
of stories, **114–20,** 129, 131
See also Writing; Stories; Reports

Declarative sentences, 29, 30, 34, 40, 43, **390, 406, 407, 428**
Description:
of action, **101–03,** 128, 130
of authors' styles, **364–65,** 382
guides for writing, **106**
of place, person, or object, **104–06,** 107, 128, 130
See Creative writing; Words
Determiners. *See* Noun signals
Dewey Decimal System, **313–14,** 315, 338, 340
Diacritical marks, **320–21**
Diagrams, sentence, **387–400**
compound elements in, 398–400
direct objects in, **391–93**
inverted order in, **388–89**
modifiers in, 392–96
prepositional phrases in, **397**
simple subject and verb in, **387–88**
subject complements in, **393, 394–95, 396, 398,** 402, 403
Dialogue, writing, **115–16, 118–20,** 129, 131
Dictionary:
accent marks in, 53, **321–22**
alphabetical order in, **318–19,** 339, 342
capitalization shown in, **326**
diacritical marks in, **320–21**
guide words in, **318–19,** 338, 341

Dictionary (*cont.*)
    hyphenation shown in, **323, 325,**
        326
    irregular verbs in, **144, 323**
    meanings of words in, **319,** 325,
        342
    pronunciations of words in, **53,
        54, 320–22**
    sample page from, **324**
    spelling of words in, **323–25**
    syllabication shown in, **53, 322**
    as a vocabulary builder, **161,** 162
    word origins in, 13
Direct objects:
    compound, **290, 291,** 303, 306,
        398, 400, 402, 403, **418**
    defined, **89, 132, 408**
    nouns as, **89–90,** 97, 99, 153, 155,
        408, 413
    pronouns as, 52, **189–90,** 191,
        192–93, 200, 203, **408, 454**
    in sentence patterns, **91**
Direct quotations. *See* Dialogue,
        writing; Quotations
Directions. *See* Explanations
Discussion. *See* Clubs
Double negatives, **252,** 254, 256,
        438, 444

Encyclopedias, **264, 316, 317,** 338,
        340
English language, the:
    American Indian contributions
        to, **12**
    Arabic contributions to, **13**
    borrowings from other languages
        in, **11–13**
    changes in, **1–2**
    French and, **8–9,** 11, 13
    German and, **7–8,** 11, 13
    German-Dutch contributions to,
        12
    Latin and, **10–11,** 13
    Middle English and, 1, 2
    Modern English and, **1, 2,** 11
    Old English and, **1, 2, 7**
    origins of, **5–11,** 13
    Spanish contributions to, **12**
    two main streams in, **11,** 13
Euphemisms, **175**
Exclamation point, 19, **29,** 30, 40,
        77, 406, 418, 427
Exclamatory sentences, 19, **29,** 30,
        40, **390, 406, 427**

Explanations:
    giving, **257–61,** 274, 276
    guides for giving, **259**
    outlining, 259
    personal notes of, **260–61**
    topic sentence in, 259, 274, 276
    unity in, **259,** 274, 276

Fragments, sentence, 18, 19, **33,
        34–35,** 39, 41, 42, 43, 384, 385,
        406–07, 409

Going Ahead:
    adjectives, 236
    articulation. 52
    building words, 166
    capitalization in dictionary, 326
    common and proper nouns, 87
    euphemisms, **175**
    improving your writing (parallel-
        ism), **298–99**
    making list of books, 367
    prefixes, 164
    pronoun plurals, 184
    pronunciation in dictionary, 54
    sentence diagrams, 400
    sentence patterns, **32, 37, 91,**
        138–39, **150–51, 188, 236,**
        246–47, **288–89**
    special vocabulary, 168
    spelling of difficult words, 333
    synonyms from Germanic and
        Latin-French, 13
    topic sentences, 111
    transitive and intransitive verbs,
        134
    voice, use of, 49
    writing an action passage, 103
    writing descriptions, 107
    writing dialogue, 120
Guide words:
    in dictionary, **318–19,** 338, 341
    in encyclopedias, **316**
Guides for:
    conversation, **56**
    giving an explanation, **259**
    interviewing, **267**
    listening in the classroom, **349**
    listening in conversation, **350**
    note-taking, **330**
    proofreading, **378**
    punctuating dialogue, **119**
    reading poetry, **369**
    storytelling, **62**

462

Memorization, of poetry (*cont.*)
  from "The World Is Too Much
  with Us" by William Wordsworth, 215
  See also Poems
Metaphors, in poetry, **369–70, 371,**
  372, 383, 385
Minutes of a meeting, **69, 70**
Model:
  of adjustment letter, **224**
  of bread-and-butter letter, **219** ′
  of business letter, **411**
  of envelope, **214**
  of friendly letter, **206**
  of invitation, **217**
  of minutes of a meeting, **69**
  of note of acceptance, **218**
  of note of apology, **218**
  of note of regret, **217**
  of note-taking, **328, 329**
  of order letter, **223, 411**
  of outline, **331**
  of personal note of explanation,
    260
  of post card, **227**
  of request letter, **222**
  of thank-you note, **216**
Motion, making a, **66–68, 70–72**

Negative adverbs, **240,** 241, 253,
  254, **416, 444**
Notes, social. *See* Social notes
Note-taking, **327–30, 339, 341**
Notice, writing a, **261–62,** 263. *See
  also* Announcements
Noun signals, **83–84, 91,** 96, 98,
  237, 412, 416
Nouns:
  abstract, **78,** 96, 98, **412**
  appositive, **93,** 97, 99, **413, 425,
    426**
  common and proper, 36, **86–87,
    88,** 97, 99, 113, 385, **412, 419–
    20, 421**
  concrete, **78,** 96, 98, **412**
  defined, **77–78, 412**
  of direct address, 19, **413, 424,
    426**
  as direct objects, **89–90,** 97, 99,
    153, 155, **408, 413**
  irregular plurals of, in dictionary,
    323, 325
  possessive, **79, 82–83,** 96, 98,
    238–39, 392, 393, 412, 423

predicate, **92, 408.** *See also* Subject complements
  in sentence patterns, **91, 94**
  signals of, **83–84, 91,** 96, 98, **237,
    412, 416**
  as simple subjects, **89–90,** 97, 99,
    407, 413
  singular and plural, **79, 80–81,**
    96, 98, **323,** 325, **412**
  as subject complements, **92,** 97,
    99, **134, 393, 408, 409, 413**

Objects of prepositions:
  compound, **194,** 195, 200, 203,
    290, 291, 303, 305, 306, **418**
  defined, **194, 279, 417**
  nouns as, **194, 278–79, 417**
  pronouns as, 52, **194–95,** 200,
    203, **287, 417, 454**
  in sentence patterns, **91, 94**
Order letter, **223,** 224, 225, 226,
  230, **411**
Outlining:
  an explanation, 259
  form for, 95, **330–31,** 339, 341,
    422, 428
  model of, **331**
  punctuation in, 95
  a report, **269–70,** 271, 272, 275,
    277
  a talk, **63–64**

Paragraphs:
  of action, **101–02,** 103
  of description, **104–05**
  developing, by details and expla-
    nation, **111–12,** 128–29, 131,
    410
  guides for writing, **112**
  indention in, **125,** 410
  topic sentence in, **108–09, 110–
    11, 125,** 128–29, 130, **410**
  unity in, **108–09, 110–11, 125,**
    128–29, 130, **272, 410**
  writing, **108–13,** 131
  in writing dialogue, **119,** 129, 131
  See also Creative writing; Writing
Parliamentary procedure. *See* Clubs
Parts of speech, **77, 412–18**
Period:
  after abbreviations, **210,** 212,
    214, 229, 231, **428**
  after declarative sentence, 29, 30,
    40, 43, **406–07, 428**

in dialogue, **119**, 129, 131

after imperative sentence, **29**, **30**, 40, 43, **406–07**, **428**

lack of, in run-ons, **33**, **34–35**, 41, 43, 384, **409**

in outlining, 19, **64**, 95, **330**, **331**, **428**

rules for using, **428**

Plagiarism, **327**, 340

Poems:

from "Casey at the Bat" by Ernest Lawrence Thayer, 361

"The Centipede" by Ogden Nash, 354

from "The Deacon's Masterpiece" by Oliver Wendell Holmes, 360

"The Eagle" by Alfred, Lord Tennyson, 355

"Felicia Ropps" by Gelett Burgess, 355

"Fog" by Carl Sandburg, 370

from "The Highwayman" by Alfred Noyes, 356

"Peter Piper," 356

from "The Skaters of Ghost Lake" by William Rose Benét, 358

"Spring Cricket" by Frances Rodman, 372

"Steam Shovel" by Charles Malam, 368

"What Do We Plant?" by Henry Abbey, 374

"The Wolf Cry" by Lew Sarett, 373

See also Memorization, of poetry

Poetry:

alliteration in, **356**, **358**, 360, 361

choral reading and, **373–74**

free verse and, **370**

guides to reading, **369**

how to read, **368–72**

listening to, **354–58**

memorizing, 334. *See also* Memorization, of poetry

meter in, **355**

mood and tone of voice in, **373**

reading, **368–74**

repetition in, **356**, **358**, 360, 361

rhyme in, **354–55**, 360, 361

rhythm in, **355–56**, 360, 361

similes and metaphors in, **369–70**, **371**, 372, 383, 385

Possessives:

adjectives as, **238–39**

apostrophe in, **79**, **82–83**, 96, 98, **184**, 185, 200, 202, **238–39**, 385, **412**, **423**

nouns as, **79**, **82–83**, 96, 98, **238–39**, **392**, 393, **412**, 423

pronouns as, 120, **184**, 185, 188, 200, 202, **238–39**, 385, **392**, 393, **415**, **449**, **455**, **458**

Post cards, writing, **227**

Predicate adjectives, **235**, **408**. *See also* Subject complements

Predicate nouns and pronouns, **191–92**, **408**. *See also* Subject complements

Predicates:

complete, **22–23**, **407**, 408

compound, **294**, 296, 303, 304, 306, **398**, **418**

defined, **20**, **407**

in interrogative sentences, **30**, 40, 43

in inverted order, **27**, 28, 40, 43, **407**, **408**

simple, **22–23**, 40, 42, **407**, **408**

See also Sentences; Verbs

Prefixes, **163–64**, 178, 180

Prepositional phrases, **194–95**, 203, **279–81**, 282, **289**, **290–91**, 303, 304, 305, 307, **397**, **417**

Prepositions:

and adverbs, **284**, 303

or adverbs, **284**, 305

defined, **278**, **417**

list of, **279**

objects of, **194–95**, 200, 203, **279**, **287**, **417**

object pronouns after, 52, **194–95**, 200, 203, **287**

in sentence patterns, **288–89**

unnecessary, **285**, 286

usage problems with, **284–85**, 286–87, 303, 305, **436**

Pronouns:

agreement with antecedents of, **187**, **196**, **198–99**, 200, 201, 202, 203, **415**, **437**

defined, **183**, **415**

as objects of prepositions, 52, **194–95**, 200, 203, **287**, 417, **454**

as objects of verbs, 52, **189–90**, 191, 192–93, 200, 203, 408, **454**

personal, **183**, 200, 202, **415**

Verbs (*cont.*)
  linking, **92, 134, 138–39, 191–92, 235, 236, 393–94**
  modified by adverbs, **240–41,** 253, 256, **416–17**
  phrases, **135–36,** 137, 138, **139,** 153, 155
  principal parts of, **142–44,** 145, 156, **440–41, 446–47**
  in sentence patterns, **91, 94, 138**
  tenses of, **141,** 153, 155, **414**
  transitive and intransitive, **132–33,** 134, 153, 155
  See also Usage; Predicates
Vocabulary:
  antonyms, **172,** 179, 181
  avoiding overworked words, **170–71**
  importance of a good, **159**
  keeping a record of new words, **160–61**
  learning from context, **161–62,** 178, 180
  learning words in specialized, **167**
  prefixes and, **163,** 164, 178, 180
  roots and, **163, 166,** 178, 180
  specialized, 159, **167–68**
  specific, **106, 176,** 179, 181, 259
  suffixes and, **163, 164–65,** 178, 180
  synonyms and, **11, 13, 169–70, 174,** 178, 181
  and use of dictionary, **161,** 162, **319**
  See also Words
Voice, **45–54**

We, us, **197**–98, 201, 203, **457**
William the Conqueror, in England, **8**
Words:
  antonyms, **172,** 179, 181
  avoiding overworked, **170–71**

choosing specific, **106, 176,** 179, 181, **259**
to convey feelings, **174**–75, 179, 181
how built, **163–66,** 178, 180
keeping a record of new, **160–61**
learning, from context, **161–62,** 178, 180
list of commonly misspelled, **431–33,** 434
in poetry, **28, 372**
recording new, **160–61**
roots of, **166,** 178, 180
in specialized vocabularies, 159, **167–68**
as symbols, **4–5**
synonyms, **11, 13, 169–70, 174,** 178, 181
vivid, 103, 104–05, **106,** 171
See also Vocabulary
Writing:
  announcements, **261–63,** 274, 276
  authors' styles in, **364–65, 383**
  business letters, **221–27,** 230, 232, **411, 424**
  choosing topics for, **121–24**
  descriptions, **101–02,** 103, **104–05, 106,** 107, 128, 130
  of dialogue, **115, 118–19,** 120, 129, 131
  friendly letters, 95, **205–15,** 229, 231, **411, 424**
  gathering information for, **264–68,** 269
  paragraphs, **108–13,** 131
  proofreading and, **125–26,** 213, **272, 378–79,** 384, 385
  reports, **272**
  social notes, **216–20,** 230, 232, **411, 424**
  stories, **114–20,** 129, 131
  See also Creative writing

Zip Code, **210, 211, 225, 411**

F
G
H
I   6
J   7